The Reproductive Rights Reader

DATE DUE

The Reproductive Rights Reader

Law, Medicine, and the
Construction of Motherhood

EDITED BY

Nancy Ehrenreich

New York University Press

NEW YORK AND LONDON

NEW YORK UNIVERSITY PRESS
New York and London
www.nyupress.org

Library of Congress Cataloging-in-Publication Data
The reproductive rights reader / edited by Nancy Ehrenreich.
p.   cm.
Includes index.
ISBN-13: 978-0-8147-2230-5 (cloth : alk. paper)
ISBN-10: 0-8147-2230-X (cloth : alk. paper)
ISBN-13: 978-0-8147-2231-2 (pbk. : alk. paper)
ISBN-10: 0-8147-2231-8 (pbk. : alk. paper)
1. Human reproduction—Law and legislation—United States. 2. Abortion—Law and legislation—United States. 3. Birth control—Law and legislation—United States.
I. Ehrenreich, Nancy.
KF3760.R47 2007
342.7308'4—dc22   2007029762

New York University Press books are printed on acid-free paper, and their binding materials are chosen for strength and durability.

Manufactured in the United States of America

c 10 9 8 7 6 5 4 3 2 1
p 10 9 8 7 6 5 4 3 2 1

In memory of my mother, Irene Shirley Ehrenreich,
who conceived ten times, bore five children,
and lost five to miscarriage

Contents

A Note from the Editor

Because this book is designed to be used principally as a reader for undergraduate and graduate/law school courses, an attempt has been made to keep the prose straightforward and accessible, and to limit the number of footnotes. Thus, the endnotes provided at the end of each reading were included primarily when necessary to provide citations for direct quotations or empirical data. Each section is preceded by a brief introduction and followed by a set of notes and review questions.

Introduction

The problem of how to obtain reproductive justice[1] for women is a problem of how to move from inequality to equality. In a world where women are not equal, to men or to each other, what policies will best produce reproductive justice for all women? This book challenges the usual answers to that question, rejecting traditional, mainstream solutions based on protecting free choice and promoting formally neutral governmental policies. Instead, it favors a critical analysis that focuses on the concrete material conditions that limit choices, the role of law and social policy in helping to create those conditions, and the gendered power dynamics that inform and are reinforced by much of the regulation of human reproduction. There are at least two distinct approaches to the question of how to attain reproductive justice for all women. The first, which I will call the "liberal individualist" approach, has been adopted by the United States Supreme Court and is frequently employed by mainstream reproductive rights analysts in this country. The second, which I will call the "critical constructivist" approach, has been the focus of increasing attention by academics and activists, and informs many of the readings in this book. But it has still not attained widespread acceptance in U.S. courts.

The Liberal Individualist Approach to Reproductive Justice

The traditional liberal[2] approach to reproductive rights sees the road to a just society as lying in a commitment to individual freedom and governmental evenhandedness. Individuals should, in general, be free to live their private lives without interference from the government; and the limited types of regulation of reproductive matters that are appropriate should be implemented in a neutral and unbiased way. In other words, legislatures instituting such regulations, and judges upholding them, should avoid imposing particular political, religious, or moral perspectives on the society at large.

Thus, the central component of the mainstream liberal approach to reproductive rights is the notion of reproductive autonomy. Each individual woman should be free from governmental control over her decisions regarding whether and when to have children, what kinds of reproductive technology to use (if any), how to protect herself from unwanted pregnancy, etc. It is this liberal focus on "choice," of course, that has given its name to the mainstream abortion rights movement of the late twentieth and early twenty-first centuries: the "pro-choice" movement. Epitomized by such slogans as "keep your laws off my body" and "my body, my choice," the mainstream reproductive rights movement has been premised upon the idea that women have a constitutional right to reproductive autonomy—to be free from governmental constraints on their reproductive decision making.[3]

This liberal view is an individualist ideal, acknowledging that different people have different needs, abilities, and situations and that the law cannot possibly anticipate each individual's particular set of preferences and constraints. For that reason (as well as because of its emphasis on free will and individual responsibility), it defers to the individual's own assessment of her needs, envisioning liberty as the route to justice. As long as the government refrains from interfering in people's personal decisions about intimate matters such as sexuality and childbearing,[4] this approach assumes, individual women will be free to make the decisions that best suit their interests and values.

In relying on this notion of governmental noninterference, the liberal ideal is also based on notions of neutrality and formal equality. "Government may not enforce a particular view, however widely held, for no individual should be compelled to surrender the freedom to make a decision for herself simply because her 'value preferences' are not shared by the majority."[5] As long as government leaves individuals alone to make their own decisions, such *non*intervention is not seen as favoring one group over another. When government stays out of women's reproductive decisions, it is not seen as discriminating against or mistreating women as a group, or any particular subset of women. Rather, under the liberal view, it is governmental *interference* with reproductive autonomy, not noninterference, that violates women's reproductive rights. Thus, the notion of "negative liberty," which equates freedom with protection from governmental interference, is central to liberal reproductive theory.[6]

Moreover, from a liberal individualist point of view, governmental noninterference in the reproductive realm not only protects women's freedom to make their own decisions but also *legitimates* the decisions they do make. By assuming women to be freely acting, rational-choice-making individuals, an ideal of noninterference rejects (so this position argues) the all-too-familiar stereotypes that assume many women to be irrational and overly emotional.[7] Treating women as capable of independent and responsible choices dignifies, humanizes, and legitimates them, thereby elevating their status and undermining harmful stereotypes.

The focus on reproductive autonomy is also central to constitutional law rules about reproductive rights. The constitutional foundation of the right to reproductive autonomy is the Due Process Clause of the Fourteenth Amendment,[8] which has been interpreted as protecting a constitutionally based right to privacy—to freedom from governmental interference in one's private decision making about intimate matters, including what happens to one's own body.[9] Applying to both women and men, this right entitles people in the United States to make their own choices, not only about termination of pregnancy but also about issues such as whom to have as a sexual partner,[10] whether to accept or refuse medical treatment,[11] and what sort of contraceptive to use.[12]

The Critical Constructivist Approach to Reproductive Justice

From Choice to Context

The critical constructivist approach—the approach embraced by this book—starts from a quite different set of assumptions than the liberal approach. Rather than seeing individual freedom from governmental interference as key, this approach instead views the *substantive conditions* that characterize women's reproductive lives as the central indicator of their reproductive equality. In short, it believes that every woman is entitled to a self-directed, fulfilling, and healthy reproductive life.

According to the critical constructivist view, individual choices are to a significant degree *socially constructed;* they are a function of preexisting conditions over which individual women have limited control. As historian Rickie Solinger puts it, "[S]ex-and-pregnancy is more than a biological event. It is also a social and political event."[13] Thus, governmental interference is sometimes affirmatively beneficial; it is needed to overcome social inequalities that interfere with the full realization of women's reproductive autonomy. For example, in order for poor women to live the reproductive lives they want and need, it may be necessary for states to fund certain services they cannot afford themselves—such as prenatal care, abortion, and childbirth services. Thus, critical constructivists reject the single-minded focus on negative liberty that characterizes liberal thinking, arguing that positive liberty—the freedom made possible when government interferes in a useful way in people's private lives—is as important as negative liberty (freedom from governmental interference).[14]

From a critical constructivist perspective, while the liberal approach in theory can seem powerfully persuasive, in practice it founders upon the shoals of material reality. In a world of political, economic, and social inequality, ideals of free choice and governmental evenhandedness often merely perpetuate those underlying inequalities. As French novelist Anatole France famously remarked, "[T]he majestic equality of the laws . . . forbid[s] rich and poor alike to sleep under bridges, to beg in the streets, and to steal . . . bread."[15] Of course, the neutrally worded prohibitions that France listed, while seemingly applying to everyone, clearly had a significantly harsher impact on the poor. His comment shows how formally equal treatment can hurt—or help—one group much more than another.

Similarly, in the reproductive law context, formally neutral governmental policies that refuse to interfere with reproductive choices, while unbiased and evenhanded in structure, can have a disparate effect. A right to make one's own choices about reproductive matters is much more meaningful to the women who have the economic, political, and informational resources to *effectuate* those choices—women who can pay for abortions, who have employment opportunities more remunerative than being a surrogate mother, who have access to information on pregnancy prevention, who can support a child on their own, etc.

As law professor Dorothy Roberts has noted,

Liberty protects all citizens' choices from the most direct and egregious abuses of governmental power, but it does nothing to dismantle social arrangements that make it impossible for some people to make a choice in the first place. Liberty guards against government intrusion; it does not guarantee social justice.[16]

Thus, many of the choices that women make in the reproductive arena either are uninformed or are voluntary in name only—Hobson's choices between the lesser of two evils in situations that offer few (if any) viable alternatives. Heterosexual young women might "choose" not to use contraceptives because they don't know where to get them or how to convince their boyfriends to agree. Poor women might "choose" to have abortions because they can't earn enough money to afford to have a child. Women who can afford it might "choose" to have endless fertility treatments because they lack adequate information about the risks, and/or because they're convinced to ignore the risks by pervasive societal messages about biological motherhood being central to female self-actualization. The reproductive decisions women make are often choices between limited, equally unsatisfactory alternatives. This is not to say, however, that they aren't still *choices,* or that women lack any decisional control over their reproductive lives whatsoever. The point of critical constructivist theory is that merely making choices cannot be equated with autonomy—or with justice and equality.

Moreover, the government often contributes substantially to the limited choices women have. Governmental policies help create the conditions that shape women's options, so that even if the state doesn't directly interfere with women's reproductive choices, it can still have an important impact on their reproductive lives. Thus, proponents of the critical approach emphasize that the government doesn't actually stay out of reproductive decisions to the extent that it is usually thought—and admonished—to do. Rather, law and governmental policies play a key role in affecting the supposedly private choices that people make about reproductive matters. Legal policies actually have a significant impact on (though they don't of course completely *determine*) whether some women will experience unwanted pregnancies; whether and when they will obtain abortions to terminate those pregnancies; who will agree to serve as "surrogate" mothers and why; and even whether substance-abusing women will get pregnant, exposing their fetuses to drugs in utero. To give one example, as Rigel C. Oliveri describes in chapter 17 of this volume, state laws imposing waiting periods and other legal constraints on women's access to abortion affect women's decisions about when to seek the procedure. Many women delay getting an abortion while they obtain the necessary funds, transportation, and lodging made necessary by such laws.

Thus, the liberal approach's narrow focus on the formal right to reproductive choice doesn't *just* miss the fact that governmental nonintervention in reproductive decision making can actually harm some women and perpetuate inequalities. It also obscures the role of biased legal and governmental policies in *creating the contexts* in which women's choices are made in the first place. Reproductive decisions are socially constructed not only in the sense that they are a function of the social conditions that structure women's lives but also in the sense that those conditions are *themselves* produced by governmental policies and practices.

For critical constructivists, then, the liberal approach to reproductive justice is not merely inadequate but actually harmful to women's interests. Instead of humanizing women and legitimating their decisions (as it purports to do), it suggests that reproductive harms are merely the results of bad choices made by some individuals. In short, it makes women seem responsible for their own subordination, thereby obscuring the role that legal and governmental policies play in producing the conditions under which reproductive choices are made.

Moreover (as discussed more fully below), critical constructivists see the liberal model as also race- and class-biased. A policy based on nonintervention is most helpful to women with resources, because resources provide those women access to a wide range of reproductive services, without their having to rely on the government to provide them. Women of color are disproportionately low-income,[17] so they, along with poor white women, are disadvantaged by this model. They are also the most stigmatized by the focus on choice, for the women most often seen as bad choice makers are low-income women and women of color. Thus, reformers should be concerned not just about stereotypes of privileged women as overly emotional and irrational but also about the stereotypes of marginalized women as affirmatively dangerous and irresponsible mothers. By blaming such women's reproductive behavior on their "free will" rather than their social circumstances, a focus on choice merely reinforces those stereotypes. In short, the liberal individualist approach, by providing meaningful autonomy primarily to economically comfortable white women, promotes a notion of reproductive rights that leaves poor women and women of color out in the cold, and stigmatizes them in the process.[18]

Note the implications that this differential effect has for the purported neutrality of the liberal individualist model. While that model is facially neutral—it advocates protection of *all* women's choices equally—its failure to recognize differences among women (and their material situations) causes it to have the harmful differential impact just described. Essentializing women (treating them as all the same) prevents the liberal approach from recognizing that its definition of reproductive rights and needs serves primarily the interests of white, economically privileged women. In contrast, the critical constructivist approach rejects the narrow, negative view of liberty relied upon by liberal theorists. As noted above,[19] it embraces the notion of "positive liberty," which sees governmental intervention as sometimes actually a good thing that *increases* liberty. From this perspective, reproductive justice includes the right to governmental *support,* when that support is necessary for women to achieve meaningful control over their reproductive lives.

Critical Constructivism and the Role of Law

In addition, the critical constructivist conclusion that governmental policies affect women's choices stems from a quite different understanding of the role of law in society than that adopted by liberal individualist writers. The liberal approach is informed by a vision of law as something separate from society—a tool used to regulate social practices. Under that vision, appropriate legal regulation is regulation that constrains individual and governmental actors in order to keep them from interfering with pre-existing, private, autonomous preferences. Inappropriate regulation unfairly limits choice and violates individual rights.

Critical constructivists believe that this model fundamentally misapprehends the nature of law. To them, law is centrally involved in *creating* the society that the liberal view sees law as merely regulating. Rather than legal rules and individual behavior being separate and distinct from each other, the two are *interrelated*. Individual choices are a function of the legal regime in which they occur; they can best be protected by establishing a set of laws and policies that eliminates inequality and thereby makes true reproductive self-determination possible.[20]

Moreover, a critical perspective on the law contends that legal rules frequently serve the needs and perspectives of those with socioeconomic power in society. This view understands the legal system—meaning not only the avowedly political legislative branch but also the courts and administrative agencies—as an arena of society in which power struggles between various social groups take place. From this perspective, while law can sometimes be a vehicle for the betterment of women's reproductive lives, it can *also* serve as an integral part of the creation, perpetuation, and obfuscation of women's inequality and subordination. Thus, among other things, law often serves as a mechanism for constructing coercive gender norms, and enforcing them on women.[21]

In this light, legal rules take on new meaning. Consider, for instance, the abortion prohibitions that prevailed in many states from the 1840s to the 1970s. It is not uncommon for U.S. Supreme Court justices to criticize Justice Blackmun's opinion in *Roe v. Wade* for ignoring the fact that abortion was illegal for much of the century preceding *Roe*.[22] But what's to be made of the fact that the *percentage* of women obtaining abortions (about one-third)[23] *hasn't* varied significantly over time?[24] Wouldn't abortion rates go down at times when it was widely viewed as criminal behavior? One way to reconcile this apparent historical contradiction—the existence of widespread abortion *practices* at times of widespread abortion *prohibition*—is to assume that the laws passed represented the views of the elite males in the society, not the females, and perhaps not the general population either.[25] Under this view, abortion prohibitions were a mechanism by which elite men (who were, after all, the ones controlling state legislatures during the nineteenth century)[26] imposed pronatalist gender norms on women, forcing them to have children when they didn't want to. Thus, the passage of laws prohibiting abortion may not necessarily indicate that the practice was widely condemned when those statutes were passed.[27] Such laws may actually reveal less about popular views towards abortion than about the relative powerlessness of certain groups of people, including women, at particular moments in history.

For these reasons, critical constructivists conclude that more can be learned about the reasons behind, and impact of, reproductive laws and policies if law is *not* seen as an arena separate from society, and if reproductive justice is *not* understood as primarily about the protection of individuals' rights to make private choices. Too often, in the reproductive rights arena, the "rights" that law grants to women don't serve the function of assuring them meaningful and empowered reproductive lives. Instead, they impose gendered and racialized roles on women, punishing those who break the rules (or are *seen* as breaking them)—those who engage in what historian Rickie Solinger calls "insubordinate reproduction."[28] Thus, for many critical constructivists, reproductive law and policy play a central role in maintaining a system of sex-based inequality. As law professor Reva Siegal puts it when discussing abortion regulations,

"Considered in social rather than physiological terms, the state's 'interest in protecting potential life' is a state interest in compelling women who are resisting motherhood to bear children."[29] For these reasons, examining reproductive issues through the lenses of race, class, and other subordinated statuses (as they intersect with gender) is central to the critical constructivist perspective.

Race, Class, and Reproductive Justice

As the discussion thus far has already suggested, the critical constructivist notion of reproductive justice recognizes the complexity and specificity of women's reproductive experiences and needs. Women's situations vary widely, and therefore so do the effects of various reproductive laws, policies, and practices on different groups of women. Thus, while reproductive justice is clearly a "women's" issue—an issue of sex equality—a critical constructivist exploration of reproductive issues refuses to focus primarily on white, affluent women or to assume that all women's situations can be subsumed into theirs. Instead, it recognizes that different groups of women struggle against different stereotypes and exist within different material realities. And it acknowledges that, as noted above, facially neutral regulations have different impacts on differently situated women.

The stereotypes frequently associated with privileged (white, affluent) women and with marginalized (poor, nonwhite) women, respectively, are strikingly different—especially in the reproductive arena.[30] While these stereotypes will be discussed more fully—and in historical context—in several of the readings included in this volume, it's useful to summarize them briefly here. (But it's important to keep in mind as well that this general summary will necessarily flatten the widely varying landscape of reproductive conditions experienced by women across the United States.) Privileged women are often treated as the reproducers of the species—and of the nation. They're assumed to be "naturally" nurturing; to be unfulfilled—and even unfeminine—if they don't have children; and to be generally more capable than men in the domestic sphere. In short, they're "good" mothers. Because of eugenic attitudes that value affluent, white babies over others, as well as the gendered stereotypes of privileged women just described, such women are often seen as owing a duty to the state to produce the future citizens of the society. Thus, throughout U.S. history, they have frequently been expected to conform to pronatalist norms[31]—norms that often require them to sacrifice their own interests (in career, health, or personal fulfillment) in order to fulfill their duty to produce (and care for) the nation's children.

In contrast, marginalized women are often stereotyped as promiscuous, irresponsible, ignorant, and/or dangerously incompetent. In short, they're "bad" mothers. And their children are frequently devalued, consistent with the general devaluation of low-income people and people of color in general in this society. Thus, these women have often had to struggle against antinatalist norms that view them as individuals who shouldn't, and don't deserve to, have children. Those norms are deployed to justify and legitimize punitive and restrictive reproductive laws, policies, and practices that, as noted above, have harsh impacts on both the decision-making autonomy and the material circumstances of poor women (many of whom are women of color).[32] In

fact, the combined effect of the wide variety of legal regulations governing human reproduction reveals that those regulations are a central mechanism by which economic
and racial subordination are effected.

Thus, when viewed *in toto,* reproductive laws and policies represent a systematic
structure of control over the sexual and reproductive lives of marginalized women—
a structure justified by derogatory class- and race-based stereotypes of low-income
women and women of color as bad mothers. Moreover, as discussed above, the liberal
individualist approach taken by most courts and commentators hides this subordination of marginalized women, making it seem instead as if the conditions of their reproductive lives are merely the result of those women's own bad choices. As Roberts
notes, "the liberal reliance on seemingly neutral principles actually legitimates the interests and experiences of white people. Government neutrality conceals the racist origins of social practices that do not overtly discriminate on the basis of race."[33] Moreover, in its focus on choice, the liberal approach prioritizes women's right to control
their fertility (that is, their right *not* to have children), ignoring the fact that, for many
marginalized women, the right to *be* a mother is of equal or greater importance. Thus,
reproductive justice is not only a sex equality issue, but one of race and class as well.

Finally, it's crucial to note the various types of *connections* among different women's
reproductive circumstances. Stereotypes of "good" and "bad" mothers, for instance,
depend upon each other; they make rhetorical sense only in tandem. The notion of a
good mother necessarily contains within it the implicit assumption that not all mothers are good; some are bad. In other words, the stereotypes that differentially affect the
different groups of women actually reinforce each other.[34] Sometimes that reinforcement can be harmful (though in different ways) to both privileged *and* subordinated
women; at other times it can harm some and benefit others. For example, privileged
women have been criticized for working instead of staying home with their children,
while women on welfare have been disparaged for *wanting* to stay home and take care
of theirs. The opposing images of both groups make possible each one's subordination
based on limiting gender stereotypes. On a more material level, the ability of privileged women to have children while pursuing careers depends upon the availability of
low-paid, low-income women to clean those women's houses and care for their children. The availability of marginalized women for those jobs is closely linked to stereotyping that excludes them from other occupations.[35] In this example, the class- and
race-based subordination of marginalized women *makes possible* the privileges enjoyed by privileged women.[36] Thus, the advantages—*and* disadvantages—that privileged women experience in their reproductive lives are related to the reproductive
conditions faced by other, less privileged women.[37]

In summary, noting the differences among different women's experiences is important not merely to assure inclusion of marginalized groups. It's also central to a complete understanding of the reproductive lives of privileged women. In other words,
even a study of the reproductive lives of *privileged* women *only* would be incomplete if
it failed to explore the ways privileged women are affected by the regulation of marginalized women's reproductive lives. Thus, appreciating the connections among different women's situations requires attending to issues of relative power among women
and instances of mutually reinforcing subordination. Only by understanding the com-

plex and interconnected nature of class, race, and gender subordination can one gain a full appreciation of the effects of reproductive law and policy on the complex realities of women's reproductive lives.

Law, Medicine, and the Coercive Enforcement of Gender Norms

As noted above, the law creates and reinforces particular gendered and racialized images of women as good and bad mothers. One of the ways this happens is through law's reliance upon—and deference to—mainstream medical understandings of human reproduction. Mainstream medicine often sees female bodies and the reproductive process as pathologically dangerous, and often operates on stereotypical assumptions about how particular types of women behave towards their children. Yet, as critical constructivists point out, the legal system too often unquestioningly accepts medical testimony and perspectives based on these biases, adding legal force to the errors imbedded in medical "truths." By deferring to medical verities, courts and legislatures place the power of law behind the culturally specific notions of appropriate female behavior that influence medical knowledge and practice. Together, law and medicine operate to enforce coercive gender norms on women.

Most people probably tend to believe that, since medical knowledge is produced through research using the scientific method, the information gleaned through such research is unbiased and more or less accurate. In recent years, however, critics of medicine have revealed that, even in the hard sciences, and even when one uses "hard" data, bias can enter in.[38] Bias can affect what sorts of questions are asked, what research projects get funded, what results are published, and so on. Heart health research, for instance, focused solely on men for many decades, despite the fact that women also suffer heart attacks, and the importance of understanding how their situations differ from men's, and why.[39] In addition, medical research priorities can be—and are—seriously affected by private corporations' increasing role in funding such research. For instance, pharmaceutical companies certainly seem likely to have had an impact on modern medicine's tendency to focus on chemical cures, rather than prevention and environmental factors. And finally, commitment to established ways of thinking can sometimes interfere with self-criticism and change. Thus, as medical anthropologist Emily Martin notes, "Scientific accounts often remain caught in puzzles produced by their models rather than examining the models themselves."[40]

Researchers have identified numerous ways in which gender-, class-, and race-based stereotypes affect both the clinical practices of individual physicians and the content of medical textbooks.[41] The famous study by Ehrenreich and English, excerpted in chapter 1 of this volume, illustrates how images of women throughout history have directly influenced the medical diagnoses and treatments that purported to objectively describe and respond to their physical conditions. Other feminist critics have made similar observations, finding patriarchal bias in the fields of genetics,[42] biology,[43] urology,[44] and even primatology.[45]

One common reaction to this information about bias in medicine is to suggest that efforts should be made to purge these sorts of flaws from research findings and practices, with the goal of producing neutral and objective medical knowledge. Such an approach aims at cleansing medical texts and practices of misperceptions and stereo-typical thinking, so as to produce truer, more accurate information. It sees the inac-curacies as existing on the margins, not as threatening the entire corpus of medical authority.[46]

But the critical constructivist view isn't so sanguine about the prospect of medical knowledge ever fully escaping the blinders that structure it. Premised upon a post-structuralist perspective that sees knowledge as socially constructed—as a product of the time and place where it is produced, and as reflecting and enforcing power dy-namics that characterize that time and place—that view assumes that it is impossible to ever produce a completely "true" set of understandings about the human body. That is, it is impossible to produce a set of understandings that is measurable by some universal set of standards for determining "truth." From this perspective, all knowl-edge is mediated by language and culture; one person's (or group's) truths are the next one's myths.[47]

According to this view, to ask merely whether mainstream medical verities are "cor-rect" is to miss important dimensions of the problem. Rather, medical knowledge should be understood as one of the numerous mechanisms by which social power is produced and perpetuated in a society. "Once we accept the social nature of knowl-edge, we must also recognize that it is 'not politically innocent,' in particular that it is intimately connected to power, its exercise, and its effects."[48] Thus, in assessing medi-cine's role in affecting judicial and legislative determinations, we might ask questions such as, How does medical "knowledge" rely upon and reinforce stereotyped images of what different sorts of women are like? Do medical descriptions of reproductive proc-esses force certain roles on women? Are differential expectations of different types of women reflected in the way medical professionals interpret those women's reproduc-tive behavior? In other words, this view raises the possibility that medicine is one of the vehicles by which particular raced and gendered constructions of the female body, its reproductive processes, and women's roles as mothers are both produced and en-forced. Medicine tells women how to be good mothers, and disparages or pathologizes those whom it sees as failing to conform to socially prescribed "good mother" norms.[49]

This critical constructivist perspective on medicine in turn raises questions about law's deference to medical expertise. Consider, for example, the infrequent, but never-theless important, practice of court-ordered Cesarean sections. Courts sometimes or-der women to undergo C-sections against their will, usually because physicians fear harm to the fetus (and/or the woman herself). This happens despite a well-established constitutional right of patients to refuse unwanted treatment. In "The Colonization of the Womb," excerpted in chapter 35 of this volume, I argue that the medical conclu-sion that a C-section is necessary is often based on biased attitudes towards the female body in general and towards low-income women of color in particular. In short, it is almost exclusively women whom doctors perceive as "bad" mothers who are subjected to forced Cesareans. Thus, judicial willingness to defer to medical opinion in this con-text implicates law, as well as medicine, in the coercive imposition of gender norms on women.

Many of the pieces included in this book are informed by this more skeptical view of medicine, and familiarity with that view is essential to understanding the feminist analyses of reproductive regulation that many of those pieces present. Under that view, law and medicine operate together to enforce raced and classed gender norms on different groups of women. While the role they play may not necessarily be apparent to particular members of medical and legal institutions, or sometimes even to the women with whom they deal as patients or litigants, understanding it is nevertheless essential to fully appreciating the issues at stake in, and the reasons behind, many reproductive laws and policies.

In summary, then, a critical constructivist perspective suggests that reproductive justice is more likely to be attained *not* by eliminating governmental intervention into women's reproductive lives but by probing the ways in which governmental laws and policies constrain the reproductive options women have, shore up systems of social inequality, and express and enforce raced, classed, and gendered social norms about women's reproductive roles. These are the concerns that inform many of the writings in this book.

The Scope and Organization of This Book

Composing an edited volume of this size—especially about the complex and ever-changing field of reproductive rights—inevitably entails difficult decisions regarding scope and focus. The lines I have drawn are necessarily arbitrary, the compromises somewhat uncomfortable. To begin with, it was necessary to decide the breadth of the terrain encompassed by the term "reproductive justice." The reproductive lives of women are, of course, significantly affected by social norms regarding, and politicolegal regulation of, both sexuality and parenting. Those lives start not with pregnancy but with the act of sex—or possibly even before, at the various social interactions (coercive or not) that lead to sex. Moreover, the conditions under which women can expect to parent their children also centrally affect their reproductive lives and decisions. Thus, this book could have addressed issues such as the politics of conception (rape, child sexual abuse, economic dependency, etc.), legal policies regarding sexually transmitted diseases (discrimination against those who are HIV-positive, liability for negligent transmission of STDs, etc.), and parenting policies (child custody and divorce, child care, etc.). Instead, although the readings allude in passing to some of those issues,[50] the book essentially focuses on the period between conception and birth. That decision admittedly creates artificial distinctions among sex, pregnancy, and childrearing—areas that actually raise overlapping and interrelated concerns.

Perhaps more importantly, this book focuses primarily on domestic reproductive rights issues in the United States, rather than engaging the wide variety of reproductive policies and practices taking place around the globe. Obviously, much can be learned by comparing other societies' approaches to reproductive issues with our own. But the more important omission necessitated by this narrow focus is the omission of any discussion of the relationship between U.S. policies and reproductive conditions abroad. Reproductive laws and regulations in this country have an impact on other nations. Sometimes that impact is direct, such as under the controversial Mexico City policy, also known as the global gag rule. That rule was first adopted in 1984 under the administration of Ronald Reagan. Bill Clinton rescinded the rule immediately upon taking office in January 1993, but it was later reinstated by George H. W. Bush on *his* first day in office in 2001. The rule prohibits foreign nongovernmental organizations (NGOs) that receive U.S. family planning funds from using their *own* funds to provide legal abortion services, lobby their governments for abortion law reform, or even provide accurate medical counseling or referrals regarding abortion.[51] The gag rule has had a huge impact on the availability of abortion (including medically necessary procedures)[52] in foreign countries and, concomitantly, on the ability of women in those countries to control their reproductive lives. Similarly, the Bush administration's controversial PEP-FAR funding for combating HIV/AIDS overseas heavily emphasizes "abstinence-only" programs, and can result in condom shortages when local authorities lack the money to supply them on their own.[53]

At other times, the impact of U.S. domestic policies on international actors is more indirect. Legal precedents, policies, and regulations that allow U.S. corporations to pollute living environments from Nigeria to India to Indonesia severely limit the reproductive rights of women in those areas by exposing their fetuses to toxins known to cause serious birth defects.[54] U.S. support of structural adjustment policies imposed by the International Monetary Fund and the World Bank on developing countries has contributed to the privatization or reduced funding of social services in those countries, depriving poor, pregnant women (among others) of needed aid.[55] U.S. reproductive policies and practices (including the legality of abortion and concomitant reduction in the number of "adoptable" babies in the United States) have created an entire industry geared to providing infants to U.S. adoptive parents.[56] Countless other examples exist as well. Nevertheless, despite the importance of such topics to a complete exploration of the subject of reproductive justice,[57] they were also excluded as simply beyond the scope and size of this modest volume.

Finally, a whole constellation of reproductive health and justice issues relates particularly to lesbians and gay men. Some of those issues, such as the impact of judicial homophobia on child custody determinations and the effect of antigay bias on HIV/AIDS policy, are beyond the scope of the conception-to-birth frame described above. Another, the bias against gays and lesbians demonstrated by providers of various types of assisted reproductive technology, is touched on briefly by Martha Ertman's piece in chapter 27 of this volume. And an issue of some interest to the GLBT (gay, lesbian, bisexual, and transgendered) community—"intersex" surgery performed on individuals with nonconforming genitalia or reproductive organs—is discussed in chapter 4. Nevertheless, because of space limitations and/or limited treatment in the literature, still other topics that could have been explored in more detail here (such as, for example, limitations on transgender individuals' access to assisted reproductive technologies) were, regrettably, not included.

The materials presented here are interdisciplinary in focus. Thus, while they include some legal cases and many law review articles, they discuss not only legal doctrine but social policy issues and social science research as well. As explained above, a critical constructivist approach to legal issues necessarily entails not only discussion of the applicable legal rules but also an exploration of the broader social context in which those rules operate, and which they help to create.

Finally, this is a feminist book. It starts from the assumption that reproductive rights and meaningful, substantive (as opposed to formal) reproductive autonomy are essential to women's equality. For these reasons, the book does not include readings from conservatives or representatives of the "pro-life" or antichoice movement. Depending on the nature and focus of the course in which the book might be used, it could certainly be supplemented with readings from other perspectives as appropriate.

The book is organized into four parts. Part I, "Questioning Science: Feminist Critiques of Medical Knowledge and Practice," interrogates mainstream understandings of medicine, drawing attention to the social construction of medical knowledge. In particular, it highlights the role played by that knowledge—upon which the law frequently relies—in producing and enforcing problematic assumptions about women's bodies, the reproductive process, and "appropriate" female behavior.

The remaining three parts treat, sequentially, the legal regulation of three different aspects of reproductive behavior: the decision to terminate a pregnancy, the decision to conceive and bear a child, and the pregnant woman's behavior during pregnancy. Part II, "Forced Motherhood: Legal Regulation of Pregnancy Termination," focuses on law's control of access to abortion. Section A, on the legal framework for abortion issues, begins with three historical treatments. It then turns to the "privacy" formulation, providing brief excerpts from two key cases that established the original parameters of the right to privacy in this context, *Roe v. Wade* and *Harris v. MacRae,* each excerpt being followed by a critique of the privacy approach. Section A continues with an introduction of the Court's current, more lenient standard toward governmental restrictions on abortion, adopted in the case of *Planned Parenthood v. Casey.*[58] In particular, it explores the numerous negative consequences that this "undue burden" standard has had for poor women of color. This section concludes with an exploration of the alternative, "equality" approach to defining reproductive rights. Section B of part II engages several specific topics within abortion jurisprudence, including late-term abortion and the Supreme Court cases of *Stenberg v. Carhart* and *Gonzales v. Carhart;* the legal regulation of minors' access to abortion; and the tension between reproductive rights and disability rights raised by the difficult issues surrounding wrongful birth suits and selective abortion.

Part III of the volume, "Motherhood Denied: Legal Regulation of Conception," examines the flip side of abortion law: limitations and constraints imposed upon women who affirmatively want to have a child. Section A addresses the wide variety of punitive restrictions on the reproductive behavior of low-income women and women of color, highlighting the extent to which reproductive rights are not only a "gender" issue but also an issue of race and class. Section B turns to another, very different, set of issues about whether the government can and should regulate women's efforts to have children: alternative reproduction. Readings in that section address racial impacts of "surrogate" motherhood, the effects of artificial insemination rules on "alternative" families such as gay men and lesbians, and the legality of reproductive cloning.

Finally, part IV of the book, "The Disciplining of Mothers-to-Be: Legal Regulation of Behavior during Pregnancy," exposes how legal regulation of behavior during pregnancy—including regulation of the actual process of carrying and delivering a child—perpetuates and facilitates the control of women's behavior in the service of coercive gender, race, and class norms. Section A of this part focuses on workplace discrimination against pregnant women, while section B considers tort and criminal liability for prenatal behavior that poses risks to the fetus. The book concludes with section C's treatment of the topic of court-ordered Cesarean sections.

Conclusion

The critical constructivist approach to reproductive justice presented in this book has significant implications for reproductive law and policy. It emphasizes the role that raced and classed gender norms play in the formation of both public policies on reproductive rights and the societal attitudes often reflected in those policies. It also demonstrates the important role that law and legal policy play in the production of individual women's reproductive choices. Reproductive law and policy are as much about enforcing unwritten rules as to what kinds of mothers various women are, and should be, as they are about rationally resolving social problems. Moreover, critical constructivism reveals that race and gender bias permeate medicine as well as law, influencing not only particular physicians' attitudes towards particular patients but also the very ways in which the medical field "sees" female bodies. As such, this approach raises questions about the law's frequent uncritical reliance on medical knowledge.

These insights in turn have implications for practical public policy and reproductive activism. The critical constructivist approach demonstrates the huge impact that government has on women's reproductive lives, even when it purports not to be interfering in those lives at all. And it highlights the importance—and legitimacy—of governmental programs that affirmatively aid poor women, in order to allow them to realize their reproductive aspirations and control their reproductive lives. It also suggests the need for collaboration among different groups of women, attention to their varying concerns, and recognition of the ways in which their interests overlap. And finally, it underlines the urgency of developing arguments that challenge the equation of reproductive choice making with reproductive equality and justice.

The work on this book was supported by several research grants from the Sturm College of Law at the University of Denver. I thank Richard Delgado and Jean Stefancic for convincing me that this was a viable project and my colleague Viva Moffat for generously providing guidance about copyright issues. This introduction benefited from helpful comments by Rickie Solinger (who also suggested some great pieces to include) and Ann Scales, although of course all errors are mine. Research librarian Diane Burkhardt provided her usual cheerful and superb research support. Joan Pope generously helped with technical problems at the eleventh hour. Many tireless research assistants assisted in the production of the book, including Amber Brink, Christina

Cavaleri, Melissa Haapala, Holly Panetta, Kate Lovelace, Stacy Porto, Elizabeth Titus, Alyssa Yatsko, Kari Zabel, and, especially, Evelyn Calvoni, Jennifer Eyl, Megan Hayes, and Blair Kanis. I am also indebted to the excellent secretarial assistance provided by the staff of the Document Technology Center of the University of Pittsburgh School of Law and for invaluable administrative assistance I received from Joy Barrett, Camilla Adams, Marianna Galstyan, Janae Kirby, Anne Beblavi, Mary Rudolph, Kristin Schneider, and Laura Wyant at the University of Denver. Finally, I thank my extremely supportive editor at NYU Press, Deborah Gershenowitz, and her assistant Salwa Jabado, as well as managing editor Despina Gimbel, for their endless patience and obliging willingness to negotiate.

NOTES

1. For reasons that should become clear later, because "reproductive rights" have been so closely associated with the notion of "choice," I prefer the term "reproductive justice." Nevertheless, for convenience and variety, I'll use both in this book.

2. By "liberal," I'm referring to a set of assumptions and intellectual commitments informed by the Enlightenment thinking of the eighteenth and nineteenth centuries, not to a particular political positioning such as that understood in the contrast between "liberal" and "conservative." *See* Elizabeth Mensch, "The History of Mainstream Legal Thought," in DAVID KAIRYS (ed.), THE POLITICS OF LAW (rev. ed. 1990) (describing liberal legal thought).

3. Other components of reproductive autonomy include the right to control one's own body, Planned Parenthood of Southeastern Pennsylvania v. Casey, 505 U.S. 833, 839 (1992) ("[T]he Constitution places limits on a State's right to interfere with a person's most basic decisions about family and parenthood, as well as bodily integrity." (citations omitted)), and the right of physicians to practice medicine without governmental interference. Roe v. Wade, 410 S.Ct. 113, 164 (1973) ("[F]or the period of pregnancy prior to [fetal viability,] the attending physician, in consultation with his patient, is free to determine, without regulation by the State, that, in his medical judgment, the patient's pregnancy should be terminated. If that decision is reached, the judgment may be effectuated by an abortion free of interference by the state.").

4. "If the right of privacy means anything, it is the right of the individual, married or single, to be free from unwarranted governmental intrusion into matters so fundamentally affecting a person as the decision whether to bear or beget a child." Eisenstadt v. Baird, 405 U.S. 438, 453 (1972).

5. Michael J. Sandel, "Moral Argument and Liberal Toleration: Abortion and Homosexuality," 77 CAL. L. REV. 521, 523 (1989) (citation omitted).

6. See generally, Susan Bandes, "The Negative Constitution: A Critique," 88 MICH. L. REV. 2271, 2273–77 (1990) (describing longstanding notion of negative liberty).

7. Actually, of course, the stereotypes of women vary depending on the particular groups of women being considered. Thus, while privileged white women have tended to be stereotyped as captives of their "womanly" emotions, many women of color and poor women are more likely to be seen as ignorant, heartless, and irresponsible—even dangerous. The critical constructivist approach to reproductive issues, described below, sees this liberal focus on combating stereotypes of white women as part of a broader inattentiveness to the needs of nonwhite women that characterizes the liberal approach. For further discussion of the different behavioral assumptions made about different groups of women and how those affect public policy, see the

readings in this volume by Austin, Davis, Ehrenreich, Gibbs et al., Oliveri, Roberts, Solinger, Todd, and Williams.

8. The Fourteenth Amendment provides: "No State shall make or enforce any law which shall abridge the privileges or immunities of citizens of the United States, nor shall any State deprive any person within its jurisdiction of the equal protection of the laws." U.S. Const. amend. XIV, § 1.

9. Roe v. Wade, 410 U.S. 113, 153 (1973). *See also* Griswold v. Connecticut, 381 U.S. 479, 482 (1965); Eisenstadt, 405 U.S. at 453.

10. Lawrence v. Texas, 539 U.S. 558, 574 (2003) (law criminalizing "deviate sexual intercourse" struck down as violative of right to privacy).

11. In re Quinlan, 70 N.J. 10, cert. denied *sub nom.* Garger v. New Jersey, 429 U.S. 922 (1976) (terminal patient has a right to refuse treatment under the constitutional right of privacy); Cruzan v. Director, Mo. Dept. of Health, 497 U.S. 261, 270 (1990) (noting that some courts have based right to refuse treatment on privacy right, and basing its own finding of a right to refuse on the "liberty" right in the Due Process clause).

12. Griswold, 381 U.S. 479 (finding a right of privacy in the Constitution and holding that it includes the right of married couples to access birth control); Eisenstadt, 405 U.S. at 453 (holding that the right of privacy protects access to contraception for single people as well as married couples).

13. Rickie Solinger, Pregnancy and Power: A Short History of Reproductive Politics in America 221 (2005) (excerpted in chapter 24 of this volume).

14. A useful example of positive liberty is the benefit society derives from traffic regulations: Those regulations constrain negative liberty, by interfering with people's freedom to drive on the left side of the road, but increase positive liberty, by making travel easier for everyone.

15. Anatole France, The Red Lilly 80 (1937).

16. Dorothy Roberts, Killing the Black Body: Race, Reproduction, and the Meaning of Liberty 294 (1997) (excerpted in this volume). As Roberts also notes, "The definition of liberty as a purely negative right serves to exempt the state from any obligation to ensure the social conditions and resources necessary for self-determination and autonomous decision making." Id. at 14.

17. "Mothers Who Receive AFDC Payments: Fertility and Socioeconomic Characteristics," Statistical Brief, Economics and Statistics Administration, U.S. Dept. of Commerce (1995), available at http://www.census.gov/population/socdemo/statebriefs/sb2-95.html; "Income, Earnings, and Poverty from the 2004 American Community Survey," American Community Survey Reports, U.S. Census Bureau (Aug. 2005), available at http://www.census.gov/prod/2005pubs/acs-01.pdf.

18. It should not be surprising, then, that many scholars writing from a critical constructivist perspective are women of color. *See, e.g.,* Roberts, supra note 16. For a sampling of works on the reproductive rights of women of color, *see* Marlene Gerber Fried (ed.), From Abortion to Reproductive Freedom: Transforming a Movement (1990); Lisa Ikemoto, "In the Shadow of Race: Women of Color in Health Disparities Policy," 39 U.C. Davis L. Rev. 1023 (2006); Lisa Ikemoto, "Racial Disparities in Health Care and Cultural Competency," 48 St. Louis U. L.J. 75 (2003); Jael Silliman, Marlene Gerber Fried, Loretta Ross, and Elena R. Gueiérrez, Undivided Rights: Women of Color Organize for Reproductive Justice (2004). Some of these authors have embraced a human rights approach to conceptualizing reproductive rights, noting that the focus of the liberal approach "on individualism and civil and political rights neglects economic, social, sexual, and cultural rights that address group or collective needs." Silliman, et al., supra, at 18.

19. See supra, p. 3.

20. An argument for seeing reproductive rights as an equality issue is presented by Reva Siegel in chapter 14 of this volume.

21. Much of this type of analysis is based upon the writings of the famous French social theorist, Michel Foucault. *See, e.g.,* Michel Foucault, "Two Lectures," in Colin Gordon (ed.), Power/Knowledge: Selected Interviews and Other Writings by Michel Foucault, 1972–1977 (Colin Gordon et al., trans., 1972).

22. See, e.g., Lawrence v. Texas, 539 U.S. 558, 588 (2003) (Justice Scalia, dissenting) (noting that Washington v. Glucksberg, 521 U.S. 702, 721 (1997), "held that *only* fundamental rights which are 'deeply rooted in this Nation's history and tradition' qualify for [heightened scrutiny under the Due Process Clause]" and noting that "*Roe* and *Casey* . . . subjected the restriction of abortion to heightened scrutiny without even attempting to establish that the freedom to abort *was* rooted in this Nation's tradition").

23. Solinger, Pregnancy and Power, supra note 13, at 210–11.

24. Id.

25. See Leslie A. Reagan, When Abortion Was a Crime: Women, Medicine, and Law in the United States, 1867–1973 1–18 (1977) (excerpted in chapter 6 of this volume).

26. Males control state legislatures today, as well. "Women currently hold 23.5 percent of legislative seats in the 50 states, a ratio that has increased only slightly over the past 10 years." Women's Legislative Network of the National Conference of State Legislatures, available at http://www.ncsl.org/programs/wln/WomenInOffice2007.htm. *See also,* Rebekah B. Steen, "Representative Government and Gender Diversity in State Legislative Bodies," 7 Pi Alpha Alpha 7, available at http://www.naspaa.org/initiatives/paa/pdf/Rebekah_Steen.pdf.

27. As Reagan notes, at any given point in history, "[p]rescribed morality and popular morality may not be identical." Reagan, supra note 25, at 6.

28. Solinger, Pregnancy and Power, supra note 13, at 221.

29. Reva B. Siegel, "Abortion as a Sex Equality Right: Its Basis in Feminist Theory," in Martha Albertson Fineman & Isabel Karpin (eds.), Mothers in Law: Feminist Theory and the Legal Regulation of Women 55 (1995) (excerpted in chapter 14 of this volume).

30. There are a number of important differences among the stereotypes applied to women of different races and ethnicities. On race, ethnicity, and reproductive rights, *see generally* Silliman et al., supra note 18 (on women of color, including chapters on African American women, Native American women, Asian and Pacific Islander women, and Latinas); Fried, supra note 18 (on women of color); and Roberts, supra note 16, at 3–21 (on African American women). *See also* Patricia Hill Collins, Black Feminist Thought: Knowledge, Consciousness, and the Politics of Empowerment (2nd ed. 2000) (on stereotypes of African American women). On class and reproductive rights, *see* Solinger, Pregnancy and Power, supra note 13; Rickie Solinger, Beggars and Choosers: How the Politics of Choice Shapes Adoption, Abortion, and Welfare in the United States (2001).

31. *See* Martha Chamallas, Introduction to Feminist Legal Theory 283–315 (2003).

32. They sometimes also have a differential impact on gay men and lesbians. *See, e.g,* Martha Ertman's discussion of alternative reproductive technology in chapter 27 of this volume.

33. Roberts, supra note 16, at 295.

34. This is not to say that they have the same effect on all women. The "good mother" image, for example, has both harmed and helped various sorts of women. As several pieces in this volume will describe, it has protected privileged women from some of the more coercive interventions that marginalized women have suffered in their reproductive lives, even as it has, as noted above, also justified pronatalist policies that restrict the choices open to such women.

And although the "bad mother" image that is its opposite seems to have had a largely negative impact, it can occasionally protect marginalized women from certain types of harmful treatment. For example, while marginalized women have often been subjected to coerced sterilizations because of their "bad mother" image, only privileged women are likely to have trouble obtaining *voluntary* sterilizations. See Nancy Ehrenreich, "Colonization of the Womb," 43 Duke L.J. 492, 509–19 (1993) (excerpted in chapter 35 of this volume). On past and recent sterilization abuse, *see* the Davis and Albiston pieces in this volume.

35. See Donna Young, "Working across Borders: Global Restructuring and Women's Work," 2001 Utah L. Rev. 1, 59–68 (2001).

36. "Some 'women's access to the high paying high status professions is facilitated through the revival of semi-indentured servitude. Put another way, one woman is exercising class and citizenship privilege to buy her way out of sex oppression.'" *Id.,* at 68n.333 (quoting Audrey Macklin, "Foreign Domestic Worker: Surrogate Housewife or Mail Order Servant?," 37 McGill L.J. 681, 751 (1992)). Despite these benefits that privileged women achieve at the expense of other women, I would argue that the privilege a particular woman enjoys along one axis (say, economic privilege) can sometimes actually *reinforce* the subordination that she suffers along another axis (say, gender). *See,* Nancy Ehrenreich, "Subordination and Symbiosis: Mechanisms of Mutual Support between Subordinating Systems," 71 UMKC L. Rev. 251, 256–57 (2002).

37. *See, e.g.,* Ehrenreich, supra note 34 (addressing the interconnections between overuse of consensual Cesarean sections experienced by privileged women and coercive use of Cesarean sections on low-income women of color).

38. *See, e.g.,* Anne Fausto-Sterling, Sexing the Body: Gender Politics and the Construction of Sexuality (2000); Donna Haraway, Primate Visions: Gender, Race and Nature in the World of Modern Science (1989); Mary Wyer, Mary Barbercheck, Donna Geisman, Hatice Orun Ozturk, and Marta Wayne (eds.), Women, Science, and Technology: A Reader in Feminist Science Studies (2001).

39. See David J. Harris and Pamela S. Douglas, "Enrollment of Women in Cardiovascular Clinical Trials Funded by the National Heart, Lung, and Blood Institute," 343 New Eng. J. Med. 475, 475–76 (2000).

40. Emily Martin, "The Fetus as Intruder: Mothers' Bodies and Medical Metaphors," *in* Robbie Davis-Floyd & Joseph Dumit (eds.), Cyborg Babies: From Techno-Sex to Techno-Tots 131 (1998).

41. See, *e.g.,* the pieces by Todd and Martin, in chapters 2 and 3, respectively, of this volume.

42. Mary Briody Mahowald, Genes, Women, Equality 39 (2000).

43. Anne Fausto-Sterling, Myths of Gender: Biological Theories about Women and Men (1985).

44. See Cheryl Chase, "'Cultural Practice' or 'Reconstructive Surgery'? U.S. Genital Cutting, the Intersex Movement, and Medical Double Standards," *in* Stanlie M. James & Claire C. Robertson (eds.), Genital Cutting and Transnational Sisterhood (2002) (excerpted in chapter 4 of this volume).

45. Haraway, supra note 38.

46. Although data on the point are hard to find, it seems likely that most legislators and judges share this first view. Even legal actors who are disposed to be more critical of medicine probably usually assume the validity and reliability of generally accepted medical knowledge, even while they're willing to entertain critiques of particular individual practitioners or authors as biased.

47. For an interesting illustration, see Shelly Tremain, "On the Government of Disability," 27

Soc. Theory & Prac. 617 (2001), in which the author criticizes disability studies theorists for assuming that scientific descriptions of bodily "impairment" are unmediated by culture.

48. Joanne Conaghan, "Schlag in Wonderland," 57 U. Miami L. Rev. 543, 562 (2003) (quoting Alessandra Tanesini, An Introduction to Feminist Epistemology 187 (1999)).

49. See the Ehrenreich and English, Todd, and Martin pieces, excerpted in chapters 1, 2, and 3, respectively, of this volume.

50. They do touch briefly, for example, on the politics of conception, with the two pieces by Dailard on the issue of sex education, excerpted together in chapter 20 of this volume.

51. Center for Reproductive Rights, "The Bush Global Gag Rule: Endangering Women's Health, Free Speech, and Democracy," July 2003, available at http://www.crlp.org/pub_fac_ggrbush.html (last visited Oct. 12, 2006); Global Gag Rule, "Background on the Policy," http://www.globalgagrule.org/background.htm (last visited Oct. 12, 2006).

52. The Global Gag Rule Impact Project, "Access Denied: U.S. Restrictions on International Family Planning," available at http://www.globalgagrule.org.

53. "The Attack on Reproductive and Sexual Freedom in the U.S. and Overseas: Analyzing the Challenges and Responses," National Lawyers Guild, "Law for the People Convention 2006," 4 (2006); The Henry Kaiser Family Foundation, Kaiser network.org,, "Daily HIV/AIDS report" (April 5, 2006), available at http://www.kaisernetwork.org/daily_reports/rep_index.cfm?hint=1&DR_ID=36429.

54. See, e.g., Julienne I. Alder, "United States' Waste Export Control Program: Burying Our Neighbors in Garbage," 40 Am. U. L. Rev. 885, 888n. 21, 909–10 (1991); Porterfield and Weir, "The Export of U.S. Toxic Wastes," The Nation, Oct. 3, 1987, 325, 341–44.

55. See Susan George, A Fate Worse than Debt 52 (1988); Michel Chossudovsky, The Globalization of Poverty 67 (2003).

56. Solinger, Beggars and Choosers, *supra* note 30, at 126.

57. *See* Chandra Talpade Mohanty, "'Under Western Eyes' Revisited: Feminist Solidarity through Anticapitalist Struggles," 28 SIGNS 499, 508–10 (2002). *See also* Rosalind Pollack Petchesky, Global Prescriptions: Gendering Health and Human Rights (2003).

58. Planned Parenthood of Southeastern Pennsylvania v. Casey, 502 U.S. 1056 (1992).

Questioning Science
*Feminist Critiques of Medical
Knowledge and Practice*

Introduction to Part I

The purpose of this part is to develop the "skeptical" view of medicine described in the Introduction. According to that view, medical knowledge about human reproduction is socially constructed. Such knowledge doesn't just represent the objective "truth" about what is going on in women's bodies, but, rather, reflects prevailing ideas about women's roles and natures—views that are the product of unequal race, class, and gender relations. And because law often relies uncritically upon mainstream medical knowledge, the legal system often enforces these problematic medical assumptions against women.

A historical piece begins part I: "The Sexual Politics of Sickness," an excerpt from *For Her Own Good*, Barbara Ehrenreich and Deirdre English's classic study of how medical and psychological experts' views of women's bodies have changed during different eras. This analysis reveals the sexist and pronatalist nature of late nineteenth- and early twentieth-century views of women, under which they were seen as primarily meant for human reproduction and as completely controlled by the uterus.

The rest of the pieces present more current illustrations of the contingency of medical knowledge. "Delusions in Discourse" is an excerpt from *Intimate Adversaries*, by Alexandra Dundras Todd, a sociological study of how doctors' assumptions about women patients compromise the effectiveness of their treatment of those patients. The author's "discourse" analysis of the words and body language used by doctors during routine office visits reveals that physicians often fail to find out crucial information about the histories, concerns, and behaviors of their patients. And "Body Narratives, Body Boundaries," by medical anthropologist Emily Martin, describes the effect of gender ideology on medical textbooks' descriptions of human conception. Her study shows that gender stereotypes penetrate descriptions of the most basic of bodily functions—such as the interaction between the egg and the sperm. It is followed by an essay by Cheryl Chase, founder of the Intersex Society of North America, in which the author indicts the widespread practice of genital normalizing surgery in the United States. Chase argues that such surgeries, performed on infants born with ambiguous genitalia, reinforce gender norms that emphasize penetrative sexuality for men and reproductive capacity for women.

As a group, these pieces illustrate the critique that has been directed at medicine by its more radical challengers. Through their descriptions of the operation of medical knowledge in concrete contexts, they show exactly how such "knowledge" both relies upon and enforces raced and classed gender norms. And in so doing, they raise important questions about what it means for legal actors to rely on medical "expertise."

Chapter 1

The Sexual Politics of Sickness

Barbara Ehrenreich and Deirdre English

When Charlotte Perkins Gilman collapsed with a "nervous disorder," the physician she sought out for help was Dr. S. Weir Mitchell, "the greatest nerve specialist in the country." . . . When Gilman met him, in the eighteen eighties, he was at the height of his career, earning over $60,000 per year (the equivalent of over $300,000 in today's dollars). His renown for the treatment of female nervous disorders had by this time led to a marked alteration of character. According to an otherwise fond biographer, his vanity "had become colossal. It was fed by torrents of adulation, incessant and exaggerated, every day, almost every hour. . . ."[1]

Gilman approached the great man with "utmost confidence. . . ." In preparation, Gilman methodically wrote out a complete history of her case. She had observed, for example, that her sickness vanished when she was away from her home, her husband, and her child, and returned as soon as she came back to them. But Dr. Mitchell dismissed her prepared history as evidence of "self-conceit." He did not want information from his patients; he wanted "complete obedience." Gilman quotes his prescription for her:

> "Live as domestic a life as possible. Have your child with you all the time." (Be it remarked that if I did but dress the baby it left me shaking and crying—certainly far from a healthy companionship for her, to say nothing of the effect on me.) "Lie down an hour after each meal. Have but two hours intellectual life a day. And never touch pen, brush or pencil as long as you live."[2]

Gilman dutifully returned home and for some months attempted to follow Dr. Mitchell's orders to the letter. The result, in her words was:

> [I] came perilously close to losing my mind. The mental agony grew so unbearable that I would sit blankly moving my head from side to side. . . . I would crawl into remote closets and under beds—to hide from the grinding pressure of that distress. . . .[3]

Finally, in a "moment of clear vision" Gilman understood the source of her illness: she did not want to be a *wife;* she wanted to be a writer and an activist. So, discarding

Barbara Ehrenreich and Deirdre English, *For Her Own Good: 200 Years of the Experts' Advice to Women* 115–54 (rev. ed. 2005).

S. Weir Mitchell's prescription and divorcing her husband, she took off for California with her baby, her pen, her brush and pencil. But she never forgot Mitchell and his near-lethal "cure." Three years after her recovery she wrote *The Yellow Wallpaper*[,] a fictionalized account of her own illness and descent into madness. If that story had any influence on S. Weir Mitchell's method of treatment, she wrote after a long life of accomplishments, "I have not lived in vain."[4]

Charlotte Perkins Gilman was fortunate enough to have had a "moment of clear vision" in which she understood what was happening to her. Thousands of other women, like Gilman, were finding themselves in a new position of dependency on the male medical profession—and with no alternative sources of information or counsel. The medical profession was consolidating its monopoly over healing,* and now the woman who felt sick, or tired, or simply depressed would no longer seek help from a friend or female healer, but from a male physician. The general theory which guided the doctors' practice as well as their public pronouncements was that women were, by nature, weak, dependent, and diseased. Thus would the doctors attempt to secure their victory over the female healer: with the "scientific" evidence that woman's essential nature was not to be a strong, competent help-giver, but to be a *patient*.

A Mysterious Epidemic

In fact at the time there were reasons to think that the doctors' theory was not so far-fetched. Women were decidedly sickly, though not for the reasons the doctors advanced. . . . The[ir] symptoms included headache, muscular aches, weakness, depression, menstrual difficulties, indigestion, etc., and usually a general debility requiring constant rest. . . . The syndrome was never fatal, but . . . [w]omen who recovered to lead full and active lives—like Charlotte Perkins Gilman and Jane Addams—were the exceptions.
. . . .

Marriage: The Sexual Economic Relation

In the second half of the nineteenth century the vague syndrome gripping middle- and upper-class women had become so widespread as to represent not so much a disease in the medical sense as a way of life. More precisely, the way this type of woman was expected to live predisposed her to sickness, and sickness in turn predisposed her to continue to live as she was expected to. The delicate, affluent lady, who was completely dependent on her husband, set the sexual romanticist ideal of femininity for women of all classes.

[As] [c]lear-headed feminists like Charlotte Perkins Gilman and Olive Schreiner . . . observed, poor women did not suffer from the syndrome. . . . A morbid aesthetic developed, in which sickness was seen as a source of female beauty, and beauty—in the

---

* *Editor's note*: For a discussion of the nineteenth-century, male-dominated medical profession's struggle to replace female healers and midwives, see the piece by Luker, in chapter 5 of this volume.

high-fashion sense—was in fact a source of sickness. . . . [T]ight-laced corsets, which [were] *de rigueur* throughout the last half of the century, . . . exerted, on the average, twenty-one pounds of pressure on [the] internal organs and extremes of up to eighty-eight pounds had been measured. . . . Some of the short-term results of tight-lacing were shortness of breath, constipation, weakness, and a tendency to violent indigestion. Among the long-term effects were bent or fractured ribs, displacement of the liver, and uterine prolapse (in some cases, the uterus would be gradually forced, by the pressure of the corset, out through the vagina).

. . . .

Femininity as a Disease

The medical profession threw itself with gusto on the languid figure of the female invalid. . . . In fact the theories which guided the doctor's practice from the late nineteenth century to the early twentieth century held that woman's *normal* state was to be sick. . . . Menstruation was a serious threat throughout life—so was the lack of it. According to Dr. Engelmann, president of the American Gynecology Society in 1900:

> Many a young life is battered and forever crippled on the breakers of puberty; if it crosses these unharmed and is not dashed to pieces on the rock of childbirth, it may still ground on the ever-recurring shallows of menstruation, and lastly upon the final bar of the menopause ere protection is found in the unruffled waters of the harbor beyond reach of sexual storms.[5]

. . . .

Ignoring the existence of thousands of working women, the doctors assumed that every woman was prepared to set aside a week or five days every month as a period of invalidism. . . . As late as 1916, Dr. Winfield Scott Hall was advising:

> All heavy exercise should be omitted during the menstrual week . . . a girl should not only retire earlier at this time, but ought to stay out of school from one to three days as the case may be, resting the mind and taking extra hours of rest and sleep.[6]

Similarly, a pregnant woman was "indisposed," throughout the full nine months. . . . Doctors stressed the pathological nature of childbirth itself—an argument which also was essential to their campaign against midwives. After delivery, they insisted on a protracted period of convalescence mirroring the "confinement" which preceded birth. . . . Finally after all this, a woman could only look forward to menopause, portrayed in the medical literature as a terminal illness—the "death of the woman in the woman."

Now it must be said in the doctors' defense that women of a hundred years ago *were,* in some ways, sicker than the women of today. . . . Without adequate, and usually without any, means of contraception, a married woman could expect to face the risk of childbirth repeatedly through her fertile years. After each childbirth a woman might suffer any number of gynecological complications, such as prolapsed (slipped) uterus or irreparable pelvic tear, which would be with her for the rest of her life.

Another special risk to women came from tuberculosis, the "white plague." . . .

So, from a statistical point of view, there was some justification for the doctors' theory of innate female frailty. But there was also, from the doctors' point of view, a strong commercial justification for regarding women as sick. . . . The theory of female frailty obviously disqualified women as healers. . . . At the same time the theory made women highly qualified as patients. . . .

Meanwhile, the health of women who were *not* potential patients—poor women—received next to no attention from the medical profession. Poor women must have been at least as susceptible as wealthy women to the "sexual storms" doctors saw in menstruation, pregnancy, etc.; and they were definitely much more susceptible to the hazards of childbearing, tuberculosis, and, of course, industrial diseases. . . . Emma Goldman, who was a trained midwife as well as an anarchist leader, described "the fierce, blind struggle of the women of the poor against frequent pregnancies" and told of the agony of seeing children grow up "sickly and undernourished"—if they survived infancy at all.[7] For the woman who labored outside her home, working conditions took an enormous toll.

. . . .

But the medical profession as a whole—and no doubt there were many honorable exceptions—sturdily maintained that it was affluent women who were most delicate and most in need of medical attention. . . . [B]etter-off women were [thought to be] sickly because of their refined and civilized lifestyle. Fortunately, however, this same lifestyle made them amenable to lengthy medical treatment. Poor and working-class women were inherently stronger, and this was also fortunate, since their [inability to take time off work] disqualified them from lengthy treatment anyway. The theory of innate female sickness, skewed so as to account for class differences in ability to pay for medical care, meshed conveniently with the doctors' commercial self-interest.

. . . .

Men Evolve, Women Devolve

But it would be overly cynical to see the doctors as mere businessmen, weighing theories of female physiology against cash receipts. The doctors of the late nineteenth century were also men of science. . . . Almost all agreed that the existing human races represented different evolutionary stages. . . . By the eighteen sixties natural scientists could pinpoint woman's place on the evolutionary ladder with some precision—she was at the level of the Negro. For example, Carl Vogt, a leading European professor of natural history, placed the Negro (male) as follows: " . . . the grown-up Negro partakes, as regards his intellectual faculties, of the nature of the child, the female, and the senile White."[8] (Where this left the Negro female one shudders to think, not to mention the "senile" female of either race.)

. . . .

[According to Darwin's theory of evolution, as applied by these scientists,] the ability [of a species] to vary in potentially successful ways . . . seemed to require a degree of cleverness and daring. It must, therefore, be a male trait. So in the grand chain of evolution, males were the innovators, . . . [m]ales produced the variations; females

merely reproduced them. . . . Females, being more primitive, were non-varying and identical in evolutionary function, and that function was to reproduce.
. . . .

The Dictatorship of the Ovaries

It was medicine's task to translate the evolutionary theory of women into the language of flesh and blood, tissues and organs. The result was a theory which put woman's mind, body and soul in the thrall of her all-powerful reproductive organs. "The Uterus, it must be remembered," Dr. F. Hollick wrote, "is the *controlling* organ in the female body." . . . To other medical theorists, it was the ovaries which occupied center stage . . . and any abnormalities, from irritability to insanity, could be traced to some ovarian disease.
. . . .

[However], the [medical theory of the] "psychology of the ovary" drew a rigid distinction between reproductivity and sexuality. . . . [D]octors said [women] had no predilection for the sex act itself. Even a woman physician, Dr. Mary Wood-Allen, wrote (perhaps from experience) that women embrace their husbands "without a particle of sex desire."[9] Hygiene manuals stated that the more cultured the woman, "the more is the sensual refined away from her nature," and warned against "any spasmodic convulsion" on a woman's part during intercourse lest it interfere with conception. Female sexuality was seen as unwomanly and possibly even detrimental to the supreme function of reproduction. . . . Underneath the complacent denials of female sexual feelings, [however,] there lurked the age-old male fascination with woman's "insatiable lust," which, once awakened, might turn out to be uncontrollable.
. . . .

[T]he uterus and ovaries . . . were . . . blamed for all possible female disorders, from headaches to sore throats and indigestion. . . . Even tuberculosis could be traced to the capricious ovaries. . . .

Since the reproductive organs were the source of disease, they were the obvious target in the treatment of disease. . . . Historian Ann Douglas Wood describes the "local treatments" used in the mid-nineteenth century for almost any female complaint:

> This [local] treatment had four stages, although not every case went through all four: a manual investigation, "leeching," "injections," and "cauterization." Dewees [an American medical professor] and Bennet, a famous English gynecologist widely read in America, both advocated placing the leeches right on the vulva or neck of the uterus, although Bennet cautioned the doctor to count them as they dropped off when satiated, lest he "lose" some. Bennet had known adventurous leeches to advance into the cervical cavity of the uterus itself, and he noted, "I think I have scarcely ever seen more acute pain than that experienced by several of my patients under these circumstances." Less distressing to a 20th century mind, but perhaps even more senseless, were the "injections" into the uterus advocated by these doctors. The uterus became a kind of catch-all, or what one exasperated doctor referred to as a "Chinese toy shop": Water,

milk and water, linseed tea, and "decoction of marshmellow . . . tepid or cold" found their way inside nervous women patients. The final step, performed at this time, one must remember with no anesthetic but a little opium or alcohol, was cauterization, either through the application of nitrate of silver, or in cases of more severe infection, through the use of much stronger hydrate of potassa, or even the "actual cautery," a "white-hot iron" instrument.[10]

In the second half of the century, these fumbling experiments with the female interior gave way to the more decisive technique of surgery—aimed increasingly at the control of female personality disorders. There had been a brief fad of clitoridectomy (removal of the clitoris) in the sixties, following the introduction of the operation by the English physician Isaac Baker Brown. Although most doctors frowned on the practice of removing the clitoris, they tended to agree that it might be necessary in cases of nymphomania, intractable masturbation, or "unnatural growth" of that organ. (The last clitoridectomy we know of in the United States was performed in 1948 on a child of five, as a cure for masturbation.)*

The most common form of surgical intervention in the female personality was ovariotomy, removal of the ovaries—or "female castration." . . . According to historian G. J. Barker-Benfield:

> Among the indications were troublesomeness, eating like a ploughman, masturbation, attempted suicide, erotic tendencies, persecution mania, simple "cussedness," and dysmenorrhea [painful menstruation]. Most apparent in the enormous variety of symptoms doctors took to indicate castration was a strong current of sexual appetitiveness on the part of women.[11]

. . . .

Patients were often brought in by their husbands, who complained of their unruly behavior. . . . The operation was judged successful if the woman was restored to a placid contentment with her domestic functions.

The overwhelming majority of women who had leeches or hot steel applied to their cervices, or who had their clitorises or ovaries removed, were women of the middle to upper classes, for after all, these procedures cost money. But it should not be imagined that poor women were spared the gynecologist's exotic catalog of tortures simply because they couldn't pay. The pioneering work in gynecological surgery had been performed by Marion Sims on black female slaves he kept for the sole purpose of surgical experimentation. He operated on one of them thirty times in four years, being foiled over and over by postoperative infections. After moving to New York, Sims continued his experimentation on indigent Irish women in the wards of New York Women's Hospital. So, though middle-class women suffered most from the doctors' actual practice, it was poor and black women who had suffered through the brutal period of experimentation.

. . . .

* *Editor's note*: For a discussion of modern clitoral surgeries, usually on children, see the piece by Cheryl Chase in chapter 4 of this volume.

Subverting the Sick Role: Hysteria

. . . .

As time goes on . . . , [m]edicine is caught in a contradiction of its own making, and begins to turn against the patient.

Doctors had established that women are sick, that this sickness is innate. . . . But at the same time, doctors *were* expected to cure. . . . [In addition, m]edicine had insisted that woman was sick *and* that her life centered on the reproductive function. But these are contradictory propositions. If you are sick enough, you cannot reproduce. . . . [And m]any women probably *were* using the sick role as a way to escape their reproductive and domestic duties. . . .

[Eventually, t]he suspicion of malingering—whether to avoid pregnancy or gain attention—cast a pall over the doctor-patient relationship. If a woman was really sick (as the doctors said she ought to be), then the doctor's efforts, however ineffective, must be construed as appropriate, justifiable, and of course reimbursable. But if she was *not* sick, then the doctor was being made a fool of.

. . . .

But it took a specific syndrome to make the ambiguities in the doctor-patient relationship unbearable, and to finally break the gynecologists' monopoly of the female psyche. The syndrome was hysteria. In many ways, hysteria epitomized the cult of female invalidism. It affected middle- and upper-class women almost exclusively; it had no discernible organic basis; and it was totally resistant to medical treatment. But unlike the more common pattern of invalidism, hysteria was episodic. It came and went in unpredictable, and frequently violent, fits. . . . It was essential to [doctors'] professional self-esteem either to find an organic basis for the disease and cure it, or to expose it as a clever charade.

There was plenty of evidence for the latter point of view. With mounting suspicion, the medical literature began to observe that hysterics never had fits when alone, and only when there was something soft to fall on. . . .

In historian Carroll Smith-Rosenberg's interpretation, the doctors' accusations had some truth to them: the hysterical fit, for many women, must have been the only acceptable outburst—of rage, of despair, or simply of *energy*—possible. . . . On the whole, however, doctors did continue to insist that hysteria was a real disease—a disease of the uterus, in fact. . . .

Carroll Smith-Rosenberg writes that doctors recommended suffocating hysterical women until their fits stopped, beating them across the face and body with wet towels, and embarrassing them in front of family and friends. . . . The more women became hysterical, the more doctors became punitive toward the disease; and at the same time, they began to see the disease everywhere themselves until they were diagnosing every independent act by a woman, especially a women's rights action, as "hysterical."

With hysteria, the cult of female invalidism was carried to its logical conclusion. Society had assigned affluent women to a life of confinement and inactivity, and medicine had justified this assignment by describing women as innately sick. In the epidemic of hysteria women were both accepting their inherent "sickness" *and* finding a way to rebel against an intolerable social role. Sickness, having become a way of life, became a way of rebellion, and medical treatment, which had always had strong over-tones of coercion, revealed itself as frankly and brutally repressive.

But the deadlock over hysteria was to usher in a new era in the experts' relation-ship to women. . . . In the course of the twentieth century psychologists and psychia-trists would replace doctors as the dominant experts in the lives of women. . . . For decades into [that] century doctors would continue to view menstruation, pregnancy, and menopause as physical diseases and intellectual liabilities. Adolescent girls would still be advised to study less, and mature women would be treated indiscriminately to hysterectomies, the modern substitute for ovariotomies. The female reproductive or-gans would continue to be viewed as a kind of frontier for chemical and surgical ex-pansionism, untested drugs, and reckless experimentation. But the debate over the Woman Question would never again be phrased in such crudely materialistic terms as those set forth by nineteenth-century medical theory—with brains "battling" uter-uses for control of woman's nature. The psychological interpretation of hysteria, and eventually of "neurasthenia" and the other vague syndromes of female invalidism, es-tablished once and for all that the brain was in command. The experts of the twenti-eth century would accept a woman's intelligence and energy: the question would no longer be what a woman *could* do, but rather, what a woman *ought* to do.

NOTES

1. Anna Robeson Burr, *Weir Mitchell: His Life and Letters* (New York: Duffield and Co., 1929), p. 289.

2. Charlotte Perkins Gilman, *The Living of Charlotte Perkins Gilman: An Autobiography* (New York: Harper Colophon Books, 1975), p. 96.

3. Gilman, loc. cit.

4. Gilman, *Autobiography,* p. 121.

5. Quoted in G. Stanley Hall, *Adolescence,* Vol. II (New York: D. Appleton, 1905), p. 588.

6. Winfield Scott Hall, Ph.D., M.D., *Sexual Knowledge* (Philadelphia: John C. Winston, 1916), pp. 202–3.

7. Emma Goldman, *Living My Life,* Vol. I (New York: Dover Publications, Inc., 1970, first published 1931), pp. 185–86.

8. Quoted in John S. Haller, Jr., and Robin M. Haller, *The Physician and Sexuality in Victo-rian America* (Urbana, Illinois: University of Illinois Press, 1974), p. 51.

9. Quoted in Haller and Haller, op. cit., p. 101.

10. Ann Douglas Wood, "The 'Fashionable Diseases': Women's Complaints and their Treat-ment in Nineteenth-Century America," *Journal of Interdisciplinary History* 4, Summer 1973, p. 30.

11. Ben Barker-Benfield, "The Spermatic Economy: A Nineteenth Century View of Sexual-ity," *Feminist Studies* I, Summer 1972, pp. 45–74.

Chapter 2

Delusions in Discourse

Alexandra Dundas Todd

I conducted in-depth interviews with women in their homes.* ... Although my study is too small to draw systematic conclusions, ... I did observe two relevant trends. First, the darker a woman's skin and/or the lower her place on the economic scale, the poorer the care and efforts at explanation she received. Women of color and/or an economically poor background were more apt to be seen as "difficult" patients when they asked questions, were more likely to be urged to use birth control pills or the IUD rather than the diaphragm in the clinic, and in the private practitioner's office, where nearly all women received the pill, they were more likely to be talked down to, scolded, and patronized.

Second, despite these important differences, there were also similarities. Women's treatment was along a continuum whereby all women received care that both reflected and reinforced society's definitions of and attitudes toward women, their bodies, and reproduction. In the interviews, as well as in my informal talks with women, a general underlying question, often only vaguely articulated, persisted. Although each woman's question took a different form and encompassed unique circumstances, there was discernible similarity or pattern in the concerns expressed. In broad outline this question was, "How can I more fully integrate my sexual activity and reproductive needs with what I want from life? How can these activities be more under my control?" Discussion about such questions was not encouraged in doctor-patient conversations, yet my interviews show them to be repeated concerns connected to contraception and health. When women did try to raise variations on this theme with their doctors, they were interrupted or cut off. Women accepted this truncation of their social lives, accepting doctors' views that such topics were beyond the scope of medical care. This dominance prevails not only in the doctor's office but often in the women's understandings of their bodies once outside the office. ...

Method

As a means of looking at these differing dynamics between what is discussed in the doctor-patient interaction and what women willingly talked about when encouraged

Alexandra Dundas Todd, *Intimate Adversaries: Cultural Conflict between Doctors and Women Patients* 77–97 (1989).
  * *Editor's note*: In this study, the author observed interactions between female patients and their doctors during office visits involving contraceptive needs, and then interviewed the patients afterwards.

	Patient	*Doctor*
Pattern 1	Has relevant information and tries to express it	Interrupts patient
Pattern 2	Unaware; does not try to express information	Has relevant information; withholds information
Pattern 3	Has relevant information; withholds information	Unaware; does not try to express information

Fig. 2.1. Categorization for information exchange between doctor and patient

to do so, a modified version of a sociolinguistic technique called "text expansion" is useful.

. . . .

[In my study,] [v]erbatim segments of the doctor-patient discourse are used in conjunction with verbatim segments of my in-depth interviews with patients. Rather than rely on doctors to explain women's behaviors, I have drawn on women's experiences to understand better their medical relationships. . . .

Organizational differences in the two settings [I studied] influenced communication, but the problems to be discussed here were similar in the clinic and private practice office: *often what the patient really needed to talk about was ignored in medical encounters.* This gap between patients' and doctors' perspectives took three main forms.

In the first pattern, the discourse displayed women trying to direct topics in the medical encounter. Women inserted their views or tried to raise their concerns about aspects of their lives important to contraceptive use and decision making but were cut off by their doctors. In the second pattern, women did not press their views or concerns. It appears as if they were unaware that their information might contribute to or change the understanding of their problems, and doctors did little to change this view. In the third pattern, women had their own agenda, which did not emerge in discussions with the doctors. Patients withheld information about their contraceptive needs from unaware doctors.

Whatever the pattern of the medical interaction, expansion of the interviews highlighted topics that were relevant to, but absent from, the discussion of contraceptive choice. These topics included technical information, but centered around contextual, social parts of women's lives and were generally defined by doctors and accepted by women as inappropriate in medical discourse. In informal conversations all of the doctors in this study expressed boredom, irritation, or both with women who tried to "tell me her life story."

I will discuss the patterns separately. . . . I examined all of the transcripts in detail to draw out recurrent themes and patterns. Once I identified these patterns, I chose a small sample to illustrate themes that appear in the data. . . .

The Doctor-Patient Discourse and Expansion of the Text

Pattern 1:

Women attempt to express their concerns in the medical interaction—doctors cut off their attempts.

MARIA MARTINEZ

. . . .

Maria Martinez is twenty-six, married, and has a tired air about her which can easily turn to animated interest if her lively sense of humor is aroused. She has four children ranging in age from eleven years to six months and a varied contraceptive history. The clinic rarely recommends the IUD for birth control, but it has been recommended to Maria because she has four children and the clinic feels this is enough for a low-income (Medicaid) family. She also has had a history of unexpected pregnancy, which places her in the clinic's category of an inept contraceptor. Maria has, somewhat reluctantly, agreed to this birth control method. Her past experience with the IUD has not been satisfactory. On this visit she comes to the doctor for the standard pre-IUD check-up, and an appointment is made for insertion of the IUD in two weeks.

Doctor (D)-Patient (P) Discourse

P: It won't hurt will it?

D: Oh, I doubt it.

P: I'm taking your word (laugh).

D: I haven't had anybody pass out from one yet.

P: The last time/

D: (cuts patient off with a joke; both patient and doctor laugh)

P: The last time when I had that Lippes Loop, oh, God/

D: (interrupts patient)/You won't even know what's going on. We'll just slip that in and you'll be so busy talking and you won't know it.

In the doctor-patient discourse Maria asks a direct question about possible pain. In two subsequent turns she tries to raise her past and painful experience with the IUD. Each time she is interrupted and cut off by the doctor. She attempts to raise the topic three times. This makes her an assertive patient. Most women in this study did not raise topics but merely responded to them.

Medical literature supports the view that women experience pain with insertion of the IUD rather than after it is in place. The doctor seems to assume this will be the case with Maria as well. This was not Maria's concern. My follow-up interview provides an expansion of what Maria was trying to express.

Expansion of the Text

P: I tried an IUD. . . . I got an IUD put in, a Lippes Loop (*interviewer* [*I*]: Uh huh), and I got that put in and I had that in August, for four months and I couldn't take it.

I: Well, what was it like using the IUD?

P: Oh, god, it was the most awful, terriblest, uncomfortable, it was awful. I hated it. . . . I had it taken out 'cause I couldn't hack it. . . .

I: How come?

P: I, it, it killed me. I was, oh, oh, that's why I'm so scared with this one, the one I'm going to get. . . . I remember the pain, yeah, it was awful.

I: When it was put in?

P: No, when it was put in it didn't hurt. . . . It was okay all month long until I started my period, like the day before I started my period, my God in heaven, I'd be on the bed crying in pain. . . . I even started taking pain killers.

I: Why did you keep it?

P: Because when I went, I went to the Public Health . . . and they just said . . . you'll have a little cramp and that's it. And you know that actually it didn't hurt a bit getting it in. (*I*: Uh huh.) It didn't bother me a bit, but it was just that I was so scared and tense (*I*: Uh huh), and nobody would tell you, relax, and you know, take it easy, or anything like that. Let you just freak out, you know, you just, then it was fine, you know, nothing bothered me. Went back to school that day and everything. And then the next month when my period started, well, the doctor had told me, "now don't be a baby and come back because you get a little pain." (*I*: uh huh.) "Don't be a big baby and come back and say you want it out. You gotta give it a couple of months chance." So I kept saying, oh, it's just getting adjusted, it's just getting, the first time, it's just, you know, just the pain, it's just going to get adjusted. (*I*: Oh.) The next month, it was "don't be a baby Maria," they said "don't be a baby; hmm, hmm, hmm."

The doctor made an assumption regarding Maria's concerns based on a generalized understanding of IUD use. Maria's experiences, however, are particularistic, based on her own history of pain after insertion. Conflict in perspective and the doctor's more powerful position to control the discourse left her concerns unaddressed. In turn, the fears the doctor assumed she was addressing (pain on insertion) were lightheartedly dismissed. . . .

Pattern 2:

Women are unaware that they need more information—doctors withhold information.

. . . .

MARIA MARTINEZ

Let us return to the medical interaction with Maria Martinez (pattern 1) to see how the various patterns can appear in different parts of the same interview. The doctors in the clinic generally present to women a very long negative oration on the IUD and a low-key push for the birth control pill. . . . In this case, however, the IUD has already been recommended. The doctor raises one question in the interview which indicates his general preference for the pill over the IUD. Maria's answer terminates any further inquiry in this direction. Maria's response does provide active direction to the medical interaction. She is not, however, consciously trying to raise issues as she was earlier with her questions on IUD insertion (Pattern 1).

Doctor-Patient Discourse

D: Uh hum. What's the pill do for you?
P: Oh, they're okay except I uh, you gotta remember how to take them.
D: True, true (initiates pre-IUD exam).

Both Maria and the doctor assume that she cannot use the birth control pill because she implies that in the past she has forgotten to take it. In fact, it is her lack of remembrance that has convinced the clinic staff that Maria needs an IUD. The doctor, having no information on Maria's social history except that she had trouble remembering to take the pill at one time and had an unexpected pregnancy as a result, proceeds with what he considers to be the most dangerous form of birth control—the IUD. He thinks it dangerous, Maria is afraid of it, yet it has been selected as the method of choice.

From this medical interaction one is likely to deduce that there are only two contraceptive methods available—the IUD and the pill. This is obviously not the case; however, there is no mention of alternatives. The clinic predominantly prescribed the pill, dispensed many diaphragms, and rarely suggested IUDs, condoms, and/or foam. Birth control pills or IUDs, however, were the main methods considered appropriate for a woman labeled a "birth control failure."

Expansion of the Text

I: How long did you use the pill?

P: Uh, let me see (inaudible) uh, two years. . . .

I: What was it like using this method?

P: Back then it was okay, because I could remember to take them. . . .

I: How come you got off of it [birth control pills]?

P: I can't remember. I guess I just, me and my husband were fighting a lot and we started fighting a lot and then we separated and I just didn't take it. I said, well I don't need them.

I: And then what happened?

P: I did need it.

I: Then what happened?

P: Michael [patient's son].

I: All right, and so, did you get on birth control after he was born?

P: Yeah . . . the pill again [husband returned].

I: Okay, and for how long did you use that pill?

P: Four years, almost five years. . . . At first it was, about the first two years it was okay, but then I, I don't know what went wrong in my head or anything, but I, I kept forgetting to take them. . . . I'd forget to take them and then I'd, I'd, you know, get scared every month. . . . And I didn't even get pregnant, you know, and then when I, about the last year, I realized I really wanted a baby, you know, and I didn't take them [birth control pills], and I didn't get pregnant. You know, I wouldn't get, I tried so hard . . . you know, my husband kept saying 'oh no, no no.' . . . I wanted to get pregnant and I knew that if I just got pregnant, that he wouldn't say nothing. You know he'd be happy and everything (*I*: Uh huh). But I wouldn't get pregnant. . . . What the hell's wrong with me? I'd do it every day for a month. . . . I kept it scheduled in my purse calendar. "I did it today—X—I did it today" . . . one whole month and I didn't get pregnant. And I thought, why, how is this possible. . . . I just felt that I may never be able to have another baby. . . . And in January, I got pregnant [nearly one year later, by which time Ms. M. had decided against another baby].

I: What kind of birth control were you using?

P: Nothing.

I: How come?

P: Because I hadn't been using it. I thought I wa——, I couldn't get pregnant, I hadn't been using it in so long . . . I didn't think I was ever going to get pregnant again.

Maria's social history with the birth control pill is confusing to her and unknown to the doctor. She has used oral contraceptives both successfully and unsuccessfully. While forgetting to take the pill, she came to realize she wanted another child and actively stopped taking the pill. She does not understand why she did not get pregnant. She did not realize that it can take up to a year after using oral contraceptives to become fertile. Thus Maria tried to become pregnant and did not. She decided she was sterile, did not use birth control, became pregnant, and was labeled a birth control failure in need of an IUD by the clinic. From Maria's birth control pill history, it seems possible that she took the pill regularly when she did not want to become pregnant and "forgot" (unconsciously and consciously) to take it with some regularity when she did want another child. . . .

Once again none of this history is explored in the medical interaction. The definition of Maria as an incompetent user of birth control is based on a slim and misleading view lacking contextual information about her contraceptive history. The doctor, whose responsibility it is to gather information relative to the decision-making process, does not explore contextual issues. Contraception as medically defined is a technical topic, not a contextual one. When social information is used by the doctor, as in this case, he draws on an abstract, stereotypic view that when women are poor and have a history of unplanned pregnancy, they are inept contraceptors.

Viewed from another perspective, doctors are inept. I never heard doctors explain to women, when prescribing the pill, the possibility of temporary infertility if they stopped using this method. This was explained if women came to the doctors to stop the pill, but many women, like Maria, stop on their own. When such basic information is not forthcoming from doctors, the results can be devastating. . . . Maria, labeled a poor contraceptive user, was denied a full discussion of all the birth control options. A fuller explanation of the possibilities and a clearer understanding of her own history would at least have left her in a position to choose a method, rather than settle for the clinic's choice. In other parts of our interview it became clear that Maria was confused about the barrier methods. She thought a diaphragm had to be inserted just before intercourse, like a condom. In fact, Maria was particularly susceptible to the clinic's persuasion because she had accepted the verdict of her contraceptive irresponsibility.

In sum, . . . Maria Martinez [is] representative of women who are unaware that they need a range of information that is not forthcoming. Doctors, having been taught that they know best, make decisions based on stereotypic attitudes toward women's behavior (as in the case of Maria's unplanned pregnancy) and a technical fix for contraception. . . .

Pattern 3:

Women withhold information—doctors are unaware.

. . . .

SALLY BARRETT

Sally Barrett is a woman in her mid-twenties, assistant manager of a bank, married with no children and no immediate plans to have any. She came to the private practitioner for a post-abortion checkup and for birth control. The doctor gave her a birth control pill prescription at the time of her abortion, and today he renews her prescription for the next three months.

Doctor-Patient Discourse:

D: You take your pills?
P: Uh hum, I still have some, maybe a week's worth.
D: I'm going to give you today a prescription for three months.
P: Okay.
D: Then I want you here when you start on the last package.
P: Okay. . . .
D: Okay? Do you read the pamphlet uh in the, well, which comes with the pills, huh?
P: Okay (nodding head).
D: And, you know, there are certain risks but you're at risk when you cross the street too. . . . All right, you dress, come and see me. I will give you a prescription, you know, and everything is fine.

But everything is not fine. As in the previous case, the doctor prescribes a method of contraception to a woman, who, it turns out, is reluctant.

Expansion of the Text

I: What was it like using the pill during that, that time?
P: It was all right. I didn't, the only physical side effect I had at that point was uh the splotchy skin, the colasma. . . . Uhm, I hated those and I got them pretty bad. . . .
I: Where were the, where were the blotchy, the blotchy skin?
P: On my face. . . . It was my own personal vanity. They were pretty dark, and they were pretty definite, and it looked like I had a moustache and (*I:* Uh huh), uh, it looked, I had them around on my cheeks and they were pretty definite. My, I didn't, make-up wouldn't cover them up or anything like that, and I never had very good skin to begin with and I didn't need to add something like that to it. . . .
I: Okay, and uhm why did you switch to the diaphragm?
P: I think it was, my sister-in-law was using a diaphragm at the time. . . . I thought I'd give it a try (*I:* Uh huh, okay), and I'm still using it. . . .
I: And when you were at Dr. M's office . . . he talked to you about being on the pill . . . and you didn't mention the diaphragm?
P: Yeah. He's pretty strong hearted and uh about that, and uh/
I: /About what?

P: Taking the pill. . . . He's been after me to take it for a while and every time that I say no, he just looks at me. . . . He's uh, he's set in his ways and so uh, the, we've had the same discussion over and over.

I: And have you tried telling him, talking to him about the fact that you, you just aren't going to use it?

P: Yeah, uhm, and he'll ask my concerns (*I*: Uh huh), and he assures me that my age, uh, is a safety factor there. Uhm, I don't know . . . that it's good. There's a lot of things that have come up about oh, clotting of blood and different things and there's a lot being tested that's so unknown, you know. . . . I think he's a good doctor, but instead of working with me, uh with the diaphragm, he'd rather see me take the pill . . . and so instead of getting into confrontations with him, because he's pretty strong willed . . . but uh he's doing it for my own good.

Like Maria Martinez, Sally Barrett has been labeled a "birth control failure" (she has had an abortion), which could account for the doctor's adamance about the pill. When this doctor (like the majority of gynecologists) prescribes and recommends the pill as the most effective nonsurgical form of birth control for women, the tendency is to minimize the dangers with such statements as "you're at risk when you cross the street too"—a statement often mirrored in patients' discourse. . . . But Sally is concerned about the safety of the birth control pill and has suffered ill effects using this method in the past.

Interestingly, although Sally would prefer to have the doctor work with her on using the diaphragm, she still feels he is basically a good doctor who looks out for her best interests. This is a good example of the basic conflict between trying to retain a trust for the doctor while concomitantly refusing his advice.

If one were to witness this doctor-patient interaction or listen to a tape of it, one would surmise that Sally was using an oral contraceptive. Her view of this method does not emerge in the encounter. Rather, she purposely withholds information from the doctor, whom she has come to and is paying for a service, to avoid an old and repeated confrontation about her reproductive control. Although this is evidence of active participation on Sally's part, it signifies an unequal relationship. The power to choose is covertly managed by the patient. The doctor's overt control in the interaction goes uncontested.

. . . Sally Barrett . . . [exemplifies] women who are uncomfortable enough with their medical care to conceal information from their doctors. Doctors, understandably unaware of withheld concerns, do not in general probe for the information concealed here.

Reflections on the Data

The medical profession has two conflicting goals with respect to delivering contraceptive services. First, the health care system is committed to help women control the reproductive function. Second, the system is organized to promote health. Doctors are caught between these two interests. At the present time, the major forms of contraception are technically efficient in that they allow sexual activity freer from risk of unwanted pregnancy than at any time in history. At the same time, these methods can create havoc for women's health. . . .

The medical profession is in the position of prescribing treatments to healthy women that can make them unhealthy, creating a paradox for women as well as doctors. Both doctors and patients are caught between the two interests—controlling reproduction and remaining healthy—with doctors generally responding predominantly to the former, often at cost to the latter. Women in my data were concerned with both. They needed to control their reproduction but did not want to do so at a cost to their health. . . .

Maria Martinez's history with the IUD is extremely negative. The doctor's misunderstanding of her fears, and his interruption of her attempts to correct his impression, leave these fears unexplored. Furthermore, none of the less dangerous barrier methods were discussed. Maria's history of birth control use when examined contextually provides a different picture of her contraceptive competence and makes alternative methods plausible. She left the clinic after this exam and did not return because by the time for her next appointment she felt too afraid of the IUD. She and her husband had resumed using condoms—a method she found distasteful. She felt reproductively insecure and sexually turned off by condoms, feelings that contributed to sexual withdrawal, resulting in her concern for her own sexuality and marital friction. These dynamics represent a pattern in which unaware doctors discourage medical discussions with patients, thus limiting women's abilities to evaluate their options and control their lives. . . .

The doctors and the patients are implicitly in conflict in these interactions. *Women come to doctors for help in understanding how to adjust their bodies to their social lives. Doctors' technical answers assume that women should adjust their social lives to their bodies.* The asymmetrical relationship between doctors and patients in our current medical model negates the possibility of open communication that would allow the doctors' technical expertise and the patients' contextual knowledge equal status, allowing participatory decision making. . . . Social information is complicated, subjective, and individual. Furthermore, to delve into such topics moves away from doctors' expertise and therefore necessitates more active participation on the part of patients. In these areas patients have more knowledge than doctors. Such equality is often resisted by the medical profession. But just as doctors are technical experts, women (people) must become contextual experts in the medical encounter if the conflict between reproductive control and health is to be resolved.

The call to incorporate social, contextual information into contraceptive and health care decision making, however, presents a double-edged sword. . . . Historically, . . . the medical establishment has broadened its power base by assimilating aspects of the social into the medical. Given the hierarchical nature of our society and health care system, access to contextual, personal history allows those in authority to exert even more control. Patients' expertise could be co-opted. . . . The Boston Women's Health Book Collective, in the *New Our Bodies, Ourselves* (1985), stresses the need for keeping doctors out of women's personal lives, where they all too often use social information to reinforce stereotypic sex roles. . . .

Thus it is not enough just to expand communication strategies. Rather, I am suggesting that along with adding contextual information to the current structure of the doctor-patient relationship, this relationship itself needs to be redefined in a more egalitarian way. . . .

Chapter 3

Body Narratives, Body Boundaries

Emily Martin

. . . .

[In medical textbooks, a sharp contrast] is set up between male and female, the male who continuously produce[s] fresh germ cells [sperm] and the female who has stock-piled germ cells [eggs] by birth and is faced with the continuous degeneration of this material. The same goes for the egg and the sperm themselves. Even though each con-tributes almost exactly half of the genetic stuff to the new individual in fertilization, it is astounding how different their roles seem and how "femininely" the egg behaves and how "masculinely" the sperm.

The egg is seen as large and passive. It does not *move or journey,* but passively "is transported," "is swept" (Guyton, 1984, p. 619 . . .), or even, in a popular account, "drifts" (Miller and Pelham, 1984) along the fallopian tube. In utter contrast, sperm are small, "streamlined," and inevitably active. They "deliver" their genes to the egg, "activate the developmental program of the egg" (Alberts et al., 1983 p. 796) and have a "velocity" which is always remarked on (Ganong, 1975, p. 322). Their tails are "strong" and efficiently powered. Together with the forces of ejaculation, they can "propel the semen into the deepest recesses of the vagina" (Guyton, 1984, p. 615). For this they need "energy," "fuel" (Solomon, 1983, p. 683), so that with a "whiplashlike motion and strong lurches" (Vander, Sherman, and Luciano, 1985, p. 580) they can "burrow through the egg coat" (Alberts et al., 1983 p. 796) and "penetrate" it.

In our cultural tradition, passivity is a quintessential female attribute, activity a male one. So one might imagine there is some cultural overlay on how egg and sperm are seen. But there is more. The egg is hidden behind a protective barrier, the egg coat, sometimes called its "vestments," a term used for sacred, religious dress. In addition the egg is said to have a "corona," a crown (Solomon 1983, p. 700), and is accompanied by "attendant cells" (Beldecos, et. al., 1988, pp. 61–76). The egg is evidently special, holy, set apart and above. As such the egg could potentially play queen to the sperm as king. In actuality her passivity dominates her royalty, which means she must depend on sperm to rescue her. Sperm have a "mission" (Alberts, et al., 1983, p. 796), which is to "move through the female genital tract in quest of the ovum" (Guyton, 1984, p. 613). An extravagant popular book, *The Facts of Life,* co-authored by Jonathan Miller (1984), the producer of the BBC series, "The Body in Question," has it that the sperm

Emily Martin, "*Body Narratives, Body Boundaries,*" in Lawrence Grossberg, Cary Nelson, and Paula A. Treichler (eds.) Cultural Studies 409–19 (1992).

carries out a "perilous journey" into the "warm darkness," where some fall away "exhausted," but other "survivors" "assault" the egg, the successful candidates "surrounding the prize" (p. 7). The journey is perilous in part because it takes place in the vagina, which is called a "hostile environment."

But the egg's journey is also perilous: "once released from the supportive environment of the ovary, an egg will die within hours unless rescued by a sperm" (Alberts et al., 1983, p. 804). The way this is phrased stresses the fragility and dependency of the egg, even though it is acknowledged elsewhere in this very text that sperm also only live a few hours (p. 801).

In one photograph from the *National Geographic,* sperm are "masters of subversion": "human sperm cells seek to penetrate an ovum. Foreigners in a hostile body, they employ several strategies to survive their mission . . ." (Jaret, 1986, p. 731). Sometimes the egg has her own defenses. In a "Far Side" cartoon, the egg is seen as a housewife besieged by clever sperm who try to get a foot inside the door. Sperm as postman says "Package for you to sign for, Ma'am." Sperm as phone repairman says "Need to check your lines, Ma'am," and sperm as insurance salesman says "Mind if I step inside?"

There is another way sperm can be made to loom in importance over the egg, despite their small size. The article in which an electron micrograph of sperm and an egg appeared is called "Portrait of a Sperm" (Nilsson, 1975). Of course, it is harder to photograph microscopic sperm than eggs, which are just large enough to see with the naked eye. But surely the use of the term "portrait," a term associated with the powerful and the wealthy, is significant. Eggs have only micrographs or pictures, not portraits.

As far as I know there is only one cultural representation in Western civilization of sperm as weak and timid instead of strong and powerful. This occurs in Woody Allen's movie, *Everything You Ever Wanted to Know About Sex But Were Afraid to Ask.* Woody Allen, playing the part of a reluctant sperm inside a man's body, is afraid to go out into the darkness, afraid of contraceptive devices, and afraid of winding up on the ceiling if the man is masturbating. In biology texts, if there is an association between strong sperm and virility, it is never directly stated. But Allen makes explicit the link between weak sperm and the impotence of the man whose body he is in.

After getting to this point in my survey of scientific and popular materials, I looked extensively at very recent research coming out of labs investigating the sperm and the egg. To summarize briefly, the views I've just outlined have been overturned: scientists have found that the forward propulsive force of the sperm's tail is extremely weak, so that rather than strongly swimming forward with purpose, the sperm actually flail side to side, swim in circles, mill around. The current picture is that adhesive molecules on the surface of the egg capture the sperm and hold it fast; otherwise, its sideways motions would lead it to escape and swim away. (As an aside, nothing is simple: in this new research, the egg comes to be described as an engulfing female aggressor, dangerous and terrifying.)

Nevertheless . . . recent scientific work also draws on virile images. . . . In research designed to help couples with sperm-related infertility, methods are being developed to force an opening in the zona, the outermost covering of the egg, and so permit the sperm to "penetrate" it. In "Zona Blasters: There's More Than One Way to Crack an Egg," a review article in *Science News*, we find an unrevised version of the saga of egg and sperm:

> The microscopic human egg floats in its fluid-filled shell. Suddenly, thousands of tiny sperm bombard it. Lashing their tails to power their entry, they bore into the shell, a tough glycoprotein coating known as the zona pellucida. One particularly vigorous sperm pierces the zona barrier, setting off a chemical reaction that shuts the others out. Then, if all goes well, the winning sperm fertilizes the egg and the miracle of human life ensues (Fackelmann, 1990, p. 376).

But trouble arises, given this view, when "the sperm can't whip their tails hard enough to bore through the tough outer shell" (p. 376). To handle this cause of infertility, "scientists are now developing imaginative methods of cracking, blasting or drilling tiny passageways through the zona envelope" (p. 376). In line with this imagery, the cover of this issue of *Science News*, captioned "Sperm at Work," shows a cartoon of three sperm ferociously attacking an egg with a jackhammer, a pickaxe, and a sledgehammer. The undertone of violence in both words and picture scarcely needs comment.

And the same goes for popular publications that purport to represent the latest scientific knowledge. In a recent issue of *Life Magazine*, the dynamic activities of sperm and the passive response of the egg are presented yet again. In "The First Days of Creation," we read, "Although few will finish, about 250 million sperm start the 5–7 inch journey from the vagina to the uterus and then to the fallopian tubes where an egg may be waiting" (Nilsson, 1990, p. 26). Two hours later, "like an eerie planet floating through space, a woman's egg or ovum . . . has been ejected by one of her ovaries into the fallopian tube. Over the next several hours sperm will begin beating their tails vigorously as they rotate like drill bits into the outer wall of the egg" (p. 28).

Other popular materials also do their part: the recent film *Look Who's Talking* begins with a simulation of a hugely magnified egg floating, drifting, gently bouncing along the fallopian tube of a woman who is in the midst of making love with a man. The soundtrack is "I Love You So" by the Chantals. Then we see, also hugely magnified, the man's sperm barreling down the tunnel of her vagina to the tune of "I Get Around" by the Beach Boys. The sperm are shouting and calling to each other like a gang of boys: "Come on, follow me, I know where I am, keep up, come on you kids, I've got the map." Then as the egg hoves into view, they shout, "This is it, yeah, this is definitely it, this is the place, Jackpot, right here, come on, dig in you kids." And when one sperm finally pushes hard enough to open a slit in the egg (a slit that looks remarkably like a vulva), that sperm (as his whole self is swallowed up) cries out, "Oh, oh, oh, I'm in!"

When I got to this point in my research, I was already wondering what social effects such vivid imagery might be having. I thought perhaps this imagery might encourage us to imagine that what results from the interaction of egg and sperm—a fertilized egg—is the result of intentional "human" action *at the cellular level.* In other words, whatever the intentions of the human couple, in this microscopic "culture," a cellular "bride" (or "femme fatale") and a cellular "groom" (or her victim) make a cellular baby. Rosalind Petchesky (1987) makes the point that through visual representations such as sonograms, we are given "images of younger and younger, and tinier and tinier, fetuses being 'saved.'" This leads to "the point of viability being 'pushed back' indefinitely" (pp. 263–92). Endowing egg and sperm with intentional action, a key aspect of personhood in our culture, lays the foundation for the point of viability being pushed back to the moment of fertilization.

Why would this matter? Because endowing cells with personhood may play a part in the breaking down of boundaries between the self and the world, and a pushing back of the boundary of what constitutes the inviolable self. In other words, whereas at an earlier time, the skin might have been regarded as the border of the individual self, now these microscopic cells are seen as tiny individual selves. This means that the "environment" of the egg and sperm, namely the human body is fair game for invasion by medical scrutiny and intervention. It is not, of course, that the interior of our bodies was not the object of study and treatment until now. But we may be experiencing an intensification of those activities (made more potent by state support) which are understood as protecting the "rights," viability, or integrity of cellular entities. It would not be that endowing cells with personhood by means of imagery in biology automatically *causes* intensification of initiatives in the legislature and elsewhere that enable protection of these new "persons." Rather, I am suggesting that this imagery may have a part in creating a general predisposition to think of the world in a certain way that can play an important role whenever legal and other initiatives do take place.

It is possible that in the 1990s what was the patient (or person) has itself begun to become an environment for a new core self, which exists at the cellular level. This change may be adding to our willingness to focus ever more attention on the internal structures of this tiny cellular self, namely its genes. In turn, such a shift in attention may encourage us to permit dramatic changes in the "environment" of the genes in the name of maintaining their welfare.

. . . .

SOURCES CITED

Alberts, Bruce et al. (1983) *Molecular Biology of the Cell.* New York: Garland.

Beldecos, A. et al. (1988) "The Importance of Feminist Critique for Contemporary Biology." *Hypatia* 3, pp. 61–76.

Fackelmann, Kathy A. (1990) "Zona Blasters." *Science News,* 138(24), pp. 376–379.

Ganong, William (1975) *Review of Medical Physiology,* 7th ed. Los Altos, CA: Lange Medical Publications.

Guyton, Arthur C. (1984) *Physiology of the Human Body,* 6th ed. Philadelphia: Saunders College Publishing.

Jaret, Peter (1986) "Our immune system: The wars within." *National Geographic,* 169(6), pp. 701–735.

Miller, Jonathan & David Pelham (1984) *The Facts of Life.* New York: Viking Press.

Nilsson, Lennart (1975) "A portrait of the sperm." In *The Functional Anatomy of the Spermatozoan.* B. Afzelius (ed). New York: Pergamon, pp. 79–82.

Nilsson, Lennart (1990) "The first days of creation." *Life,* 13(10), pp. 26–43.

Petchesky, Rosalind (1987) "Fetal images: The power of visual culture in the politics of reproduction." *Feminist Studies,* 13(2), pp. 263–292.

Solomon, Eldra Pearl (1983) *Human Anatomy and Physiology.* New York: CBS College Publishing.

Vander, Arthur, James Sherman and Dorothy Luciano (1985) *Human Physiology: The Mechanics
of Body Function,* 3rd ed. New York: McGraw Hill.

Chapter 4

"Cultural Practice" or "Reconstructive Surgery"?

U.S. Genital Cutting, the Intersex Movement, and Medical Double Standards

Cheryl Chase

. . . .

"New Law Bans Genital Cutting in United States" read the headlines on the front page of the *New York Times*.[1] The law seems clear enough: "Whoever knowingly circumcises, excises, or infibulates the whole or any part of the labia majora or labia minora or clitoris of another person who has not attained the age of eighteen years shall be fined under this title or imprisoned not more than five years, or both."[2] Yet this law was not intended and has not been interpreted to protect the approximately five children per day in the United States who are subjected to excision of part or all of their clitoris and inner labia simply because doctors believe their clitoris is too big.

Sexual anatomies, genitals in particular, come in many sizes and shapes. U.S. doctors label children whose sexual anatomies differ significantly from the cultural ideal "intersexuals" or "hermaphrodites" (a misleading term because these children are born with intermediate genitals, not two sets). Medical practice today holds that possession of a large clitoris, or a small penis, or a penis that has the urethra placed other than at its tip is a "psychosocial emergency." The child would not be accepted by the mother, would be teased by peers, and would not be able to develop into an emotionally healthy adult. The medical solution to this psychosocial problem is surgery—before the child reaches three months of age or even before the newborn is discharged from hospital. Although parental emotional distress and rejection of the child and peer harassment are cited as the primary justifications for cosmetic genital surgery, there has never been an investigation of non-surgical means—such as professional counseling or peer support—to address these issues.

The federal Law to Ban Female Genital Mutilation notwithstanding, girls born with large clitorises are today routinely "normalized" by excising parts of the clitoris and burying the remainder deep within the genital region. And boys with small penises? Current medical practice holds that intersex children "can be raised successfully as members of either sex if the process begins before 2½ years."[3] Because surgeons cannot create a large penis from a small one, the policy is to remove testes and raise these

Cheryl Chase, "'Cultural Practice'" or 'Reconstructive Surgery'? U.S. Genital Cutting, the Intersex Movement, and Medical Double Standards," in STANLIE M. JAMES AND CLAIRE C. ROBERTSON (eds), GENITAL CUTTING AND TRANSNATIONAL SISTERHOOD 126 (2002).

children as girls. This is accomplished by "carv[ing] a large phallus down into a clitoris, [and] creat[ing] a vagina using a piece of [the child's] colon," marveled a science writer who spoke only to physicians and parents, not to any of the intersex people subjected to this miracle technology.[4] Efforts to create or extend a penile urethra in boys whose urethra exits other than at the tip of the penis—a condition called hypospadias—frequently lead to multiple surgeries, each compounding the harm. Heartrending stories of physical and emotional carnage are related by victims of these surgeries in "Growing up in the Surgical Maelstrom" and, with black humor, in "Take Charge: A Guide to Home Catheterization."[5]

"Reconstructive" surgeries for intersex infant genitals first came into widespread practice in the 1950s. Because intersexuality was treated as shameful and physicians actively discouraged open discussion by their patients—indeed, recommended lying to parents and to adult intersex patients—until recently most victims of these interventions suffered alone in shame and silence.

By 1993 the accomplishments of a progression of social justice movements—civil rights, feminism, gay and lesbian, bisexual and transgender—helped make it possible for intersex people to speak out. Initially, physicians scoffed at their assertions that intersexuality was not shameful and that medically unnecessary genital surgeries were mutilating and should be halted.

. . . .

Hermaphrodites: Medical Authority and Cultural Invisibility

. . . .

Although the male/female binary is constructed as natural and therefore presumably immutable, the phenomenon of intersexuality offers clear evidence that physical sex is not binary. . . . The concept of bodily sex, in popular usage, refers to multiple characteristics, including karyotype (organization of sex chromosomes); gonadal differentiation (e.g., ovarian or testicular); genital morphology; configuration of internal reproductive organs; and pubertal sex characteristics such as breasts and facial hair. These characteristics are assumed and expected to be concordant in each individual—either all-male or all-female.

Because medicine intervenes quickly in intersex births to change the infant's body, the phenomenon of intersexuality has been, until recently, largely unknown outside specialized medical practices. . . . The techniques and protocols for physically transforming intersexed bodies were developed primarily at Johns Hopkins University in Baltimore during the 1920s and 1930s under the guidance of urologist Hugh Hampton Young. . . . By the 1950s, the principle of rapid postnatal detection and intervention for intersex infants had been developed at Johns Hopkins, with the stated goal of completing surgery early enough so the child would have no memory of it. One wonders whether the insistence on early intervention was not at least partly motivated by the resistance offered by adult intersex people to "normalization" through surgery. Frightened parents of ambiguously sexed infants were much more open to suggestions of normalizing surgery than were intersex adults, and the infants themselves could, of course, offer no resistance whatsoever.

Most of the theoretical foundations justifying these interventions are attributable to psychologist John Money, a sex researcher invited to Johns Hopkins by Lawson Wilkins, founder of pediatric endocrinology. . . . In 1998 Suzanne Kessler noted that Money's ideas enjoyed a "consensus of approval rarely encountered in science."[6] But the revelation in 2000 that Money had grossly misrepresented and mishandled the famous "John/Joan" case (in which an infant was castrated and raised as a girl after his penis was destroyed in a circumcision accident) sent Money's stock into a steep decline.

In keeping with the Hopkins model, the birth of an intersex infant is today deemed a "psychosocial emergency" that propels a multi-disciplinary team of intersex specialists into action. . . . The team examines the infant and chooses either male or female as a "sex of assignment," then informs the parents that this is the child's true sex. Medical technology, including surgery and hormones, is then used to make the child's body conform as closely as possible to the assigned sex.

Current protocols for choosing a sex are based on phallus size: to qualify for male assignment the child must possess a penis at least one inch long; clitorises may not exceed three-eighths inch. Infants with genital appendages in the forbidden zone of three-eighths to one-inch are assigned female and the phallus trimmed to an acceptable size. The only exception to this sorting rule is that even a hypothetical possibility of female fertility must be preserved by assigning the infant as female, disregarding masculine genitals and a phallus longer than one inch.

The sort of deviation from sex norms exhibited by intersex people is so highly stigmatized that emotional harm due to likely parental rejection and community stigmatization of the intersex child provides physicians with their most compelling argument to justify medically unnecessary surgical interventions. Intersex status is considered to be so incompatible with emotional health that misrepresentation, concealment of facts, and outright lying (both to parents and later to the intersex person) are unabashedly advocated in professional medical literature.

The Impact of "Reconstructive" Surgeries

. . . .

This system of hushing up the fact of intersex births and using technology to normalize intersex bodies has caused profound emotional and physical harm to intersex people and their families. The harm begins when the birth is treated as a medical crisis, and the consequences of that initial treatment ripple out ever afterward. The emotional impact of this treatment is so devastating that until the middle of the 1990s people whose lives have been touched by intersexuality maintained silence about their ordeal. As recently as 1995, no one publicly disputed surgeon Milton Edgerton when he wrote that in forty years of clitoral surgery on children "not one has complained *of loss of sensation, even when the entire clitoris was removed*" (emphasis in the original).[7]

The tragic irony in all this is that while intersexual anatomy occasionally indicates an underlying medical problem such as adrenal disorder, ambiguous genitals are, in and of themselves, neither painful nor harmful to health. The often debilitating pediatric genital surgeries are entirely cosmetic in function. Surgery is essentially a destructive process. It can remove tissue and to a limited extent relocate it, but it cannot create new structures. This technical limitation, taken together with the framing of the feminine as a condition of lack, leads physicians to assign 90 percent of anatomically ambiguous infants as female by excising genital tissue. Surgeons justify female assignment because "you can make a hole, but you can't build a pole."[8] Heroic efforts shore up a tenuous masculine status for the one-tenth assigned male, who are subjected to multiple operations—twenty-two in one case—with the goal of straightening the penis and constructing a urethra to enable standing urinary posture. For some, the surgeries end only when the child grows old enough to resist.

Children assigned female are subjected to surgery that removes the troubling hypertrophic (i.e., large) clitoris. This is the same tissue that would have been a troubling micropenis (i.e., small penis) had the child been assigned male. Through the 1960s, feminizing pediatric genital surgery was openly labeled "clitoridectomy" and was compared favorably to the African practices that have now become the focus of such intense scrutiny. As three Harvard surgeons noted, "Evidence that the clitoris is not essential for normal coitus may be gained from certain sociological data. For instance, it is the custom of a number of African tribes to excise the clitoris and other parts of the external genitals. Yet normal sexual function is observed in these females."[9] Authors Robert E. Gross, Judson Randolph, and John E. Crigler apparently understand normal female sexual function only as passive penetration and fertility. A modified operation that removes most of the clitoris and relocates a bit of its tip is variously (and euphemistically) called clitoroplasty, clitoral reduction, or clitoral recession and described as a simple cosmetic procedure in order to differentiate it from the now-infamous clitoridectomy. The operation, however, is far from benign.

Johns Hopkins surgeons Joseph E. Oesterling, John P. Gearhart, and Robert D. Jeffs have described their technique. They make an incision around the clitoris, at the corona, then dissect the skin away from its underside. Next they dissect the skin away from the upper side and remove as much of the clitoral shaft as necessary to create an "appropriate size clitoris." Then they place stitches from the pubic area along both sides of the entire length of what remains of the clitoris; when they tighten these stitches, the tissue folds, like pleats in a skirt, and recesses into a concealed position behind the pubic mound. If they think the result still "too large," they further reduce the tip of the clitoris by cutting away a pie-shaped wedge.

For many intersex people, this sort of arcane, dehumanized medical literature, illustrated with close-ups of genital surgery and naked children with blacked-out eyes, is the only available version of *Our Bodies, Ourselves*. Thus, even as fierce arguments over gender identity, gender role development, and social construction of gender rage in psychology, feminism, and queer theory, we have literally delegated to medicine the authority to police the boundaries of male and female, leaving intersex people to recover as best they can, alone and silent, from violent normalization.

My own case, as it turns out, was not unusual. I was born with ambiguous genitals. A doctor specializing in intersexuality deliberated for three days—and sedated my mother each time she asked what was wrong with her baby—before concluding that I was male, with micropenis, complete hypospadias, undescended testes, and a strange extra opening behind the urethra. A male birth certificate was completed for me, and my parents began raising me as a boy. When I was a year and a half old, my parents consulted a different set of intersex experts, who admitted me to a hospital for "sex determination." "Determine" is a remarkably apt word for this context, meaning both to *ascertain* by investigation and to *cause* to come to a resolution. It perfectly described the two-level process whereby science produces through a series of masked operations what it claims merely to observe. Doctors told my parents that a thorough medical investigation, including exploratory surgery, would be necessary to determine (that is, ascertain) what my "true sex" was. They judged my genital appendage to be inadequate as a penis, too short to effectively mark masculine status or to penetrate females. As a female, however, I would be penetrable and potentially fertile. My anatomy having now been re-labeled as vagina, urethra, labia, and outsized clitoris, my sex was determined (in the second sense) by amputating my genital appendage—clitoridectomy. Following doctors' orders, my parents then changed my name; combed their house to eliminate all traces of my existence as a boy (photographs, birthday cards, etc.); engaged a lawyer to change my birth certificate; moved to a different town; instructed extended family members to no longer refer to me as a boy; and never told anyone else —including me—just what had happened. My intersexuality and change of sex were the family's dirty little secrets.

At age eight, I was returned to the hospital for abdominal surgery that trimmed away the testicular portion of my gonads, each of which was partly ovarian and partly testicular in character. No explanation was given to me then for the long hospital stay or the abdominal surgery, nor for the regular hospital visits afterward in which doctors photographed my genitals and inserted fingers and instruments into my vagina and anus. These visits ceased as soon as I began to menstruate. At the time of the sex change, doctors had assured my parents that their once-son/now-daughter would grow into a woman who could have a normal sex life and babies. With the confirmation of menstruation, my parents apparently concluded that the prediction had borne out and their ordeal was behind them. For me, the worst part of the nightmare was just beginning.

As an adolescent, I became aware that I had no clitoris or inner labia and was unable to experience orgasm. By the end of my teens, I began to research in medical libraries, trying to discover what might have happened to me. When I finally determined to obtain my personal medical records, it took three years to overcome the obstruction of the doctors whom I asked for help. When I did obtain a scant three pages from my medical files, I learned for the first time that I was a "true hermaphrodite" who had been my parents' son for a year and a half, with a name that was unfamiliar to me. The records also documented my clitoridectomy. . . . . I was so traumatized by discovering the circumstances that produced my embodiment that I could not speak of these matters with anyone.

Nearly fifteen years later, in my middle thirties, I suffered an emotional meltdown. In the eyes of the world I was a highly successful businesswoman, a principal in an international high-tech company. To myself, I was a freak, incapable of loving or being loved, filled with shame about my status as a hermaphrodite, about the imagined appearance of my genitals before surgery (I thought "true hermaphrodite" meant that I had been born with a penis), and about my sexual dysfunction. Unable to make peace with these facts about myself, I finally sought help from a professional therapist, only to find my experience denied. . . . Increasingly desperate, I confided my story to several friends who shrank away in embarrassed silence. I was in emotional agony and found myself utterly alone, with no possible way out. I decided to kill myself.

Confronting suicide as a real possibility proved to be my personal epiphany in contemplating my own death. I fantasized killing myself quite messily and dramatically in the office of the surgeon who had sliced out my clitoris, forcibly confronting him with the horror he had imposed on my life. But in acknowledging that desire to put my pain to some use, not to waste my life completely, I turned a crucial corner, finding a way to direct my rage productively out into the world rather than aim it destructively at myself. My breakdown became my breakthrough, and I vowed that, whatever it took, I would heal myself. Still, I had no conceptual framework for developing a more positive self-consciousness. I knew only that I felt mutilated, not fully woman, less than fully human even, but I was determined to heal. I struggled for weeks in emotional chaos, unable to eat or sleep or work. I could not accept my image of a hermaphroditic body any more than I could accept the butchered one left me by the surgeons. Thoughts of myself as a Frankenstein patchwork alternated with longings for escape by death, only to be followed by outrage, anger, and determination to survive. I could not accept that it was just or right or good to treat any person as I had been treated—my sex changed, my genitals cut up, my experience silenced and rendered invisible. I bore a private hell within me, wretchedly alone in my condition without even my tormentors for company. Finally, I began to envision myself standing in a driving rain storm with clear skies and a rainbow visible in the distance. I was still in agony, still alone, but I was beginning to see the painful process in which I was caught up in terms of revitalization and rebirth, a means of investing my life with a new sense of authenticity possessing vast potentials for further transformation. Since then I have seen this experience described by other intersex and transsexual activists.
. . . .

I began a search for community that brought me to San Francisco in the fall of 1992. . . . I started telling my story to everyone I met. Before long I learned of six other intersex people—including two who had been fortunate enough to escape medical attention. Realizing that intersexuality, rather than being extremely rare, must be relatively common, I decided to create a support network. Soon I was receiving several letters per week from intersex people throughout the United States and Canada and a few from further afield. Although details varied, the letters gave a remarkably coherent picture of the emotional consequences of medical intervention:

> All the things my body might have grown to do, all the possibilities, went down the hall with my amputated clitoris to the pathology department. The rest of me went to the recovery room—I'm still recovering.
>
> —Morgan Holmes

> I am horrified by what has been done to me and by the conspiracy of silence and lies. I am filled with grief and rage, but also relief finally to believe that maybe I am not the only one.
>
> —Angelo Moreno

. . . .

Doctors never consulted me. . . . [T]he idea of asking for my opinion about having my penis surgically altered apparently never occurred to them. . . . Far too many people allow social stigma to cloud their judgment. It's OK to be different.

—Randy

I pray that I will have the means to repay, in some measure, the American Urological Association for all that it has done for my benefit. I am having some trouble, though, in connecting the timing mechanism to the fuse.

—Thomas

Toward Social Justice

The peer support network that I formed grew into the Intersex Society of North America (ISNA). ISNA's long-term and fundamental goal is to change the way intersex infants are treated. We advocate that surgery not be performed on children born with ambiguous genitals unless there is a medical reason (to prevent physical pain or illness) and that parents be given the conceptual tools and emotional support to accept their children's physical differences. We also advocate that children be raised either as boys or girls, according to which designation seems likely to offer the child the greatest future sense of comfort. Advocating gender assignment without resorting to normalizing surgery is a radical position given that it requires the willful disruption of the assumed concordance between body shape and gender category. However, this is the only position that prevents irreversible physical damage to the intersex person's body, that preserves the intersex person's agency regarding their own flesh, and that recognizes genital sensation and erotic functioning to be at least as important as reproductive capacity. If an intersex child or adult decides to change gender or to undergo surgical or hormonal alteration of his/her body, that decision should also be fully respected and facilitated. The key point is that intersex subjects should not be violated for the comfort and convenience of others.

. . . .

[T]he medical management of intersexuality has changed shockingly little in the more than forty years since my first surgery—doctors still cut up children's genitals and still perpetuate invisibility and silence around intersex lives. Kessler expresses surprise that " . . . there are no meta-analyses from within the medical community on levels of success."[10] Surgeons admit to not knowing whether their former patients are "silent and happy or silent and unhappy."[11] There is no research effort to improve erotic functioning for adult intersex people whose genitals have been cut, nor are there psychotherapists who specialize in working with adult intersex clients trying to heal from the trauma of medical intervention.

. . . .

Public Discourse on Pediatric Genital Surgeries

. . . .

ISNA initially found direct, nonconfrontational interactions with medical specialists who determine policy on the treatment of intersex infants and actually carry out the surgeries to be both difficult and ineffective. . . . Surgeon Richard Schlussel, at a pediatric plastic surgery symposium (which had rejected ISNA's offer to provide a patients' panel) at Mount Sinai Medical Center in New York City in 1996 proclaimed, "The parents of children with ambiguous genitals are more grateful to the surgeon than any—more grateful even than parents whose children's lives have been saved through open heart surgery."[12]

. . . .

[A] physician participating in [an Internet discussion on intersexuality], in a marvelous example of the degree to which practitioners of science can be blind in their complicity in constructing the objects they study, asked what was for him obviously a rhetorical question: "Who is the enemy? I really don't think it's the medical establishment. Since when did we establish the male/female hegemony?" John Hopkins surgeon Gearhart, quoted in a *New York Times* article on ISNA, summarily dismissed us as "zealots," but professional meetings in the fields of pediatrics, urology, genital plastic surgery, and endocrinology are abuzz with anxious and defensive discussions of intersex activism.[13] In response to a 1996 protest by Hermaphrodites with Attitude at the American Academy of Pediatrics annual meeting, that organization felt compelled to hold a press conference and issue a statement: "The Academy is deeply concerned about the emotional, cognitive, and body image developments of intersexuals, and believes that successful early genital surgery minimizes these issues." The academy refused, however, to speak with intersex people picketing its meeting.

The roots of resistance in the medical establishment to the truth-claims of intersex people run deep. Not only does ISNA's existence imply a critique of the normativistic biases couched within most scientific practice but it also advocates a treatment protocol for intersex infants that disrupts conventional understandings of the relationship between bodies and genders. On a level more personally threatening to medical practitioners, ISNA's position implies that they have—unwittingly at best and through willful denial at worst—spent their careers inflicting a profound harm from which their patients will never fully recover. ISNA's position threatens to destroy the foundational assumptions motivating an entire medical subspecialty, thus jeopardizing their continued ability to perform what surgeons find to be technically fascinating work. Science writer Melissa Hendricks notes that Gearhart is known to colleagues as an "artist" who can "carve a large phallus down into a clitoris" with consummate skill.[14] Given these deep and mutually reinforcing reasons for opposing ISNA's position, it is hardly surprising that medical intersex specialists have, for the most part, turned a deaf ear toward us. . . .

. . . .

Conclusion

. . . .

Most medical intersex management is a form of violence based on a sexist devaluing of female pain and female sexuality: Doctors consider the prospect of growing up male with a small penis to be a worse alternative than living as a female without a clitoris, ovaries, or sexual gratification. Medical intervention literally transforms transgressive bodies into ones that can safely be labeled female and subjected to the many forms of social control with which women must contend. Why then have most feminists failed to engage the issue of medical abuse of intersex people?

I suggest that intersex people have had such difficulty generating mainstream feminist support not only because of the racist and colonialist frameworks that situate clitoridectomy as a practice foreign to proper subjects within the first world but also because intersexuality undermines the stability of the category "woman" that undergirds much first-world feminist discourse. We call into question the assumed relation between genders and bodies and demonstrate how some bodies do not fit easily into male/female dichotomies. We embody viscerally the truth of Judith Butler's dictum that "sex," the concept that accomplishes the materialization and naturalization of culturally constructed gender differences, has really been "gender all along."[15] By refusing to remain silenced, we queer the foundations upon which depend not only the medical management of bodies but also widely shared feminist assumptions of properly embodied female subjectivity.

. . . .

To the extent that we are not normatively female or normatively women, we are not the proper subjects of feminist concern. Western feminism has represented African genital cutting as primitive, irrational, harmful, and deserving of condemnation. The Western medical community has represented its genital cutting as modern, scientific, healing, and above reproach. When will Western feminists realize that their failure to examine either of these claims "others" African women and allows the violent medical oppression of intersex people to continue unimpeded?

NOTES

My appreciation goes to Susan Stryker for her extensive contribution to the development of this essay. An earlier version appeared as "Hermaphrodies with Attitude: Mapping the Emergence of Intersex Political Activism," *GLQ: A Journal of Gay and Lesbian Studies* 4, no. 2 (1998): 189–211 © 1998. All rights reserved. Used by permission of Duke University Press.

1. Celia Dugger, "New Law Bans Genital Cutting in the United States," *New York Times*, Oct. 12, 1996, 1.

2. Department of Defense Appropriations Act, Public Law 104-208, Sept. 30, 1996.

3. American Academy of Pediatrics Section on Urology, "Timing of Elective Surgery on the Genitalia of Male Children with Particular Reference to the Risks, Benefits, and Psychological Effects of Surgery and Anesthesia," *Pediatrics* 97, no. 4 (1996): 590.

4. Melissa Hendricks, "Is It a Boy or a Girl?" *Johns Hopkins Magazine* 45, no. 5 (1993): 10.

5. Howard Devore, "Growing Up in the Surgical Maelstrom," and Sven Nicholson, "Take Charge: A Guide to Home Catheterization," both in *Intersex in the Age of Ethics*, ed. Alice Domurat Dreger (Hagerstown: University Publishing Group, 1999), 78–81.

6. Suzanne Kessler, "The Medical Construction of Gender: Case Management of Intersexual Infants," *Signs: Journal of Women in Culture and Society* 16, no. 1 (1990): 3–26, quotation on 7.

7. Milton T. Edgerton, "Discussion: Clitoroplasty for Clitoromegaly Due to Adrenogenital Syndrome without Loss of Sensitivity," *Plastic and Reconstructive Surgery* 91, no. 5 (1993): 956.

8. Hendricks, "Is It a Boy or a Girl?" Quotation on 15.

9. Robert E. Gross, Judson Randolph, and John F. Crigler, "Clitorectomy for Sexual Abnormalities: Indications and Technique," *Surgery* 59, no. 2 (1966): 300–308, quotation on 307.

10. Suzanne Kessler, *Lessons from the Intersexed* (New Brunswick: Rutgers University Press, 1998), quotation on 53.

11. Ellen Barry, "United States of Ambiguity," *Boston Phoenix,* Nov. 22, 1996, style section, 6–8.

12. Mt. Sinai School of Medicine, Conference on Pediatric Plastic and Reconstructive Surgery, New York City, May 16, 1996.

13. Natalie Angier, "Intersexual Healing: An Anomaly Finds a Group," *New York Times,* Feb. 4, 1996, 76.

14. Hendricks, "Is It a Boy or a Girl?" More than one ISNA member has discovered that the surgeons who operated on them did so at no charge. A 1994 wire service news article (Tom Majeski, "Surgery Changes Russian Child's Sex," *San Jose Mercury News,* July 25, 1994, A11) relates how a Moscow family, driven to thoughts of murder-suicide by their one-year-old son Misha's anatomy, searched high and low until they connected with an American pediatric urologist. The urologist operated for free, the hospital donated its services, and an airline footed the expenses for a round trip to St. Paul for the entire family. Doctors removed Misha's penis, testis, and ovary and instructed the family to rename him and to move. The family plans never to reveal any part of the story to relatives or to their now-daughter Masha. The medical establishment's fascination with its power to change sex and its drive to rescue parents from intersex children are so strong that intervention can be delivered across national borders and without regard to the commercial model that ordinarily governs U.S. medical services.

15. Judith Butler, *Gender Trouble: Feminism and the Subversion of Identity* (New York: Routledge, 1990): 8.

Questions and Comments

1. According to Ehrenreich and English, how did doctors' assumptions that affluent women were naturally weak and dependent, and that pregnancy and childbirth were pathological, benefit the medical profession in the nineteenth century? What, if anything, does their analysis suggest about the reliability and objectivity of modern medical knowledge? In this light, consider a recent article about the increasing tendency of physicians in the United States to prescribe bed rest for pregnant women. Taking to bed, usually ordered to protect an at-risk fetus, is prescribed in one in five U.S. pregnancies, significantly more than in other countries. And physicians in the United States have been found both to "discount . . . the side effects of bed rest and to believe in its value in the face of evidence to the contrary." Sarah Bilston, "Don't Take This Lying Down," NEW YORK TIMES, March 24, 2006, p.A19.

2. Ehrenreich and English suggest that the nineteenth-century disease of "hysteria" was actually a form of female resistance to male domination. What types of resistance to physician (and male?) authority does Todd describe in her account of doctor/patient interactions today?

3. What did the physicians observed by Todd think they "knew" about their patients? What prompted those assumptions? Why/how were they wrong? In a more recent study (of doctor/patient interactions involving prescription contraceptives), Todd found many of the same dynamics she identified in the study excerpted here. For example, physicians in those interactions dominated the questioning, operated on stereotypical notions of women's roles, and considered social information about patients' lives irrelevant to health care delivery. *See* Alexandra Dundas Todd, "A Diagnosis of Doctor-Patient Discourse in the Prescription of Contraception," in ALEXANDRA DUNDAS TODD AND SUE FISHER (eds.), THE SOCIAL ORGANIZATION OF DOCTOR-PATIENT COMMUNICATION 206 (1993).

4. Are the authors of the medical textbooks Martin describes just trying to "liven up" their descriptions for their overworked medical student readers, or is something else going on?

5. What does Chase mean when she says, "Science produces through a series of masked operations what it claims merely to observe"? What does this suggest about the role medicine plays in creating a binary understanding of sex (and gender)?

Forced Motherhood?
Legal Regulation of Pregnancy Termination

A. Abortion: The Legal Framework

Introduction to Part II(A)

Part II, "Forced Motherhood: Legal Regulation of Pregnancy Termination," focuses on law's control of access to abortion. Section A introduces the legal framework for abortion issues, beginning (in subsection 1) with three historical treatments. The chapter from Kristin Luker's *Abortion: The Politics of Motherhood* raises questions about the "objectivity" of the medical establishment's opposition to abortion rights—and of the knowledge upon which it purportedly based that opposition. She describes how the effect of medical opposition to abortion during the nineteenth century was to construct the issue of abortion as a factual rather than a moral one, and how relegation of abortion to medical control caused the moral dimensions of the issue to disappear from public debate.

The excerpt from Leslie J. Reagan's book, *When Abortion Was a Crime,* explores how the threat of prosecution turned nineteenth-century medicine into an arm of the state, coercing even those physicians who were motivated to help pregnant women into, instead, collaborating in the enforcement of abortion prohibitions. Reagan also compares medical and popular understandings of pregnancy in the eighteenth and early nineteenth centuries, and her findings provide a vivid illustration of the ways in which medicine reinforces raced and gendered views of women's bodies, and enforces prescribed gender norms.

During the late nineteenth century, Reagan explains, people tended to refer to early terminations of pregnancies as the curing of "blocked menses," rather than as the ending of a fetal life. But Regan doesn't present this viewpoint as an *error* that was later *corrected* by modern medicine. Seeing medical knowledge as socially constructed, she instead emphasizes that *social understandings* of physiological processes vary over time, implying that there is no one "correct" way to interpret the various stages in the process by which a fertilized egg eventually becomes a child. Moreover, Reagan reveals that the medical view introduced during this period—to wit, that widely accepted popular practices aimed at "restoration of menses" were really immoral "abortions"—was aimed at solidifying the emerging medical profession's power and undermining women's fight for gender equality. That view wasn't any more or less "correct" than the popular one, for each was a culturally specific frame for understanding biological processes that have no inherent *social* meaning. Thus, Reagan's analysis suggests, the medical view ultimately prevailed not because it was "right" but rather because its proponents were more powerful.

Reagan's findings provide powerful insights when read in this way. From a critical constructivist perspective that sees medical knowledge as socially constructed, Reagan's account illustrates a larger set of changes that took place during the nineteenth and early twentieth centuries. During that period, doctors were successfully installed as experts on human physiology. In the area of human reproduction, their knowledge about women's bodies came to be seen as more accurate and impartial than individual women's knowledge about themselves. And this medical monopoly on "accurate" descriptions of the human body—a monopoly that continues to this day—plays a central role in informing and justifying many aspects of modern reproductive law and policy.

Finally, Angela Davis's essay, "Racism, Birth Control, and Reproductive Rights" (originally published in 1981), critiques the white women's abortion rights movement, during both the nineteenth and the twentieth centuries. Davis indicts that movement for having focused on eugenics (the effort to purge "undesirable" traits and people from the human race by limiting reproduction of supposedly inheritable traits), as well as for being insensitive to the concerns of women of color. The focus on the right to terminate a pregnancy (the right to avoid motherhood), Davis shows, ignored important issues about the *denial* of motherhood to certain segments of the female population—issues such as sterilization abuse and the financial barriers to having children.

Subsection 2 of section A introduces the "privacy" formulation adopted by the U.S. Supreme Court for dealing with abortion issues. The privacy concept was first applied in the reproductive rights context in the case of *Griswold v. Connecticut,*[1] in which the Court held that a state statute denying married couples access to contraceptives violated the Constitution. *Griswold* was followed seven years later by *Eisenstadt v. Baird,*[2] which also relied on the privacy right to strike down a law that prohibited the distribution of contraceptives to *unmarried* people. Subsection 2 begins with the landmark case of *Roe v. Wade,* decided a year later, and also includes another important abortion case, *Harris v. MacRae;* both cases were founded upon the privacy rationale introduced in *Griswold* and *Eisenstadt.*

Each of those two cases is followed by a critique of the privacy approach. Rosalind Petchesky, in the excerpt from her influential book, *Abortion and Woman's Choice,* argues that proponents of reproductive justice should focus less on choice and more on the social conditions in which choices are made. And my article entitled "Surrogacy as Resistance?" contends that the privacy formulation relies upon incoherent distinctions between governmental interference and individual autonomy, and between action and inaction, obscuring the race and sex biases that have influenced judicial rulings in this area.

The next subsection in section A examines the "undue burden" standard currently used for deciding abortion cases. The case of *Planned Parenthood v. Casey* (excerpted in chapter 12), which adopted the standard in a plurality opinion in 1992, formally supports *Roe.* But arguably, in substance, it abandons some of the most important protections provided by the original privacy right. As the amicus brief following the case describes, the wide variety of abortion restrictions allowed by *Casey's* "undue burden" test has had numerous negative consequences for poor women, many of whom are women of color.

Subsection 4 concludes section A of part II with an exploration of the alternative, "equality" approach to defining reproductive rights. Reva B. Siegel's essay, "Abortion as a Sex Equality Right: Its Basis in Feminist Theory," presents the findings of her prodigious study of the history of abortion regulation. Siegel first summarizes her argument that abortion prohibitions are the equivalent of forced motherhood and, as such, are a form of gender caste regulation. She then canvasses several different versions of the equality argument, arguing that an equality analysis would succeed under the Equal Protection Clause—the constitutional provision that governs antidiscrimination law in general and sex discrimination in particular—if the Court were willing to move to the "antisubordination" approach to defining equality. A brief by Kathleen M. Sullivan and Susan R. Estrich illustrates how one might articulate an equality argument for the abortion right within traditional Equal Protection doctrine, without changing to the antisubordination approach.

NOTES

1. 381 U.S. 479 (1965).
2. 405 U.S. 438 (1972).

1. Social and Historical Context

Chapter 5

Medicine and Morality in the Nineteenth Century

Kristin Luker

. . . .

Abortion in Nineteenth-Century America

. . . .

Contrary to our assumptions about "Victorian morality," the available evidence suggests that abortions were frequent [in the first half of the nineteenth century]. . . . Discreet advertisements for "clinics for ladies" where menstrual irregularities "from whatever cause" could be treated (and where confidentiality and even private off-street entrances were carefully noted in the advertisement itself) were common.

. . . .

[V]arious attempts were made during this period to estimate the frequency of induced abortion as we now understand it. These estimates were primarily the work of physicians who wanted to convince the public that abortion was a problem of great magnitude, and so their estimates must be treated cautiously. Nonetheless, estimates from differing sources yield roughly comparable results. An Ohio medical investigation concluded that one-third of all "live births" (*sic*) ended in induced abortion. Dr. Horatio Storer, one of the most visible anti-abortionists of the era, estimated that there was one abortion for every four pregnancies; a survey of Michigan physicians found between 17 and 34 percent of all pregnancies ending in abortion; and an 1871 American Medical Association committee concluded that 20 percent of all pregnancies were deliberately aborted.[1] . . . Contemporary observers . . . were in unanimous agreement that the women who engaged in abortion did not believe they were doing anything wrong. [Women felt] . . . , they argued, . . . that abortion before quickening was morally blameless, only slightly different from preventing a conception in the first place.

Physicians and Abortion

In the second half of the nineteenth century abortion began to emerge as a social problem: newspapers began to run accounts of women who had died from "criminal abortions," although whether this fact reflects more abortions, more lethal abortions,

Kristin Luker, *Abortion and the Politics of Motherhood* 11–39 (1984).

or simply more awareness is not clear. Most prominently, physicians became involved, arguing that abortion was both morally wrong and medically dangerous.

The membership of the American Medical Association (AMA), founded in 1847 to upgrade and protect the interests of the profession, was deeply divided on many issues. But by 1859 it was able to pass a resolution condemning induced abortion and urging state legislatures to pass laws forbidding it. . . . Meanwhile, a number of physicians . . . began to publish books designed to convince the public that abortion was a medical and a moral wrong. Most of these men were elite "regular" physicians and associated with university-based medical schools. . . . In all, scholarship on the nineteenth-century abortion debate has been hard-pressed to find any other group of anti-abortion activists as central and visible as physicians.

Why should nineteenth-century physicians have become so involved with the question of abortion? The physicians themselves gave two related explanations for their activities, and these explanations have been taken at face value ever since. First, they argued, they were compelled to address the abortion question because American women were committing a moral crime based on ignorance about the proper value of embryonic life. According to these physicians, women sought abortions because the doctrine of quickening led them to believe that the embryo was not alive, and therefore aborting it was perfectly proper. Second, they argued, they were obliged to act in order to save women from their own ignorance because only physicians were in possession of new scientific evidence which demonstrated beyond a shadow of a doubt that the embryo was a child from conception onward.

The physicians were probably right in their belief that American women did not consider abortion—particularly early abortion—to be morally wrong. . . . [T]hat attitude would have been consistent with a long moral and legal tradition. But the core of the physicians' claim—the assertions that women practiced abortion because they were ignorant of the biological facts of pregnancy and that physicians were opposed to it because they were in possession of new scientific evidence—had no solid basis in fact. . . . Women (and the general public) knew that pregnancy was a *biologically* continuous process from beginning to end, and physicians were not in possession of remarkable new scientific discoveries to use to prove the case.

Both popular and medical writings of the period suggest that for many years prior to the first "right-to-life" movement, the nineteenth-century public agreed with the anti-abortion physicians' belief that pregnancy was, biologically speaking, a continuous process that led to the birth of a child. Where they disagreed was upon the *moral* implications of these biological facts. The public did not consider the embryo "not alive" in the biological sense, as the anti-abortion physicians asserted. Rather, public (and much medical) opinion seems to have been that embryos were, morally speaking, simply not *as alive* as the mother, at least until quickening—and sometimes later than that, if the pregnancy threatened the life of the woman. . . .

This preference for maternal life over embryonic life reflects standard medical practice, at least according to textbooks in use at the time. William Dewees, the author of a classic obstetrical textbook published in 1826 and reprinted nine times over the next twenty-five years, denounced abortion when practiced by women, yet quoted approvingly the traditional notion that the life of the child was "incomparably small" when pitted against that of its mother. Similarly, Gunning Bedford, another well-respected obstetrical expert whose work was reprinted eight times, argued in favor of abortion: "Without the operation, two lives would certainly be sacrificed, while, with it, it is more than probable that one would be saved." Charles Meigs, the author of another much-reprinted obstetrical textbook, agreed: "Whenever a clear indication for the sacrifice of the tender embryo exists, no evil is done in procuring the greater good of the mother; on the contrary, the act by which it is destroyed is as purely good as the saving of a man's life. The lesser, in morals, must yield to the greater; the lesser is always included in the greater."[2]

What the anti-abortion physicians achieved, therefore, was a subtle transformation of the grounds of the debate. By asserting that women had abortions because they were ignorant of scientific knowledge, doctors shifted the focus of the debate from moral *values* to empirical *facts*. But judging by the available evidence, the public, the medical profession in general, and the anti-abortion physicians in particular were *not* at odds with one another over the facts about what went on during pregnancy. With greater or lesser degrees of detail, all seem to have drawn on relatively widely available and popularly accepted beliefs about the development of the embryo. Popular (and legal) acceptance of abortion was not based on ignorance of "the facts," as physicians asserted, but on *a different moral evaluation of the facts*.

Motives for Mobilization

Thus, the question remains: why, in the middle of the nineteenth century, did some physicians become active anti-abortionists? James Mohr, in a pioneering work on this topic, argues that the proliferation of healers in the nineteenth century created a competition for status and clients.[3] The "regular" physicians, who tended to be both wealthier and better educated than members of other medical sects, therefore sought to distinguish themselves both scientifically and socially from competing practitioners. Support of anti-abortion activity was admirably suited to this need. By taking an anti-abortion stand, regular physicians could lay claim to superior scientific knowledge, based on the latest research developments and theories (usually from abroad) to buttress their claim that pregnancy was continuous and that any intervention in it was immoral. . . . The abortion issue thus gave them a way of demonstrating that they were both more scientifically knowledgeable and more morally rigorous than their competitors.

Mohr suggests that there were several more practical reasons why regular physicians should have opposed abortion. On the one hand, outlawing abortion would remove a lucrative source of income from competitors they called "quacks" and perhaps remove that temptation from the path of the "regulars" as well. In addition, the "regulars" were predominantly white, upper-income, and native-born; as such, they belonged to precisely the same group that was thought to harbor the primary users of abortion. As a result, they were likely to be concerned both about the depopulation of

their group in the face of mounting immigration (and the higher fertility of immigrants) and about "betrayal" by their own women (because abortion required less male control and approval than the other available forms of birth control).
. . . .

It is certainly true, as Mohr claims, that the mobilization of American physicians against abortion took place in the context of a profound dilemma within the medical profession, a dilemma produced by the lack of a traditional guild structure, the proliferation of competing medical sects and dissension within the ranks of the regulars themselves. Physicians wanted to upgrade their profession by obtaining licensing laws that would restrict medical practice to only the best and the best-trained among them. But lacking such licensing laws and given the ease with which one could become even a "trained" physician by attending one of the proliferating "proprietary" medical schools, regular physicians had no way of proving that they were any better than their competitors.

Nineteenth-century physicians needed to be "better" than their competition in order to persuade the public that licensing laws were not simply a self-serving "restraint of trade," designed only to raise the price of a doctor's bill by eliminating the competition. (The "restraint of trade" complaint arose routinely whenever regular physicians pressed for licensing laws.) But they could not be "better" until they had licensing laws that would purge their own numbers of the inadequate or the incompetent.

As we know, regular physicians succeeded in their campaign for licensing laws. More than almost any other profession, medicine now rigorously exercises the right to control who shall enter the profession, how they shall practice, and how competitors will be treated; its nineteenth-century stand against abortion contributed substantially to this ultimate success. It is in the context of this drive for professionalization that the political activity of American physicians against abortion must be understood. When examined closely in this context, their actual behavior raises serious doubts about whether they had, as Mohr and Degler claim, an unparalleled commitment to the "sanctity of life" of the embryo.

The traditional explanation of how one group of medical practitioners in America, the regulars, successfully strove for and obtained the attributes that we now associate with modern medicine (and that, incidentally, squeezed out the competition) . . . attribute[s] this success to the superior education and understanding of the regulars and to their adoption of a new way of looking at the problem of disease, namely, "the scientific method." . . . On the other hand, recent studies of medical professionalization have tended to focus on another dimension, on what Charles Rosenberg has called the "sordid realities of the marketplace." This approach emphasizes the fact that regular physicians (and in particular those who *organized* on behalf of the regulars) tended to be of a higher social status than their sectarian competitors and tended to cater primarily to an upper-class clientele. The expenses of a medical education—especially when it was combined, as it often was for elite physicians, with a tour of study at a European university—tended to restrict the ranks of the regulars to the well-to-do. Notwithstanding the generally higher level of education among regulars, however, the actual content of the medical training they received was problematic. For much of the century, medical education was extremely informal, and by the latter part of the century, an increasing part of it, even for regulars, took place in proprietary schools that were very close to being "diploma mills."

Since most medical historians agree that regular physicians began to mobilize for licensing laws that would restrict competing practitioners *before* they could convincingly demonstrate that they were better healers in practice, writers in this second school have tended to see the success of the regulars as more frankly political. They argue that because the regulars were largely members of the elite, they were able to use their class standing and educational credentials to argue that they were "better" than the sectarians and the doctors trained by apprenticeship.

As is often the case, the full truth probably lies somewhere between the view of the first school, which stresses the improvement of technical understanding among physicians, and the view of the second, which stresses their use of political rather than technical skills. Anyone who reads nineteenth-century medical textbooks cannot fail to be impressed by the explosion of knowledge that occurred in the last third of the century. . . . In a real sense, medicine in the 1880s was closer to our own era than it was to the medicine of a mere forty years before.

Nonetheless, it is also true, as the second school of thought argues, that regular physicians had begun to mobilize politically *before* this explosion of new knowledge had effectively taken place. The AMA, for example, was founded in 1847, before many of these technical accomplishments were made and long before physicians were able to translate these accomplishments into better survival rates for their patients. At best it can be argued that the drive for professionalization was concurrent with scientific progress; it is virtually impossible to argue, as the first school did, that professionalization was the *product* of such progress. Finally, it may be argued that until the level of scientific progress is dramatically higher than it was during the nineteenth century, the ordinary consumer cannot differentiate between a "scientific" practitioner and a folk healer. Given the standard of living in the nineteenth century and the relatively primitive (though rapidly improving) state of medical knowledge, it remains to be demonstrated whether the average person would have been able to rank varieties of practitioners by effectiveness.

By the middle of the nineteenth century, therefore, American physicians had few if any of the formal attributes of a profession. The predominance of proprietary medical schools combined with the virtual absence of any form of licensing meant that the regulars could control neither entry into the profession nor the performance of those who claimed healing capacities. With the possible exceptions of the thermometer, the stethoscope, and the forceps, the technological tools of modern medicine were yet to come; and lacking the means of professional control, regular physicians were hard put to keep even those simple instruments out of the hands of the competition. Because they could offer no direct, easily observable, and dramatic proof of their superiority, regular physicians were forced to make an indirect, *symbolic* claim about their status. By becoming visible activists on an issue such as abortion, they could claim both *moral stature* (as a high-minded, self-regulating group of professionals) and *technical expertise* (derived from their superior training).

Therefore, the physicians' choice of abortion as the focus of their moral crusade was carefully calculated. Abortion, and only abortion, could enable them to make symbolic claims about their status. Unlike the other medico-moral issues of the time —alcoholism, slavery, venereal disease, and prostitution—only abortion gave physicians the opportunity to claim to be saving human lives. Given the primitive nature of medical practice, persuading the public that embryos were human lives and then persuading state legislatures to protect these lives by outlawing abortion may have been one of the few life-saving projects actually available to physicians.

Physicians, therefore, had to exaggerate the differences between themselves and the lay public. Anti-abortion physicians had to claim that women placed *no* value on embryonic life whereas they themselves ranked the embryo as a full human life, namely, as a baby. But these two positions, when combined, created an unresolvable paradox for physicians, a paradox that would haunt the abortion debate until the present day.

If the embryo is a full human life, as these physicians claimed, then abortion can never be morally right, even when undertaken to save the life of the mother; the Western tradition does not permit even physicians to "set aside one life for another," as the Jewish Mishnah puts it. The only logical moral position was that of Bishop Kenrick of Philadelphia, who declared with respect to abortion in 1841 that two deaths were better than one murder.

But if abortion is never morally right, then nineteenth-century physicians had no grounds for claiming it as a medical issue that required their *professional* regulation. Once they had alerted Americans to the "fact" that abortion was murder, the logical move would have been to turn the issue over to their "competition"—clergymen who would deal with its moral consequences and lawyers who would deal with its legal consequences. Ironically, what the physicians did, in effect, was to simultaneously claim both an *absolute* right to life for the embryo (by claiming that abortion is always murder) and a *conditional* one (by claiming that doctors have a right to declare some abortions "necessary").

. . . .

If these regular doctors were as actively opposed to abortion as their public rhetoric suggested, we would expect the result of their efforts to be laws that either forbade abortions entirely or, at the very least, carefully defined the few kinds of abortions that could take place. On the other hand, if physicians were trying to both *create* and *control* a moral problem at the same time, we would expect laws that would forbid non-physicians to perform abortions but would give physicians a great deal of legal discretion to perform abortions when they wanted to—a discretion hard to reconcile with their public contention that abortion was always murder.

And, in fact, an inspection of most nineteenth-century state laws suggests that this latter course was the one taken. By 1900 only six states did not include a "therapeutic exception" in their abortion laws, a clause stating that any abortion undertaken by or on the advice of a physician to preserve the life of the mother was legal. These laws in effect gave physicians almost unlimited discretion in deciding when an abortion was necessary. . . . [N]one of these laws described exactly what constituted a threat to life. For example, must the threat be immediate or can it be long term? Similarly, they did not specify the confidence level needed. Must the pregnancy be an unquestionable threat to maternal life, or could the threat be only probable?

. . . .

[P]hysicians wanted to create a category of "justifiable" abortion and to make themselves the custodians of it. Some anti-abortion physicians actually opposed legislative attempts to tighten or spell out what exactly was entailed in the therapeutic exception. . . . In short, the opposition of the regulars to abortion could become quite tempered when it appeared that abortion could be suppressed only at the cost of increased social and legislative control of the medical profession.

Nineteenth-century anti-abortionist literature, gynecology textbooks, and articles in medical journals indicate still another important consequence of the physicians' paradox: the terms chosen to define physician boundaries—"saving the life" of the woman—were perhaps deliberately vague. The word *life* may mean physical life in the narrow sense of the word (life or death), or it may mean the social, emotional, and intellectual life of a woman in the broad sense (style of life). . . .

Physicians were willing to induce (and in their writings to advocate inducing) abortions under both of these definitions of the term *life*. Not only were cardiac disease, "consumption," and pernicious vomiting causes for abortion, so also were "neurasthenia" (an all-purpose diagnosis for complaints from "high-strung" women) and many other complaints that would compromise the woman's life in the broader sense of the word. The range of acceptable grounds for abortion is demonstrated by T. Gaillard Thomas, an outstanding obstetrician-gynecologist and a strong anti-abortionist. He believed that abortion was indicated when pregnancy would "destroy the life or intellect, or permanently ruin the health of the mother."[4] Even Horatio Storer, in many ways the most prominent anti-abortionist of his day, subscribed to a broad view of what "saving the life" of a woman entailed. While arguing that the decision to induce an abortion is a weighty one and must always be taken in consultation with colleagues, his list of indications for abortion includes other considerations besides strict preservation of maternal life, notably what would later be called health and "fetal" indications:

> There are other instances that might be cited, cases of dangerous organic disease, as cancer of the womb, in which, however improbable it might seem, pregnancy does occasionally occur; *cases of insanity, of epilepsy, or of other mental lesion, where there is fear of transmitting the malady* to a line of offspring; cases of general ill health, where there is perhaps a chance of the patient becoming an invalid for life [emphasis added].[5]

All the available evidence suggests, therefore, that rhetoric notwithstanding, nineteenth-century anti-abortion physicians who were successful in securing the first statute laws prohibiting abortion never believed that embryos had an absolute right to life. Instead, like most of those around them (and indeed, like most Americans of the present day), they believed that although embryos had rights, these rights were subordinate to the life of the mother, in both the broad *and* the narrow sense.

The important difference between the nineteenth-century physicians' stand and the previous public and legal toleration for abortion does not lie in a radically new view of the nature of the embryo or of its rights. . . . In practice, . . . physicians agreed that the embryo's rights were in fact conditional. What was at the core of their movement, therefore, was a *reallocation* of social responsibility for assessing the conditional rights of the embryo against the woman's right to life, both narrowly and broadly defined. From the late nineteenth century until the late 1960s, it was doctors, not women, who held the right to make that assessment.

Consequences of the Physicians' Crusade

. . . .

Because doctors successfully asserted professional control over the [abortion] issue, a major part of it disappeared from view. There continued to be concern about women who performed abortions on themselves, and the newly defined criminal abortionists were prosecuted; but, in general, physicians made their decisions on abortion without public scrutiny. . . .

Meanwhile, the ideological sleight of hand performed by the physicians left its imprint on the debate for the ensuing century. Because the profession had successfully achieved the right to handle this thorny public issue within the confines of its own domain—because in effect the American public accepted the profession's claim that it was capable of juggling the conflicting rights of the abortion decision—the physician's paradox disappeared from view. Thus, both "strict" and "liberal" constructionists—the inheritors, in other words, of both the neo-Pythagorean view that the embryo is a baby and the Stoic view that it is not—could rest assured that the issue had been turned over to a morally rigorous and self-evidently upstanding profession, which in turn would make wise decisions. The intrinsic conflict between the two interpretations was therefore hidden from view: partisans of each interpretation could feel confident that theirs was the dominant one—that all abortion was murder or that physicians could, should, and would do abortions when the circumstances warranted. As a result, abortion as a major social, political, and ethical issue could disappear beneath the cloak of an emerging profession's claims, there to rest quietly for almost a century.

NOTES

1. For the Ohio medical investigation, see, Arthur W. Calhoun, *The Social History of the American Family,* 3:243 (New York: Barnes and Noble, 1919). The one-to-four ratio is suggested in Horatio Storer and Franklin Fiske Heard, *Criminal Abortion: Its Nature, Its Law, Its Evidence* (Cambridge, Mass., 1868). Storer and Heard conflated criminal and spontaneous abortions, but the authors assert that the vast majority of these abortions are induced (pp. 28–34). For the Michigan survey (1882), see Edward Cox et al., *Report of the Special Committee on Criminal Abortion, in* NINTH ANNUAL REPORT OF THE SECRETARY OF THE STATE BOARD OF HEALTH OF THE STATE OF MICHIGAN 164–88 (Lansing, 1882). For the AMA committee report, see *Transactions of the AMA* 22, 250–51 (1871).

2. Dewees, William P. *A Compendious System of Midwifery* 477. Philadelphia: Blanchard & Lea, 1847. Bedford, Gunning. *Principles and Practice of Obstetrics* 679. 3rd ed. New York: William Wood & Co., 1866. Meigs, Charles D. *Woman: Her Diseases and Remedies* 552. Philadelphia: Blanchard & Lea, 1859.

3. Mohr, James C. *Abortion in America: The Origins and Evolution of National Policy* 147–70. New York: Oxford University Press, 1978.

4. Thomas, T. Gaillard. *Abortion and Its Treatment: From the Standpoint of Practical Experience* 99. New York: D. Appleton, 1894.

5. Storer, Horatio R. *Why Not? A Book for Every Woman* 25. Boston: Lea & Shepard, 1866.

Chapter 6

When Abortion Was a Crime
Women, Medicine, and Law in the United States, 1867–1973

Leslie J. Reagan

. . . .

[In the era of criminalization,] [m]uch of the regulation of abortion was carried out not by government agents, but by voluntary agencies and individuals. The state expected the medical profession to assist in enforcing the law.

. . . .

It would have been virtually impossible for the state to enforce the criminal abortion laws without the cooperation of physicians. State officials won medical cooperation in suppressing abortion by threatening doctors and medical institutions with prosecution or scandal. Physicians learned to protect themselves from legal trouble by reporting to officials women injured or dying as a result of illegal abortions. By the 1940s and 1950s, physicians and hospitals had become so accustomed to this regulatory stance toward women and abortion that they instituted new regulations to observe and curb the practice of abortion in the hospital. The medical profession and its institutions acted as an arm of the state.

Yet the medical profession's position was contradictory. While physicians helped control abortion, they too were brought under greater control. State officials demanded that the profession police the practices of its members. The duty of self-policing and physicians' fears of prosecution for abortion created dilemmas for doctors who at times compromised their duties to patients in order to carry out their duties to the state.

Furthermore, plenty of physicians provided abortions. . . .

Punishment for violation of the law and sexual norms has been gendered. In abortion cases, the investigative procedures themselves constituted a form of punishment and control for women. Publicity and public exposure of women's transgressions further served as punishment. This form of punishment served, in Michel Foucault's words, as "a school." The shame of public exposure was for all of "the potentially guilty," not only the individual who had been caught. . . .

The illegality of abortion has hidden the existence of an unarticulated, alternative, popular morality, which supported women who had abortions. This popular ethic contradicted the law, the official attitude of the medical profession, and the teachings

Leslie J. Reagan, *When Abortion Was a Crime: Women, Medicine, and the Law in the United States, 1867–1973* 1–18 (1997).

of some religions. Private discussions among family and friends, conversations between women and doctors, and the behavior of women (and the people who aided them) suggest that traditional ideas that accepted early abortions endured into the twentieth century. Furthermore, through the 1920s at least, working-class women did not make a distinction between contraceptives and abortion. What I call a popular morality that accepted abortion was almost never publicly expressed but was rooted in people's daily lives. Americans have a long history of accepting abortion in certain situations as a necessity and as a decision that, implicitly, belongs to women to make. This popular attitude made itself felt in the courts and in doctors' offices: prosecutors found it difficult to convict abortionists because juries regularly nullified the law by acquitting abortionists, and few physicians escaped the pressure from women for abortions. Throughout the period of illegal abortion, women asserted their need for abortion and, in doing so, implicitly asserted their sense of having a right to control their own reproduction.

I am not suggesting a "gap" between people's beliefs and their ability to live up to them, but different, even oppositional, moral perspectives. The values expressed by ordinary people deserve to be taken seriously rather than categorized and dismissed as sinful or mistaken. Though some felt guilt about abortion and found ways to justify their behavior, others never held the official antiabortion views. Prescribed morality and popular morality may not be identical. Analysis of women's practices and ideas—popular behavior and belief—rather than exclusive focus on the statements of male theologians and philosophers suggests that it is incorrect to conclude that hostility to abortion is "almost an absolute value in history."[1] The reverse may be more accurate.

Although this book takes note of religious teachings and the religious background of women who had abortions, it does not focus on religious opinion. Organized religion had little interest in abortion until it entered the public, political arena in the late 1950s and early 1960s. There was no reason to energetically fight abortion when, for nearly a century, abortion was a crime and no social movement suggested otherwise. From the 1920s on, however, there was much religious interest in, and division over, another method of reproductive control: contraception. Birth control became a topic of interest because a movement advocated women's right to reproductive control. Further, it is incorrect to assume that the Catholic Church has always organized against abortion or that all Catholics subscribe to the views of their church leaders. Indeed, many Catholics shared what I have described as a popular ethic accepting abortion. A good history of religion and reproductive control would examine not only theology and sermons, but also the attitudes and actions of the congregations, with particular attention to women.

Women who had abortions did so within a context of illegality and religious disapproval, but the prohibitions were ambiguous. Christian traditions had tabooed abortion since antiquity, but the acceptance of abortion in order to save the life of a pregnant woman had a long tradition as well. Until the mid-nineteenth century, the Catholic Church implicitly accepted early abortions prior to ensoulment. Not until 1869, at about the same time that abortion became politicized in this country, did the church condemn abortion; in 1895, it condemned therapeutic abortion. Protestant churches accepted abortion when pregnancy threatened a woman's life, a view shared by the

medical profession and written into the nation's laws. Jewish tradition clearly viewed the woman's life as primary. The Mishnah, a code of ancient Jewish law that guided later rabbinic thought, required abortion when childbirth threatened a woman's life, for "her life takes precedence over its life."
. . . .

Medical discourse has convinced some scholars that physicians did not perform abortions in the period of illegal abortion, and most press coverage of abortion in the early twentieth century gives the misleading impression that abortion was universally condemned and generally fatal. These conclusions are not correct. Analysis of discourse alone would miss the ongoing medical practice of abortion in total contradiction of official medical mores. . . . The publicly articulated and published discussion of abortion rarely included the voices or perspectives of women who had abortions, except to provide shocking examples of depraved womanhood. Women who had abortions did not intervene to explain themselves, but instead, in other nonpublic arenas, made their perspectives known and acted to obtain a much-needed method for preventing births. More tolerant attitudes toward abortion, rooted in material experiences, persisted in the face of a public discourse that denounced it. . . .

Common Law and the Criminalization of Abortion

Abortion was not always a crime. During the eighteenth and early nineteenth centuries, abortion of early pregnancy was legal under common law. Abortions were illegal only after "quickening," the point at which a pregnant woman could feel the movements of the fetus (approximately the fourth month of pregnancy). The common law's attitude toward pregnancy and abortion was based on an understanding of pregnancy and human development as a process rather than an absolute moment. Indeed, the term abortion referred only to the miscarriages of later pregnancies, after quickening. What we would now identify as an early induced abortion was not called an "abortion" at all. If an early pregnancy ended, it had "slipp[ed] away," or the menses had been "restored." At conception and the earliest stage of pregnancy before quickening, no one believed that a human life existed; not even the Catholic Church took this view. Rather, both the popular ethic regarding abortion and [the] common law were grounded in the female experience of their own bodies.

Colonial and early-nineteenth-century women, historians have learned, perceived conception as the "blocking" or "obstructing" of menstruation, which required attention. The cessation of the menses indicated a worrisome imbalance in the body and the need to bring the body back into balance by restoring the flow. This idea of menstruation corresponded with medical and popular understanding of sickness and health. The body was a delicate system of equilibrium that could easily be thrown out of balance—by a change in weather or diet, for example—and that then needed to be restored through active intervention. A disruption in the healthy body, in the world view of patients and physicians, required a visible, often violent, physical response to treatment in order to restore equilibrium. This theory underlay eighteen-and-nineteenth-century regular medical practice, which emphasized heroic measures—bleeding, blistering, purging, and puking—in response to sickness. The response to the blocking of the menses was part of this shared understanding of the body: women took drugs in order to make their menses regular and regarded the ensuing vomiting and evacuation as evidence of the drugs' effective action.

Restoring the menses was a domestic practice. The power of certain herbs to restore menstruation was widely known. . . .

Both of these concepts, blocked menses and quickening, must be taken seriously by late-twentieth-century observers. Blocked menses cannot be dismissed as an excuse made by women who knew they were pregnant. Quickening was a moment recognized by women and by law as a defining moment in human development. Once quickening occurred, women recognized a moral obligation to carry the fetus to term. This age-old idea underpinned the practice of abortion in America. The legal acceptance of induced miscarriages before quickening tacitly assumed that women had a basic right to bodily integrity.

By the mid-eighteenth century, the most common means of inducing abortion— by taking drugs—was commercialized. The availability of abortifacients was so well-known that a common euphemism described their use. When Sarah Grosvenor, a Connecticut farm girl, confided to her sister in 1742 that she was "taking the trade," her sister understood. That Grosvenor successfully conveyed her meaning to her sister in three metaphoric words tells us a great deal about the world of mid-eighteenth-century New England. Many New Englanders, including these sisters, knew of the possibility of inducing an abortion by purchasing and ingesting drugs. The need for a euphemism tells of the difficulty of speaking openly about sex and reproductive control and of the need for secrecy. Yet it reveals an awareness that women could and did regulate their own fertility through abortion. Furthermore, abortifacients had become a profitable product sold by doctors, apothecaries, and other healers.

The first statutes governing abortion in the United States, James Mohr has found, were poison control measures designed to protect pregnant women like Grosvenor by controlling the sale of abortifacient drugs, which often killed the women who took them. The proliferation of entrepreneurs who openly sold and advertised abortifacients may have inspired this early legislation, passed in the 1820s and 1830s. The 1827 Illinois law, which prohibited the provision of abortifacients, was listed under "poisoning."

It is crucial to recognize what these early-nineteenth-century laws did not cover: they did not punish women for inducing abortions, and they did not eliminate the concept of quickening. Even as poison control measures, they said nothing about growing the plants needed in one's own garden or mixing together one's own home remedy in order to induce an abortion. The legal silence on domestic practices suggests that the new laws were aimed at the commercialization of this practice and, implicitly, retained to women the right to make their own decisions about their pregnancies before quickening.

By the 1840s, the abortion business boomed. Despite the laws forbidding the sale of abortifacients, they were advertised in the popular press and could be purchased from physicians or pharmacists or through the mail. If drugs failed, women could go to a practitioner who specialized in performing instrumental abortions. Advertisements and newspaper exposés made it appear that what had been an occasional domestic practice had become a daily occurrence performed for profit in northern cities. Madame Restell, for example, openly advertised and provided abortion services for thirty-five years. Restell began her abortion business in New York City in the late 1830s; by the mid-1840s, she had offices in Boston and Philadelphia and traveling agents who sold her "Female Monthly Pills." Restell became the most infamous abortionist in the country, but she was not the only abortionist.[2] The clientele of these busy clinics were primarily married, white, native-born Protestant women of the upper and middle classes.

In 1857, the newly organized AMA initiated a crusade to make abortion at every stage of pregnancy illegal. The antiabortion campaign grew in part, James Mohr has shown, out of regular physicians' desire to win professional power, control medical practice, and restrict their competitors, particularly homeopaths and midwives. . . . Though professional issues underlay the medical campaign, gender, racial, and class anxieties pushed the criminalization of abortion forward. The visible use of abortion by middle-class married women, in conjunction with other challenges to gender norms and changes in the social makeup of the nation, generated anxieties among American men of the same class. Birth rates among the Yankee classes had declined by midcentury while immigrants poured into the country. Antiabortion activists pointed out that immigrant families, many of them Catholic, were larger and would soon outpopulate native-born white Yankees and threaten their political power. Dr. Horatio R. Storer, the leader of the medical campaign against abortion, envisioned the spread of "civilization" west and south by native-born white Americans, not Mexicans, Chinese, Blacks, Indians, or Catholics. "Shall" these regions, he asked, "be filled by our own children or by those of aliens? This is a question our women must answer; upon their loins depends the future destiny of the nation."[3] Hostility to immigrants, Catholics, and people of color fueled this campaign to criminalize abortion. White male patriotism demanded that maternity be enforced among white Protestant women.

The antiabortion campaign was antifeminist at its core. Women were condemned for following "fashion" and for avoiding the self-sacrifice expected of mothers. "The true wife," Storer declared, did not seek "undue power in public life, . . . undue control in domestic affairs, . . . [or] privileges not her own."[4] The antiabortion campaign was a reactionary response to two important efforts of the nineteenth-century women's movements: the fight to admit women into the regular medical profession and the battle to make men conform to a single standard of sexual behavior. The antiabortion campaign coincided with the fight by male Regulars to keep women out of their medical schools, societies, and hospitals. Boston and Harvard University, Storer's hometown and alma mater, were key sites of struggle over women's place in medicine, and Storer was personally engaged in the battle against female physicians. Advocates of women in medicine argued that women doctors would protect women patients from sexual violation. Regular male doctors degraded female physicians by accusing them, along with midwives, of performing abortions.

The relative morality of men and women was of crucial importance to this campaign. For the specialists, whose interest in the female reproductive system raised questions about their sexual morality, the antiabortion campaign was a way to proclaim their own high morality in contrast to their competitors, their female patients, and even the ministers who tolerated abortion. It was at the same time a backlash against the women's movement's critique of male sexual behavior and feminist claims to political power. Nineteenth-century feminists expressed their anger with male sexual domination and promiscuity in a number of movements, including the campaigns against prostitution and slavery and the fight for temperance. All sections of the women's movement advocated "voluntary motherhood," a slogan that addressed both men's sexual violation of their wives and women's desire to control childbearing. Women saw themselves as morally superior and urged men to adopt a single standard —the female standard of chastity until marriage, followed by monogamy and moderation. The campaign against abortion challenged this feminist analysis of men by condemning women for having abortions. Indeed, Storer compared abortion to prostitution and, in so doing, called into question all claims made by middle-class nineteenth-century women on the basis of moral superiority. "There is little difference," he proclaimed, "between the immorality" of the man who visited prostitutes and the woman who aborted.[5] The nineteenth-century women's movements never defended abortion, but activist women and women doctors were blamed for the practice of abortion nonetheless.

The antiabortion campaign attempted to destroy the idea of quickening. As physicians targeted quickening, they discredited women's experiences of pregnancy and claimed pregnancy as medical terrain. "Quickening," as Storer described it, "is in fact but a sensation." A sensation that had emotional, social, and legal meaning was thus denigrated. Quickening was based on women's own bodily sensations—not on medical diagnosis. It made physicians, and obstetricians in particular, dependent on female self-diagnosis and judgment. Quickening could not be relied upon as an indicator of fetal life because, Storer argued, it did not occur at a standard moment. "Many women never quicken at all," he joked about women's perceptions, "though their children are born living."[6] Storer's propaganda aimed to erase the distinctions between earlier and later stages of pregnancy, thereby redefining the restoration of the menses. What had previously been understood as a blockage and a restoration of the menses prior to quickening was now associated with inducing a miscarriage after quickening by labeling it abortion. Furthermore, Storer equated abortion with infanticide.

. . . .

The new laws passed across the country between 1860 and 1880 regarded abortion in an entirely different light from common law and the statutes regulating abortifacients. In general, the laws included two innovations: they eliminated the common-law idea of quickening and prohibited abortion at any point in pregnancy. Some included punishment for the women who had abortions. The "Comstock Law" passed in 1873 included abortion and birth control in federal antiobscenity legislation; states and municipalities passed similar ordinances.

The antiabortion laws made one exception: physicians could perform therapeutic abortions if pregnancy and childbirth threatened the woman's life. . . . Physicians entered a new partnership with the state and won the power to set reproductive policy. In the process, women's perceptions of pregnancy were delegitimated and women lost what had been a common-law right.

Periodization: Changing Patterns of Illegal Abortion

During the more than one hundred years that abortion was illegal in the United States, the patterns, practice, policing, and politics of abortion all changed over time, though not always simultaneously. . . . Abortion was widely available throughout much of the era when abortion was a crime. Yet periods of tolerance were punctuated by moments of severe repression. . . . In the nineteenth century, abortion came under attack at a moment when women were claiming political power; in the twentieth century, it came under attack when they claimed sexual freedom. Abortion, like contraception, means that women can separate sex and procreation—still a controversial notion. Antiabortion campaigns developed when women asserted sexual independence, as during the Progressive Era and since the 1970s. When abortion was most firmly linked to the needs of family rather than the freedoms of women, as during the Depression, it was most ignored by those who would suppress it. Periods of antiabortion activity mark moments of hostility to female independence.

The epoch of illegal abortion may be broken down into four periods. The first covers the time from the criminalization of abortion state-by-state, accomplished nationwide by 1880, to 1930. This period, covering fifty years, is heavily marked by continuity. As other historians have also found, the reproductive lives of most women and the day-to-day practice of most physicians changed slowly. In this period, abortion was widely accepted and was practiced in women's homes and in the offices of physicians and midwives. The diversity of practitioners, the privacy of medical practice, and the autonomy of physicians in the late nineteenth and early twentieth centuries made the widespread medical practice of abortion possible. A crackdown on abortion occurred between 1890 and 1920 as specialists in obstetrics renewed the earlier campaign against abortion, and the medical profession was drawn into the state's enforcement system.

The structural transformation that occurred during the 1930s, the second period, was crucial for the history of abortion. Abortion became more available and changed location. As the practice moved from private offices and homes to hospitals and clinics, abortion was consolidated in medical hands and became more visible. The changes wrought by the Depression accelerated the pace of change in the coming decades, particularly in the methods of enforcing the criminal abortion laws.

The third period was marked by increasing restrictions on abortion by state and medical authorities and intensifying demand for abortion from women of all groups. This period begins in 1940, when the new methods of controlling abortion were first instituted, and continues through 1973, when they were dismantled. In reaction to the growing practice of abortion as well as apparent changes in female gender and reproductive patterns, a backlash against abortion developed. 1940 marks a dividing line as hospitals instituted new policies, and police and prosecutors changed their tactics. The repression of abortion was part of the repression of political and personal deviance that took place in the 1940s and 1950s. Yet even in this period, the practice of abortion expanded in new directions in response to relentless demand. The new repression of abortion, however, was devastating for women. A dual system of abortion, divided by race and class, developed. During the postwar period, the criminalization of abortion produced its harshest results.

A new stage in the history of abortion, the movement to legalize it, overlaps with the third period. The movement to decriminalize abortion began in the mid-1950s and arose out of the difficult experiences resulting from the repression of abortion in the 1940s and 1950s. In the 1950s, a handful of physicians began to challenge the very abortion laws their profession had advocated a century earlier. The progress of that challenge attests to the continuing power of the medical profession to make public policy regarding reproduction. As legal reform moved forward, a new feminist movement arose, which radically transformed the movement for legal change. When the women's movement described abortion as an aspect of sexual freedom, they articulated a new feminist meaning for abortion; when they demanded abortion as a right, they echoed generations of women.

. . . .

NOTES

1. John T. Noonan Jr., "An Almost Absolute Value in History," in *The Morality of Abortion: Legal and Historical Perspectives,* edited by John T. Noonan Jr. (Cambridge, Mass.: Harvard University Press, 1970), 1–59.

2. James C. Mohr, *Abortion in America: The Origins and Evolution of National Policy, 1800–1900* (New York: Oxford University Press, 1978), 47–59, 70–71; Carroll Smith-Rosenberg, *Disorderly Conduct: Visions of Gender in Victorian America* (New York: Oxford University Press, 1985), 225–227.

3. Mohr, *Abortion in America,* 166–168. Quotation from Horatio Robinson Storer, *Why Not? A Book for Every Woman* (Boston: Lee and Shepard, 1868); reprinted as *A Proper Bostonian on Sex and Birth Control* (New York: Arno Press, 1974), 85.

4. Quotation from Horatio Robinson Storer, *Is It I? A Book for Every Man* (Boston: Lee and Shepard, 1868); reprinted as *A Proper Bostonian on Sex and Birth Control,* 134; Smith-Rosenberg, *Disorderly Conduct,* 224–228, 236–239; Mohr, *Abortion in America,* 107–108, 168–170.

5. Storer, *Why Not?,* 76, 83.

6. Ibid., 32.

Chapter 7

Racism, Birth Control, and Reproductive Rights

Angela Davis

. . . .

[T]he birth control movement has seldom succeeded in uniting women of different social backgrounds, and rarely have the movement leaders popularized the genuine concerns of working-class women. Moreover, arguments advanced by birth control advocates have sometimes been based on blatantly racist premises.

. . . .

The ranks of the abortion rights campaign [in the early 1970s] did not include substantial numbers of women of color. Given the racial composition of the larger women's liberation movement, this was not at all surprising. When questions were raised about the absence of racially oppressed women in both the larger movement and in the abortion rights campaign, two explanations were commonly proposed in the discussions and literature of the period: women of color were overburdened by their people's fight against racism, and/or they had not yet become conscious of the centrality of sexism. But the real meaning of the almost lily-white complexion of the abortion rights campaign was not to be found in ostensibly myopic or underdeveloped consciousness among women of color. The truth lay buried in the ideological underpinnings of the birth control movement itself.

The failure of the abortion rights campaign to conduct a historical self-evaluation led to a dangerously superficial appraisal of Black people's suspicious attitudes toward birth control in general. Granted, when some Black people unhesitatingly equated birth control with genocide, it did appear to be an exaggerated—even paranoiac—reaction. Yet white abortion rights activists missed a profound message, for underlying these cries of genocide were important clues about the history of the birth control movement. This movement, for example, had been known to advocate involuntary sterilization—a racist form of mass "birth control." If ever women would enjoy the right to plan their pregnancies, legal and easily accessible birth control measures and abortions would have to be complemented by an end to sterilization abuse.

As for the abortion rights campaign itself, how could women of color fail to grasp its urgency? They were far more familiar than their white sisters with the murderously clumsy scalpels of inept abortionists seeking profit in illegality. In New York, for instance, during the several years preceding the decriminalization of abortions in that

Angela Davis, "Racism, Birth Control, and Reproductive Rights," in Marlene Gerber Fried (ed.), From Abortion to Reproductive Freedom: Transforming a Movement 15–26 (1990).

state, some 80 percent of the deaths caused by illegal abortions involved Black and Puerto Rican women.[1] Immediately afterward, women of color received close to half of all the legal abortions. If the abortion rights campaign of the early 1970s needed to be reminded that women of color wanted desperately to escape the back-room quack abortionists, they should also have realized that these same women were not about to express pro-abortion sentiments. They were in favor of *abortion rights*, which did not mean that they were proponents of abortion. When Black and Latina women resort to abortions in such large numbers, the stories they tell are not so much about the desire to be free of their pregnancy, but rather about the miserable social conditions which dissuade them from bringing new lives into the world.

Black women have been aborting themselves since the earliest days of slavery. . . . Why were self-imposed abortions and reluctant acts of infanticide such common occurrences during slavery? Not because Black women had discovered solutions to their predicament, but rather because they were desperate. Abortions and infanticides were acts of desperation, motivated not by the biological birth process but by the oppressive conditions of slavery. Most of these women, no doubt, would have expressed their deepest resentment had someone hailed their abortions as a stepping stone toward freedom.

During the early abortion rights campaign, it was too frequently assumed that legal abortions provided a viable alternative to the myriad problems posed by poverty. As if having fewer children could create more jobs, higher wages, better schools, etc. This assumption reflected the tendency to blur the distinction between *abortion rights* and the general advocacy of *abortions*. The campaign often failed to provide a voice for women who wanted the *right* to legal abortions while deploring the social conditions that prohibited them from bearing more children.

. . . .

[Nineteenth-century] women's consciousness of their reproductive rights was born within the organized movement for women's political equality. . . . [W]omen's new dreams of pursuing careers and other paths of self-development outside marriage and motherhood could only be realized[, organizers knew,] if they could limit and plan their pregnancies. In this sense, the slogan "voluntary motherhood" contained a new and genuinely progressive vision of womanhood. At the same time, however, this vision was rigidly bound to the lifestyle enjoyed by the middle classes and the bourgeoisie. The aspirations underlying the demand for "voluntary motherhood" did not reflect the conditions of working-class women, engaged as they were in a far more fundamental fight for economic survival. Since this first call for birth control was associated with goals which could only be achieved by women possessing material wealth, vast numbers of poor and working-class women would find it rather difficult to identify with the embryonic birth control movement.

Toward the end of the nineteenth century the white birth rate in the United States suffered a significant decline. Since no contraceptive innovations had been publicly introduced, the drop in the birth rate implied that women were substantially curtailing their sexual activity. By 1890, the typical native-born white woman was bearing no more than four children. Since U.S. society was becoming increasingly urban, this new birth pattern should not have been a surprise. While farm life demanded large families, they became dysfunctional within the context of city life. Yet this phenomenon was publicly interpreted in a racist and anti-working-class fashion. . . . Since native-born white women were bearing fewer children, the specter of "race suicide" was raised in official circles.

In 1905 President Theodore Roosevelt concluded his Lincoln Day Dinner speech with the proclamation that "race purity must be maintained."[2] By 1906, he blatantly equated the falling birth rate among native-born whites with the impending threat of "race suicide." In his State of the Union message that year, Roosevelt admonished the well-born white women who engaged in "willful sterility—the one sin for which the penalty is national death, race suicide."[3] These comments were made during a period of accelerating racist ideology and of great waves of race riots and lynchings on the domestic scene.

. . . .

How did the birth control movement respond to Roosevelt's accusation that their cause was promoting race suicide? The President's propagandistic ploy was a failure, according to a leading historian of the birth control movement, for, ironically, it led to greater support for its advocates. Yet, as Linda Gordon maintains, this controversy " . . . also brought to the forefront those issues that most separated feminists from the working class and the poor."[4]

> This happened in two ways. First, the feminists were increasingly emphasizing birth control as a route to careers and higher education—goals out of reach of the poor with or without birth control. In the context of the whole feminist movement, the race-suicide episode was an additional factor identifying feminism almost exclusively with the aspirations of the more privileged women of the society. Second, the pro-birth control feminists began to popularize the idea that poor people had a moral obligation to restrict the size of their families, because large families create a drain on the taxes and charity expenditures of the wealthy and because poor children were less likely to be "superior."[5]

. . . .

Thus class bias and racism crept into the birth control movement when it was still in its infancy. More and more, it was assumed within birth control circles that poor women, Black and immigrant alike, had a "moral obligation to restrict the size of their families."[6] What was demanded as a "right" for the privileged came to be interpreted as a "duty" for the poor.

. . . .

By 1919, the eugenic influence on the birth control movement was unmistakably clear. In an article published by Margaret Sanger in the American Birth Control League's journal, she defined "the chief issue of birth control" as "more children from the fit, less from the unfit."[7] Around this time the American Birth Control League (ABCL) heartily welcomed the author of *The Rising Tide of Color Against White World Supremacy* into its inner sanctum. Lothrop Stoddard, Harvard professor and theoretician of the eugenics movement, was offered a seat on the ABCL board of directors. In the pages of the ABCL journal, articles by Guy Irving Birch, director of the American Eugenics Society, began to appear. Birch advocated birth control as a weapon to

". . . prevent the American people from being replaced by alien or Negro stock, whether it be by immigration or by overly high birth rates among others in this country."[8]

By 1932, the Eugenics Society could boast that at least 26 states had passed compulsory sterilization laws and that thousands of "unfit" persons had already been surgically prevented from reproducing. Margaret Sanger offered her public approval for this development. "Morons, mental defectives, epileptics, illiterates, paupers, unemployables, criminals, prostitutes and dope fiends" ought to be surgically sterilized, she argued in a radio talk.[9] She did not wish to be so intransigent as to leave them with no choice in the matter; if they wished, she said, they should be able to choose a lifelong segregated existence in labor camps.

Within the ABCL, the call for birth control among Black people acquired the same racist edge as the call for compulsory sterilization. In 1939, its successor, the Birth Control Federation of America, planned a "Negro Project." In the Federation's words, "[t]he mass of Negroes, particularly in the South, still breed carelessly and disastrously, with the result that the increase among Negroes, even more than among whites, is from that portion of the population least fit, and least able to rear children properly."[10]

Calling for the recruitment of Black ministers to lead local birth control committees, the Federation proposal suggested that Black people should be rendered as vulnerable as possible to their birth control propaganda. "We do not want word to get out," wrote Margaret Sanger in a letter to a colleague, "that we want to exterminate the Negro population and the minister is the man who can straighten out that idea if it ever occurs to any of their more rebellious members."[11]

This episode in the birth control movement confirmed the ideological victory of the racism associated with eugenic ideas. It had been robbed of its progressive potential, advocating for people of color not the individual right to *birth control*, but rather the racist strategy of *population control*. The birth control campaign would be called upon to serve in an essential capacity in the execution of the U.S. government's imperialist and racist population policy.

The abortion rights activists of the early 1970s should have examined the history of their movement. Had they done so, they might have understood why so many of their Black sisters adopted a posture of suspicion toward their cause. They might have understood how important it was to undo the racist deeds of their predecessors, who had advocated birth control as well as compulsory sterilization as a means of eliminating the "unfit" sectors of the population. Consequently, the young white feminists might have been more receptive to the suggestion that their campaign for abortion rights include a vigorous condemnation of sterilization abuse, which had become more widespread than ever.

It was not until the media decided that the casual sterilization of two Black girls in Montgomery, Alabama, was a scandal worth reporting that the Pandora's box of sterilization abuse was finally flung open. But by the time the case of the Relf sisters broke, it was practically too late to influence the politics of the abortion rights movement. It was the summer of 1973 and the Supreme Court decision legalizing abortions had already been announced in January. Nevertheless, the urgent need for mass opposition to sterilization abuse became tragically clear. The facts surrounding the Relf sisters' story were horrifyingly simple. Minnie Lee, who was 12 years old, and Mary Alice, who was 14, had been unsuspectingly carted into an operating room, where surgeons irrevocably robbed them of their capacity to bear children. The surgery had been ordered by the HEW-funded Montgomery Community Action Committee after it was discovered that Depo-Provera, a drug previously administered to the girls as a birth prevention measure, caused cancer in test animals.

After the Southern Poverty Law Center filed suit on behalf of the Relf sisters, the girls' mother revealed that she had unknowingly "consented" to the operation, having been deceived by the social workers who handled her daughters' case. They had asked Mrs. Relf, who was unable to read, to put her "X" on a document, the contents of which were not described to her. She assumed, she said, that it authorized the continued Depo-Provera injections. As she subsequently learned, she had authorized the surgical sterilization of her daughters.

In the aftermath of publicity exposing the Relf sisters' case, similar episodes were brought to light. In Montgomery alone, 11 girls, also in their teens, had been similarly sterilized. HEW-funded birth control clinics in other states, as it turned out, had also subjected young girls to sterilization abuse. Moreover, individual women came forth with equally outrageous stories. Nial Ruth Cox, for example, filed suit against the state of North Carolina. At the age of 18—eight years before her suit—officials had threatened to discontinue her family welfare payments if she refused to submit to surgical sterilization. Before she assented to the operation, she was assured that her infertility would be temporary.

Nial Ruth Cox's lawsuit was aimed at a state which had diligently practiced the theory of eugenics. Under the auspices of the Eugenics Commission of North Carolina, so it was learned, 7,686 sterilizations had been carried out since 1933. Although the operations were justified as measures to prevent the reproduction of "mentally deficient persons," about 5,000 of the sterilized persons had been Black.[12] According to Brenda Feigen Fasteau, the ACLU attorney representing Nial Ruth Cox, North Carolina's recent record was not much better. "As far as I can determine, the statistics reveal that since 1964, approximately 65 percent of the women sterilized in North Carolina were Black and approximately 35 percent were white."[13]

As the flurry of publicity exposing sterilization abuse revealed, the neighboring state of South Carolina had been the site of further atrocities. Eighteen women from Aiken, South Carolina, charged that they had been sterilized by a Dr. Clovis Pierce during the early 1970s. The sole obstetrician in that small town, Pierce had consistently sterilized Medicaid recipients with two or more children. According to a nurse in his office, Dr. Pierce insisted that pregnant welfare women "will have to submit [sic] to voluntary sterilization" if they wanted him to deliver their babies.[14] While he was ". . . tired of people running around and having babies and paying for them with my taxes,"[15] Dr. Pierce received some $60,000 in taxpayers' money for the sterilizations he performed. During his trial he was supported by the South Carolina Medical Association, whose members declared that doctors " . . . have the moral and legal right to insist on sterilization permission before accepting a patient, if it is done on the initial visit."[16]

Revelations of sterilization abuse during the time exposed the complicity of the federal government. At first the Department of Health, Education and Welfare claimed that approximately 16,000 women and 8,000 men had been sterilized in 1972 under the auspices of federal programs. Later, however, these figures underwent a drastic revision. Carl Shultz, director of [the] HEW Population Affairs Office, estimated that between 100,000 and 200,000 sterilizations had actually been funded that year by the federal government. During Hitler's Germany, incidentally, 250,000 sterilizations were carried out under the Nazis' Hereditary Health Law. Is it possible that the record of the Nazis, through the years of their reign, may have been almost equaled by the U.S. government-funded sterilizations in the space of a single year?

Given the historical genocide inflicted on the native population of the United States, one would assume that Native American Indians would be exempted from the government sterilization campaign. But according to Dr. Connie Uri's testimony in a Senate committee hearing, by 1976 some 24 percent of all Indian women of childbearing age had been sterilized. "Our blood lines are being stopped," the Choctaw physician told the Senate committee. "Our unborn will not be born. . . . This is genocide to our people."[17] According to Dr. Uri, the Indian Health Services Hospital in Claremore, Oklahoma, had been sterilizing one out of every four women giving birth in that federal facility.

. . . .

The domestic policy of the U.S. government has [had] an undeniably racist edge. Native American, Chicana, Puerto Rican and Black women continue to be sterilized in disproportionate numbers. According to a national fertility study conducted in 1970 by Princeton University's Office of Population Control, 20 percent of all married Black women [had] been permanently sterilized. Approximately the same percentage of Chicanas [had] been rendered surgically infertile. Moreover, 43 percent of the women sterilized through federally subsidized programs were Black.

The astonishing number of Puerto Rican women who have been sterilized reflects a special government policy that can be traced back to 1939. In that year, President Roosevelt's Interdepartmental Committee on Puerto Rico issued a statement attributing the island's economic problems to the phenomenon of overpopulation. This committee proposed that efforts be undertaken to reduce the birth rate to no more than the level of the death rate. Soon afterward, an experimental sterilization campaign was undertaken in Puerto Rico. Although the Catholic Church initially opposed this experiment and forced the cessation of the program, in 1946, it was converted during the early 1950s to the teachings and practice of population control. In this period, over 150 birth control clinics were opened, resulting in a 20 percent decline in population growth by the mid-1960s. By the 1970s, over 35 percent of all Puerto Rican women of childbearing age had been surgically sterilized.

. . . .

The prevalence of sterilization abuse during the latter 1970s may [have been] greater than ever before. Although the Department of Health, Education and Welfare issued guidelines in 1974, which were ostensibly designed to prevent involuntary sterilizations, the situation nonetheless deteriorated. When the American Civil Liberties

Union Reproductive Freedom Project conducted a survey of teaching hospitals in 1975, it discovered that 40 percent of those institutions were not even aware of the regulations issued by HEW. Only 30 percent of the hospitals examined by the ACLU were even attempting to comply with the guidelines.

The 1977 Hyde Amendment added yet another dimension to coercive sterilization practices. As a result of this law passed by Congress, federal funds for abortions were eliminated in all cases but those involving rape and the risk of death or severe illness. According to Sandra Salazar of the California Department of Public Health, the first victim of the Hyde Amendment was a 27-year-old Chicana woman from Texas. She died as a result of an illegal abortion in Mexico shortly after Texas discontinued government-funded abortions. There have been many more victims—women for whom sterilization has become the only alternative to abortions, which are currently beyond their reach. Sterilizations continue to be federally funded and free, to poor women, on demand.

. . . .

Within organizations representing the interests of middle-class white women, there has been a certain reluctance to support the demands of the campaign against sterilization abuse, for these women are often denied their individual rights to be sterilized when they desire to take this step. While women of color are urged, at every turn, to become permanently infertile, white women enjoying prosperous economic conditions are urged, by the same forces, to reproduce themselves. They therefore sometimes consider the "waiting period" and other details of the demand for "informed consent" to sterilization as further inconveniences for women like themselves. Yet whatever the inconveniences for white middle-class women, a fundamental reproductive right of racially oppressed and poor women is at stake. Sterilization abuse must be ended.

NOTES

1. Edwin M. Gold *et al.,* "Therapeutic Abortions in New York City: A Twenty-Year Review," *American Journal of Public Health,* Vol. LV (July, 1965), pp. 964–972. Quoted in Lucinda Cisler, "Unfinished Business: Birth Control and Women's Liberation," in Robin Morgan, ed., *Sisterhood Is Powerful: An Anthology of Writings from the Women's Liberation Movement* (New York: Vintage Books, 1970), p. 261. Also quoted in Robert Staples, *The Black Woman in America* (Chicago: Nelson Hall, 1974), p. 146.

2. Melvin Steinfeld, *Our Racist Presidents* (San Ramon, California: Consensus Publishers, 1972), p. 212.

3. Bonnie Mass, *Population Target: The Political Economy of Population Control in Latin America* (Toronto, Canada: Women's Educational Press, 1977), p. 20.

4. Linda Gordon, *Woman's Body, Woman's Right: A Social History of Birth Control in America* (New York: Penguin Books, 1976), p. 157.

5. Ibid., p. 158.

6. Ibid.

7. Ibid., p. 281.

8. Ibid., p. 283.

9. Gena Corea, *The Hidden Malpractice* (New York: A Jove/HBJ Book, 1977), p. 149.

10. Gordon, *op. cit.,* p. 332.

11. Ibid., pp. 332–333.

12. Harold X., "Forced Sterilization Pervades South," *Muhammed Speaks,* October 10, 1975.

13. Jack Slater, "Sterilization, Newest Threat to the Poor," *Ebony,* Vol. XXVIII, No. 12 (October, 1973), p. 150.

14. Les Payne, "Forced Sterilization for the Poor?" *San Francisco Chronicle,* February 26, 1974.

15. Ibid.

16. Ibid.

17. Arlene Eisen, "They're Trying to Take Our Future—Native American Women and Sterilization," *The Guardian,* March 23, 1972.

Questions and Comments

1. According to Luker, how did physicians' opposition to abortion during the nineteenth century aid the efforts of the emerging medical profession to gain legitimacy and political power?

2. Do these readings provide any insights into the role of law in the reproductive arena? For example, what does Reagan's distinction between "popular" morality and "prescribed" morality suggest about whether anti-abortion laws of the nineteenth century reflected popular views of the time? If law did not reflect popular views, whose views *did* it reflect?

3. Reagan argues that the anti-abortion campaign of the nineteenth century was "antifeminist" and attempted to impose restrictive roles on women. How did abortion regulations passed during that period reflect and enforce a particular view about the appropriate role(s) of women in society? Do you think that today's abortion laws also reflect a particular view about women's role(s)?

4. According to Davis, how did the women's movement of the nineteenth century misperceive the reproductive needs and interests of women of color? Has the modern pro-choice movement made the same mistakes? For instance, has it done a good job of making people aware of the differing reproductive needs and interests of women of color today?

5. The modern era of abortion rights advocacy arguably was prompted by outrage over what happened to Sherri Finkbine. Here is one commentator's description of her case:

> The 1962 Sherri Finkbine case brought the abortion issue into the public eye. While pregnant with her fifth child, she discovered that her sleeping pills contained defect-causing Thalidomide. Her doctor scheduled an abortion, and he assured her that the hospital board was only a formality. Concerned that other pregnant women might have been exposed to Thalidomide, she allowed a friend to use her experience for a newspaper story. While her name was not mentioned, her abortion was cancelled because of an ensuing public outcry over the idea that women would get an abortion even if their lives were not in danger. Finkbine's name became public when her husband filed a court order to allow the abortion, and she eventually had to go to Sweden to get it. Margaret Foley, "The Body Politic" (book review), available at http://www.mothersmovement.org/books/reviews/05/politics_of_motherhood .htm.

6. Frances Olsen has argued (possibly facetiously) that, if the government really wanted to reduce the number of abortions, it would outlaw the impregnation of

women who don't want to be pregnant. Frances Olsen, *Unraveling Compromise,* 103 HARV. L REV. 40, 130 (1989). Do you agree? Is this suggestion likely to be accepted by state legislatures? If not, why not?

2. The "Privacy" Formulation and Its Critics

Chapter 8

Roe v. Wade

Mr. Justice BLACKMUN delivered the opinion of the Court.

. . . .

This Texas federal appeal and its Georgia companion, *Doe v. Bolton,* present constitutional challenges to state criminal abortion legislation.

We forthwith acknowledge our awareness of the sensitive and emotional nature of the abortion controversy, of the vigorous opposing views, even among physicians, and of the deep and seemingly absolute convictions that the subject inspires. . . .

Our task, of course, is to resolve the issue by constitutional measurement, free of emotion and of predilection. We seek earnestly to do this, and, because we do, we have inquired into, and in this opinion place some emphasis upon, medical and medical-legal history and what that history reveals about man's attitudes toward the abortion procedure over the centuries. . . .

I

The Texas statutes that concern us here . . . make it a crime to "procure an abortion," as therein defined, or to attempt one, except with respect to "an abortion procured or attempted by medical advice for the purpose of saving the life of the mother." Similar statutes are in existence in a majority of the States.

. . . .

II

[Jane] Roe alleged that she was unmarried and pregnant; that she wished to terminate her pregnancy by an abortion "performed by a competent, licensed physician, under safe, clinical conditions"; that she was unable to get a "legal" abortion in Texas because her life did not appear to be threatened by the continuation of her pregnancy; and that she could not afford to travel to another jurisdiction in order to secure a legal abortion under safe conditions.

. . . .

VI

It perhaps is not generally appreciated that the restrictive criminal abortion laws in effect in a majority of States today are of relatively recent vintage. . . . [A]bortion was

Roe v. Wade, 410 U.S. 113 (1973).

practiced in Greek times as well as in the Roman Era. . . . Most Greek thinkers . . . commended abortion, at least prior to viability. . . . [At] common law, abortion performed *before* "quickening"—the first recognizable movement of the fetus in utero, appearing usually from the 16th to the 18th week of pregnancy—was not an indictable offense. . . . Gradually, in the middle and late 19th century the quickening distinction disappeared from the statutory law of most States and the degree of the offense and the penalties were increased. By the end of the 1950's, a large majority of the jurisdictions banned abortion, however and whenever performed, unless done to save or preserve the life of the mother. . . . In the past several years, however, a trend toward liberalization of abortion statutes has resulted in adoption, by about one-third of the States, of less stringent laws.

It is thus apparent that at common law, at the time of the adoption of our Constitution, and throughout the major portion of the 19th century, abortion was viewed with less disfavor than under most American statutes currently in effect. Phrasing it another way, a woman enjoyed a substantially broader right to terminate a pregnancy than she does in most States today. At least with respect to the early stage of pregnancy, and very possibly without such a limitation, the opportunity to make this choice was present in this country well into the 19th century. Even later, the law continued for some time to treat less punitively an abortion procured in early pregnancy.

VII

. . . .

Parties challenging state abortion laws have sharply disputed in some courts the contention that a purpose of these laws, when enacted, was to protect prenatal life. Pointing to the absence of legislative history to support the contention, they claim that most state laws were designed solely to protect the woman. Because medical advances have lessened this concern, at least with respect to abortion in early pregnancy, they argue that with respect to such abortions the laws can no longer be justified by any state interest. There is some scholarly support for this view of original purpose. The few state courts called upon to interpret their laws in the late 19th and early 20th centuries did focus on the State's interest in protecting the woman's health rather than in preserving the embryo and fetus. Proponents of this view point out that in many States, including Texas, by statute or judicial interpretation, the pregnant woman herself could not be prosecuted for self-abortion or for cooperating in an abortion performed upon her by another. They claim that adoption of the "quickening" distinction through received common law and state statutes tacitly recognizes the greater health hazards inherent in late abortion and impliedly repudiates the theory that life begins at conception.

It is with these interests, and the weight to be attached to them, that this case is concerned.

VIII

The Constitution does not explicitly mention any right of privacy. In a line of decisions, however, going back perhaps as far as Union Pacific R. Co. v. Botsford, 141 U.S. 250, 251 (1891), the Court has recognized that a right of personal privacy, or a guarantee of certain areas or zones of privacy, does exist under the Constitution. . . .

This right of privacy, whether it be founded in the Fourteenth Amendment's concept of personal liberty and restrictions upon state action, as we feel it is, or, as the District Court determined, in the Ninth Amendment's reservation of rights to the people, is broad enough to encompass a woman's decision whether or not to terminate her pregnancy. The detriment that the State would impose upon the pregnant woman by denying this choice altogether is apparent. Specific and direct harm medically diagnosable even in early pregnancy may be involved. Maternity, or additional offspring, may force upon the woman a distressful life and future. Psychological harm may be imminent. Mental and physical health may be taxed by child care. There is also the distress, for all concerned, associated with the unwanted child, and there is the problem of bringing a child into a family already unable, psychologically and otherwise, to care for it. In other cases, as in this one, the additional difficulties and continuing stigma of unwed motherhood may be involved. All these are factors the woman and her responsible physician necessarily will consider in consultation.

On the basis of elements such as these, appellant and some amici argue that the woman's right is absolute and that she is entitled to terminate her pregnancy at whatever time, in whatever way, and for whatever reason she alone chooses. With this we do not agree. Appellant's arguments that Texas either has no valid interest at all in regulating the abortion decision, or no interest strong enough to support any limitation upon the woman's sole determination, are unpersuasive. The Court's decisions recognizing a right of privacy also acknowledge that some state regulation in areas protected by that right is appropriate. . . .

IX

. . . .

A

The appellee and certain amici argue that the fetus is a "person" within the language and meaning of the Fourteenth Amendment. . . . If this suggestion of personhood is established, the appellant's case, of course, collapses, for the fetus' right to life would then be guaranteed specifically by the Amendment. The appellant conceded as much on reargument. On the other hand, the appellee conceded on reargument that no case could be cited that holds that a fetus is a person within the meaning of the Fourteenth Amendment. The Constitution does not define "person" in so many words. . . . [The particular uses of the word "person" in the Constitution], together with our observation, supra, that throughout the major portion of the 19th century prevailing legal abortion practices were far freer than they are today, persuades us that the word "person," as used in the Fourteenth Amendment, does not include the unborn.

. . . .

B

The pregnant woman cannot be isolated in her privacy. She carries an embryo and, later, a fetus. . . . The situation therefore is inherently different from marital intimacy, or bedroom possession of obscene material, or marriage, or procreation, or education, with which *Eisenstadt* [*v. Baird,* 405 U.S. 438 (1972)], and *Griswold* [*v. Connecticut,* 381 U.S. 479 (1965)], *Stanley* [*v. Georgia,* 394 U.S. 557 (1969)], *Loving* [*v. Virginia,* 388 U.S. 1 (1967)], *Skinner* [*v. Oklahoma,* 316 U.S. 535 (1942)], *Pierce* [*v. Society of Sisters,* 268 U.S. 510 (1925)], and *Meyer* [*v. Nebraska,* 262 U.S 390 (1923)] were respectively concerned. . . .

Texas urges that, apart from the Fourteenth Amendment, life begins at conception and is present throughout pregnancy, and that, therefore, the State has a compelling interest in protecting that life from and after conception. We need not resolve the difficult question of when life begins. When those trained in the respective disciplines of medicine, philosophy, and theology are unable to arrive at any consensus, the judiciary, at this point in the development of man's knowledge, is not in a position to speculate as to the answer.

It should be sufficient to note briefly the wide divergence of thinking on this most sensitive and difficult question. There has always been strong support for the view that life does not begin until live birth. . . . As we have noted, the common law found greater significance in quickening. Physicians and their scientific colleagues have regarded that event with less interest and have tended to focus either upon conception, upon live birth, or upon the interim point at which the fetus becomes "viable," that is, potentially able to live outside the mother's womb, albeit with artificial aid. Viability is usually placed at about seven months (28 weeks) but may occur earlier, even at 24 weeks. . . .

In areas other than criminal abortion, the law has been reluctant to endorse any theory that life, as we recognize it, begins before live birth or to accord legal rights to the unborn. . . . In short, the unborn have never been recognized in the law as persons in the whole sense.

X

In view of all this, we do not agree that, by adopting one theory of life, Texas may override the rights of the pregnant woman that are at stake. We repeat, however, that the State does have an important and legitimate interest in preserving and protecting the health of the pregnant woman . . . and that it has still another important and legitimate interest in protecting the potentiality of human life. These interests are separate and distinct. Each grows in substantiality as the woman approaches term and, at a point during pregnancy, each becomes "compelling."

With respect to the State's important and legitimate interest in the health of the mother, the "compelling" point, in the light of present medical knowledge, is at approximately the end of the first trimester. This is so because of the now-established medical fact that until the end of the first trimester mortality in abortion may be less than mortality in normal childbirth. It follows that, from and after this point, a State may regulate the abortion procedure to the extent that the regulation reasonably relates to the preservation and protection of maternal health. Examples of permissible state regulation in this area are requirements as to the qualifications of the person who is to perform the abortion; as to the licensure of that person; as to the facility in which the procedure is to be performed, that is, whether it must be a hospital or may be a clinic or some other place of less-than-hospital status; as to the licensing of the facility; and the like.

This means, on the other hand, that, for the period of pregnancy prior to this "compelling" point, the attending physician, in consultation with his patient, is free to determine, without regulation by the State, that, in his medical judgment, the patient's pregnancy should be terminated. If that decision is reached, the judgment may be effectuated by an abortion free of interference by the State.

With respect to the State's important and legitimate interest in potential life, the "compelling" point is at viability. This is so because the fetus then presumably has the capability of meaningful life outside the mother's womb. State regulation protective of fetal life after viability thus has both logical and biological justifications. If the State is interested in protecting fetal life after viability, it may go so far as to proscribe abortion during that period, except when it is necessary to preserve the life or health of the mother.

Measured against these standards, Art. 1196 of the Texas Penal Code, in restricting legal abortions to those "procured or attempted by medical advice for the purpose of saving the life of the mother," sweeps too broadly. The statute makes no distinction between abortions performed early in pregnancy and those performed later, and it limits to a single reason, "saving" the mother's life, the legal justification for the procedure. The statute, therefore, cannot survive the constitutional attack made upon it here.

XI

To summarize and to repeat:

1. A state criminal abortion statute of the current Texas type, that excepts from criminality only a life-saving procedure on behalf of the mother, without regard to pregnancy stage and without recognition of the other interests involved, is violative of the Due Process Clause of the Fourteenth Amendment.

(a) For the stage prior to approximately the end of the first trimester, the abortion decision and its effectuation must be left to the medical judgment of the pregnant woman's attending physician.

(b) For the stage subsequent to approximately the end of the first trimester, the State, in promoting its interest in the health of the mother, may, if it chooses, regulate the abortion procedure in ways that are reasonably related to maternal health.

(c) For the stage subsequent to viability, the State in promoting its interest in the potentiality of human life may, if it chooses, regulate, and even proscribe, abortion except where it is necessary, in appropriate medical judgment, for the preservation of the life or health of the mother.

. . . .

This holding, we feel, is consistent with the relative weights of the respective interests involved, with the lessons and examples of medical and legal history, with the lenity of the common law, and with the demands of the profound problems of the present day. The decision leaves the State free to place increasing restrictions on abortion as the period of pregnancy lengthens, so long as those restrictions are tailored to the recognized state interests. The decision vindicates the right of the physician to administer medical treatment according to his professional judgment up to the points where important state interests provide compelling justifications for intervention. Up to those points, the abortion decision in all its aspects is inherently, and primarily, a medical decision, and basic responsibility for it must rest with the physician. . . .
. . . .

Mr. Justice WHITE, with whom Mr. Justice Rehnquist joins, dissenting.

At the heart of the controversy in these cases are those recurring pregnancies that pose no danger whatsoever to the life or health of the mother but are, nevertheless, unwanted for any one or more of a variety of reasons—convenience, family planning, economics, dislike of children, the embarrassment of illegitimacy, etc. The common claim before us is that for any one of such reasons, or for no reason at all, and without asserting or claiming any threat to life or health, any woman is entitled to an abortion at her request if she is able to find a medical advisor willing to undertake the procedure.

The Court for the most part sustains this position: During the period prior to the time the fetus becomes viable, the Constitution of the United States values the convenience, whim, or caprice of the putative mother more than the life or potential life of the fetus; the Constitution, therefore, guarantees the right to an abortion as against any state law or policy seeking to protect the fetus from an abortion not prompted by more compelling reasons of the mother.

With all due respect, I dissent. . . .

Mr. Justice REHNQUIST, dissenting.
. . . .

If the Court means by the term "privacy" no more than that the claim of a person to be free from unwanted state regulation of consensual transactions may be a form of "liberty" protected by the Fourteenth Amendment, there is no doubt that similar claims have been upheld in our earlier decisions on the basis of that liberty. I agree with the statement of Mr. Justice STEWART in his concurring opinion that the "liberty," against deprivation of which without due process the Fourteenth Amendment protects, embraces more than the rights found in the Bill of Rights. But that liberty is not guaranteed absolutely against deprivation, only against deprivation without due process of law. The test traditionally applied in the area of social and economic legislation is whether or not a law such as that challenged has a rational relation to a valid state objective. The Due Process Clause of the Fourteenth Amendment undoubtedly does place a limit, albeit a broad one, on legislative power to enact laws such as this. If the Texas statute were to prohibit an abortion even where the mother's life is in jeopardy, I have little doubt that such a statute would lack a rational relation to a valid state objective under the test stated. . . . But the Court's sweeping invalidation of any restrictions on abortion during the first trimester is impossible to justify under that standard, and the conscious weighing of competing factors that the Court's opinion apparently substitutes for the established test is far more appropriate to a legislative judgment than to a judicial one. . . .

Chapter 9

Beyond "A Woman's Right to Choose"
Feminist Ideas about Reproductive Rights

Rosalind Pollack Petchesky

. . . .

Two essential ideas underlie a feminist view of reproductive freedom. The first is . . . an extension of the general principle of "bodily integrity," or "bodily self-determination," to the notion that women must be able to control their bodies and procreative capacities. The second is a "historical and moral argument" based on the social position of women and the needs that such a position generates. It states that, insofar as women, under the existing division of labor between the sexes, are the ones most affected by pregnancy, since they are the ones responsible for the care and rearing of children, it is women who must decide about contraception, abortion, and childbearing. . . .

My argument is that reproductive freedom—indeed, the very nature of reproduction—is social and individual at the same time; it operates "at the core of social life" as well as within and upon women's individual bodies. . . . For even if it were true, as some "right-to-lifers" have charged, that the women's movement is self-contradictory in demanding both control by women over reproductive matters and greater sharing of responsibility for such matters between women and men, both these goals are indispensable to a feminist program for reproductive freedom. We have to struggle for a society in which responsibility for contraception, procreation, and childrearing is no longer relegated to women primarily; and, at the same time, we have to defend the principle of control over our bodies and our reproductive capacities. In the long run, we have to ask whether women's control over reproduction is what we want, whether it is consistent with equality; in the short run, we have never experienced the concrete historical conditions under which we could afford to give it up.

Controlling Our Bodies

. . . .

Control over one's body is an essential part of being an individual with needs and rights, a concept that is the most powerful legacy of the liberal political tradition. . . . [T]he "bodily integrity" principle has an undeniable biological component. As long as

Rosalind Petchesky, *Abortion and Women's Choice: The State, Sexuality, and Reproductive Freedom* 2–18 (rev. ed. 1990).

women's bodies remain the medium for pregnancies, the connection between women's reproductive freedom and control over their bodies represents not only a moral and political claim but also, on some level, a material necessity. This acknowledgment of biological reality should not be mistaken for biological determinist thinking about women; my point is simply that biology is a *capacity* as well as a limit.

. . . .

It is important, however, to keep in mind that woman's reproductive situation is never the result of biology alone, but of biology mediated by social and cultural organization. That is, it is not inevitable that women, and not men, should bear the main consequences of unintended pregnancy and thus that their sexual expression be inhibited by it. Rather, it is the result of the socially ascribed primacy of motherhood in women's lives. . . .

[T]he idea of "a woman's right to choose" as the main principle of reproductive freedom is insufficient and problematic at the same time as it is politically compelling. For one thing, this principle evades moral questions about when, under what conditions, and for what purposes reproductive decisions should be made. . . . Should women get an abortion on the grounds that they prefer a different gender, which amniocentesis can now determine? Such a decision would be blatantly sexist, and nobody's claim to "control over her body" could make it right or compatible with feminist principles. That is, "a woman's right to control her body" is not absolute, but we have not developed a socialist-feminist morality that would tell us what the exceptions should be. . . . [T]he potential danger in the assertion of women's right to control over reproduction as absolute or exclusive, [is that] it can be turned back on us to reinforce the view of all reproductive activity as the special, biologically destined province of women. This danger grows out of the concept of "rights" in general, a concept that is inherently static and abstracted from social conditions. Rights are by definition claims staked within a given order of things. They are demands for access for oneself, or for "no admittance" to others; but they do not challenge the social structure, the social relations of production and reproduction. The claim for "abortion rights" seeks access to a necessary service, but by itself fails to address the social relations and sexual divisions around which responsibility for pregnancy and children is assigned. In real-life struggles, this limitation exacts a price, for it lets men and society neatly off the hook.

. . . .

Finally, the idea of a "woman's right to choose" is vulnerable to political manipulation, as demonstrated in recent legislative and judicial debates. Thus "right-to-lifers" exploit the liberal concept of "informed consent" by promoting legislation that would require abortion patients to be "informed" in graphic detail of the fetus's physiological characteristics at each stage of development. Physicians opposing the federal, California, and New York City regulations to curb involuntary sterilization, particularly the requirement of a thirty-day waiting period, have claimed that such regulation is "paternalistic" and inhibits women's "right to choose" sterilization.[1] . . . [T]he ease with which the principle of individuality and control over one's own body may be perverted into bourgeois individualism . . . should make us pause, clear our heads, and think through more rigorously the social conditions of individual control.

The Social Relations of Reproduction

. . . .

A woman does not simply "get pregnant" and "give birth" like the flowing of tides and seasons. She does so under the constraint of *material conditions* that set limits on "natural" reproductive processes—for example, existing birth control methods and technology and access to them; class divisions and the distribution/financing of health care; nutrition; employment, particularly of women; and the state of the economy generally. And she does so within a specific network of *social relations* and social arrangements involving herself, her sexual partner(s), her children and kin, neighbors, doctors, family planners, birth control providers and manufacturers, employers, the church and the state.

. . . .

Today, class and race divisions in reproductive health care determine not only women's access to decent gynecological services, counseling, and the like, but their risk of exposure to involuntary sterilization, dangerous contraceptive drugs, or unnecessary hysterectomy.

. . . .

[T]he critical issue for feminists is not so much the content of women's choices, or even the "right to choose," as it is the social and material conditions under which choices are made. The "right to choose" means little when women are powerless. In cultures where "illegitimacy" is stigmatized or where female infants are devalued, women may resort to abortion or infanticide with impunity; but that option clearly grows out of female subordination. Similarly, women may have autonomy over reproduction and childbirth, as in New Guinea, while being totally excluded from everything else. Or, like the women employees at the American Cyanamid plant in West Virginia, they may "choose" sterilization as the alternative to losing their jobs. To paraphrase Marx, women make their own reproductive choices, but they do not make them just as they please; they do not make them under conditions they create but under conditions and constraints they, as mere individuals, are powerless to change. That individuals do not determine the social framework in which they act does not nullify their choices nor their moral capacity to make them. It only suggests that we have to focus less on "choice" and more on how to transform the social conditions of choosing, working, and reproducing.

. . . .

[The] conjuncture of medical, corporate, and state interests in the "management" of reproduction has defined the choices of all women, but in a way that is crucially different depending on one's class and race. . . . For example, private doctors in Maryland were found to provide abortions with much greater regularity to their middle-class than to their lower-class patients.[2] Similarly, cases of sterilization abuse by physicians in the public health services have occurred almost entirely among black, Native American, and Mexican-American welfare recipients, as well as women who are prisoners or mentally retarded. Low-income and non–English-speaking women are regularly denied information about safer, "nonmedical" methods of birth control because of racist and class-biased assumptions that they are not "competent" to "manage" such methods. Moreover, it is poor and Third World women who are likely to be used as experimental subjects in international population control programs for testing or "dumping" contraceptive chemicals or implants whose safety has been questioned by the FDA. Finally, in a capitalist society, class is the mightiest determinant of the material resources that help make having and raising children joyful rather than burdensome.

On what principle is women's struggle to secure control over the terms and conditions of reproduction based? . . . Because it is primarily women who bear the consequences of pregnancy and the responsibility for children, the conditions of reproduction and contraception affect them directly and in every aspect of their lives. Therefore, it is women primarily who should have control over whether, when, and under what conditions to have children. . . .

On the other hand, . . . [f]or most of history women's "choices" over reproduction have been exercised in a framework in which reproduction and motherhood have determined their relationship to society. A materialist (and feminist) view looks forward to an eventual transcendence of the existing social relations of reproduction so that gender is not ultimately the determinant of responsibility. This implies that society be transformed so that men, or society itself, bear an equal responsibility for nurturance and child care. Then the basis of the need would have changed and control over reproduction might not belong primarily to women. . . .

Reproductive Politics, Past and Future

How do we break out of the apparent contradiction between "women's right to control" over reproduction and their need not to be defined by reproduction? How do we transform the social relations of reproduction to bring men, as potential fathers, into those relations on an equal basis? How would such a transformation affect the principle of "control over our bodies"?
. . . .

The tendency . . . is [for] measures such as liberalized abortion and abolishing illegitimacy [to] unleash a rise in sexual activity, abortions, and divorce followed by a period of backlash in which there is an outcry against the "breakup of the family," women are blamed and accused of "selfishness," and the society is chided by population experts about its declining birthrate. In the absence of either adequate material support (incomes, child care, health care, housing) or shared male responsibility for contraception and childrearing, women are left, after [pro-abortion] reforms, in some ways more vulnerable than before.
. . . .

In a class- and race-divided society, "pronatalist" and "antinatalist" policies coincide (e.g., restrictions on abortion *and* involuntary sterilization), making it necessary for "reproductive rights" proponents to articulate continually that "reproductive freedom means the freedom to have as well as not to have children."[3] Because women are subordinate economically, politically, and legally, a policy emphasizing male sharing of childrearing responsibility could well operate to divest women of control over their children in a situation where they have little else. (We are currently getting a foretaste of this danger, with increasing losses of custody fights by women, particularly lesbian mothers.) The [notion of collective childrearing responsibility] could [also] play into the suggestions of "right-to-lifers" that the responsibility for childbearing is too important to be left to women.

On the other hand, . . . a policy emphasizing improved benefits and services to encourage childbearing may ease the material burdens of motherhood; but it may also operate to perpetuate the existing sexual division of labor and women's social subordination. . . . [I]t is easy to imagine an accretion of reforms such as pregnancy disability benefits, child-care centers, and maternity leave provisions, which, if unaccompanied by demands for transforming the total position of women, can be used to rationalize that position. The point is not that present attempts to secure funded abortion, pregnancy and maternity benefits, child-care services, and other reforms should be abandoned but that those attempts must be moved beyond the framework of "a woman's right to choose" and connected to a broader . . . movement that addresses all the conditions for women's liberation.

A feminist and socialist transformation of the existing conditions of reproduction would seek to unleash the possibilities for material (economic and technological) improvements in reproduction from traditional family and sexual forms, to place those positive changes in a new set of social relations. . . . The changes we require are total; " . . . no decisive changes can be brought about by measures aimed at women alone, but, rather, the division of functions between the sexes must be changed in such a way that men and women have the same opportunities to be active parents and to be gainfully employed. . . . The care of children becomes a fact which society has to take into consideration."[4]

Under different conditions from any that now exist, it may become possible to transcend some of the individualist elements of feminist thinking about reproductive freedom and move toward a concept of reproduction as an activity that concerns all of society. At the same time, a basis could be created for the genuine reproductive freedom of individuals, ending systems of domination that inhibit their control over their bodies. We need to envision what those conditions would be, even though they seem far from present reality. Charting the development of reproductive politics in the past, especially abortion, and rigorously analyzing their conditions in the present, ought to help us transform those politics in the future.

NOTES

1. Patricia Donovan, "Sterilizing the Poor and Incompetent," *Hastings Center Report* 6 (October 1976): 5; and Petchesky, "Reproduction, Ethics and Public Policy: The Federal Sterilization Regulations," *Hastings Center Report* 9 (October 1979): 29–42, 35.

2. Constance A. Nathanson and Marshall H. Becker, "The Influence of Physicians' Attitudes on Abortion Performance, Patient Management and Professional Fees," *Family Planning Perspectives* 9 (July/August 1977): 158–63.

3. Committee for Abortion Rights and against Sterilization Abuse (CARASA), *Women Under Attack: Abortion, Sterilization Abuse, and Reproductive Freedom* 9 (New York: CARASA 1979): p.9.

4. Hilda Scott, *Does Socialism Liberate Women?* (Boston: Beacon, 1974), p. 159.

Chapter 10

Harris v. McRae

Mr. Justice STEWART delivered the opinion of the Court.

This case presents statutory and constitutional questions concerning the public funding of abortions. . . . The constitutional question . . . is whether the Hyde Amendment, by denying public funding for certain medically necessary abortions, contravenes the liberty or equal protection guarantees of the Due Process Clause of the Fifth Amendment. . . .

I

. . . .

One . . . requirement [under the federal Medicaid program] is that a participating State agrees to provide financial assistance to the "categorically needy" [including hospital services, family planning services, and services of physicians]. . . .

Since September 1976, Congress has prohibited . . . the use of any federal funds to reimburse the cost of abortions under the Medicaid program except under certain specified circumstances. This funding restriction is commonly known as the "Hyde Amendment." . . .

[Plaintiffs filed this lawsuit seeking that the provision be enjoined]. They alleged that the Hyde Amendment violated the First, Fourth, Fifth, and Ninth Amendments of the Constitution insofar as it limited the funding of abortions to those necessary to save the life of the mother, while permitting the funding of costs associated with childbirth.

. . . .

III

. . . .

A

We address first the appellees' argument that the Hyde Amendment, by restricting the availability of certain medically necessary abortions under Medicaid, impinges on the "liberty" protected by the Due Process Clause as recognized in *Roe v. Wade,* 410 U.S. 113 (1973), and its progeny.

. . . .

In *Maher v. Roe,* 432 U.S. 464 (1977), the Court was presented with the question whether the scope of personal constitutional freedom recognized in *Roe* v. *Wade* included an entitlement to Medicaid payments for abortions that are not medically

Harris v. McRae, 448 U.S. 297 (1980).

necessary. At issue in *Maher* was a Connecticut welfare regulation under which Medicaid recipients received payments for medical services incident to childbirth, but not for medical services incident to nontherapeutic abortions. . . . The doctrine of *Roe v. Wade*, the Court held in *Maher*, "protects the woman from unduly burdensome interference with her freedom to decide whether to terminate her pregnancy," such as the severe criminal sanctions at issue in *Roe v. Wade*, or the absolute requirement of spousal consent for an abortion challenged in *Planned Parenthood of Central Missouri v. Danforth*, 428 U.S. 52 (1976).

But the constitutional freedom recognized in *Wade* and its progeny, the *Maher* Court explained, did not prevent Connecticut from making "a value judgment favoring childbirth over abortion, and . . . implement[ing] that judgment by the allocation of public funds." 432 U.S., at 474. As the Court elaborated:

> The Connecticut regulation places no obstacles—absolute or otherwise—in the pregnant woman's path to an abortion. An indigent woman who desires an abortion suffers no disadvantage as a consequence of Connecticut's decision to fund childbirth; she continues as before to be dependent on private sources for the service she desires. The State may have made childbirth a more attractive alternative, thereby influencing the woman's decision, but it has imposed no restriction on access to abortions that was not already there. The indigency that may make it difficult—and in some cases, perhaps, impossible—for some women to have abortions is neither created nor in any way affected by the Connecticut regulation. *Id.*

. . . .

In explaining [its ruling,] . . . the Court cited the "basic difference between direct state interference with a protected activity and state encouragement of an alternative activity consonant with legislative policy. Constitutional concerns are greatest when the State attempts to impose its will by force of law; the State's power to encourage actions deemed to be in the public interest is necessarily far broader." 432 U.S., at 475–476 (footnote omitted). . . .

[However,] . . . the appellees argue that because the Hyde Amendment affects a significant interest not present or asserted in *Maher*—the interest of a woman in protecting her health during pregnancy—and because that interest lies at the core of the personal constitutional freedom recognized in *Wade*, the present case is constitutionally different from *Maher*.

. . . .

Regardless of whether the freedom of a woman to choose to terminate her pregnancy for health reasons lies at the core or the periphery of the due process liberty recognized in *Wade*, it simply does not follow that a woman's freedom of choice carries with it a constitutional entitlement to the financial resources to avail herself of the full range of protected choices. The reason why was explained in *Maher*: although government may not place obstacles in the path of a woman's exercise of her freedom of choice, it need not remove those not of its own creation. Indigency falls in the latter category. . . .

[T]he fact remains that the Hyde Amendment leaves an indigent woman with at least the same range of choice in deciding whether to obtain a medically necessary abortion as she would have had if Congress had chosen to subsidize no health care costs at all. We are thus not persuaded that the Hyde Amendment impinges on the constitutionally protected freedom of choice recognized in *Wade.*[1] . . .

B

[The Court also held that the statute didn't violate the prohibition of state support for religion found in the Establishment Clause of the First Amendment, because it had a secular purpose and just "happened to coincide" with the tenets of the Roman Catholic Church.]

C

[The Court also held that indigence is not a "suspect class" requiring "strict scrutiny" of the provision. Applying the less demanding "rational basis" review, the Court concluded that the statute was rationally related to the state interest in "protecting the potential life of the fetus."]

. . . .

Mr. Justice BRENNAN, with whom Mr. Justice MARSHALL and Mr. Justice BLACK-MUN join, dissenting.

. . . .

The proposition for which [*Roe* and its progeny] stand . . . is not that the State is under an affirmative obligation to ensure access to abortions for all who may desire them; it is that the State must refrain from wielding its enormous power and influence in a manner that might burden the pregnant woman's freedom to choose whether to have an abortion. The Hyde Amendment's denial of public funds for medically necessary abortions plainly intrudes upon this constitutionally protected decision, for both by design and in effect it serves to coerce indigent pregnant women to bear children that they would otherwise elect not to have.[2]

. . . .

[T]he discriminatory distribution of the benefits of governmental largesse can discourage the exercise of fundamental liberties just as effectively as can an outright denial of those rights through criminal and regulatory sanctions. Implicit in the Court's reasoning is the notion that as long as the Government is not obligated to provide its citizens with certain benefits or privileges, it may condition the grant of such benefits on the recipient's relinquishment of his constitutional rights.

. . . .

[W]e have heretofore never hesitated to invalidate any scheme of granting or withholding financial benefits that incidentally or intentionally burdens one manner of exercising a constitutionally protected choice. To take but one example of many, *Sherbert v. Verner,* 374 U.S. 398 (1963), involved a South Carolina unemployment insurance statute that required recipients to accept suitable employment when offered, even if the grounds for refusal stemmed from religious convictions. Even though the recipients possessed no entitlement to compensation, the Court held that the State could not cancel the benefits of a Seventh-Day Adventist who had refused a job requiring her to work on Saturdays. The Court's explanation is particularly instructive for the present case:

> The ruling forces her to choose between following the precepts of her religion and forfeiting benefits, on the one hand, and abandoning one of the precepts of her religion in order to accept work, on the other hand. Governmental imposition of such a choice puts the same kind of burden upon the free exercise of religion as would a fine imposed against appellant for her Saturday worship.
>
> Nor may the South Carolina court's construction of the statute be saved from constitutional infirmity on the ground that unemployment compensation benefits are not appellant's "right" but merely a "privilege." It is too late in the day to doubt that the liberties of religion and expression may be infringed by the denial of or placing of conditions upon a benefit or privilege. . . . [To] condition the availability of benefits upon this appellant's willingness to violate a cardinal principle of her religious faith effectively penalizes the free exercise of her constitutional liberties. *Id.,* at 404–406.

. . . .

The Medicaid program cannot be distinguished from these other statutory schemes that unconstitutionally burdened fundamental rights.[3] Here, as in *Sherbert,* the government withholds financial benefits in a manner that discourages the exercise of a due process liberty: The indigent woman who chooses to assert her constitutional right to have an abortion can do so only on pain of sacrificing health-care benefits to which she would otherwise be entitled. . . .

> [The state] may not impose conditions which require the relinquishment of constitutional rights. If the state may compel the surrender of one constitutional right as a condition of its favor, it may, in like manner, compel a surrender of all. It is inconceivable that guaranties embedded in the Constitution of the United States may thus be manipulated out of existence. *Frost & Frost Trucking Co. v. Railroad Comm'n,* 271 U.S. 583, 593–94 (1926).

I respectfully dissent.

Mr. Justice STEVENS, dissenting.

. . . .

If a woman has a constitutional right to place a higher value on avoiding either serious harm to her own health or perhaps an abnormal childbirth[4] than on protecting potential life, the exercise of that right cannot provide the basis for the denial of a benefit to which she would otherwise be entitled. The Court's sterile equal protection analysis evades this critical though simple point. . . .

[I]t is misleading to speak of the Government's legitimate interest in the fetus without reference to the context in which that interest was held to be legitimate. For *Roe v. Wade* squarely held that the States may not protect that interest when a conflict with the interest in a pregnant woman's health exists.

. . . .

NOTES

1. A substantial constitutional question would arise if Congress had attempted to withhold all Medicaid benefits from an otherwise eligible candidate simply because that candidate had exercised her constitutionally protected freedom to terminate her pregnancy by abortion. This would be analogous to *Sherbert v. Verner,* 374 U.S. 398 (1963), where this Court held that a State may not, consistent with the First and Fourteenth Amendments, withhold *all* unemployment compensation benefits from a claimant who would otherwise be eligible for such benefits but for the fact that she is unwilling to work one day per week on her Sabbath. But the Hyde Amendment, unlike the statute at issue in *Sherbert,* does not provide for such a broad disqualification from receipt of public benefits. Rather, the Hyde Amendment, like the Connecticut welfare provision at issue in *Maher,* represents simply a refusal to subsidize certain protected conduct. A refusal to fund protected activity, without more, cannot be equated with the imposition of a "penalty" on that activity.

2. My focus throughout this opinion is upon the coercive impact of the congressional decision to fund one outcome of pregnancy—childbirth—while not funding the other—abortion. [While] I believe this alone renders the Hyde Amendment unconstitutional, . . . I concur completely, . . . in my Brother STEVENS' [conclusion] . . . that the congressional decision to fund all medically necessary procedures except for those that require an abortion is entirely irrational either as a means of allocating health-care resources or otherwise serving legitimate social welfare goals. . . . Nonpregnant women may be reimbursed for all medically necessary treatments. Pregnant women with analogous ailments, however, will be reimbursed only if the treatment involved does not happen to include an abortion. Since the refusal to fund will in some significant number of cases force the patient to forgo medical assistance, the result is to refuse treatment for some genuine maladies not because they need not be treated, cannot be treated, or are too expensive to treat, and not because they relate to a deliberate choice to abort a pregnancy, but merely because treating them would as a practical matter require termination of that pregnancy. . . . Antipathy to abortion, in short, has been permitted not only to ride roughshod over a woman's constitutional right to terminate her pregnancy in the fashion she chooses, but also to distort our Nation's health-care programs. As a means of delivering health services, then, the Hyde Amendment is completely irrational. As a means of preventing abortions, it is concededly rational—brutally so. But this latter goal is constitutionally forbidden.

3. . . . [T]here is "more" than a simple refusal to fund a protected activity in this case; instead, there is a program that selectively funds but one of two choices of a constitutionally protected decision, thereby penalizing the election of the disfavored option. Moreover, it is no answer to assert that no "penalty" is being imposed because the State is only refusing to pay for the specific costs of the protected activity rather than withholding other Medicaid benefits to which the recipient would be entitled or taking some other action more readily characterized as "punitive." Surely the government could not provide free transportation to the polling booths only for those citizens who vote for Democratic candidates, even though the failure to provide the same benefit to Republicans "represents simply a refusal to subsidize certain protected conduct," and does not involve the denial of any other governmental benefits. . . . [I]t cannot interfere with a constitutionally protected decision through the coercive use of governmental largesse.

4. . . . The Maher opinion repeatedly referred to the policy of favoring "normal childbirth." But this case involves a refusal to fund abortions which are medically necessary to avoid abnormal childbirth.

Chapter 11

Surrogacy as Resistance?

The Misplaced Focus on Choice in the Surrogacy and Abortion Funding Contexts

Nancy Ehrenreich

. . . .

Abortion Law and Women's Autonomy

In a line of cases spanning nearly fifteen years, the Supreme Court has upheld various limitations on the use of state or federal money to finance abortion-related activities, repeatedly asserting that the constraints faced by low-income women seeking abortions are imposed by their poverty, not by the government. Consistent with this body of precedent, the Court held in *Rust v. Sullivan*[1] that the Title X "gag" rules, prohibiting federally funded physicians from [providing their patients with abortion counseling or referrals], did not constitute governmental interference with low-income women's reproductive decision making. Chief Justice Rehnquist wrote for the majority:

> The Government has no affirmative duty to "commit" any resources to facilitating abortions," . . . and its decision to fund childbirth but not abortion "places no *governmental* obstacle in the path of a woman who chooses to terminate her pregnancy. . . ." Congress' refusal to fund abortion counseling and advocacy leaves a pregnant woman with the same choices as if the government had chosen not to fund family-planning services at all.[2]

The Court's position here . . . treat[s] the private interaction at issue—. . . obtaining an abortion—as no different from other [market] interactions, and thus as appropriately subject to market pressures. . . .

The Court's conclusion is [also] informed by a vision of the social setting in which conception occurs that is . . . unrealistically individualistic . . . [, ignoring] the crucial importance of the context in which individual choices and governmental "inaction" take place. . . . [G]overnmental failure to fund abortion counseling and services, against a backdrop of federal funding of childbirth and extensive state structuring of the economic life of low-income people, constitutes interference.

Nancy Ehrenreich, "Surrogacy as Resistance? The Misplaced Focus on Choice in the Surrogacy and Abortion Funding Contexts," 41 DePaul L.Rev. 1369 (1992) (reviewing CARMEL SHALEV, BIRTH POWER: THE CASE FOR SURROGACY (1989)).

The federal government subsidizes birth by providing Title X funds for counseling and referral to prenatal care facilities, as well as Medicaid payments for childbirth. The *Rust* majority held that such a practice, combined with the lack of governmental support for abortion, "'places no governmental obstacle in the path of a woman who chooses to terminate her pregnancy, but rather . . . encourages alternate activity.'"[3] Because the woman has the same *range* of choice with or without government funding, the Court concluded, subsidizing birth does not unduly burden that choice.

This argument assumes that we are in fact dealing with two rights here, a right to terminate a pregnancy and a right to continue it. But clearly there is only one right—that of reproductive decision making. The essence of *Roe* is its protection of a woman's freedom to choose between termination and continuation. A woman has only two options here: Her decision must inevitably be either to end the pregnancy or to carry the fetus to term. Thus, by subsidizing only one side of the decisional equation, the government has undeniably skewed the outcome, making one option more appealing than the other. As Justice Brennan noted in discussing governmental refusal to fund therapeutic abortions, "[T]here is 'more' than a simple refusal to fund a protected activity in this case; instead, there is a program that selectively funds but one of two choices of a constitutionally protected decision, thereby penalizing the election of the disfavored option."[4] The point is equally applicable to *Rust*, where the government selectively funds the provision of information about only one of two choices.

Through Title X and its regulations, the government has actively interfered in the private sphere: It has established a family planning program that makes it more difficult for a woman to decide to terminate a pregnancy than it would be if no such program existed at all. . . . [W]ithout any family planning program, a woman would necessarily have to spend more of her own money to deal with her pregnancy, either to terminate it or to bear a child. Since she would have to pay either way, her *poverty* would not make it any harder for her to choose one option or the other. Under the program established by the *Maher*-to-*Rust* line of cases, however, it becomes more difficult for her to choose abortion because that is the only course of action that requires her to spend her own limited funds. Thus it is precisely the existence of the federal program that causes her poverty to burden her reproductive choice.

The Title X regulations burden a woman's decision not only because they expressly support childbirth but also because they remove this one area of health care—abortion—from the otherwise encompassing web of governmental subsidies. As Mark Tushnet has stated in discussing *Maher* and *McRae*:

[Those decisions assume that] the basic rule is that goods are not allocated by market processes. If the government allocates some or many goods, relegating some particular good to the market isolates that good from the rest, presumably because the government wishes to see less consumption of the good. . . . And actions designed to discourage consumption place burdens on the decision to consume in any reasonable understanding. In our society, the government allocates most of the goods that poor people consume. Their shelter is subsidized in public housing, their consumption of food is subsidized by food stamps, their use of most medical services is subsidized by Medicaid, and they have few remaining resources to devote to purchases of unsubsidized goods. Thus, they are in precisely the situation described, where a decision not to sub-sidize constitutes a burden.[5]

This point is equally applicable to the "gag" rules, which similarly burden low-income women by excluding abortion counseling and referral from the otherwise comprehensive obstetric and gynecological services subsidized by the government under Title X.

Finally, one could argue that governmental interference in women's abortion decisions is in fact unavoidable. Frances Olsen has pointed out, in another context, that governmental refusal to criminalize spouse abuse does not preserve the state's neutrality towards the family, because courts will still have to rule on whether the past abuse should be a mitigating or excusing factor when the victimized spouse kills the abuser.[6] Similarly, even if the government fails to fund abortion services, it must still decide how to treat people's responses to that policy—as, for example, when a woman steals the money to pay for an abortion and then raises the defense of necessity.

In summary, then, it makes just as much sense to see a refusal to subsidize abortion services and counseling for low-income women as governmental interference in reproductive decision making—and the births that result as instances of forced motherhood—as it does to see nonfunding as noninterference. In fact, the Court's conclusory equation of state inaction with noninterference reflects an abstract and highly debatable conceptualization of coercion that is totally inattentive to the circumstances in which reproductive decisions are made. Nevertheless, my point here is not that the Court's decisions were illogical, but rather that they simply were not inevitable. The doctrinal discourse allows one to argue either that failure to fund the exercise of a constitutional right is burdensome or that it is not.

Why, then, has the Court repeatedly refused to find that failure to fund in the reproductive realm burdens fundamental rights, despite its (at least occasional) willingness to do so in other contexts? In the next section, I show how the conclusion that an abortion decision constitutes a choice, and the conclusion that the governmental failure to subsidize it is noninterference, are based upon a belief in . . . patriarchal images of women. . . . I argue that it is only by unearthing the hidden assumptions about women and reproductive roles that inform decisions like *Rust* that we can come to understand what makes the jurists deciding those cases conclude that the behaviors they are assessing are chosen rather than coerced.

Abortion Law and Images of Women

To the extent that it treats the situation of low-income women with unwanted pregnancies as freely chosen, the *Rust* line of cases assumes that women deserve their pregnancies (and their poverty), implying that these women's situations are somehow the result of their own irresponsibility. Thus, at the most obvious level, such cases rely upon and perpetuate negative stereotypes of women, or perhaps just of low-income women, as immature, unreliable, and overemotional individuals to whom important moral decisions about life and death should not be delegated. But more subtle messages are presented by these cases as well.

For instance, it is interesting to note how differently women who are thinking of aborting their fetuses and women who are thinking of putting their children up for adoption are treated. In both situations the woman is faced with an unwanted pregnancy. In either situation, her lack of money might cause her to do something she does not want to do—give up the baby or carry the pregnancy to term (and keep the child). Yet in the adoption situation the law takes great pains to protect her from being coerced by her circumstances into making a decision she will later regret. In virtually all states, adoptions are closely regulated to prevent private "sales," and many states also protect women with required waiting periods during which they cannot consent to termination of their parental rights. In contrast, *Rust* and its predecessors reveal that neither Congress nor the Supreme Court sees any need to insulate a woman's decision about whether to continue a pregnancy from market pressures.

Why is the law so willing to conceive that a woman might be coerced by indigency into *giving up* a child but not that a woman might be coerced by indigency into *bearing* one? It is hard to escape the conclusion that the coerced loss of a child through adoption is considered a harm to women, but forced motherhood is not. . . . The fact that the law treats relinquishing one's child for adoption as an injury both reflects and reinforces the notion that being a woman means being someone who would love to be a parent and is devoted to her offspring. "Good" girls love their children and thus suffer a harm if they lose them. On the other hand, the fact that the law does not treat bearing an unwanted child as an injury reflects and reinforces the flip side of the message: If all "good" girls love children, then forcing a woman to have a child cannot possibly do her harm. Or, to put it less charitably, a woman who would stray so far from the societal role of devoted mother as to actually perceive having a child as a harm to herself must be "bad," and therefore is undeserving of state protection. Thus, the existing legal rules protect the woman who conforms to pronatalist gender expectations and punish the one who does not.

Public Power and Reproductive "Choice"

Given the indeterminacy of the distinctions between choice and coercion, noninterference and interference, the Court's attitudes towards women provide a better explanation for its rulings in this area. But the public/private dichotomy that grounds abortion doctrine hides these negative attitudes, focusing attention and argumentation on whether women's reproductive decisions are burdened by governmental action. . . . [T]he traditional formulation of the abortion funding issue diverts attention from fundamental questions about how to structure our reproductive lives and who should bear the burden of reproducing the citizenry. Moreover, it serves an apologetic function here as [elsewhere] . . . , legitimating a world vision that obscures the operation of state power in the realm of supposedly "private" conduct.

Privacy doctrine assumes that there is a separate and discrete realm of reproductive decision making that is untouched by governmental power. While the two sides of the debate might disagree as to where the line between "private" choice and public coercion should be drawn, both agree that it is that line which marks the difference between legitimate and illegitimate governmental policies. In conceptualizing the problem in this way, however, both positions ignore the extent to which the "private" conditions in which the government is not supposed to interfere are themselves produced by the state. . . . [T]he *Rust* court fails to recognize that the public hand is present in the very pregnancy that makes a woman's reproductive decision necessary.

What causes unwanted pregnancies? The Supreme Court, and many citizens, believe they are primarily the product of a conscious and irresponsible choice on the part of a woman to engage in unprotected sex—to "take the risk" of getting pregnant. Indeed, the fact that currently proposed abortion prohibitions frequently contain exceptions for rape and incest, as did many pre-*Roe* statutes, reinforces the notion that all pregnancies that do not fall within those exceptions are freely willed, even if later regretted. . . . [Thus,] focusing on coercion in the abortion context . . . conveys the notion that most sex in our society is consensual and that most pregnancies are the result of conscious risk-taking. It thereby hides the aspects of sexual interactions and contraceptive practices that many would characterize as neither consensual nor irresponsible, respectively.

Such images severely misunderstand and misrepresent the social etiology of unwanted pregnancies, and completely ignore the state's contribution to this social problem. In the same way that a tortious act is said to cause the injury that follows as long as that injury was a foreseeable result of the act, so many pregnancies (and abortions) that occur in this society are caused by the government, in the sense that they are the foreseeable result of its policies.

At the most obvious level, the state affects the number of unwanted pregnancies by allowing sex assaults to persist in the private sphere in alarming numbers. Thousands of women are raped each year; only a fraction of those attacks are ever reported. While it is obviously private actors who actually perpetrate these attacks, the ignominious history of judicial unreceptivity to rape claims, as well as the explicit doctrinal barriers placed in the way of rape prosecutions, at a minimum provide a sense of impunity to those attackers and at worst actually legitimate their conduct. Moreover, some such assaults—rapes by husbands in states that retain the marital rape exclusion*—are expressly authorized by the state. Like rape, incest and child sexual abuse are also severely under reported and difficult to prosecute. As a result, official statistics on these various types of sexual assault do not begin to capture the actual prevalence of such attacks, nor do they provide any realistic means of estimating how many of them result in pregnancies.

Moreover, governmental programs and policies are implicated in low-income women's unwanted pregnancies even aside from any question of state-allowed attacks. It is not uncommon for public family planning clinics to be insensitive to the health concerns and comfort of their low-income patients. For example, these clinics consis-

---

* *Editor's note*: Today, all states criminalize rape in marriage but many still treat it less severely than nonmarital rape.

tently prescribe oral contraceptives, which pose more serious health risks and are often accompanied by uncomfortable side effects, rather than safer methods of contraception such as the diaphragm. They also frequently fail to fully explain a woman's options to her, leading many women to believe that their only safe choice is to use the method recommended or nothing at all. As a result, a significant proportion of women who engage in unprotected sex may be doing so because, due to inadequate and incorrect information about contraception, they know of no other way to protect themselves from health risks and/or significant discomfort. In addition, inadequate sex education programs in public schools prevent teenagers from being fully informed about birth control methods, resulting in many ineffective efforts at contraception.*

State power affects sexual relations in much more subtle ways as well, suggesting yet another set of reasons why it is unproductive to ask whether or not government interferes with women's abortion decisions. For example, economic dependence, produced in part by unequal pay scales unaddressed by comparable worth law and by inadequate maintenance awards given at the dissolution of marriages, can cause a woman to accede to her partner's sexual demands because she sees such compliance as a necessary *quid* for the *quo* of financial support. In addition, judicial unreceptiveness to rape cases has helped to create the current climate in which a concern with not appearing sexually available—whether because such availability is not considered appropriate for women or because it can be used later to support allegations that an individual consented—can prevent a woman from using a contraceptive at all.

Moreover, governmental policies not only prevent women from avoiding pregnancy, but also prevent them from carrying a pregnancy to term once a child is conceived. In a society where governmentally subsidized childcare is virtually nonexistent and parental leave policies are among the worst in the industrialized world; where advancement in many jobs is predicated upon such total "dedication" to the employer as to preclude any meaningful role as a parent; in which women as a group earn 68.6 cents for every dollar earned by men; and where the major financial, social, and emotional burdens of parenthood still fall, and are thought properly to fall, on women, it is not surprising that having a child is not a viable economic option for many women who would otherwise like to have one. These economic realities are not merely the product of private action in the "private" sphere, but are directly related to existing governmental policies. Judicial and legislative resistance to meaningful pay equity reform buttresses existing wage inequalities; governmental failure to apply maximum hour legislation to many workplaces allows and legitimates inhumanely long work weeks; the absence of state-subsidized childcare and medical care—or governmental regulations requiring employers to provide certain basic necessities for workers, such as childcare, health insurance, and nurturing leave—is what makes child rearing prohibitively expensive for many.

Thus the interference/noninterference debate in the abortion context . . . relies upon the inaccurate assumption that at least some reproductive behavior occurs in a realm of pure choice, unaffected by governmental power. It both assumes and perpetuates

* *Editor's note*: For a discussion of the prevalence of abstinence-based sex education programs in public schools today, see chapter 20 in this volume, by Cynthia Dailard.

the legitimacy of the public/private distinction, thereby deflecting attention from the question of how, rather than whether, government should affect reproductive practices. In so doing, it obscures both the attitudinal explanations for judicial conclusions and the structural constraints on all women's exercises of choice.

Conclusion

In summary, . . . the body of abortion law created by the Supreme Court in the abortion funding cases both relies upon and reproduces the harmful notion that motherhood is an unadulterated benefit to women (and society). Furthermore, . . . the *Rust* majority's focus on whether the Title X "gag" rules constitute state interference with reproductive rights diverts attention from the underlying question of what we mean by those rights, of why women experience unwanted pregnancies, and of how we should structure sexual and reproductive relations in this society.

Whether one argues that a woman's decisions are freely chosen or coerced, a focus on choice diverts attention from the fundamental questions of substantive justice that should inform social policy. . . . [T]he focus should not be on whether something or someone actively interfered with women's choices, but rather on what conditions characterize the society in which reproductive activities are carried out. Legal rules about abortion are most likely to produce humane and fulfilling reproductive relations if they result from a focus on how and why women experience unwanted pregnancies, not on whether they "freely chose" them. No one relishes the idea of an abortion. It is a necessary, but not a preferred, option. Protecting women from coerced sex, developing safe and effective contraceptive techniques (as well as providing men and women with the information they need to use them correctly), undermining harmful sex role stereotypes, and restructuring the workplace to accommodate the reproductive and child-rearing activities of both sexes would go far—and certainly much farther than the post hoc, punitive approach legalized by *Rust* and its predecessors—towards reducing the number of unwanted pregnancies and producing meaningful reproductive lives for all women.

NOTES

1. 111 S. Ct. 1759 (1991).

2. Id. at 1776–77 (quoting Webster v. Reproductive Health Serv., 492 U.S. 490, 511 (1989) and Harris v. McRae, 448 U.S. 297, 315 (emphasis added)).

3. Id. at 1976–77 (quoting Harris v. McRae, 448 U.S. at 315).

4. Id. at 336 n.6 (Brennan, J., dissenting).

5. GEOFFREY R. STONE ET AL., CONSTITUTIONAL LAW 942 (1991) (quoting Mark V. Tushnet, "The Supreme Court on Abortion," in ABORTION, MEDICINE AND THE LAW (J. Douglas Butler & David F. Walbert eds., 1985)).

6. Frances Olsen, "The Family and the Market," 96 HARV. L. REV. 1497, 1509 (1983). . . .

Questions and Comments

1. In his majority opinion in *Roe*, does Justice Blackmun conclude that the fetus is a person? If not, when and why is it important to protect "potential life," according to the Court?

2. What are the implications of Blackmun's assertion that abortion is "primarily a medical decision"? How does the history recounted by Luker in section A help to explain this view of abortions?

3. *Roe's* trimester approach was later changed by the Supreme Court. *See Planned Parenthood v. Casey,* excerpted in chapter 12 of this volume, and *Gonzales v. Carhart,* excerpted in chapter 18.

4. In *Bray v. Alexandria Women's Health Clinic,* 506 U.S. 263 (1993), an organization called Feminists for Life submitted a brief describing certain feminist objections to abortion during the nineteenth century. The brief argued that those nineteenth-century opponents saw abortion as a byproduct of both politicoeconomic inequality between the sexes and the sexual domination of women. Thus, they "did not view legalized abortion as a solution to, but rather, as an abhorrent consequence of, the oppressions and disenfranchisement of women"—including "a sexual double standard which permitted men to behave in an irresponsible fashion but punished the women being victimized. . . ." Amicus Brief of Feminists for Life in *Bray v. Alexandria Women's Health Clinic,* quoted in BECKER ET AL, FEMINIST JURISPRUDENCE: TAKING WOMEN SERIOUSLY 522, 524 (2001). Do you find this argument relevant to today? For example, do you think the right to obtain abortions is not much of a right as long as there are still many other burdens on women's reproductive choices —such as low wages for women, inadequate sex education, unaffordable child care, and violence (including rape) in intimate relationships?

5. At one point Petchesky states, "[T]he critical issue for feminists is not so much the content of women's choices, or even the 'right to choose,' as it is the social and material conditions under which choices are made." In light of this and other statements that Petchesky makes in her piece, is her analysis more consistent with the liberal individualist approach to reproductive justice or the critical constructivist approach?

6. Petchesky suggests that, in a completely egalitarian society, women should share the right to decide about abortion with men. Why does she say this? Do you agree? If not, what would justify female control of reproduction even where men's and women's situations were completely equal?

7. As the *Rust v. Sullivan* case discussed in chapter 11 illustrates, a line of Supreme Court cases following (and often citing to) *Harris v. McRae* has used arguments

similar to those in *McRae* to uphold a wide range of abortion regulations. In *Webster v. Reproductive Health Services,* 492 U.S. 490 (1989), the Court upheld laws prohibiting the use of public funds for abortion counseling and requiring that abortions not be performed by state employees or in public (state-funded) medical facilities (except, as to both, where the mother's life was in danger). And in *Rust,* it protected restrictions that mandated that federally funded family planning clinics refrain from advocating, counseling, or referring patients for abortion. Here's what one commentator had to say about this line of cases:

> This constitutional structure, with its privileging of regulatory government benefit allocations, unleashes the power of the legislature to oppressively control the constitutional rights of the poor who depend upon government largesse for survival. In contrast, the constitutional rights of those fortunate enough not to depend upon government benefits for their subsistence are protected because, to inflict harm upon them, the government cannot merely refuse to give to them but instead must take away something that they have. This confiscation constitutes an unconstitutional burden or penalty on the constitutional rights. Consequently, the rights of the "haves" are protected because the government lacks constitutional weapons to affect their rights. In contrast, the rights of the "have-nots" are jeopardized because the government constitutionally retains weapons to affect their rights, namely, the deprivation of subsistence government aid. Yvette Marie Barksdale, "And the Poor Have Children: A Harm-Based Analysis of Family Caps and the Hollow Procreative Rights of Welfare Beneficiaries," 14 L. & INEQUALITY 1, 28–29 (1995).

8. In chapter 11, Ehrenreich argues that "it makes just as much sense to see a refusal to subsidize abortion services and counseling for low-income women as governmental interference in reproductive decision making—and the births that result as instances of forced motherhood—as it does to see [such] nonfunding as noninterference." What explains, then (according to this argument), the Supreme Court's consistent refusal to find that nonfunding violates women's constitutional rights? Why does the Court prefer that conclusion over the other?

9. The U.S. Supreme Court recently relied upon the privacy right in holding unconstitutional a Texas statute that criminalized consensual sexual activity between adult males, *Lawrence v. Texas,* 539 U.S. 558 (2003), stating, "The petitioners are entitled to respect for their private lives. The State cannot demean their existence or control their destiny by making their private sexual conduct a crime." Id. at 578.

3. The "Undue Burden" Test

Chapter 12

Planned Parenthood of Southeastern Pennsylvania v. Casey

Justice O'CONNOR, Justice KENNEDY, and Justice SOUTER announced the judgment of the Court and delivered the opinion of the Court with respect to Parts I, II, III, V-A, V-C, and VI, an opinion with respect to Part V-E, in which Justice STEVENS joins, and an opinion with respect to Parts IV, V-B, and V-D.

I

Liberty finds no refuge in a jurisprudence of doubt. Yet 19 years after our holding that the Constitution protects a woman's right to terminate her pregnancy in its early stages, *Roe v. Wade,* 410 U.S. 113 (1973), that definition of liberty is still questioned. Joining the respondents as *amicus curiae,* the United States, as it has done in five other cases in the last decade, again asks us to overrule *Roe.*

At issue in these cases are five provisions of the Pennsylvania Abortion Control Act of 1982, as amended in 1988 and 1989. 18 Pa. Cons. Stat. § § 3203–3220 (1990). . . . The Act requires that a woman seeking an abortion give her informed consent prior to the abortion procedure, and specifies that she be provided with certain information at least 24 hours before the abortion is performed. § 3205. For a minor to obtain an abortion, the Act requires the informed consent of one of her parents, but provides for a judicial bypass option if the minor does not wish to or cannot obtain a parent's consent. § 3206. Another provision of the Act requires that, unless certain exceptions apply, a married woman seeking an abortion must sign a statement indicating that she has notified her husband of her intended abortion. § 3209. The Act exempts compliance with these three requirements in the event of a "medical emergency."
. . . .

Before any of these provisions took effect, the petitioners, who are five abortion clinics and one physician representing himself as well as a class of physicians who provide abortion services, brought this suit seeking declaratory and injunctive relief.
. . . .

After considering the fundamental constitutional questions resolved by *Roe,* principles of institutional integrity, and the rule of *stare decisis,* we are led to conclude this: the essential holding of *Roe v. Wade* should be retained and once again reaffirmed.

Planned Parenthood of Southeastern Pennsylvania v. Casey, 505 U.S. 833 (1992).

It must be stated at the outset and with clarity that *Roe's* essential holding, the holding we reaffirm, has three parts. First is a recognition of the right of the woman to choose to have an abortion before viability and to obtain it without undue interference from the State. Before viability, the State's interests are not strong enough to support a prohibition of abortion or the imposition of a substantial obstacle to the woman's effective right to elect the procedure. Second is a confirmation of the State's power to restrict abortions after fetal viability, if the law contains exceptions for pregnancies which endanger the woman's life or health. And third is the principle that the State has legitimate interests from the outset of the pregnancy in protecting the health of the woman and the life of the fetus that may become a child. These principles do not contradict one another; and we adhere to each.

. . . .

Our law affords constitutional protection to personal decisions relating to marriage, procreation, contraception, family relationships, child rearing, and education. *Carey v. Population Services International,* 431 U.S. 678, 685 (1977). Our cases recognize "the right of the *individual,* married or single, to be free from unwarranted governmental intrusion into matters so fundamentally affecting a person as the decision whether to bear or beget a child." *Eisenstadt v. Baird,* 405 U.S. 438 (1972) . . . (emphasis in original). Our precedents "have respected the private realm of family life which the state cannot enter." *Prince v. Massachusetts,* 321 U.S. 158 (1944). These matters, involving the most intimate and personal choices a person may make in a lifetime, choices central to personal dignity and autonomy, are central to the liberty protected by the Fourteenth Amendment. At the heart of liberty is the right to define one's own concept of existence, of meaning, of the universe, and of the mystery of human life. Beliefs about these matters could not define the attributes of personhood were they formed under compulsion of the State.

. . . .

Though abortion is conduct, it does not follow that the State is entitled to proscribe it in all instances. That is because the liberty of the woman is at stake in a sense unique to the human condition and so unique to the law. The mother who carries a child to full term is subject to anxieties, to physical constraints, to pain that only she must bear. That these sacrifices have from the beginning of the human race been endured by woman with a pride that ennobles her in the eyes of others and gives to the infant a bond of love cannot alone be grounds for the State to insist she make the sacrifice. Her suffering is too intimate and personal for the State to insist, without more, upon its own vision of the woman's role, however dominant that vision has been in the course of our history and our culture. The destiny of the woman must be shaped to a large extent on her own conception of her spiritual imperatives and her place in society.

. . . .

While we appreciate the weight of the arguments made on behalf of the State in the cases before us, arguments which in their ultimate formulation conclude that *Roe* should be overruled, the reservations any of us may have in reaffirming the central holding of *Roe* are outweighed by the explication of individual liberty we have given combined with the force of *stare decisis.* We turn now to that doctrine.

III

A

. . . .

2

The inquiry into reliance counts the cost of a rule's repudiation as it would fall on those who have relied reasonably on the rule's continued application.

. . . .

[F]or two decades of economic and social developments, people have organized intimate relationships and made choices that define their views of themselves and their places in society, in reliance on the availability of abortion in the event that contraception should fail. The ability of women to participate equally in the economic and social life of the Nation has been facilitated by their ability to control their reproductive lives. See, e.g., R. Petchesky, *Abortion and Woman's Choice* 109, 133, n.7 (rev. ed. 1990). The Constitution serves human values, and while the effect of reliance on *Roe* cannot be exactly measured, neither can the certain cost of overruling *Roe* for people who have ordered their thinking and living around that case be dismissed.

. . . .

4

We have seen how time has overtaken some of *Roe's* factual assumptions: advances in maternal health care allow for abortions safe to the mother later in pregnancy than was true in 1973, and advances in neonatal care have advanced viability to a point somewhat earlier. But these . . . divergences from the factual premises of 1973 have no bearing on the validity of *Roe's* central holding, that viability marks the earliest point at which the State's interest in fetal life is constitutionally adequate to justify a legislative ban on nontherapeutic abortions. The soundness or unsoundness of that constitutional judgment in no sense turns on whether viability occurs at approximately 28 weeks, as was usual at the time of *Roe,* at 23 to 24 weeks, as it sometimes does today, or at some moment even slightly earlier in pregnancy, as it may if fetal respiratory capacity can somehow be enhanced in the future. Whenever it may occur, the attainment of viability may continue to serve as the critical fact, just as it has done since *Roe* was decided; which is to say that no change in *Roe's* factual underpinning has left its central holding obsolete, and none supports an argument for overruling it.

. . . .

IV

. . . .

The woman's right to terminate her pregnancy before viability is the most central principle of *Roe v. Wade.* It is a rule of law and a component of liberty we cannot renounce.

. . . .

Though the woman has a right to choose to terminate or continue her pregnancy before viability, it does not at all follow that the State is prohibited from taking steps to ensure that this choice is thoughtful and informed. Even in the earliest stages of pregnancy, the State may enact rules and regulations designed to encourage her to know that there are philosophic and social arguments of great weight that can be brought to bear in favor of continuing the pregnancy to full term and that there are procedures and institutions to allow adoption of unwanted children as well as a certain degree of state assistance if the mother chooses to raise the child herself. " 'The Constitution does not forbid a State or city, pursuant to democratic processes, from expressing a preference for normal childbirth.' " *Webster v. Reproductive Health Services,* 492 U.S. at 511 (opinion of the Court) (quoting *Poelker v. Doe,* 432 U.S. 519, 521 (1977)). It follows that States are free to enact laws to provide a reasonable framework for a woman to make a decision that has such profound and lasting meaning. This, too, we find consistent with *Roe's* central premises, and indeed the inevitable consequence of our holding that the State has an interest in protecting the life of the unborn.

We reject the trimester framework, which we do not consider to be part of the essential holding of *Roe.* Measures aimed at ensuring that a woman's choice contemplates the consequences for the fetus do not necessarily interfere with the right recognized in *Roe,* although those measures have been found to be inconsistent with the rigid trimester framework announced in that case. A logical reading of the central holding in *Roe* itself, and a necessary reconciliation of the liberty of the woman and the interest of the State in promoting prenatal life, require, in our view, that we abandon the trimester framework as a rigid prohibition on all previability regulation aimed at the protection of fetal life. The trimester framework suffers from these basic flaws: in its formulation it misconceives the nature of the pregnant woman's interest; and in practice it undervalues the State's interest in potential life, as recognized in *Roe.*

As our jurisprudence relating to all liberties save perhaps abortion has recognized, not every law which makes a right more difficult to exercise is, *ipso facto,* an infringement of that right.

. . . .

The fact that a law which serves a valid purpose, one not designed to strike at the right itself, has the incidental effect of making it more difficult or more expensive to procure an abortion cannot be enough to invalidate it. Only where state regulation imposes an undue burden on a woman's ability to make this decision does the power of the State reach into the heart of the liberty protected by the Due Process Clause.

. . . .

Not all governmental intrusion is of necessity unwarranted; and that brings us to the other basic flaw in the trimester framework: even in *Roe's* terms, in practice it undervalues the State's interest in the potential life within the woman.

. . . .

Roe began the contradiction by using the trimester framework to forbid any regulation of abortion designed to advance [the interest in protecting fetal life or potential life] before viability. 410 U.S. at 163. . . . . This treatment is, in our judgment, incompatible with the recognition that there is a substantial state interest in potential life throughout pregnancy. The very notion that the State has a substantial interest in potential life leads to the conclusion that not all regulations must be deemed unwarranted. Not all burdens on the right to decide whether to terminate a pregnancy will be undue. In our view, the undue burden standard is the appropriate means of reconciling the State's interest with the woman's constitutionally protected liberty.

. . . .

A finding of an undue burden is a shorthand for the conclusion that a state regulation has the purpose or effect of placing a substantial obstacle in the path of a woman seeking an abortion of a nonviable fetus. A statute with this purpose is invalid because the means chosen by the State to further the interest in potential life must be calculated to inform the woman's free choice, not hinder it. And a statute which, while furthering the interest in potential life or some other valid state interest, has the effect of placing a substantial obstacle in the path of a woman's choice cannot be considered a permissible means of serving its legitimate ends.

. . . .

Some guiding principles should emerge. What is at stake is the woman's right to make the ultimate decision, not a right to be insulated from all others in doing so. Regulations which do no more than create a structural mechanism by which the State, or the parent or guardian of a minor, may express profound respect for the life of the unborn are permitted, if they are not a substantial obstacle to the woman's exercise of the right to choose. Unless it has that effect on her right of choice, a state measure designed to persuade her to choose childbirth over abortion will be upheld if reasonably related to that goal. Regulations designed to foster the health of a woman seeking an abortion are valid if they do not constitute an undue burden.

. . . .

We give this summary:

(a) To protect the central right recognized by *Roe v. Wade* while at the same time accommodating the State's profound interest in potential life, we will employ the undue burden analysis as explained in this opinion. An undue burden exists, and therefore a provision of law is invalid, if its purpose or effect is to place a substantial obstacle in the path of a woman seeking an abortion before the fetus attains viability.

(b) We reject the rigid trimester framework of *Roe v. Wade.* To promote the State's profound interest in potential life, throughout pregnancy the State may take measures to ensure that the woman's choice is informed, and measures designed to advance this interest will not be invalidated as long as their purpose is to persuade the woman to choose childbirth over abortion. These measures must not be an undue burden on the right.

(c) As with any medical procedure, the State may enact regulations to further the health or safety of a woman seeking an abortion. Unnecessary health regulations that have the purpose or effect of presenting a substantial obstacle to a woman seeking an abortion impose an undue burden on the right.

(d) Our adoption of the undue burden analysis does not disturb the central holding of *Roe v. Wade,* and we reaffirm that holding. Regardless of whether exceptions are made for particular circumstances, a State may not prohibit any woman from making the ultimate decision to terminate her pregnancy before viability.

(e) We also reaffirm *Roe's* holding that "subsequent to viability, the State in promoting its interest in the potentiality of human life may, if it chooses, regulate, and even proscribe, abortion except where it is necessary, in appropriate medical judgment, for the preservation of the life or health of the mother." *Roe v. Wade*, 410 U.S. at 164–165.

These principles control our assessment of the Pennsylvania statute, and we now turn to the issue of the validity of its challenged provisions.

V

. . . .

A

Under the statute, a medical emergency is

that condition which, on the basis of the physician's good faith clinical judgment, so complicates the medical condition of a pregnant woman as to necessitate the immediate abortion of her pregnancy to avert her death or for which a delay will create serious risk of substantial and irreversible impairment of a major bodily function. 18 Pa. Cons. Stat. § 3203 (1990).

. . . .

We . . . conclude that, as construed by the Court of Appeals, the medical emergency definition imposes no undue burden on a woman's abortion right.

B

We next consider the informed consent requirement. 18 Pa. Cons. Stat. § 3205 (1990). Except in a medical emergency, the statute requires that at least 24 hours before performing an abortion a physician inform the woman of the nature of the procedure, the health risks of the abortion and of childbirth, and the "probable gestational age of the unborn child." The physician or a qualified nonphysician must inform the woman of the availability of printed materials published by the State describing the fetus and providing information about medical assistance for childbirth, information about child support from the father, and a list of agencies which provide adoption and other services as alternatives to abortion. An abortion may not be performed unless the woman certifies in writing that she has been informed of the availability of these printed materials and has been provided them if she chooses to view them.

. . . .

[R]equiring that the woman be informed of the availability of information relating to fetal development and the assistance available should she decide to carry the pregnancy to full term is a reasonable measure to ensure an informed choice, one which might cause the woman to choose childbirth over abortion. This requirement cannot be considered a substantial obstacle to obtaining an abortion, and, it follows, there is no undue burden.

. . . .

We also disagree with the District Court's conclusion that the "particularly burdensome" effects of the waiting period on some women require its invalidation. A particular burden is not of necessity a substantial obstacle. Whether a burden falls on a particular group is a distinct inquiry from whether it is a substantial obstacle even as to the women in that group. And the District Court did not conclude that the waiting period is such an obstacle even for the women who are most burdened by it. Hence, on the record before us, and in the context of this facial challenge, we are not convinced that the 24-hour waiting period constitutes an undue burden.

. . . .

C

Section 3209 of Pennsylvania's abortion law provides, except in cases of medical emergency, that no physician shall perform an abortion on a married woman without receiving a signed statement from the woman that she has notified her spouse that she is about to undergo an abortion. The woman has the option of providing an alternative signed statement certifying that her husband is not the man who impregnated her; that her husband could not be located; that the pregnancy is the result of spousal sexual assault which she has reported; or that the woman believes that notifying her husband will cause him or someone else to inflict bodily injury upon her. A physician who performs an abortion on a married woman without receiving the appropriate signed statement will have his or her license revoked, and is liable to the husband for damages.

. . . .

The spousal notification requirement is . . . likely to prevent a significant number of women from obtaining an abortion. It does not merely make abortions a little more difficult or expensive to obtain; for many women, it will impose a substantial obstacle. We must not blind ourselves to the fact that the significant number of women who fear for their safety and the safety of their children are likely to be deterred from procuring an abortion as surely as if the Commonwealth had outlawed abortion in all cases.

Respondents attempt to avoid the conclusion that § 3209 is invalid by pointing out that it imposes almost no burden at all for the vast majority of women seeking abortions. They begin by noting that only about 20 percent of the women who obtain abortions are married. They then note that of these women about 95 percent notify their husbands of their own volition. Thus, respondents argue, the effects of § 3209 are felt by only one percent of the women who obtain abortions. . . . For this reason, it is asserted, the statute cannot be invalid on its face. We disagree with respondents' basic method of analysis.

The analysis does not end with the one percent of women upon whom the statute operates; it begins there. Legislation is measured for consistency with the Constitution by its impact on those whose conduct it affects. For example, we would not say that a law which requires a newspaper to print a candidate's reply to an unfavorable editorial is valid on its face because most newspapers would adopt the policy even absent the law. The proper focus of constitutional inquiry is the group for whom the law is a restriction, not the group for whom the law is irrelevant. . . . The unfortunate yet persisting conditions we document above will mean that in a large fraction of the cases in which § 3209 is relevant, it will operate as a substantial obstacle to a woman's choice to undergo an abortion. It is an undue burden, and therefore invalid.

. . . .

D

[The Court upheld the parental notification provision in the statute.]

E

[The Court upheld a record-keeping provision requiring abortion providers to report abortions they perform to the state, but struck down a requirement that the report include a married woman's "reason for failing to provide notice to her husband."]

Justice BLACKMUN, concurring in part, concurring in the judgment in part, and dissenting in part.

[Justice Blackmun concurred in O'Connor's confirmation of *Roe* (see parts I and III), but not in her rejection of the trimester framework (see part IV). He also concurred in O'Connor's conclusion as to the medical exception and the husband consent provision.]

. . . .

Three years ago, in *Webster v. Reproductive Health Services*, 492 U.S. 490 (1989), four Members of this Court appeared poised to "cast into darkness the hopes and visions of every woman in this country" who had come to believe that the Constitution guaranteed her the right to reproductive choice. Id. at 557 (BLACKMUN, J., dissenting). All that remained between the promise of *Roe* and the darkness of the plurality was a single, flickering flame. Decisions since *Webster* gave little reason to hope that this flame would cast much light. But now, just when so many expected the darkness to fall, the flame has grown bright.

I do not underestimate the significance of today's joint opinion. Yet I remain steadfast in my belief that the right to reproductive choice is entitled to the full protection afforded by this Court before *Webster*. And I fear for the darkness as four Justices anxiously await the single vote necessary to extinguish the light.

I

Make no mistake, the joint opinion of JUSTICES O'CONNOR, KENNEDY, and SOUTER is an act of personal courage and constitutional principle. In contrast to previous decisions in which JUSTICES O'CONNOR and KENNEDY postponed reconsideration of *Roe v. Wade*, 410 U.S. 113, 35 L. Ed. 2d 147, 93 S. Ct. 705 (1973), the authors of the joint opinion today join JUSTICE STEVENS and me in concluding that "the essential holding of *Roe v. Wade* should be retained and once again reaffirmed." In brief, five Members of this Court today recognize that "the Constitution protects a woman's right to terminate her pregnancy in its early stages."

. . . .

II

Today, no less than yesterday, the Constitution and decisions of this Court require that a State's abortion restrictions be subjected to the strictest of judicial scrutiny. Our precedents and the joint opinion's principles require us to subject all non-de-minimis abortion regulations to strict scrutiny. Under this standard, the Pennsylvania statute's provisions requiring content-based counseling, a 24-hour delay, informed parental consent, and reporting of abortion-related information must be invalidated.

A

. . . .

State restrictions on abortion violate a woman's right of privacy in two ways. First, compelled continuation of a pregnancy infringes upon a woman's right to bodily integrity.

. . . .

Further, when the State restricts a woman's right to terminate her pregnancy, it deprives a woman of the right to make her own decision.

. . . .

A State's restrictions on a woman's right to terminate her pregnancy also implicate constitutional guarantees of gender equality. State restrictions on abortion compel women to continue pregnancies they otherwise might terminate. By restricting the right to terminate pregnancies, the State conscripts women's bodies into its service, forcing women to continue their pregnancies, suffer the pains of childbirth, and in most instances, provide years of maternal care. The State does not compensate women for their services; instead, it assumes that they owe this duty as a matter of course. This assumption—that women can simply be forced to accept the "natural" status and incidents of motherhood—appears to rest upon a conception of women's role that has triggered the protection of the Equal Protection Clause. The joint opinion recognizes that these assumptions about women's place in society "are no longer consistent with our understanding of the family, the individual, or the Constitution."

. . . .

III

. . . .

I am 83 years old. I cannot remain on this Court forever, and when I do step down, the confirmation process for my successor well may focus on the issue before us today. That, I regret, may be exactly where the choice between the two worlds will be made.

CHIEF JUSTICE REHNQUIST, with whom Justice WHITE, Justice SCALIA, and Justice THOMAS join, concurring in the judgment in part and dissenting in part.

The joint opinion, following its newly minted variation on *stare decisis,* retains the outer shell of *Roe v. Wade,* but beats a wholesale retreat from the substance of that

case. We believe that *Roe* was wrongly decided, and that it can and should be overruled consistently with our traditional approach to *stare decisis* in constitutional cases.
. . . .

[T]he Court in *Roe* read the earlier opinions upon which it based its decision much too broadly. Unlike marriage, procreation, and contraception, abortion "involves the purposeful termination of a potential life." *Harris v. McRae,* 448 U.S. 297, 325, 65 L. Ed. 2d 784, 100 S. Ct. 2671 (1980). . . . One cannot ignore the fact that a woman is not isolated in her pregnancy, and that the decision to abort necessarily involves the destruction of a fetus. See *Michael H. v. Gerald D.* 491 U.S. 110, 124 n.4 (1989) (To look "at the act which is assertedly the subject of a liberty interest in isolation from its effect upon other people [is] like inquiring whether there is a liberty interest in firing a gun where the case at hand happens to involve its discharge into another person's body").
. . . .

The sum of the joint opinion's labors in the name of *stare decisis* and "legitimacy" is this: *Roe v. Wade* stands as a sort of judicial Potemkin Village, which may be pointed out to passers-by as a monument to the importance of adhering to precedent. But behind the facade, an entirely new method of analysis, without any roots in constitutional law, is imported to decide the constitutionality of state laws regulating abortion. Neither *stare decisis* nor "legitimacy" are truly served by such an effort.

We have stated above our belief that the Constitution does not subject state abortion regulations to heightened scrutiny. Accordingly, we think that the correct analysis is that set forth by the plurality opinion in *Webster.* A woman's interest in having an abortion is a form of liberty protected by the Due Process Clause, but States may regulate abortion procedures in ways rationally related to a legitimate state interest.
. . . .

Chapter 13

Brief Amici Curiae of the National Council of Negro Women, Inc., et al., Submitted in *Webster v. Reproductive Health Services*

*Joan Gibbs, Mary M. Gundrum, Rhonda Copelon,
Wendy Brown, Cathy Bell, and Barbara Wolvovitz*

. . . .

I. The Reversal of Roe v. Wade *Would Have a Disproportionate
Adverse Impact on Poor Women*

A. Poor Women and Women of Color Will Resort to Illegal Abortions in
Disproportionately High Numbers As They Did before Roe

While *Roe v. Wade* benefitted women of all classes, races and ages, its effect on the health and mortality of poor women, particularly women of color, was, and still is, especially significant. At the time of this Court's decision in *Roe v. Wade,* abortions were illegal in most of the United States. In a majority of states, abortions were permitted only to save the life of pregnant women; in 14 others, more "liberal" laws allowed abortions to prevent grave impairment to the woman's health. *Roe v. Wade,* 410 U.S. at 118, n.2. . . . While a small number of upper and middle class women had access to safe, sanitary abortions in private hospitals and doctors' offices, and some others were able to afford to travel to safer illegal providers, poor women, unable to afford the cost of either long distant [sic] trips or private doctors, were forced to resort to illegal abortions under the most frightening, unhygienic and often life-threatening conditions. Permanent loss of reproductive capacity or death were not uncommon. . . . [W]omen of color risked their lives at much higher rates than did white women if they chose not to continue their pregnancy. In 1965, in New York, for example, although there were 4 abortion deaths for every 100,000 live births for white women; for non-white women there were 56 abortion deaths per 100,000; for Puerto Rican women, there were 61. N.Y.C. Dept. of Health Statistics (October 14, 1969).

The overall maternal mortality rate from illegal abortions reveals a similar disparity. Between 1951 and 1962, that rate was nine times higher for African-American women than for white women in New York City. Gold, "Therapeutic Abortions in New York; A 20 Year Review," 55 AM. J. PUB. HEALTH 964–65 (1965). Half of all deaths

Brief for National Council of Negro Women, et al., Submitted as *Amici Curiae* in *Webster v. Reproductive Health Services,* 492 U.S. 490 (No. 88–605) (1989).

of women of color associated with pregnancy were due to complications following an abortion, while only one-fourth of all white maternal deaths resulted from such complications. Id.

. . . .

II. The Impact of Adopting an Undue Burden Threshold Will Be to Preclude Legal and Safe Abortions for Poor Women, Who Are Disproportionately Women of Color; Strict Scrutiny of All Significant Burdens Is Needed to Avert That Impact

The State of Missouri proposes that even if the Court continues to recognize the right to abortion as fundamental, the Court should adopt a higher threshold for triggering strict scrutiny than for other fundamental rights. Brief for Appellants at 19. Under the proposed standard, unless state regulations constitute an "undue burden" on the fundamental right to choose abortion, strict scrutiny need never be applied and state laws need only be rationally related to any state interest, including the state interest in potential life. *See Akron v. Akron Center for Reproductive Health*, 462 U.S. 416, 453 (1983) (O'Connor, J., dissenting).

Although this proposed change in the standard of review appears to be an innocuous, less sweeping means of undoing the *Roe v. Wade* framework, the result would be essentially identical to a wholesale judicial rejection of the fundamental right to abortion for most women.

Because equality with respect to the exercise of fundamental rights is a paramount aspect of equal justice, because an "undue burden" standard is indeterminate and subject to arbitrary application, and because it would effectively foreclose millions of poor women, women of color and young women from the ability to exercise their fundamental right, this Court should reject any modification of the threshold for the application of strict scrutiny established in *Roe v. Wade* and reaffirmed in *Akron*.

A. Strict Scrutiny of All Significant Burdens on the Fundamental Right to Abortion Is Required under the Equal Protection Clause in Order to Avert Disproportionate Impact Based on Wealth and Race

. . . .

This Court has shown special solicitude for the disproportionate impact of fundamental rights-restrictive legislation on the basis of wealth or class. Thus, the Court has invalidated relatively minor financial restrictions on electoral participation, not because the poor are a suspect class, but because it is essential to guarantee the right to vote equally regardless of wealth. The right of privacy has been likewise protected against such disproportionate impact. In *Boddie v. Connecticut*, 401 U.S. at 383 the Court invalidated a $45 filing fee for divorce because of the state's monopoly over the means of obtaining a divorce and the fundamental nature of the privacy interest. In *Zablocki v. Redhail*, 434 U.S. at 387, the Court struck down a statute conditioning the right to marry on a judicial determination that support obligations were not in arrears and not likely to be affected. While finding that the statute created an impermissible procedural burden for those who could afford it, the Court emphasized that for the poor, the statute would operate as an absolute bar. Id. at 388.

From a constitutional perspective, there is no difference between a statute imposing a filing fee and one which increases the cost of abortion. The added cost and its preclusive effect is imposed by the state and is not simply a consequence of an individual's poverty. Strict scrutiny of any significant increase in cost is the only way to assure that only necessary costs, carefully tailored to a compelling interest, will be imposed so that the preclusive effect of state regulation on the poor will be kept to a minimum.

In assessing whether a restriction has an impermissible effect on the exercise of a fundamental right, the Court examines its deterrent as well as its penalizing effect. *Shapiro v. Thompson,* 394 U.S. 618 (1969); *Dunn v. Blumstein,* 405 U.S. 330 (1972); *Memorial Hospital v. Maricopa County,* 415 U.S. 250 (1974). Poor women will be significantly deterred from seeking legal abortions by burdensome regulations. Moreover, even for those women who should succeed, the added cost, procedural hurdles and delay, which escalate health risks and emotional distress, constitute a penalty on the exercise of the right. Id. at 255–256 (increased health risk from delayed health care is a penalty on the right to travel).

Finally, it is critical to stress the importance of assuring equality in the exercise of procreative rights. *Skinner v. Oklahoma,* 316 U.S. at 541. In *Skinner,* the Court recognized the danger of giving the state power to select who was eligible to reproduce. The power to force unwanted pregnancy is no less destructive of the dignity of women and their right to shape their lives, express their values or create their families. To eliminate strict scrutiny of burdensome regulation in this area invests the state with power to coerce the childbearing decisions of the poor.

B. An "Undue Burden" Threshold for Strict Scrutiny of Abortion Restrictions Is Indeterminate and Will Lead to Confusion, to Prejudice or to No Standard at All

. . . .

C. The Cumulative Impact of Restrictive Regulations Which Would Be Permissible under an "Undue Burden" Standard Will Effectively Preclude Abortion for Poor Women Who Are Disproportionately Women of Color

The effect of state regulations that restrict abortion, both individually and cumulatively, would be to create virtually impenetrable barriers between a woman and her ability to obtain a safe, legal abortion. Such obstruction would not save potential human life, but rather would force poor women and women of color to resort to illegal abortion with its resultant risks of death, maiming, trauma, and familial, social and economic disintegration.

1. LAWS REQUIRING THAT ALL ABORTIONS BE PERFORMED IN HOSPITALS WOULD EFFECTIVELY PRECLUDE ABORTIONS FOR POOR WOMEN AND WOMEN OF COLOR

It has been suggested that a requirement that all abortions be performed in hospitals might not be found to be an "undue burden," and therefore, might be upheld under minimal scrutiny. *See Akron,* 462 U.S. at 466–67 (O'Connor, J., dissenting). *Amici* will examine the adverse consequences of this requirement in order to exemplify the preclusive effect of an "undue burden" threshold for strict scrutiny on poor women and women of color.

a. Poor Women Do Not Have Access to Hospitals for Abortions. To require that abortions be performed in hospitals will place an added burden on the already inadequate delivery of health care to the poor. For general health care, poor families are dependent on public hospitals which are severely overcrowded and understaffed.

Even though hospitals are the ordinary source of medical care for the poor, access to abortions in hospitals is limited and in most communities unavailable. In 1979–1980 only 17% of all public hospitals in the United States reported doing at least one abortion and only 22% of all abortions took place in hospitals, with a mere 32% of those hospitals providing abortions after 14 weeks of pregnancy.[1] For Native American women who live on reservations, and African-American women in the rural South, there has been even less access. To require that all abortions be performed at hospitals would severely restrict the numbers of abortion providers. Additionally, it would render abortion inaccessible to women in most communities in the country.

b. Hospitalization Requirements Will Increase the Cost of Abortions By at Least Five Times. If states are permitted to require hospitalization for abortion throughout pregnancy, the cost of an abortion will increase artificially. The cost of abortions in hospitals is at least five times greater than the cost of clinic abortions. Although a first-trimester abortion in a clinic costs $200–$300, the same abortion in a hospital costs $1200–$1300. The cost for women who require second-trimester hospital abortions is even greater.

The cost of an in-hospital first-trimester abortion would be almost four times the average monthly AFDC payment ($375) for a family of three.[2] Medicaid-eligible women who receive an average of $375 per month for themselves and their children cannot afford $200-$300 for a first-trimester clinic abortion. Yet many women, living in states which do not fund abortions, have managed to pay this sum by using all or part of their meager grants for daily living expenses. Increasing the cost to $1200 or $1300 will foreclose that option, making illegal abortion, once again, the only choice for poor women.

The increased cost of abortion is only part of the financial burden created by a hospitalization requirement. The cost of travel, of overnight stays, of childcare and of lost time from employment need to be factored in. The impact of a hospitalization requirement would fall especially heavily upon teenagers from poor families or those with no independent access to resources.
. . . .

d. Delay Which Results in Increased Danger to Life and Health and in Increased Costs Would Be Inevitable. Requirements that increase the cost of abortion will also endanger women's health by delaying the performance of the procedure. Each week of delay in obtaining an abortion increases the risk of serious health complications by 20% and risk of death by 50%.[3] Legalization has allowed most abortions to be performed earlier. While only 10% of all abortions between 1972 and 1977 were second-trimester abortions, 57% of the deaths following legal abortions involved late abortions.[4] Between 1972 and 1977 African-American women having second-trimester abortions were three times more likely to die than white women.[5]

African-American, young, single and poor women were significantly more likely than others to have later abortions. In 1982, Medicaid-eligible women had abortions two to three weeks later than others and 42% said that they delayed pregnancy testing or abortion for financial reasons.[6] Of the 29% of women who delayed abortion due to problems in making arrangements for them, 60% said they needed more time to raise money, 33% said that the first provider contacted did not offer the services,[7] 25% said they did not find a provider nearby and had to arrange transportation. Torres & Forrest, *Why Do Women Have Abortions?* 20 FAM. PLAN. PERSP. 169, 175 (1988). In 1982, 22% of Medicaid-eligible women who had second-trimester abortions would have had first trimester abortions if there had been no financial delay.[8]

. . . .

2. THE CUMULATIVE IMPACT OF MANY RESTRICTIVE REGULATIONS WILL FURTHER DENY ACCESS

Rigid in-hospital requirements are only one example of a broad range of regulations that would result from an undue burden standard. Each additional requirement which escapes strict scrutiny increases the physical, emotional and economic burdens. They must not be considered in isolation from one another.

In addition to hospitalization, a number of regulations struck down by this and lower courts under the *Roe v. Wade* framework might not be considered sufficiently burdensome as to trigger strict scrutiny analysis. Intrusive and distorted "informed consent" requirements designed to frighten women from obtaining abortions, and onerous recordkeeping and public disclosure requirements, which were intended to harass patients and providers, were struck down in *Thornbourgh v. American College of Obstetricians and Gynecologists,* 476 U.S. 747 (1986). These and more preclusive parental consent and notices rules, or more intrusive spousal consent or notice requirements, *Planned Parenthood of Central Missouri v. Danforth,* 428 U.S. 52 (1976), might survive an unduly burdensome threshold.

That these and other requirements burden the choice of poor women and women of color is suggested by several additional examples. . . . Depending on the length of the waiting period, and the number of weeks pregnant, women will suffer increased risk to health because of delay. Once again, the impact will fall most severely upon the most vulnerable. When Tennessee mandated a waiting period, low-income women incurred a 48% increase in the cost of abortion, as opposed to a 14% increase for higher-income women.

Obviously, where women must travel great distances, such as in North Dakota, the cost of two trips or two overnight stays could become prohibitive.

Anti-abortion statutes have also increased costs by mandating expensive and unnecessary requirements. In Louisiana, the state required frequent warrantless inspections of clinics, restrictive licensing and hospitalization. *Margaret S. v. Edwards,* 488 F. Supp. 181 (E.D. La. 1980). After this statute was declared unconstitutional, Louisiana enacted a new law requiring, among other things, mandatory hospitalization, a waiting period, ultra-sound testing for every abortion (adding $60-$195 to the cost in 1984) and that physicians personally counsel patients.

In the *Webster* case before this Court, Missouri requires useless and expensive viability tests which risk the health of the pregnant woman and substantially increase the cost. Whereas these requirements are plainly unconstitutional under the current framework, they could multiply and yet survive deferential and often "toothless" minimal scrutiny.

3. CUMULATIVE EFFECT OF AN UNDUE BURDEN THRESHOLD WILL FORCE POOR WOMEN TO OBTAIN ILLEGAL ABORTIONS

Any one of these requirements could tip the balance and lead a woman to take the drastic, but less procedurally complicated, step of illegal or self-abortion. Certainly this will be the result in states whose hostility to abortion will be expressed through several expensive, intimidating, unnecessary, and time consuming restrictions.

. . . .

NOTES

1. Henshaw, Forrest, Sullivan and Tietze, "Abortion Services in the U.S., 1979–1980," 14 Fam. Plan. Persp. 5, 6, 11, 12 (1982).

2. Comm. on Ways and Means, U.S. House of Representatives, 100th Cong., 2d Sess., Background Material and Data on Programs Within The Jurisdiction of The Committee on Ways and Means 428 (Comm. Print 1988).

3. Center for Disease Control, U.S. Dept. of Health and Human Services, Abortion Surveillance Report, 1978 (1980).

4. Benditt, "Second-Trimester Abortion in the United States," 11 Fam. Plan. Persp. 358 (1979); Torres and Forrest, "Why Do Women Have Abortions?" 20 Fam. Plan. Persp. 169 (1988). Among women who experienced abortion complications requiring a hospital visit, those who were Medicaid eligible in non-funding states had a two to four week later average gestational age than did those who were not poor. Trussell, Menken, Lindheim, and Vaughan, "The Impact of Restricting Medicaid Financing for Abortion," 12 Fam. Plan. Persp. 120, 129 (1980).

5. Benditt, "Second-Trimester Abortion in the United States," supra note 4, at 359.

6. Henshaw and Wallisch, "The Medicaid Cutoff and Abortion Services for the Poor," 16 Fam. Plan. Persp. 170 (1984). Since the Medicaid cutoffs, delay has increased for poor women. 50% had abortions at 10 weeks or later compared to 37% in 1977. Id.

7. In 1982, 63% of hospitals and 43% of abortion clinics did not provide abortions after 12 weeks. Henshaw, Forrest and Blaine, Abortion Services in the United States, 1981 and 1982 125 (1984).

8. Henshaw and Wallisch, supra note 7.

Questions and Comments

1. How does *Casey* change the constitutional analysis introduced in *Roe?* Does it essentially overrule *Roe* without saying so (as Justice Scalia alleged in his dissent), or does it uphold the core holding of *Roe* (as Justice O'Connor's opinion maintains)?

2. As the *amicus* brief authored by Gibbs et al. for the National Council of Negro Women makes clear, the impact of waiting periods, "informed consent" provisions, record-keeping rules, facilities regulations, and the like is increased delay, and the increased costs that accompany it. Those cost increases, in turn, are likely to have the greatest impact on those with the fewest resources. In this sense, does *Casey* establish a two-tiered abortion system? Does it preserve the privacy rights of economically privileged women, while eliminating those of poor and working-class women?

3. Despite those disparate effects, it seems likely, after *Casey,* that most of the common types of abortion regulations being passed by states today will be upheld by the courts. As a result, the post-*Casey* era has seen a proliferation of "TRAP" (targeted regulation of abortion providers) laws (and bills), which impose (or, in the case of bills, consider imposing) a wide variety of restrictions on clinics—restrictions such as "informed consent" provisions that require physicians to give the woman specific, often biased information about the fetus before her abortion; ceiling height and hallway width regulations that can mandate costly changes in clinic facilities; and residency requirements mandating that physicians live in the state where they provide services.

   However, the case of *Planned Parenthood of Minnesota v. Rounds,* 467 F.3d 716 (8th Cir., 2006), demonstrates that at least one federal appellate court believes there is a limit to how far these sorts of statutes can go. In that case, the Circuit Court of Appeals for the Eighth Circuit blocked enforcement of a South Dakota law that would have required physicians to tell women that an abortion would "terminate the life of a whole, separate, unique, living human being." The law, the court said, raised questions about the First Amendment rights of physicians, as well as possibly violating the undue burden standard of *Casey.*

4. The *Casey* plurality opinion makes it clear that promoting childbirth is a legitimate state objective, and that states can regulate abortions even in the first trimester to further that goal. Is promoting childbirth the same thing as discouraging abortion? If not, what's the difference? If they *are* the same, is it possible for women to have a meaningful right to reproductive autonomy within the confines of a legal regime that allows states to try to tip the scales in favor of birth?

5. Note that one positive aspect of *Casey,* for those concerned about women's reproductive rights, is the language in the plurality opinion that recognizes the equality

dimensions of the abortion issue. In noting that the suffering caused by carrying a child to term "is too intimate and personal for the State to insist, without more, upon its own vision of the woman's role," Justice O'Connor acknowledges that abortion regulations have been used to coerce women into motherhood, a role that has historically been used to justify limiting some women's access to careers and public lives. For more on equality-based arguments for the abortion right, see the next subsection.

4. The Equality Approach

Chapter 14

Abortion as a Sex Equality Right
Its Basis in Feminist Theory

Reva B. Siegel

The abortion right is generally discussed as a negative liberty, a right of privacy, a right to be let alone. . . . Conversations about the abortion right typically occur within a framework that is individualist, antistatist, and focused on the physiology of reproduction—that is, on matters of sex, not gender. This mode of speaking about the abortion right shares important features in common with the framework the Supreme Court adopted in *Roe v. Wade.*

The abortion right is also sometimes discussed as an issue of equality for women, both in feminist circles and in the community at large. The Court's opinion in *Roe,* however, is generally oblivious to such concerns; indeed, *Roe* defines the abortion right in such a way as to make it difficult to speak about in sex equality terms. Recently, as judicial criticism of *Roe* has mounted, a growing number of scholars have attempted to re-conceptualize the abortion right in a sex equality framework. . . . I will discuss the theoretical basis of one such argument, developed in my article "Reasoning from the Body: A Historical Perspective on Abortion Regulation and Questions of Equal Protection" (Siegel 1992). . . .

Analyzing Abortion Restrictions as Gender Status Regulation

Legal and popular debate over abortion tends to focus on matters concerning the physical relations of reproduction. But, . . . [w]hen abortion restrictions are analyzed in a sociohistorical perspective, it is possible to identify constitutionally significant features of [abortion] laws otherwise obscured by the naturalistic framework in which courts now analyze them.

America's criminal abortion laws were first enacted in the nineteenth century, the product of a campaign led by the medical profession, then in its infancy. . . . Obstetricians and gynecologists . . . [argued] against birth control practices, thereby infusing social arguments for criminalizing birth control with the authority of science.

Analyzing the record of the nineteenth-century criminalization campaign reveals

Reva B. Siegel, "Abortion as a Sex Equality Right: Its Basis in Feminist Theory," in Martha Albertson Fineman and Isabel Karpin (eds.), Mothers in Law: Feminist Theory and the Legal Regulation of Motherhood (1995).

how social discourses concerning women's roles have converged with physiological discourses concerning women's bodies, as two distinct but compatible ways of reasoning about women's obligations as mothers. As I will show, the physiological discourses that currently dominate the abortion debate have roots in the nineteenth-century anti-abortion campaign, where they were employed interchangeably with arguments emphasizing the need to enforce women's duties as wives and mothers. Simply put, in debates over abortion, issues we habitually conceptualize in terms of women's bodies in fact involve questions concerning women's roles. An examination of the nineteenth-century criminalization campaign thus provides a new basis for analyzing abortion-restrictive regulation, illuminating its lineage and function as gender-caste regulation.

The Nineteenth-Century Campaign to Criminalize Abortion

. . . .

The [medical] profession's antiabortion arguments focused on the physiology of reproduction, the structure of the family, and the dynamics of population growth.

DOCTORS' ANTIABORTION ARGUMENTS

The doctors who led the criminalization campaign sought, first of all, to discredit the customary and common law concept of quickening. Considered from the standpoint of medical science, the doctors argued, human development was continuous from the point of conception; therefore, quickening had no special physiological significance. The doctors then sought to use this scientific critique of quickening to demonstrate that life begins at conception, and thus that abortion at any point after conception was tantamount to murder.

As doctors sought to equate abortion with the murder of a born person, however, they invested physiological facts with particular social significance. Doctors observed that the embryo/fetus had the physiological capacity to develop into a human being, and pointed to this capacity for physical growth as evidence that the embryo was an *autonomous* form of life. . . . Dr. Horatio Storer, leader of the criminalization campaign, contended that the embryo/fetus was for all practical purposes *outside* of the woman bearing it—even going so far as to compare the embryo/fetus to a kangaroo gestating in its mother's abdominal pouch. . . .

To defend the claim that life begins at conception, nineteenth-century physicians offered a "scientific" account of human development that treated women's role in reproduction as a matter of minor consequence. . . . [But] authorities of the era [also] emphasized that mothers had a unique capacity to shape a child's development, during gestation and after. . . . Doctors repeatedly argued that women had a duty to bear children. Implicitly or explicitly, they were discussing *married* women. . . .

The only way that a wife could ensure her health was to bear children, pregnancy being "a normal physiological condition, and often absolutely necessary to the physical and moral health of woman" (Hale 1867:6n.).

By defining the obligations of marriage in medical terms, doctors claimed special authority to mediate between a married woman and the state. . . . The profession's claim of expertise justified the so-called therapeutic exception to birth control laws that vested in physicians authority to determine whether their patients might have legal access to abortion and contraception. In this way, . . . a woman's choices regarding birth control were made subject to a man's consent, where no such requirement existed at common law before.

Just as doctors translated concepts of marital duty into physiological terms, they also analyzed matters of civic governance in reproductive paradigms. . . . [T]he same doctors who condemned abortion as "feticide" condemned abortion and contraception as a form of "race suicide" (Calhoun 1919:225–54). . . . Individually and collectively, these arguments suggested that regulating the physical act of reproduction was necessary to ensure reproduction of the social order.

ANTIABORTION AS ANTIFEMINISM

The campaign against abortion and contraception was quite specifically concerned with controlling the conduct of women. . . . Physicians suggested that women's interest in controlling birth was incited by feminist advocacy, and depicted abortion and contraception as an expression of women's resistance to marital and maternal obligations. The same doctors who called abortion feticide also described the moral evils of abortion in the following terms:
. . . .

> "Woman's rights" now are understood to be, that she should be a man, and that her physical organism, which is constituted by Nature to bear and rear offspring, should be left in abeyance, and that her ministrations in the formation of character as mother should be abandoned for the sterner rights of voting and law making. (Pallen 1869: 205–6)

Or, as another doctor put it:

> There are lecturers "to ladies only" who profess to be actuated simply by good-will toward their unfortunate sisters, who yet call woman's highest and holiest privilege by the name of slavery, and a law to protect the family from the first step toward extinction, tyranny.
>
> There are apostles of woman's rights who, in their well-meaning but misdirected efforts to arouse women to claim privileges now denied them, encourage their sisters to feel ashamed of the first and highest right which is theirs by the very idea of their nature.
>
> There are advocates of education who seek to deter woman by false pride, from performing the one duty she is perfectly sure of being able to do better than a man! And there are those who teach that their married sisters may save time and vitality for high and noble pursuits by "electing" how few children shall be born to them. (Pomeroy 1888:95–96)

As these polemics suggest, doctors who opposed abortion and contraception were engaged in a wide-ranging debate with the feminist movement of the era. It was not feminist support for abortion rights that drew the physicians' ire; the nineteenth-century woman's rights movement in fact condemned abortion. But the movement did seek reproductive autonomy for wives, in the form of a demand for "voluntary motherhood": the claim that a married woman was entitled to refuse her husband's sexual advances (Gordon 1976:108–11). . . . Indeed, the movement's criticisms of the legal and customary structure of the marriage relationship were sufficiently far-reaching that, while the movement did not openly support abortion, many feminists of the era tacitly condoned abortion as an act of self-defense under prevailing conditions of "forced motherhood" (Siegel 1992:308).

By contrast, physicians used antiabortion arguments to *oppose* the demands of the woman's rights movement. . . . In short, doctors urged legislators to criminalize abortion in order to preserve traditional gender roles in matters of sexuality and motherhood, education and work, and affairs of suffrage and state.

Even this cursory examination of the arguments advanced by the nineteenth-century criminalization campaign reveals that opposition of abortion was powerfully shaped by judgments rooted in relations of gender, race, ethnicity, and class. Those who sought to criminalize abortion were interested in protecting unborn life; yet it is equally clear that they viewed protecting the unborn as a means to control rebellious middle-class women and teeming immigrant populations, and it is in this context that their judgments about the morality of abortion and contraception must be understood. Concerns of gender, race, ethnicity, and class were not peripheral to this ethic, but were instead an integral part of it.

CRIMINALIZING BIRTH CONTROL: A NEW MODE OF
REGULATING GENDER STATUS

. . . .

Restrictions on abortion and contraception were enacted at a time when state legislatures were liberalizing the marital status doctrines of the common law. . . . [P]hysicians offered the American public a *new* way of regulating wives' conduct, one that deviated in method and preoccupation from traditional doctrines of marriage and family law. . . .

To appreciate the campaign's role in transforming discourses of gender status, it is helpful to examine the 1908 case of *Muller v. Oregon.* In *Muller,* the Supreme Court upheld protective labor legislation regulating women's employment and justified this result on unprecedented constitutional grounds. To explain why the state of Oregon could restrict women's freedom of contract as it could not men's, the Court pointed to women's "physical structure," invoking women's bodies as the basis for gender-differentiated regulation of women's conduct in a fashion that no court of the early nineteenth century ever would. The Court understood that it was discussing matters of gender status in a fashion that broke with the conventions of the common law. The Court began its analysis in *Muller* by noting that Oregon had recently reformed the common law to allow wives to form binding contracts, yet the Court ruled that the state could impose new restrictions on women's capacity to form employment contracts, for reasons relating to their reproductive role:

> Though limitations upon personal and contractual rights may be removed by legislation, there is that in her disposition and habits of life which will operate against a full assertion of those rights. . . . [Woman's] physical structure and a proper discharge of

her maternal functions—having in view not merely her own health, but the well-being of the race—justify legislation to protect her from the greed as well as the passion of man. . . . Many words cannot make this plainer. The two sexes differ in structure of body, in the functions to be performed by each. . . . This difference justifies a difference in legislation and upholds that which is designed to compensate for some of the burdens which rest upon her. (*Muller,* 422–23)

In *Muller,* the Court employed claims about women's bodies to reach a result that some decades earlier it might have justified by invoking the common law of marital status. The campaign to criminalize abortion did not supplant marital status law, nor did it eliminate the use of marriage concepts in explaining women's social status. Instead it gave them a more "modern," scientific sense. As the *Muller* opinion illustrates, the campaign enabled the Court to repudiate traditional norms of gender status and still find reasons for enforcing women's roles—reasons now rooted in immutable facts of nature rather than transitory and contestable social norms.

Comparing the Abortion Debate, Past and Present

. . . .

Today secular arguments about abortion are conducted in a medical framework, just as they were in the nineteenth century. In fact, one can discern the legacy of the criminalization campaign in *Roe* itself. *Roe* recognizes that a woman has a privacy right to make decisions about abortion, and describes this right in medical terms: it is a right to be exercised under the guidance of a physician. . . . The opinion derives the state's interest in protecting potential life from a purely medical definition of pregnancy:

The pregnant woman . . . carries an embryo, and later a fetus, if one accepts the medical definition of the developing young in the human uterus. See Dorland's *Medical Illustrated Dictionary.* . . . The situation is therefore inherently different from [all other privacy precedents]. (Roe, 159)

Recognizing both a woman's right to make decisions about abortion and the state's prerogative to regulate those decisions, *Roe* reconciles the conflict by means of its trimester framework, with the strength of each constitutional interest determined by [the] temporal progress of gestation itself.

The medico-physiological reasoning that supports *Roe* also undergirds secular arguments opposing the right *Roe* recognized. To take one example, an editorial in the *New York Post* urged its readers to examine a photo essay depicting the formation of a human being, observing:

Here in graphic color is living, thrilling irrefutable proof that within hours of conception, a unique distinctive human being has been formed. The magazine says that within 20 hours of conception, when the sperm enters the ovum, "the result is a single nucleus that contains the entire biological blueprint for a new individual, genetic information governing everything from the length of the nose to the diseases that will be inherited." (Kerrison 1990:2)

The editorial asserts, without more, that these photographs "virtually render obsolete the whole abortion debate" (ibid., 2).

In debating the abortion question today, we reason within a physiological framework that abstracts the conflict from the social context in which judgments about abortion are formed and enforced. To understand the reasons why women seek to have children or to avoid having them, as well as the reasons why their choices are communally acceptable or not, one has to examine the social relations of reproduction and not merely its physiology. But the naturalistic rhetorics of the abortion debate deter this. As a consequence, we conceptualize the abortion question as a question concerning women's bodies, not women's roles. That women are the object of abortion-restrictive regulation is considered to be a matter of physiological necessity: women are where the embryo/fetus *is*. Indeed, as the *New York Post* editorial illustrates, medico-physiological discourses often present the fetus as if it were an autonomous form of life, depicting the process of human development as if it scarcely involved women at all. Thus, . . . [a]n anti-abortion pamphlet observes "[n]othing has been added to the fertilized ovum you once were except nutrition" (Willke, n.d., quoted in Olsen 1989:128), just as Horatio Storer once argued that the "total independence" of the unborn could be discerned in the fact that "its subsequent history after impregnation is merely one of development, its attachment merely for nutrition and shelter" (Storer and Heard 1868:10–11).

While opponents of abortion no longer make claims about women's roles of the sort that dominated the nineteenth-century campaign, gender-based judgments do continue to inform arguments for regulating women's reproductive conduct: *today these judgments can be articulated in the physiological modes of reasoning the campaign inaugurated.* . . . [C]ritics of *Roe*'s trimester framework[, for example,] contend that the state's interest in protecting potential life "exists throughout the pregnancy."[1] This proposition bears consideration. Considered in social rather than physiological terms, the state's "interest in protecting potential life" is a state interest in compelling women who are resisting motherhood to bear children. Of course, legislators would dispute this characterization of the state's interest in regulating abortion. To do so, they would invoke the discourse of reproductive physiology, that is, they would argue that the state has no interest in the pregnant woman, save for the fact that she is where the embryo/fetus is. But this rejoinder does not alter the fact that a state forbidding abortion to protect potential life *is* forcing women who are resisting motherhood to bear children. Should legislators protest that they wish to prohibit abortion out of concern for the unborn and entertain no thoughts about the women on whom they would impose motherhood, such a defense would reveal that the policy was premised on gendered assumptions with deep roots in the nineteenth-century campaign: that the embryo/fetus is somehow "outside" women, like a kangaroo gestating in its mother's pouch— or that women are little more than reproductive organs. Alternatively, if legislators attempted to explain why they believed they were justified in forcing a pregnant woman to bear a child, each of the putatively gender-neutral explanations they might provide (e.g., consent, fault) could in turn be traced to a set of status-linked judgments about women.

In short, claims about abortion that focus on the physical relations of reproduction often express judgments about abortion rooted in the social relations of reproduction. In *Abortion and the Politics of Motherhood*, Kristin Luker traces value judgments about protecting unborn life to value judgments about the structure of family life, contending that "[t]he abortion debate is so passionate and hard-fought because it is a referendum on the place and meaning of motherhood" (Luker 1984:193). As Luker persuasively demonstrates, divergent modes of reasoning about the unborn correlate with divergent modes of reasoning about the nature of sexuality, work, and family commitments in women's lives (ibid., 192–215). Thus, while the separate spheres tradition no longer receives official public sanction, the sex-role concepts it fostered continue to play a crucial role in the abortion controversy, supplying norms of sexual and maternal comportment for women that inform public judgments about the propriety of abortion. A 1990 poll of Louisiana residents indicated that 89 percent favored providing women access to abortion when pregnancy occurred because of rape or incest, while 79 percent opposed abortion "when childbirth might interrupt a woman's career" (Hill 1990). The most widespread support for abortion depended on a judgment about the sexual relations in which unborn life was conceived, and the most widespread opposition to abortion reflected a judgment about women's pursuit of career opportunities in conflict with the maternal role.

We can thus recharacterize the interest in regulating abortion. Those who seek to protect unborn life want to regulate the conduct of women who fail to act as good mothers should. . . .

If one considers the means conventionally employed to protect the unborn, one finds ample evidence that fetal-protective policies do in fact reflect judgments about women, as well as the unborn life they bear. For example, . . . [w]hy . . . is it that antiabortion laws do not assist pregnant women in coping with the social consequences of gestating and raising a child? Would every jurisdiction interested in prohibiting abortion do so if it were obliged to make women whole for the costs of bearing and raising a child? Do jurisdictions that wish to prohibit abortion employ all available *noncoercive* means to promote the welfare of unborn life, assisting those women who do want to become mothers so that they [can] bear and rear healthy children? . . .

Analyzing reproductive regulation in historical perspective thus yields several critical insights. . . .

1. *In the abortion debate, the discourse of reproductive physiology functions as a discourse of gender status.* . . . Modes of describing the maternal/fetal relation and the process of human development that would seem to be purely empirical are in fact specific to the abortion debate; they have a rhetorical history and a conceptual bias consistent with this history. These rhetorics of the body are part of a discourse of gender status, long used to justify regulating women's reproductive conduct. Consequently, in contemporary debates about abortion, gendered judgments can be articulated in the physiological discourses the nineteenth-century campaign inaugurated. (The "state's interest in protecting potential life" is an expression of this discursive tradition; the Court's reasoning in *Roe* unfolds within, and not against, the logic of the criminalization campaign.)

2. *Laws criminalizing abortion and contraception compel motherhood, and from an historical perspective can be understood as a form of gender status regulation.* In the

nineteenth century, the criminalization of abortion and contraception was advocated as a method of ensuring that women performed their duties as wives and mothers. Laws criminalizing birth control enacted in this period can be understood as a new form of gender status regulation, adopted in an era in which the older common law regime of marital status was under feminist attack and undergoing liberalization. Today, as in the past, public interest in regulating women's reproductive conduct has grown as older forms of patriarchal regulation have declined in legitimacy. Now, as then, new forms of reproductive regulation are justified with reference to "facts of nature" rather than to relations of social status, a justificatory stance necessitated by the waning legitimacy of overtly patriarchal discourses. . . . (With the appearance of modern equal protection doctrines forbidding discrimination on the basis of sex, arguments grounded in reproductive physiology constitute one of the strongest constitutional rationales for class-based regulation of women's conduct.)

3. *The nineteenth-century campaign to criminalize birth control was shaped by concerns of gender, race, and class—notwithstanding the apparent universality of its physiological polemics; the same is true of contemporary interest in reproductive regulation.* In the nineteenth century, the "native" American middle class responded to the populationist "threat" posed by immigrant and African-American families by regulating the reproductive conduct of its own women. Today, . . . [a]n integrated approach to analyzing reproductive regulation will attempt to ascertain the gender, race, and class salience of such regulation, whether birth-compelling, or birth-deterring in form.

4. *All regulation directed at women's reproductive conduct reflects judgments about women and the children they might bear; to determine whether such regulation is animated by benign judgments, judgments infected by gender, class, or racial bias, or some amalgam of both, it is necessary to analyze the structure of the regulation in light of the social, as well as physical, relations of reproduction—an inquiry that should include an examination of the historical lineage or antecedents of the practice.* Reproductive regulation has served to enforce or maintain caste relations in times past. For this reason, examining past regulatory practices can illuminate tacit forms of bias structuring present regulatory practices. . . .

The Legal Context: Developments in Feminist Jurisprudence Since Roe

The foregoing analysis of abortion restrictions draws upon and contributes to social construction theory—the body of feminist theory exploring the social organization of reproductive relations. But this method of analyzing reproductive regulation shares little in common with the framework the Supreme Court employs in interpreting the Constitution. . . . Feminist jurisprudence now offers an alternative constitutional framework for analyzing restrictions on abortion—one that can draw on social construction theory in ways the prevailing constitutional framework does not. . . .

Roe protected women's right to make the abortion decision as a right of privacy not equality. In fact, when *Roe* was decided in 1973, the Court had not yet interpreted the equal protection clause to require government adherence to principles of sex equality. As important, *Roe* could not be easily incorporated into the constitutional sex discrimination tradition that would develop shortly thereafter. The modern equal protection tradition defines equality as a relation of similarity and discrimination as an illegitimate act of differentiation. *Roe,* however, analyzed abortion restrictions in physiological terms. Considered from a physiological standpoint, no man is similarly situated to the pregnant woman facing abortion restrictions; hence, state action restricting a woman's abortion choices does not seem to present a problem of sex discrimination.

In the mid-1970s, shortly after *Roe* was decided, the Court began to apply the equal protection clause to questions of sex discrimination. In a series of precedent-setting decisions, the Court declared that it would scrutinize sex-based regulation closely and invalidate the legislation if it was premised on "old notions of role typing" or other vestiges of the separate spheres tradition[2] (such as the assumption that women are "child-rearers" (*Califano v. Webster*) or the assumption that "the female [is] destined solely for the home and the rearing of the family" (*Stanton v. Stanton*)). But the Court refused to analyze legislation regulating women's reproductive role similarly. In *Geduldig v. Aiello,* the Court ruled that a law governing pregnancy was not sex-based state action for purposes of equal protection doctrine, and thus did not warrant heightened constitutional scrutiny; on other occasions, the Court observed that the reality of reproductive differences between the sexes justified their differential regulatory treatment.

While feminists protested the *Geduldig* decision, few were concerned about its implications for the abortion right. . . .

By the 1980s, . . . [a]s jurisprudential criticism of the *Roe* decision mounted, legal academics began to explore alternative constitutional foundations for the abortion right. . . . During this same period . . . [a] number of feminist legal scholars began to repudiate equality theory focused on issues of similarity and difference and to argue for an inquiry focused on issues of hierarchy and subordination. This approach removed a crucial stumbling block to analyzing abortion in a sex equality framework. No longer was it necessary to demonstrate sex discrimination by comparing the treatment of women to a group of similarly situated men; instead, as Catharine MacKinnon argued, it was enough to show that "the policy or practice in question integrally contributes to the maintenance of an underclass or a deprived position because of gender status" (MacKinnon 1979:117). Indeed, as MacKinnon conceptualized the problem of inequality, gender-differentiated practices such as rape, pornography, and abortion-restrictive regulation played a central role in women's subordination (MacKinnon 1983a; 1983b:646–55; 1987:40–45). This paradigm shift facilitated equal protection challenges to abortion restrictions. For example, in 1984 Sylvia Law drew on MacKinnon's work in one of the first major articles to explore the abortion right in a sex equality framework, "Rethinking Sex and the Constitution." Law argued that because women's capacity to bear children represented a real and significant biological difference between the sexes, reproductive regulation should be evaluated under an antisubordination framework; at the same time, she contended that the traditional comparative treatment approach to equal protection analysis should be retained for all other forms of sex-based regulation (1984:1007–13).

From Privacy to Equality: Analyzing Abortion
Restrictions as Caste Regulation

A growing number of constitutional scholars now defend the abortion right on sex equality grounds. . . .

Sex Equality Arguments for the Abortion Right

As it is currently interpreted, the equal protection clause imposes virtually no re-straints on state regulation of women's reproductive lives. Together, the Court's physi-ological view of reproduction and its comparative understanding of equality present formidable obstacles to equal protection analysis of abortion restrictions. Yet, ana-lyzed in historical perspective, it is clear that restrictions on abortion are deeply at odds with the values and commitments informing the constitutional guarantee of equal protection. . . . [L]aws restricting abortion do not just regulate women's bodies; they regulate women's roles. Because abortion restrictions can enforce caste or status relations, such laws implicate constitutional guarantees of equality as well as privacy.

While the Court often reasons comparatively in interpreting the equal protection clause of the fourteenth amendment, it has also drawn upon a cluster of concepts as-sociated with social status or caste. As Kenneth Karst observes "[T]he equality that matters in our Supreme Court is not the simple abstraction that likes should be treated alike. . . . The equal citizenship principle that is the core of the fourteenth amendment . . . is presumptively violated when the organized society treats someone as an inferior, as part of a dependent caste, or as a non-participant" (Karst 1983:248). . . . Commentators who would replace the "equal treatment principle" with a mediat-ing principle focused on issues of group subordination also invoke concepts associ-ated with caste to describe the practices prohibited by the fourteenth amendment (Fiss 1976:157; MacKinnon 1979:117; Tribe 1988:1520).

As this paper demonstrates, restrictions on abortion are readily analyzed as a form of caste regulation. In the nineteenth century, restrictions on abortion and contracep-tion were enacted for the explicit purpose of forcing married women to bear children. Abortion restrictions were used to enforce the gender status norms of the separate spheres tradition; they perform a similar function today. Today, no less than in the past, restrictions on abortion force women to assume the status and perform the work of motherhood. . . .

An increasing number of scholars have advanced equal protection arguments against abortion restrictions. While these equality arguments do not specifically in-voke the history of criminal abortion laws or analyze the regulation in a caste frame-work, they do emphasize that abortion restrictions are (1) a form of class legislation that (2) reflects status-based judgments about women and (3) inflicts status-based in-juries on women. The new equal protection arguments point out that:

1. *Abortion restrictions single out women for an especially burdensome and invasive form of public regulation.* . . .

2. *Abortion restrictions are gender-biased in justification and structure, reflecting di-verse forms of status-based reasoning about women's roles.* [J]ustifications for abortion

restrictions . . . rest on a distinctive set of judgments about the unborn, not consistently expressed in other social settings and often controverted by other social practices. . . . The regulations are selective, imposing a duty of lifesaving on pregnant women not otherwise imposed on citizens or family members who have the capacity to save the life of another (Olsen 1989:129–30; Regan 1979; Siegel 1992:335–47; 366; Sunstein 1992:33–36). The selectivity of the compulsion is rarely noted because women are expected to perform the work of motherhood, and this role expectation makes reasonable, or invisible, the impositions of forced motherhood. . . .

3. *Restrictions on abortion injure women by compelling motherhood, forcing women to assume a role and to perform work that has long been used to subordinate them as a class.* The injuries inflicted on women by abortion restrictions are not attributable to nature, but instead reflect institutional practices of the society that would force women to bear children. . . . Because abortion-restrictive regulation coerces women to perform the work of motherhood without altering the conditions that continue to make such work a principal cause of their subordinate social status, it is a form of status-reinforcing state action that offends constitutional guarantees of equal protection. . . .

4. *Too often, legal restrictions on abortion do not save fetal lives but instead subject women, especially poor women, to unsafe, life-threatening medical procedures.* . . . If the state is genuinely interested in promoting the welfare of the unborn, it can and should do so by means that support women in the work of bearing and rearing children. . . .

Judicial Reception of the Sex Equality Argument

In the years since *Roe* the Court has grown to better appreciate the gendered character of the abortion conflict. In part this is because the Court has acquired experience in interpreting the federal law prohibiting pregnancy discrimination in employment. . . . But the Court's understanding of the abortion conflict has also been shaped by sex equality arguments for the abortion right.

In its most recent pronouncement on the abortion right, *Planned Parenthood of Southeastern Pennsylvania v. Casey,* the Court . . . identified constitutional reasons for protecting this privacy right not discussed in *Roe.* The Court observed that the state was obliged to respect a pregnant woman's decisions about abortion because her "suffering is too intimate and personal for the State to insist . . . upon its own vision of the woman's role, however dominant that vision has been in the course of our history and our culture. The destiny of the woman must be shaped to a large extent on her own conception of her spiritual imperatives and her place in society" (Casey, 2807). In short, the Court ruled that laws prohibiting abortion offend the Constitution because they use the power of the state to impose traditional sex roles on women. . . .

Justice Blackmun, who authored *Roe,* endorsed the gender-conscious reasoning of the *Casey* decision and drew upon it to advance the argument that restrictions on abortion offend constitutional guarantees of *equality* as well as privacy. In this equality argument, Justice Blackmun emphasized that abortion restrictions are gender-biased in impetus and impact. When the state restricts abortion, it exacts the work of motherhood from women without compensating their labor because it assumes that it is women's "natural" duty to perform such labor:

The State does not compensate women for their services; instead, it assumes that they owe this duty as a matter of course. This assumption—that women can simply be forced to accept the "natural" status and incidents of motherhood—appears to rest upon a conception of women's role that has triggered the protection of the Equal Protection Clause. (Ibid., 2847; citations and footnote omitted)

. . . .

While the abortion controversy is typically discussed as a conflict between an individual's freedom of choice and the community's interest in protecting unborn life, Justice Blackmun's opinion reframes the conflict. The community's decision to intervene in women's lives is no longer presumptively benign; its decision to compel motherhood is presumptively suspect, one more instance of the sex-role restrictions imposed on women throughout American history.

While Justice Blackmun has recently retired from the Court, Justice Ruth Bader Ginsburg, who has recently joined the Court, shares the view that restrictions on abortion may violate constitutional guarantees of sex equality (Ginsburg 1985:1992). The Court as a whole is by no means ready to embrace the view that restrictions on abortion violate guarantees of equal protection; but its opinion in *Casey* makes clear, as *Roe* did not, that "[t]he ability of women to participate equally in the economic and social life of the Nation has been facilitated by their ability to control their reproductive lives" (Casey, 2809).

What the Equality Argument Illuminates: Advantages of Analyzing Abortion Restrictions as Caste- or Status-Enforcing State Action

There are several advantages to analyzing abortion restrictions as caste- or status-enforcing state action. First, [such an analysis] . . . call[s] into question the "benign" justifications conventionally offered for fetal-protective regulation. As *Casey* illustrates, the Court will oppose abortion restrictions when it believes they are gender biased in impetus or impact, even if the Court is not ready to adopt the equal protection clause as the constitutional basis for protecting the abortion right.

Second, the caste framework offers a basis for discriminating between subordinating and emancipating forms of state intervention in women's reproductive lives. Because the inquiry focuses attention on the normative premises of reproductive regulation and its practical impact on women's lives, it supplies a framework that reconciles feminist objections to state involvement in matters of reproduction with feminist demands for state involvement in matters of reproduction.

Third, the caste framework is useful because it shifts the focus of critical inquiry from the physical to the social relations of reproduction—from the maternal/fetal relation to the network of social relations in which women conceive, gestate, and raise children. . . . Focusing analysis on the social conditions of motherhood . . . demonstrates that this society's professed concern for the welfare of future generations is pervasively contradicted by the manner in which it treats children and the women who raise them. Thus, the very analysis that reveals discriminatory bias in abortion restrictions and other forms of fetal-protective regulation simultaneously advances an argument that this society needs to reform the social conditions of motherhood if it in fact intends to promote the welfare of future generations. In this way, objections to coercive intervention in women's reproductive lives lead to demands for supportive intervention in women's reproductive lives, so that legislative support for the Freedom of Choice Act, adequate child care, the Family and Medical Leave Act, and supplemental nutrition programs are tied together, as they are not under a privacy analysis. When the abortion question is reconfigured in this fashion, it is possible to argue for abortion rights without seeming to oppose motherhood; the charge that women seeking abortions devalue children and the work of raising them can be turned on its head and aimed at the society that would regulate their conduct. The argument for abortion rights is thus transformed into a dare and a demand: that this society honor the commitments putatively expressed in fetal-protective regulation by supporting those who are struggling to raise children.

Finally, . . . examining equality arguments for the abortion right can help identify elements of pro-choice rhetoric that are dysfunctional artifacts of early second-wave feminism. For example, some arguments in defense of the abortion right have equated freedom of choice with freedom from motherhood, without demanding the social reforms that would enable women to choose motherhood freely, i.e., without status-linked consequences for their welfare or autonomy. Moreover, defenses of the abortion right rarely address the ways that racism has shaped reproductive policies in this nation—focusing on birth-compelling regulation without acknowledging the history of birth-deterring regulation directed at poor peoples of color. Analyzing the case for abortion rights in a caste or equality framework illuminates these antimaternalist and race-essentialist tendencies in pro-choice arguments, and so explains why such arguments may alienate many women and men who otherwise might support the abortion right. For this reason and others, developing equality arguments for the abortion right can in fact reinvigorate privacy discourse. The exercise in translation should encourage us to identify the peculiar strengths of privacy discourse and to articulate privacy-based claims in ways that complement, rather than contradict, equality-based arguments for the abortion right.

NOTES

1. *City of Akron v. Akron Center for Reproductive Health,* 462 U.S. 416, 461 (1983) (O'Connor, J., dissenting) ("[P]otential life is not less potential in the first weeks of pregnancy than it is at viability or afterward. . . . Accordingly, I believe that the State's interest in protecting human life exists throughout the pregnancy.").

2. See *Craig v. Boren,* 429 U.S. 190, 198 (1976); ibid., 198–99 (rejecting statutory schemes premised on "increasingly outdated misconceptions concerning the role of females in the home rather than in the 'marketplace and world of ideas'") (quoting *Stanton v. Stanton,* 421 U.S. 7, 14–15 [1975]).

SOURCES CITED

Calhoun, Arthur W. 1919. *A Social History of the American Family from Colonial Times to the Present.* Cleveland: Arthur H. Clark.

Califano v. Webster, 430 U.S. 313, 317 (1977).

City of Akron v. Akron Center for Reproductive Health, 462 U.S. 416, 461 (1983).

Fiss, Owen M. 1976. "Groups and the Equal Protection Clause." *Philosophy & Public Affairs* 5, no. 2:107–77.

Geduldig v. Aiello, 417 U.S. 484 (1974).

Ginsburg, Ruth Bader. 1985. "Some Thoughts on Autonomy and Equality in Relation to *Roe v. Wade*." *North Carolina Law Review* 63, no. 2:375–86.

Gordon, Linda. 1976. *Woman's Body, Woman's Rights: A Social History of Birth Control in America*. New York: Grossman.

Hale, Edwin M. 1867. *The Great Crime of the Nineteenth Century*. Chicago: C.S. Halsey.

Hill, John. 1990. "New Poll: Abortion Veto OK." Gannet News Service (September 7). Available LEXIS, NEXIS Library, GNS File.

Karst, Kenneth L. 1983. "Why Equality Matters." *Georgia Law Review* 17:245–89.

Kerrison, Ray. 1990. "Backdrop to Bush's Court Selection; Pictures Show What Abortion Is About." *New York Post* (July 25):2.

Law, Sylvia A. 1984. "Rethinking Sex and the Constitution." *University of Pennsylvania Law Review* 132:955–1040.

Luker, Kristin. 1984. *Abortion and the Politics of Motherhood*. Berkeley: University of California Press.

MacKinnon, Catharine A. 1979. *Sexual Harassment of Working Women*. New Haven: Yale University Press.

———. 1983a. "The Male Ideology of Privacy: A Feminist Perspective on the Right to Abortion." *Radical America* 17, no. 4:23–38.

———. 1983b. "Feminism, Marxism, Method, and the State: Toward Feminist Jurisprudence." *Signs* 8:636–58.

———. 1987. *Feminism Unmodified: Discourses on Life and Law*. Cambridge: Harvard University Press.

Muller v. Oregon, 208 U.S. 412 (1908).

Olsen, Frances E. 1989. "Unraveling Compromise." *Harvard Law Review* 103:105–35.

Pallen, Montrose A. 1869. "Foeticide, or Criminal Abortion." *Medical Archives* 3:193–206.

Planned Parenthood of Southeastern Pennsylvania v. Casey, 112 S. Ct. 2791 (1992).

Pomeroy, H. S. 1888. *The Ethics of Marriage*. New York: Funk and Wagnalls.

Regan, Donald H. 1979. "Rewriting *Roe v. Wade*." *Michigan Law Review* 77:1568–646.

Roe v. Wade, 410 U.S. 113 (1973).

Siegel, Reva B. 1992. "Reasoning from the Body: A Historical Perspective on Abortion Regulation and Questions of Equal Protection." *Stanford Law Review* 44:262–381.

Stanton v. Stanton, 421 U.S. 7, 14 (1975).

Storer, Horatio R. and Franklin Fiske Heard. 1868. *Criminal Abortion: Its Nature, Its Evidence, and Its Law*. Boston: Little, Brown.

Sunstein, Cass R. 1992. "Neutrality in Constitutional Law (with Special Reference to Pornography, Abortion, and Surrogacy)." *Columbia Law Review* 92:1–52.

Tribe, Laurence H. 1988. *American Constitutional Law*. 2d ed. Minneola: Foundation Press.

Willke, J. n.d. *Did You Know* (antiabortion pamphlet) (on file at the Harvard Law School Library), quoted in Frances Olsen, "Unraveling Compromise." *Harvard Law Review* 103 (1989): 105, 128n93.

Chapter 15

Brief Amici Curiae of 274 Organizations in Support of *Roe v. Wade,* Submitted in *Turnock v. Ragsdale*

Kathleen M. Sullivan and Susan R. Estrich

. . . .

Because abortion restrictions both discriminate uniquely against women, and do so in a way that intrudes on women's basic interests in bodily integrity, procreation, and health, such laws should trigger strict scrutiny.

A. Sex Classifications That Interfere with Bodily Integrity and Procreation Are Impermissible in the Absence of Compelling Justification

This court has held that measures classifying on the basis of gender are unconstitutional unless the party supporting the measure can "carry the burden of showing an 'exceedingly persuasive justification' for the classification." *Mississippi University for Women v. Hogan,* 458 U.S. 718, 724 (1982). A "searching analysis" is required because gender-based measures often reflect the "mechanical application," of " 'old notions' and 'archaic and overbroad' generalizations," and operate to "put women not on a pedestal, but in a cage." Thus, this Court has repeatedly struck down legislation that restricted the exercise by both men and women of liberty in social roles, recognizing that "[n]o longer is the female destined solely for the home and the rearing of family, and only the male for the marketplace and the world of ideas."

Exacting as it is, this scrutiny escalates to the highest level where, as here, legislation that discriminates on the basis of gender also intrudes on basic interests in bodily integrity, procreation, health, family, and sometimes life itself. The "fundamental rights" branch of equal protection jurisprudence makes clear that, where legislation classifies with respect to such basic interests, any deference that would otherwise be given the legislature attenuates. Rather, such legislation may be upheld only if it survives the strictest and most searching kind of review. Thus, in *Skinner v. Oklahoma,* 316 U.S. 535, this Court applied strict scrutiny under the Equal Protection Clause to a compulsory sterilization law that discriminated among categories of thieves—a kind of line drawing that otherwise would not have been suspect. . . . If cases such as *Skinner* . . . treat

Brief for 274 Organizations in Support of *Roe v. Wade,* Submitted as *Amici Curiae* in *Turnock v. Ragsdale,* Nos. 88-790 and 88-805 (1989), in Mary Becker, Cynthia Grant Bowman, and Morrison Torrey (eds.), Feminist Jurisprudence: Taking Women Seriously: Cases and Materials 470–72 (3d ed., 1994).

impact on the fundamental rights to procreate and to marry as escalating the standard of review from minimal to strict, then surely the impingement of abortion laws on procreation, health, marriage, and family interests should escalate judicial scrutiny the lesser distance from heightened to strict review. Thus, the gender-based discrimination worked by restrictive abortion laws should be reviewed strictly.

B. Restrictive Abortion Laws Classify on the Basis of Sex

The direct impact of abortion restrictions falls, exclusively, on a class of people that consists only of women. Only women get pregnant; only women have abortions; only women will be forced to endure unwanted pregnancies and adverse health consequences if abortions are restricted; only women are injured by dangerous, illegal abortions where legal ones are unavailable; and only women will bear children if abortions are unavailable.

The fact that the laws do not mention "women" is irrelevant. A law restricting "all abortions" is the precise equivalent of a law restricting "all abortions sought by women." A classification based on pregnancy is, by biological definition, a classification based on gender.

. . . .

Moreover, abortion restrictions, like the most classic gender-based restriction on women seeking to participate in the worlds of work and ideas, have historically rested on archaic stereotypes of women as persons whose "paramount destiny and mission . . . [is] to fulfill the noble and benign office of wife and mother." *Bradwell v. Illinois,* 16 Wall. 130, 142 (1873) (Bradley, J., concurring). Legislation prohibiting abortion, largely a product of the years between 1860 and 1880, reflected precisely the same ideas about the natural and proper role of women as did the legislation of the same period—long-since discredited—that prohibited women from serving on juries or participating in the professions, including the practice of law.

Perhaps not surprisingly, modern studies have found that support for laws banning abortion continues to be an outgrowth of the same sort of stereotypical notions that women's only appropriate roles are those of mother and housewife; in many cases, such laws have emerged as a direct reaction to the increasing number of women who work outside the home. See generally K. Luker, *Abortion and the Politics of Motherhood* 192–215 (1984). It is, of course, precisely such stereotypes, as they are reflected in legislation, that have over and over again been the focus of this Court's modern equal protection cases.

C. The Political Process Is Inadequate to Protect Access to Abortion for All Women

. . . .

This Court has long interpreted the Equal Protection Clause to require even-handedness in legislation, lest the powerful few too casually trade away for others key liberties that they are careful to reserve for themselves. For example, the Court once struck down under the Equal Protection Clause a law permitting castration of recidivist chicken thieves but sparing white-collar embezzlers the knife. *Skinner v. Oklahoma,* 316 U.S. 535. The implication of *Skinner* was that, put to an all-or-nothing choice, legislators would rather sterilize no one than jeopardize people like themselves. Thus equality serves as a backstop to liberty.

Every restrictive abortion law has been passed by a legislature in which men constitute a numerical majority. And every restrictive abortion law, by definition, contains an unwritten clause exempting all men from its strictures. To rely on state legislatures to protect women against "abortion regulation reminiscent of the dark ages," *Webster,* 109 S. Ct. 3058, ignores the fact that the overwhelming majority of "those who serve in such bodies," like the Oklahoma legislators who supported sterilization for working-men's crimes, are not directly affected at all by the penalties they are imposing. It is precisely in such cases that strict scrutiny is required, to protect against the very real danger that those in power will too casually impose burdens on others, in this case on women, that they would not have imposed upon themselves.

That is particularly so where, as here, the women most likely to be affected are those whom the political process protects least well. A world without *Roe* will not be a world without abortion, but a world in which abortion is accessible according to one's constitutional caste. While affluent women will travel to jurisdictions where safe and legal abortion is available, paying whatever is required, restrictive abortion laws—and with them, the life threatening prospect of the back-alley abortion—will disproportionately descend upon "those without . . . adequate resources" to avoid them. *Griswold,* 381 U.S. at 503 (White, J., concurring). Those for whom the burdens of an unwanted pregnancy may be the most crushing—the young, the poor, women whose color already renders them victims of discrimination—will be the ones least able to secure a safe abortion.

In the years prior to *Roe,* "[p]oor and minority women were virtually precluded from obtaining safe, legal procedures, the overwhelming majority of which were obtained by white women in the private hospital services on psychiatric indications."[1] Women denied access to safe and legal abortions often had dangerous and illegal ones. Mishandled criminal abortions were, one detailed study found, the principal cause of maternal deaths in the 1960's, and mortality rates for African-American women were as much as nine times higher than for white women. In 1972, women of color accounted for sixty-four percent of the deaths associated with illegal abortions in this country.

To trust the political process to protect these women is to ignore completely the lessons of history. Time and again, this Court has recognized its special duties to protect minorities whose rights can too easily be trampled by legislative majorities.

. . . .

NOTES

1. Polgar & Fried, "The Bad Old Days: Clandestine Abortions among the Poor in New York City before Liberalization of the Abortion Law," 8 Fam. Plan. Persp. 125 (1976).

Questions and Comments

1. Siegel's notion of "gender-caste" regulation refers to laws that reinforce women's subordinate status in society—by, for example, forcing women to perform traditional gender roles such as those of nurturer and mother. What does Siegel mean when she says that abortion regulations are "gender-caste" regulations? Is it appropriate to see abortion restrictions as a form of forced motherhood?

2. What is Siegel's critique of the "physiological discourse" often used in legal discussions of the abortion issue? What consequences flow, according to her, from rooting abortion-talk in consideration of the biological "facts" about women's bodies rather than in discussion of social issues such as women's roles?

3. How does the brief by Sullivan and Estrich articulate the equality view? How does it use the sterilization case of *Skinner v. Oklahoma* to make its argument?

4. Some proponents of an equality approach to abortion law have argued that this approach provides a stronger argument against cases like *Harris v. McRae* than does the privacy approach. State law provides some support for that position. Thus, despite the U.S. Supreme Court's upholding of the Hyde Amendment and similar statutes, several state supreme courts have invalidated similar state rules as contrary to those *states'* constitutions. Often the decision is based upon a state Equal Rights Amendment that specifically prohibits sex discrimination and subjects sex-based statutory distinctions to strict scrutiny—rather than the intermediate scrutiny used for sex-based distinctions under federal constitutional law. *See, e.g., New Mexico Right to Choose/NARAL v. Johnson*, 975 P.2d 841 (1998) (holding that law restricting state funding for medically necessary abortions for poor women constituted sex discrimination under state's Equal Rights Amendment). Thus, these cases ground their results on the prohibition against sex discrimination, rather than the right to privacy. The New Mexico case, for example, held that the state's restrictions on state funding of abortions for Medicaid-eligible women violated the state constitution because they restricted women's access to medically necessary health care even though the state covered all medically necessary procedures for men. *Accord, Low-Income Women of Texas v. Bost*, 38 S.W.3d 689 (Tex. App.-Austin, 2000), *reversed, Bell v. Low Income Women of Texas*, 95 S.W.3d 253 (Tex., 2002).

5. There is some indication that the "undue burden" test introduced in *Casey* may be migrating to the Equal Protection context. Consider, for example, the case of *Tucson Women's Clinic v Eden*, 379 F.3d 531 (9th Cir., 2004), in which an Equal Protection challenge was brought against an abortion statute on the grounds that the state did not similarly regulate comparably risky procedures sought by men. In that case, the federal Court of Appeals for the Ninth Circuit acknowledged that "the right to

obtain an abortion is tied to the right to be free from sex discrimination in a manner unlike any other medical service that only one gender seeks." Id. at 549. But the court refused to apply the intermediate scrutiny test usually used in gender discrimination cases, ruling that, for "laws singling out abortion . . . [that] facially promote maternal health or fetal life, *Casey* replaces the intermediate scrutiny such a law would normally receive under the equal protection clause with the undue burden standard." Id.

B. Abortion: Special Topics

Introduction to Part II(B)

Section B of part II continues this part's exploration of the abortion issue, engaging several specific topics within abortion jurisprudence. Subsection 1 presents the two Supreme Court cases on late-term abortion, as well as Rigel Oliveri's trenchant critique of the efforts by opponents of late-term abortion statutes to prevent their passage. In *Stenberg v. Carhart,* the Court declared unconstitutional a Nebraska statute that prohibited "partial birth abortion." Oliveri's piece, "Crossing the Line: The Political and Moral Battle over Late-Term Abortion," shows how pro-choice activists' attempts to hide—rather than explain—the use of late-term abortion by poor women and women of color ultimately contributed to the failure of their efforts to prevent passage of the federal late-term abortion statute. Her account presents a particularly poignant illustration of the connections between the reproductive interests of different groups of women, and of how privileged women ignore those connections at their peril. That account is made yet more telling when read against the backdrop of the most recent Supreme Court case in this area, *Gonzales v. Carhart,* decided as this book was going to press. In that landmark (and highly controversial) case, the Court upheld the Federal act, even though its provisions include no exception to protect the health of the mother.

Subsection 2 explores the legal regulation of minors' access to abortion and sex education, excerpting Deborah Rhode's "Politics and Pregnancy: Adolescent Mothers and Public Policy" and two pieces by Cynthia Dailard on sex education. Rhode shows that inadequate social support for teen parents might be a central cause of the harms of teen pregnancy, and that restrictions on minors' access to abortion might have little impact on parent-teen communication or teen sexual behavior. Dailard's anaylsis of abstinence-only education also highlights the effect of social policy on teen behavior, connecting abstinence-only programs to unwanted pregnancy.

Finally, subsection 3 of section B presents a fascinating pair of articles on the difficult issue of wrongful birth and selective abortion. Julie F. Kowitz, in "Not Your Garden Variety Tort Reform: Statutes Barring Claims for Wrongful Life and Wrongful Birth Are Unconstitutional under the Purpose Prong of *Planned Parenthood v. Casey,*" maintains that statutes barring wrongful birth and wrongful life claims[1] violate the constitutional rights of women who wish to sue their doctors for burdening their right to reproductive autonomy. In contrast, Marsha Saxton, in "Disability Rights and Selective Abortion," presents a disability rights argument against both selective abortions and wrongful birth suits, raising important questions about whether problematic eugenic attitudes account for some of the abortions of disabled fetuses. Finally, in subsection 4, Rachel Roth discusses the range of serious limitations imposed on the reproductive rights of women in prison.

NOTE

1. The typical wrongful birth claim is brought by parents of a disabled child against the physician whose negligent treatment prevented the parents from discovering their child's disability early enough to terminate the pregnancy before birth. Wrongful life claims are similar claims brought on behalf of the disabled infant (instead of the parents), and claiming that the defendant's negligence harmed the already-disabled child by causing the child to be born (with disabilities) rather than aborted.

1. Late-Term Abortion

Chapter 16

Stenberg v. Carhart

Justice BREYER delivered the opinion of the Court.

We again consider the right to an abortion. We understand the controversial nature of the problem. Millions of Americans believe that life begins at conception and consequently that an abortion is akin to causing the death of an innocent child; they recoil at the thought of a law that would permit it. Other millions fear that a law that forbids abortion would condemn many American women to lives that lack dignity, depriving them of equal liberty and leading those with least resources to undergo illegal abortions with the attendant risks of death and suffering. Taking account of these virtually irreconcilable points of view . . . this Court, in the course of a generation, has determined and then redetermined that the Constitution offers basic protection to the woman's right to choose. Roe v. Wade, 410 U.S. 113 (1973); Planned Parenthood of Southeastern Pa. v. Casey, 505 U.S. 833 (1992). We shall not revisit those legal principles. Rather, we apply them to the circumstances of this case.

Three established principles determine the issue before us. We shall set them forth in the language of the joint opinion in Casey. . . . " '[S]ubsequent to viability, the State in promoting its interest in the potentiality of human life may, if it chooses, regulate, and even proscribe, abortion except where it is necessary, in appropriate medical judgment, for the preservation of the life or health of the mother.' " 505 U.S. at 879 (quoting Roe v. Wade, 410 U.S. at 164–165).

We apply these principles to a Nebraska law banning "partial birth abortion." The statute reads as follows:

> No partial birth abortion shall be performed in this state, unless such procedure is necessary to save the life of the mother whose life is endangered by a physical disorder, physical illness, or physical injury, including a life-endangering physical condition caused by or arising from the pregnancy itself. Neb. Rev. Stat. Ann. §28–328(1) (Supp. 1999)

The statute defines "partial birth abortion" as "an abortion procedure in which the person performing the abortion partially delivers vaginally a living unborn child before killing the unborn child and completing the delivery." §28–326(9). It further defines "partially delivers vaginally a living unborn child before killing the unborn child" to mean "deliberately and intentionally delivering into the vagina a living unborn child, or a substantial portion thereof, for the purpose of performing a procedure that

Stenberg v. Carhart, 530 U.S. 914 (2000).

the person performing such procedure knows will kill the unborn child and does kill the unborn child." Id.

The law classifies violation of the statute as a "Class III felony" carrying a prison term of up to 20 years, and a fine of up to $25,000. §§28–328(2), 28–105. It also provides for the automatic revocation of a doctor's license to practice medicine in Nebraska. §28–328(4).

We hold that this statute violates the Constitution.

I

. . . .

B

. . . .

[W]e shall describe the relevant methods of performing abortions in technical detail. The evidence before the trial court, as supported or supplemented in the literature, indicates the following:*

1. About 90% of all abortions performed in the United States take place during the first trimester of pregnancy, before 12 weeks of gestational age. During the first trimester, the predominant abortion method is "vacuum aspiration," which involves insertion of a vacuum tube (cannula) into the uterus to evacuate the contents. Such an abortion is typically performed on an outpatient basis under local anesthesia. Vacuum aspiration is considered particularly safe. The procedure's mortality rates for first trimester abortion are, for example, 5 to 10 times lower than those associated with carrying the fetus to term. . . .

2. Approximately 10% of all abortions are performed during the second trimester of pregnancy (12 to 24 weeks). Today . . . the medical profession . . . [uses] surgical procedures for most second trimester abortions. The most commonly used procedure is called "dilation and evacuation" (D&E). That procedure (together with a modified form of vacuum aspiration used in the early second trimester) accounts for about 95% of all abortions performed from 12 to 20 weeks of gestational age.

3. . . .

Between 13 and 15 weeks of gestation:

D&E is similar to vacuum aspiration except that the cervix must be dilated more widely because surgical instruments are used to remove larger pieces of tissue. . . . Because fetal tissue is friable and easily broken, the fetus may not be removed intact. The walls of the uterus are scraped with a curette to ensure that no tissue remains.

After 15 weeks:

Because the fetus is larger at this stage of gestation (particularly the head), and because bones are more rigid, dismemberment or other destructive procedures are more likely to be required than at earlier gestational ages to remove fetal and placental tissue.

After 20 weeks:

Some physicians use intrafetal potassium chloride or digoxin to induce fetal demise prior to a late D&E (after 20 weeks), to facilitate evacuation.

---

* *Editor's note*: The authorities cited by the Court to support its factual conclusions here have been admitted.

There are variations in D&E operative strategy. However, the common points are that D&E involves (1) dilation of the cervix; (2) removal of at least some fetal tissue using nonvacuum instruments; and (3) (after the 15th week) the potential need for instrumental disarticulation or dismemberment of the fetus or the collapse of fetal parts to facilitate evacuation from the uterus.

4. When instrumental disarticulation incident to D&E is necessary, it typically occurs as the doctor pulls a portion of the fetus through the cervix into the birth canal....

5. The D&E procedure carries certain risks. The use of instruments within the uterus creates a danger of accidental perforation and damage to neighboring organs. Sharp fetal bone fragments create similar dangers. And fetal tissue accidentally left behind can cause infection and various other complications. Nonetheless ... the risks of mortality and complication that accompany the D&E procedure between the 12th and 20th weeks of gestation are significantly lower than those accompanying induced labor procedures (the next safest mid-second trimester procedures).

6. At trial, Dr. Carhart and Dr. Stubblefield described a variation of the D&E procedure, which they referred to as an "intact D&E." [It] ... involves removing the fetus from the uterus through the cervix "intact," i.e., in one pass, rather than in several passes. It is used after 16 weeks at the earliest.... If the fetus presents head first (a vertex presentation), the doctor collapses the skull; and the doctor then extracts the entire fetus through the cervix. If the fetus presents feet first (a breech presentation), the doctor pulls the fetal body through the cervix, collapses the skull, and extracts the fetus through the cervix. The breech extraction version of the intact D&E is also known commonly as "dilation and extraction," or D&X. In the late second trimester, vertex, breech, and traverse/compound (sideways) presentations occur in roughly similar proportions.

....

Despite the technical differences we have just described, intact D&E and D&X are sufficiently similar for us to use the terms interchangeably.

9. Dr. Carhart testified he attempts to use the intact D&E procedure during weeks 16 to 20 because [it] (1) ... reduces the dangers from sharp bone fragments passing through the cervix, (2) minimizes the number of instrument passes needed for extraction and lessens the likelihood of uterine perforations caused by those instruments, (3) reduces the likelihood of leaving infection-causing fetal and placental tissue in the uterus, and (4) could help to prevent potentially fatal absorption of fetal tissue into the maternal circulation.... The District Court concluded ... that "the evidence is both clear and convincing that Carhart's D&X procedure is superior to, and safer than, the ... other abortion procedures used during the relevant gestational period in the 10 to 20 cases a year that present to Dr. Carhart." 11 F. Supp. 2d at 1126.

10. The materials presented at trial referred to the potential benefits of the D&X procedure in circumstances involving nonviable fetuses, such as fetuses with abnormal fluid accumulation in the brain (hydrocephaly) [because it reduces the size of the cranium]. Others have emphasized its potential for women with prior uterine scars, or for women for whom induction of labor would be particularly dangerous.

11. There are no reliable data on the number of D&X abortions performed annually. Estimates have ranged between 640 and 5,000 per year.

II

The question before us is whether Nebraska's statute, making criminal the performance of a "partial birth abortion," violates the Federal Constitution. . . . We conclude that it does for at least two independent reasons. First, the law lacks any exception "'for the preservation of the . . . health of the mother.'" Casey, 505 U.S. at 879 (joint opinion of O'CONNOR, KENNEDY, and SOUTER, JJ). Second, it "imposes an undue burden on a woman's ability" to choose a D&E abortion, thereby unduly burdening the right to choose abortion itself. 505 U.S. at 874. . . .

A

. . . .

[T]he governing standard requires an exception [to allowable abortion regulations] "where it is necessary, in appropriate medical judgment, for the preservation of the life or health of the mother," Casey, supra, at 879, for this Court has made clear that a State may promote but not endanger a woman's health when it regulates the methods of abortion. Thornburgh v. American College of Obstetricians and Gynecologists, 476 U.S. 747 (1986); Colautti v. Franklin, 439 U.S. 379 (1979); [Planned Parenthood of Central Mo. v.] Danforth, 428 U.S. 52, 76–79 (1973).

Justice THOMAS says that the cases just cited limit this principle to situations where the pregnancy *itself* creates a threat to health. He is wrong. The cited cases, reaffirmed in Casey, recognize that a State cannot subject women's health to significant risks both in that context, *and also* where state regulations force women to use riskier methods of abortion. Our cases have repeatedly invalidated statutes that in the process of regulating the *methods* of abortion, imposed significant health risks. They make clear that a risk to a women's health is the same whether it happens to arise from regulating a particular method of abortion, or from barring abortion entirely. Our holding does not go beyond those cases, as ratified in Casey.

1

[The Court noted that there is significant medical authority that in some circumstances D&X is safer than D&E, discussing the District Court's findings to that effect.]

2

Nebraska . . . says (1) that the D&X procedure is "little-used," (2) by only "a handful of doctors." It argues (3) that D&E and labor induction are at all times "safe alternative procedures." . . .

3

We find these . . . arguments insufficient to demonstrate that Nebraska's law needs no health exception. For one thing, certain of the arguments are beside the point. The D&X procedure's relative rarity (argument (1)) is not highly relevant. The D&X is an infrequently used abortion procedure; but the health exception question is whether protecting women's health requires an exception for those infrequent occasions. A rarely used treatment might be necessary to treat a rarely occurring disease that could strike anyone—the State cannot prohibit a person from obtaining treatment simply by pointing out that most people do not need it. Nor can we know whether the fact that only a "handful" of doctors use the procedure (argument (2)) reflects the comparative rarity of late second term abortions, the procedure's recent development, . . . the controversy surrounding it, or, as Nebraska suggests, the procedure's lack of utility.

For another thing, the record responds to Nebraska's (and amici's) medically based arguments. In respect to argument (3), for example, the District Court agreed that alternatives, such as D&E and induced labor, are "safe" but found that the D&X method was significantly *safer* in certain circumstances. 11 F.Supp.2d, at 1125–1126.

. . . .

4

[The Court concluded that "necessary to preserve the health of the mother" does not mean absolutely necessary. Because of the division of medical opinion and the chance that D&X could be a safer procedure, a health exception is necessary.]

B

. . . .

Nebraska does not deny that the statute imposes an "undue burden" if it applies to the more commonly used D&E procedure as well as to D&X. And we agree with the Eighth Circuit that it does so apply.

. . . .

The statute forbids "deliberately and intentionally delivering into the vagina a living unborn child, or a substantial portion thereof, for the purpose of performing a procedure that the person performing such procedure knows will kill the unborn child." We do not understand how one could distinguish, using this language, between D&E (where a foot or arm is drawn through the cervix) and D&X (where the body up to the head is drawn through the cervix). . . . Indeed D&E involves dismemberment that commonly occurs only when the fetus meets resistance that restricts the motion of the fetus: "The dismemberment occurs between the traction of . . . [the] instrument and the counter-traction of the internal os of the cervix." 11 F. Supp. 2d at 1128. And these events often do not occur until after a portion of a living fetus has been pulled into the vagina. Id. . . .

Even if the statute's basic aim is to ban D&X, its language makes clear that it also covers a much broader category of procedures. The language does not track the medical differences between D&E and D&X—though it would have been a simple matter, for example, to provide an exception for the performance of D&E and other abortion procedures. . . . Thus, the dissenters' argument that the law was generally intended to bar D&X can be both correct and irrelevant. The relevant question is *not* whether the legislature wanted to ban D&X; it is whether the law was intended to apply *only* to D&X. The plain language covers both procedures.

. . . .

In sum, using this law some present prosecutors and future Attorneys General may choose to pursue physicians who use D&E procedures, the most commonly used method for performing previability second trimester abortions. All those who perform abortion procedures using that method must fear prosecution, conviction, and imprisonment. The result is an undue burden upon a woman's right to make an abortion decision. We must consequently find the statute unconstitutional.

The judgment of the Court of Appeals is Affirmed.

Justice O'CONNOR, concurring.

. . . .

If Nebraska's statute limited its application to the D&X procedure and included an exception for the life and health of the mother, the question presented would be quite different than the one we face today. . . . If there were adequate alternative methods for a woman safely to obtain an abortion before viability, it is unlikely that prohibiting the D&X procedure alone would "amount in practical terms to a substantial obstacle to a woman seeking an abortion." 505 U.S. at 884. Thus, a ban on partial-birth abortion that only proscribed the D&X method of abortion and that included an exception to preserve the life and health of the mother would be constitutional in my view.

. . . .

Justice GINSBURG, with whom Justice STEVENS joins, concurring.

I write separately only to stress that amidst all the emotional uproar caused by an abortion case, we should not lose sight of the character of Nebraska's "partial birth abortion" law. As the Court observes, this law does not save any fetus from destruction, for it targets only "a *method* of performing abortion." Nor does the statute seek to protect the lives or health of pregnant women. Moreover, as Justice STEVENS points out (concurring opinion), the most common method of performing previability second trimester abortions is no less distressing or susceptible to gruesome description. Seventh Circuit Chief Judge Posner correspondingly observed, regarding similar bans in Wisconsin and Illinois, that the law prohibits the D&X procedure "not because the procedure kills the fetus, not because it risks worse complications for the woman than alternative procedures would do, not because it is a crueler or more painful or more disgusting method of terminating a pregnancy." Hope Clinic v. Ryan, 195 F.3d 857, 881 (CA7 1999) (dissenting opinion). Rather, Chief Judge Posner commented, the law prohibits the procedure because the State legislators seek to chip away at the private choice shielded by Roe v. Wade, even as modified by Casey. Id. at 880–82. . . . Again as stated by Chief Judge Posner, "if a statute burdens constitutional rights and all that can be said on its behalf is that it is the vehicle that legislators have chosen for expressing their hostility to those rights, the burden is undue." Id. at 881.

Justice SCALIA, dissenting.

I am optimistic enough to believe that, one day, Stenberg v. Carhart will be assigned its rightful place in the history of this Court's jurisprudence beside Korematsu and Dred

Scott. The method of killing a human child—one cannot even accurately say an entirely unborn human child—proscribed by this statute is so horrible that the most clinical description of it evokes a shudder of revulsion. And the Court must know (as most state legislatures banning this procedure have concluded) that demanding a "health exception"—which requires the abortionist to assure himself that, in his expert medical judgment, this method is, in the case at hand, marginally safer than others (how can one prove the contrary beyond a reasonable doubt?)—is to give live-birth abortion free rein. The notion that the Constitution . . . prohibits the States from simply banning this visibly brutal means of eliminating our half-born posterity is quite simply absurd.

. . . .

[M]y judgment that Casey does not support today's tragic result can be traced to the fact that what I consider to be an "undue burden" is different from what the majority considers to be an "undue burden"—a conclusion that can not be demonstrated true or false by factual inquiry or legal reasoning. It is a value judgment, dependent upon how much one respects (or believes society ought to respect) the life of a partially delivered fetus, and how much one respects (or believes society ought to respect) the freedom of the woman who gave it life to kill it. Evidently, the five Justices in today's majority value the former less, or the latter more, (or both), than the four of us in dissent. Case closed. There is no cause for anyone who believes in Casey to feel betrayed by this outcome. It has been arrived at by precisely the process Casey promised —a democratic vote by nine lawyers, not on the question whether the text of the Constitution has anything to say about this subject (it obviously does not); nor even on the question (also appropriate for lawyers) whether the legal traditions of the American people would have sustained such a limitation upon abortion (they obviously would); but upon the pure policy question whether this limitation upon abortion is "undue"—i.e., goes too far.

. . . .

And those who believe that a 5-to-4 vote on a policy matter by unelected lawyers should not overcome the judgment of 30 state legislatures have a problem, not with the *application* of Casey, but with its *existence*. Casey must be overruled.

. . . .

Justice KENNEDY, with whom the CHIEF JUSTICE joins, dissenting.

. . . .

Justice O'CONNOR assures the people of Nebraska they are free to redraft the law to include an exception permitting the D&X to be performed when "the procedure, in appropriate medical judgment, is necessary to preserve the health of the mother." Ante, at 5. The assurance is meaningless. She has joined an opinion which accepts that Dr. Carhart exercises "appropriate medical judgment" in using the D&X for every patient in every procedure, regardless of indications, after 15 weeks' gestation. Ante, at 18–19 (requiring any health exception to "tolerate responsible differences of medical opinion" which "are present here."). A ban which depends on the "appropriate medical judgment" of Dr. Carhart is no ban at all. He will be unaffected by any new legislation. This, of course, is the vice of a health exception resting in the physician's discretion. . . .

Chapter 17

Crossing the Line
The Political and Moral Battle over Late-Term Abortion

Rigel C. Oliveri

Introduction

. . . .

This Article will examine the proposed legislation, lobbying, and debate surrounding "partial birth abortion," and the representational difficulties faced by opponents of the [federal statute banning it]. . . .

The History of the Ban

The first version of the legislation, House Resolution 1833, was introduced in the House on June 14, 1995[,] . . . with an incredible 162 cosponsors. HR 1833 imposed both criminal and civil penalties on doctors who performed a procedure defined as: "an abortion in which the person performing the abortion partially vaginally delivers a living fetus before killing the fetus and completing the delivery." Doctors convicted under the proposed law would face a fine and up to two years in prison. The father of a fetus aborted through the D&X procedure, as well as the parents of a woman under the age of eighteen, would have a civil cause of action against the doctor, enabling them to claim damages for psychological injury and additional monetary damages of up to three times the cost of the procedure.

. . . .

The "Partial Birth Abortion Ban of 1996" [HR 1833] . . . was vetoed by President Clinton on April 10, 1996. In his veto message, Clinton expressed his disappointment with Congress' refusal to include a maternal health exception. . . . The House overrode the veto on September 19, 1996. However, a few days later the Senate's override attempt failed by a margin of thirteen votes. For the time being, the fight appeared to be over, but the issue was far from settled. . . . As a result [of a controversy over whether opponents of the act had underrepresented the frequency of and reasons for the abortion

Rigel C. Oliveri, "Crossing the Line: The Political and Moral Battle over Late-Term Abortion," 10 YALE J.L. & FEMINISM 397 (1998).

procedures at issue,] the Ban was revitalized on January 21, 1997. . . . President Clinton vetoed House Resolution 1122 on October 10, 1997.*

. . . .

A Note on Terminology

. . . .

The procedure at the center of this controversy is known by several different medical terms, including "intact dilation and evacuation," "dilation and extraction," and "intrauterine cranial decompression." "Partial-birth abortion" is the term coined by the congressional proponents of the Ban. This is neither an accepted medical nor legal term, and is not used by abortion practitioners or the medical community at large. Rather, as I will discuss later, this term was purposefully created to be both inflammatory and misleading. I will refer to the procedure by the more-accepted medical term "dilation and extraction" ("D&X"). The D&X procedure is used in the second and third trimesters of pregnancy, from 18 to 32 weeks of gestation. The woman's cervix is partially dilated, enabling the doctor to move the fetus into the birth canal. At this stage of pregnancy, the fetus' head is usually too large to be removed from the uterus without inducing full-blown labor. In order to remove it, the doctor may have to collapse the fetus' skull. This is usually accomplished by creating a puncture at the base of the fetus' skull, either with scissors or a scalpel, and suctioning out the brain and/or skull contents with a vacuum aspirator. The fetus is then removed, largely intact, and the umbilical cord is cut.

The procedure is essentially the same regardless of when in the pregnancy it is performed. However, the timing of the procedure relative to fetal viability is of great moral and legal significance. Therefore, when I refer to the D&X procedure I will clarify whether it is a "pre-viability" or "post-viability" D&X. . . . [C]urrent medical technology places viability as early as 23 to 24 weeks of gestation. It is important to note that viability varies from case to case; one fetus may be viable at 25 weeks and another may not. . . .

[T]here are several ways that a woman's health can be jeopardized by a problem pregnancy, leading a woman to seek an abortion. The pregnancy itself may be dangerous to the woman's health, even if she is otherwise healthy, particularly if the fetus is severely deformed. Fetal death, seizures, stiffening, or malformation place the mother at risk of a variety of complications, including severe hemorrhaging, . . . ruptured uterus, and blood poisoning and shock. . . . Also, the treatments of some life-threatening ailments, such as chemotherapy for cancer or intensive drug therapy for HIV, may be incompatible with pregnancy. . . .

Two Versions of the Truth

Disagreement and the Truth

During the lobbying period and the congressional debates, anti-Ban activists insisted that the procedure was rarely performed. They estimated the number of D&X

---

* *Editor's note*: Congress ultimately repassed the Act, with nearly identical language to that used in 1997, and President George W. Bush signed it into law.

abortions performed each year as between 450 and 600 nationwide. Meanwhile, pro-Ban activists produced their own statistics, including estimates from doctors and clinics who perform the procedure, . . . indicating that the annual number of D&X abortions performed nationwide was between 3,000 and 5,000. . . . [A]nti-Ban activists seemed to argue that the D&X procedure is only performed when there are serious fetal defects or other severe risks to maternal health. Bill proponents, on the other hand, had evidence that the vast majority—between 80 and 90%—of D&X abortions are performed for purely elective reasons or for minor health indications.

While it seemed impossible to reconcile the two sets of information, in fact a simple explanation could account for both. It is probably true, as the pro-Ban activists argued, that between 3,000 and 5,000 D&X abortions are performed each year. However, it is also probably true that of these, only between 450 and 600 (roughly 10–20%) are performed after fetal viability. Likewise, it is probably true that between 80 and 90% of all D&X abortions are performed on an elective basis. But, as the anti-Ban forces argued, 100% of post-viability D&X abortions were performed because of serious fetal abnormalities and maternal health endangerment. Thus, both sets of data were accurate but based on different classifications of the measured group. Seekers of the "truth" would discover that finding the answer wasn't as simple as picking a side; instead, a true understanding of D&X abortions would only come from understanding who the relevant groups of women were and why they were classified in different ways.

Reasons for the Confusion

This disparity came about for several reasons. . . . But the deeper explanation of how these two different pictures developed can be found within the framework of the debate itself. The Ban's proponents combined information about the pre- and post-viability procedures to create the most damaging possible scenario. Their rhetoric centered around post-viability abortions, describing healthy fully-formed fetuses who they claimed were mere inches from being born infants. However, they used pre-viability data about the numbers of, and reasons for, the procedure—claiming that thousands were performed each year for elective reasons. As a result, they painted a completely inaccurate picture of an America in which tens of thousands of elective abortions are performed on healthy fetuses during the final weeks of pregnancy. This type of confusion, deliberate or not, was extremely common during the floor debates in Congress, in articles written by proponents of the Ban, and in the pro-Ban lobbying materials. . . .

The anti-Ban forces responded to the mixed data by focusing solely on post-viability abortions. Narrowing the issue allowed them to refute the arguments that the procedure was used on fetuses that were both healthy and near-term. The Ban's opponents instead were able to focus on the severe maternal and health indications that many of the Ban's supporters minimized. . . .

When they discussed the numbers of and reasons for the procedure, the anti-Ban activists used accurate information but only for the third-trimester. They could claim in all truthfulness that the procedure was only done for severe health reasons, and that only 450–600 D&X abortions were performed per year if they limited their discussion to post-viability abortions. They correctly characterized the post-viability scenario but completely ignored the numbers of and reasons for pre-viability D&X abortions. Consequently, both sides presented their data deceptively. Pro-Ban activists presented more complete information but did so in a confusing and inaccurate way. In responding, anti-Ban activists presented a partially-accurate but incomplete set of data. Even though both sides are to blame for the dissemination of inaccurate and incomplete information and for the confusion that resulted in the debate over HR 1833, the resulting furor unquestionably harmed the anti-Ban forces more than their opponents.

Critique of the Anti-Ban Strategy

. . . .

Negative

Despite the beneficial aspects of the focus on Group 1 [those who received medically necessary, post-viability D&X abortions], the strategy proved ultimately to be harmful to the anti-Ban cause and may have negative implications for the broader abortion rights movement. Tactically, the strategy's backfire resulted in a terrible public relations and legislative backlash. From a broader representational perspective, the contest over the Ban highlighted the fact that a significant number of women are being ignored by the movement which purports to speak for their interests.

TACTICAL DISADVANTAGES

By failing to explain their statistics adequately, the anti-Ban forces gave the appearance that they were hiding something. . . . The appearance of deception made them appear as the pro-Ban side portrayed them: callous, cold and manipulative, unwilling to accept the reality of their positions. Their attempts to clarify the terms and methods supporting their arguments came only after the furor had erupted and were viewed by many as an attempt to cover up their deceit. . . .

REPRESENTATIONAL DISADVANTAGES

While the immediate fallout from the statistics scandal damaged the anti-Ban activists' credibility, their choice of tactics may have indicated and re-enforced deeper representational problems within the broader pro-choice community. The whole controversy boiled down to the fact that the anti-Ban forces had attempted to minimize (or deny) the existence of thousands of women whose interests were directly implicated in the D&X debate. Women in Group 2 [those who received pre-viability, elective D&X abortions] make up roughly nine-tenths of the approximately 4,000 women who seek the procedure each year. That a powerful coalition of abortion-rights lobbyists and representatives of abortion providers should deliberately ignore such a big segment of a group whose interests they were purportedly representing indicates that the pro-choice movement may be uncertain about how—or whether—to represent these women.

That the anti-Ban lobbyists failed to represent Group 2 in the contest over HR 1833 is clear. The oft-repeated D&X narrative was in fact the "medically necessary post-viability termination of a wanted pregnancy" narrative. The "elective D&X abortion of a pre-viable fetus" narrative was never told. No one sought to identify or interview women from Group 2 to assist in the lobbying efforts. The women of Group 2 were not asked to testify before congressional committees or brought around to meet members of Congress for one-on-one lobbying sessions. Their stories were never circulated in anti-Ban fact sheets or press releases. Their numbers, purposely left out of the totals compiled by the anti-Ban statistics gatherers, surfaced later as an embarrassment to be explained away.[1] Despite the fact that the women of Group 2 outnumber the women of Group 1 ten to one, the anti-Ban forces scarcely acknowledged their existence, even as Ban proponents were touting the statistics that proved it.

Although they may have felt backed into a rhetorical corner, the truth is that anti-Ban activists were not "forced" into the representational strategy they pursued. . . . Indeed, the pro-choice movement as a whole seems to have a blind spot when it comes to women who have second-term, pre-viability, elective abortions—D&X or otherwise. These women occupy a netherworld between the millions of women who undergo brief elective abortions at around 6–8 weeks gestation and the handful of women who have three-day-long post-viability abortions under the most tragic of circumstances. They are women who have, frustratingly, waited until the latest stage of pregnancy in which it is possible to legally obtain an elective abortion. Pro-choice advocates seldom talk to or about these women; often the very reasons that they wait so long to have abortions—youth, ignorance, trauma, poverty—make them both unlikely participants in the organized pro-choice movement and unattractive "faces" to put on it. While there are a variety of explanations for their behavior (detailed further below), and despite the fact that Supreme Court precedent protects the right to elective abortions at any point prior to viability, the women of Group 2 have become the pro-choice movement's "dirty little secret."[2]

Problems of Non-Representation: Reinforcement. The "invisibility" of the women in Group 2—to the anti-Ban activists, the pro-choice movement, and society as a whole —. . . means that women in Group 2 are conceptually isolated from and played against the women of Group 1 in a manner that reinforces traditional attitudes about abortion and the role of women in society.

Practical Issues: The Need for a Voice in Politics and Beyond. The anti-Ban activists' failure to acknowledge the women of Group 2 effectively "disenfranchised" them. Because the anti-Ban activists conducted their research, lobbying, and public relations as though Group 2 did not exist, they may be forced to disregard the group's interests in later political contests. The most obvious "worst-case" scenario would be if a maternal health exception were added to the Ban, eliminating the threat of a Presidential veto. This would give the women of Group 1—all of whom require post-viability abortions because of severe health risks—access to the D&X procedure. But the women of Group 2, who for the most part do not suffer from severe health risks, would be denied such access and so would be left worse off than before. By setting up the lack of a maternal health exception as the sole stumbling block for the legislation, anti-Ban advocates presented their foes with a powerful opportunity to limit abortion access for the much larger group of women who would be unable to claim the exception. . . . [S]hould [anti-Ban forces] achieve the "victory" of a maternal health exception, . . . it is difficult to imagine that the activists would have any success [if they then began to argue] that women with *no* health indications should be allowed access to the procedure under a kind of "pre-viability exception." . . .

It is important to note at this point that, while such a shift in argument may be unacceptable to politicians or the American public, [prior federal court decisions, such as *Women's Medical Professional Corp. v. Voinovich* and *Planned Parenthood of Missouri v. Danforth,* indicate that] courts are likely to protect the rights of women to choose the safest available method of abortion and to obtain elective pre-viability abortions in the second trimester. This prediction is based on how federal courts have ruled on state prohibitions of specific abortion methods as well as more general restrictions on second-trimester abortions. . . .

Possible judicial protection notwithstanding, the representative gap is important because it has had negative consequences beyond the struggle over the Ban. Few attempts have been made to determine who the members of Group 2 are and why they wait so long to have abortions. . . ." Instead of brushing those second-trimester abortions to the side," one critic recognized, "we should talk about the women who have them and why they have them so late."[3] . . . Evidence from a variety of sources indicates that many of these women are vulnerable due to their age and/or lack of resources, and delay abortion, not because of apathy but because of the inability to recognize pregnancy and difficulty arranging and paying for the abortion.

For example, many of the women in Group 2 delay abortion because they are extremely young and are likely either to have irregular menstrual cycles that make it difficult to recognize pregnancy, or to be uneducated and inexperienced in recognizing the signs of pregnancy. In addition, teenagers, especially the very young, are more likely to experience confusion, fear, and denial over an unwanted pregnancy than adult women. Dr. James McMahon, a practitioner who used the D&X method, stated that, "if there is any . . . single factor that inflates the number of late abortions, it is youth. Often, teenagers don't recognize the first signs of pregnancy."[4] In 1981, forty-three percent of abortions after twenty weeks were performed for minors, as compared to twenty-eight percent of all abortions.[5] For girls fourteen and under, the proportion of late abortions is almost four times the national average.[6] In fact, nearly one in four abortions performed on girls below the age of fifteen are performed in the second trimester.[7] Joyce Strauss, a clinic administrator in Los Angeles, explains that "the doctor does abortions up to 26 weeks because he does not feel he can turn a 12 . . . year-old away and send her to be a mother."[8]

Parental consent laws have also had the unintended effect of causing many minors to delay abortion until the second trimester. Sixty-three percent of minors surveyed said that difficulty notifying and obtaining consent from their parents caused them to delay until after sixteen weeks. . . . [9] While most of these states have judicial bypass provisions, the process of going to court and obtaining the consent of a judge also leads to delays.

Other women in Group 2 may not have had the money on hand to pay for an earlier abortion or the means to travel promptly to an abortion clinic. In one 1988 survey of women obtaining abortions after sixteen weeks, fifty percent of the participants indicated that they delayed abortion in part because it was difficult for them to make arrangements.[10] Sixty percent of this group said that problems coming up with the money for an abortion lead [sic] to the delay. . . . [11] It is estimated that twenty-two percent of women having second-trimester abortions would have had them in the first trimester if funding had been available.[12] A clinic administrator for a Manhattan abortion clinic declares bluntly, "This is a poverty issue. Don't let anybody tell you any different. . . ."[13]

Other women may lack the means to travel to an abortion clinic. In the 1988 survey, over half of the women who indicated problems making arrangements (twenty-six percent of the total surveyed) said that difficulties getting to an abortion clinic had lead [sic] to the delay.[14] . . . Other demographic factors associated with late abortion are race and level of education. Nonwhite women are significantly more likely than their white counterparts to have second-trimester abortions.[15] . . .

Thus, while it is true that a woman can legally receive a second-trimester pre-viability abortion for purely elective reasons, the evidence indicates that the women and girls getting these abortions are likely to have compelling physical, mental, emotional, economic and other reasons for seeking them so late. . . . Dr. David Grimes, a leading expert on late term abortion, sums up this situation, saying "although these late abortions are infrequent, they are terribly important, because the women who need them need them desperately."[16] . . . Indeed, the fact that some of the very young women in Group 2 were even having sex at all is cause for concern. . . . As long as the women of Group 2 remain invisible, they will continue to experience unwanted pregnancies and to seek late abortions, their powerlessness becoming more entrenched. . . .

Theoretical Issues: Dichotomy and the Status Quo. Rather than enjoying any meaningful inclusion in the D&X narrative, Group 2 served merely as the necessary implicit foil for Group 1 in defining who should have access to the D&X procedure, and why. The anti-Ban forces set up the women in Group 1 as deserving of access to the D&X procedure because they are everything that the women in Group 2 are not. The plea made by one congresswoman during the debates was typical: "The women involved are older, they are married, the pregnancies are wanted, planned for, joyously anticipated. . . ."[17] . . . The sense from the stories and descriptions of the women in Group 1 was that they were all "good women" who were forced to make "bad" choices by a set of terrible circumstances. . . .

The implied converse of these arguments . . . is that a woman with an unwanted pregnancy who seeks to terminate it for elective reasons does not deserve access to a second-trimester abortion. . . . By seeming to condition access to late-term abortion on severity of circumstances, anti-Ban forces may have unwittingly bought into the pro-Ban arguments that an abortion performed for any other than life-threatening health problems is unjustified. . . .

In setting up a dichotomy between groups of women, the anti-Ban activists may have inadvertently played into the same sets of assumptions and stereotypes that limit women's reproductive options and confine their roles within society as a whole. First, this approach sets women against one another in a competition for social, medical, and legislative resources. Such a "contest" only makes sense against a backdrop in which abortion is a limited commodity. . . .

The statements of Ellen Goodman, a pro-choice columnist, illustrate this danger. She muses that, "if I could make a trade-off that would limit late second-trimester abortions for healthy women with healthy fetuses in return for freely and widely available abortion in the first trimester, I would be sorely tempted."[18] . . .

Second, the weighing of moral worthiness places all of the focus on the character of the women themselves. This diverts attention from other important pieces of the abortion puzzle, such as the institutional and social barriers that make raising a child as a single parent so difficult, the persistent lack of access to reliable birth control technology, and the ridiculously high rate of unwanted pregnancy in the United States. . . .

Problems Underlying Non-Representation: Moral Uncertainty. The problems the anti-Ban activists encountered in representing the full range of women who undergo D&X abortions bespeak a deeper tension within the pro-choice movement. . . . Supporters of abortion rights believe in a woman's right to choose, but most also hope that the woman herself will exercise this right with the circumspection and deference that such a serious decision warrants. . . .

The focus on Group 1 gave the anti-Ban activists a way out. It enabled them to argue against the Ban without having to delve into the more complicated territory of elective second trimester abortions. . . .

However, assigning culpability is not the mission of the pro-choice movement. The movement seeks to guarantee reproductive freedom to all women, regardless of who they are and what the circumstances surrounding their decision might be. Indeed, one of the underlying principles of the abortion rights movement is that the reproductive decisions are intensely personal, and that women seeking abortions should have the freedom to do so without having their lives, morals, and motives scrutinized by doctors, legislators, or the public. . . .

In order for the right to abortion to remain meaningful, it must exist for all women. . . . First Amendment rights are guaranteed to all precisely because the selective protection of individuals would distort the very purpose of the right to freedom of expression no matter who the expressor is and what he is saying. Similarly, women who seek Constitutionally-permitted abortions must be free to do so no matter who they are and why they want one. . . . As one abortion rights supporter argues, "we need to defend women's freedom to choose when and if to become mothers—not just the right of women to choose abortion over serious injury or death."[19] . . .

Still, the pro-choice movement is left in an admittedly uncomfortable situation. . . . When pro-choice people critically assess their own positions, they open themselves up for a flood of opportunistic pro-life criticism. . . .

Perhaps the best solution would be for anti-Ban advocates and the broader pro-choice movement to admit that pre-viability late term abortions are tragic choices. . . . [A]ctivists will have to change the focus. They will have to start talking more about improved education and health care to decrease the number of women and girls who delay abortion because of ignorance, poverty, or lack of health facilities. They could start focusing on the disturbingly young age of many of the girls who are seeking D&X abortions, emphasizing that it is not just the fact that these girls are pregnant or seeking abortions that is a social problem, but the fact that they are having sex in the first place. And they might try to highlight the lack of options that such women face should they carry their babies to term, and their improved prospects should they delay childbearing until they are ready. As one scholar argues, "that individuals do not determine the social framework in which they act does not nullify their choices nor their moral capacity to make them. It only suggests that we have to focus less on 'choice' and more on how to transform the social conditions of choosing."[20] Anti-Ban activists can recognize elective late term abortions as the tragedies that they are, while simultaneously focusing on the backdrop of youth and poverty in which they occur. "Those circumstances," argues one commentator, "are the real abortion scandal."[21]

. . . .

NOTES

1. Renee Chelian, the president of the National Coalition of Abortion Providers and a member of the National Abortion Federation, stated, "I got caught up: What do we do about this secret? Who do we tell and what happens when we tell?" Ruth Padawer, "Pro-Choice Advocates Admit to Deception," The Record, Feb. 27, 1997.

2. Ron Fitzsimmons described this deception as making him feel like "a dirty little abortionist with a dirty little secret." Diane M. Gianelli, "Abortion Rights Leader Urges End to 'Half Truths,'" Am. Med. News, Mar. 3, 1997, at 3.

3. Katha Pollitt, "Secrets and Lies," The Nation, Mar. 31, 1997, at 9 ("The big anti-choice lie was obscured by the consistent merging of third-trimester abortions . . . with second-trimester abortions . . . as in live-baby-who-could-survive-if-not-murdered-by-doctor, and also as in, Gross!").

4. Dr. James McMahon, quoted in Karen Tumulty, "Abortions of Last Resort," L.A. Times Mag., Jan. 7, 1990. But see David A. Grimes, "Second-Trimester Abortions in the United States," 16 Fam. Plan. Persp. 260, 262 (1984) (arguing that a history of irregular menses is the most important determinant of delay).

5. See United States Centers for Disease Control, Abortion Surveillance 1981, 37, tbl. 14 (Nov. 1985).

6. See id.

7. See Grimes, supra note 4, at 260.

8. Quoted in Tumulty, supra note 4. Strauss describes bringing coloring books and teddy bears to the clinic for 10- and 11-year old girls having second-trimester abortions because of sexual abuse. See id.

9. See Aida Torres & Jacqueline Darroch Forrest, "Why Do Women Have Abortions?," 20 Fam. Plan. Persp. 169, 174–75, (July–Aug. 1988).

10. See id. at 174.

11. See id.

12. See AGI, Facts in Brief: Abortion in the United States 2 (1995).

13. Anne Walshe, quoted in Tumulty, supra note 4.

14. See Torres & Forrest, supra note 9, at 175.

15. See Laurie Nsiah-Jefferson, "Reproductive Laws, Women of Color, and Low-Income Women," in REPROD. LAWS FOR THE 1990s 23, 25 (Sherrill Cohen & Nadine Taub eds., 1989).

16. Quoted in Tumulty, supra note 4.

17. 141 Cong. Rec. H11604–01, H11614 (1995) (statement of Rep. Rivers).

18. Ellen Goodman, "Abortion Spin-Cycle Is Nonstop," Dayton Daily News, Mar. 8, 1997, at A13.

19. Pollitt, supra note 3.

20. Rosalind Petchesky, Abortion and Woman's Choice: The State, Sexuality, and Reproductive Freedom 4 (rev. ed. 1990).

21. Pollitt, supra note 3.

Chapter 18

Gonzales v. Carhart

Justice KENNEDY delivered the opinion of the Court.

These cases require us to consider the validity of the Partial-Birth Abortion Ban Act of 2003(Act), 18 U.S.C. §1531 (2000 ed., Supp. IV), a federal statute regulating abortion procedures.... We conclude the Act should be sustained ...
. . . .

I

A

. . . .

The surgical procedure referred to as "dilation and evacuation" or "D&E" is the usual abortion method in [the second] trimester.... [A variation of this standard procedure] was the impetus for the numerous bans on "partial-birth abortion," including [this] Act....

B

. . . .

The Act responded to *Stenberg* in two ways. First, Congress made factual findings. ... Congress found, among other things, that "[a] moral, medical, and ethical consensus exists that the practice of performing a partial-birth abortion ... is a gruesome and inhumane procedure that is never medically necessary and should be prohibited." 18 U.S.C. §1531 (2000 ed., Supp.IV), at 767, ¶ (1).... Second, and more relevant here, the Act's language differs from that of the Nebraska statute struck down in *Stenberg*. ... The operative provisions of the Act provide in relevant part:

(a) Any physician who, in or affecting interstate or foreign commerce, knowingly performs a partial-birth abortion and thereby kills a human fetus shall be fined under this title or imprisoned not more than 2 years, or both. This subsection does not apply to a partial-birth abortion that is necessary to save the life of a mother whose life is endangered by a physical disorder, physical illness, or physical injury, including a life-endangering physical condition caused by or arising from the pregnancy itself....
(b) As used in this section—

Gonzales v. Carhart, No. 05-38 0 (slip opinion) (2007).

(1) the term 'partial-birth abortion' means an abortion in which the person performing the abortion—

(A) deliberately and intentionally vaginally delivers a living fetus until, in the case of a head-first presentation, the entire fetal head is outside the body of the mother, or, in the case of breech presentation, any part of the fetal trunk past the navel is outside the body of the mother, for the purpose of performing an overt act that the person knows will kill the partially delivered living fetus; and

(B) performs the overt act, other than completion of delivery, that kills the partially delivered living fetus;

. . . .

(e) A woman upon whom a partial-birth abortion is performed may not be prosecuted under this section, for a conspiracy to violate this section, or for an offense under section 2, 3, or 4 of this title based on a violation of this section." 18 U.S.C. §1531 (2000 ed., Supp. IV).

The Act also includes a provision authorizing civil actions that is not of relevance here.
. . . .

II

We assume the following principles for the purposes of this opinion. Before viability, a State "may not prohibit any woman from making the ultimate decision to terminate her pregnancy." *Planned Parenthood of Southeastern Pa. v. Casey*, 505 U.S. 833, 879 (1992) (plurality opinion). It also may not impose upon this right an undue burden . . . On the other hand, "[r]egulations which do no more than create a structural mechanism by which the State, or the parent or guardian of a minor, may express profound respect for the life of the unborn are permitted, if they are not a substantial obstacle to the woman's exercise of the right to choose." *Id.*, at 877, 112 S.Ct. 2791. *Casey*, in short, struck a balance. The balance was central to its holding. We now apply its standard to the cases at bar.

III

. . . .

[T]he Act . . . regulates and proscribes, with exceptions or qualifications to be discussed, performing the intact D & E procedure. . . . We conclude that the Act is not void for vagueness, does not impose an undue burden from any overbreadth, and is not invalid on its face.

A

. . . .

First, the . . . Act . . . is inapplicable to abortions that do not involve vaginal delivery (for instance, hysterotomy or hysterectomy). The Act does apply both previability and postviability because, by common understanding and scientific terminology, a fetus is a living organism while within the womb, whether or not it is viable outside the womb.

. . . .

B

Respondents contend the language [of the statute] is indeterminate, and they thus argue the Act is unconstitutionally vague on its face. . . . Unlike the statutory language in *Stenberg* that prohibited the delivery of a " 'substantial portion' " of the fetus —where a doctor might question how much of the fetus is a substantial portion— the Act defines the line between potentially criminal conduct on the one hand and lawful abortion on the other. . . . Doctors performing D & E will know that if they do not deliver a living fetus to an anatomical landmark they will not face criminal liability.

. . . .

This conclusion is buttressed by the intent that must be proved to impose liability. The Court has made clear that scienter requirements alleviate vagueness concerns. . . . [A] doctor performing a D&E will not face criminal liability if he or she delivers a fetus beyond the prohibited point by mistake . . . Respondents have likewise failed to show that the Act should be invalidated . . . because it encourages arbitrary or discriminatory enforcement. [The Act's requirements] provide doctors with objective standards . . . and limit prosecutorial discretion. . . .

C

We next determine whether the Act imposes an undue burden, as a facial matter, because its restrictions on second-trimester abortions are too broad. . . .

1

. . . .

The Act excludes most D & Es in which the fetus is removed in pieces, not intact. If the doctor intends to remove the fetus in parts from the outset, the doctor will not have the requisite intent to incur criminal liability. A doctor performing a standard D & E procedure can often "tak[e] about 10–15 'passes' through the uterus to remove the entire fetus." *Planned Parenthood*, 320 F.Supp.2d, at 962. Removing the fetus in this manner does not violate the Act because the doctor will not have delivered the living fetus to one of the anatomical landmarks or committed an additional overt act that kills the fetus after partial delivery. . . .

A comparison of the Act with the Nebraska statute . . . confirms this point. The statute in *Stenberg* prohibited " 'deliberately and intentionally delivering into the vagina a living unborn child, or a substantial portion thereof . . .' " . . . The Court concluded that this statute encompassed D & E because "D & E will often involve a physician pulling a 'substantial portion' of a still living fetus, say, an arm or leg, into the vagina prior to the death of the fetus." 530 U.S. at 939. . . . D & E does not involve the delivery of a fetus because it requires the removal of fetal parts that are ripped from the fetus as

they are pulled through the cervix. . . . Interpreting the Act so that it does not prohibit standard D & E is the most reasonable reading and understanding of its terms.
. . . .

IV

. . . .

The abortions affected by the Act's regulations take place both previability and postviability . . . The question is whether the Act . . . imposes a substantial obstacle to late-term, but previability, abortions. The Act does not on its face impose a substantial obstacle . . .

A

. . . .

[The fact that] the State, from the inception of the pregnancy, maintains its own regulatory interest in protecting the life of the fetus that may become a child, cannot be set at naught by interpreting *Casey's* requirement of a health exception so it becomes tantamount to allowing a doctor to choose the abortion method he or she might prefer. Where it has a rational basis to act, and it does not impose an undue burden, the State may use its regulatory power to bar certain procedures and substitute others, all in furtherance of its legitimate interests in regulating the medical profession in order to promote respect for life, including life of the unborn.
. . . .

While we find no reliable data to measure the phenomenon, it seems unexceptionable to conclude some women come to regret their choice to abort the infant life they once created and sustained. . . . In a decision so fraught with emotional consequence some doctors may prefer not to disclose precise details of the means that will be used, confining themselves to the required statement of risks the procedure entails. . . . The State has an interest in ensuring so grave a choice is well informed. It is self-evident that a mother who comes to regret her choice to abort must struggle with grief more anguished and sorrow more profound when she learns, only after the event, what she once did not know: that she allowed a doctor to pierce the skull and vacuum the fast-developing brain of her unborn child, a child assuming the human form.

It is a reasonable inference that a necessary effect of the regulation and the knowledge it conveys will be to encourage some women to carry the infant to full term, thus reducing the absolute number of late-term abortions. . . . In sum, we reject the contention that the congressional purpose of the Act was "to place a substantial obstacle in the path of a woman seeking an abortion."

B

. . . .

[T]the next question is] . . . whether the Act has the effect of imposing an unconstitutional burden on the abortion right because it does not allow use of the barred procedure where "'necessary, in appropriate medical judgment, for [the] preservation of the . . . health of the mother.'" *Ayotte [v. Planned Parenthood of Northern New Eng.,* 546 U.S. 320], 327–8 (quoting *Casey, supra,* at 879 (plurality opinion)). . . .

Respondents presented evidence that intact D & E may be the safest method of abortion. . . . There is documented medical disagreement whether the Act's prohibition would ever impose significant health risks on women. . . . The question becomes whether the Act can stand when this medical uncertainty persists. . . . The Court has given state and federal legislatures wide discretion to pass legislation in areas where there is medical and scientific uncertainty. . . . [That uncertainty] . . . provides a sufficient basis to conclude in this facial attack that the Act does not impose an undue burden.

The conclusion that the Act does not impose an undue burden is supported by other considerations. Alternatives are available to the prohibited procedure. As we have noted, the Act does not proscribe D & E. . . . In addition the Act's prohibition only applies to the delivery of "a living fetus." 18 U.S.C. §1531(b)(1)(A) (2000 ed., Supp. IV). If the intact D & E procedure is truly necessary in some circumstances, it appears likely an injection that kills the fetus is an alternative under the Act that allows the doctor to perform the procedure.

. . . .

In reaching the conclusion the Act does not require a health exception we reject certain arguments made by the parties on both sides of these cases. On the one hand, the Attorney General urges us to uphold the Act on the basis of the congressional findings alone. . . . The Court retains an independent constitutional duty to review factual findings where constitutional rights are at stake. . . . On the other hand, relying on the Court's opinion in *Stenberg,* respondents contend that an abortion regulation must contain a health exception "if 'substantial medical authority supports the proposition that banning a particular procedure could endanger women's health.'" Brief for Respondents in No. 05-380, p. 19 (quoting 530 U.S., at 938, 120 S.Ct. 2597) . . . This is too exacting a standard to impose on the legislative power. . . . Considerations of marginal safety, including the balance of risks, are within the legislative competence when the regulation is rational and in pursuit of legitimate ends. When standard medical options are available, mere convenience does not suffice to displace them; and if some procedures have different risks than others, it does not follow that the State is altogether barred from imposing reasonable regulations. The Act is not invalid on its face where there is uncertainty over whether the barred procedure is ever necessary to preserve a woman's health, given the availability of other abortion procedures that are considered to be safe alternatives.

Justice GINSBURG, with whom Justice STEVENS, Justice SOUTER, and Justice BREYER join, dissenting.

. . . .

Today's decision is alarming. It refuses to take *Casey* and *Stenberg* seriously. It tolerates, indeed applauds, federal intervention to ban nationwide a procedure found necessary and proper in certain cases by the American College of Obstetricians and Gynecologists (ACOG). It blurs the line, firmly drawn in *Casey,* between previability and postviability abortions. And, for the first time since *Roe,* the Court blesses a prohibition with no exception safeguarding a woman's health.

. . . .

I

A

As *Casey* comprehended, at stake in cases challenging abortion restrictions is a woman's "control over her [own] destiny. . . ." 505. U.S. at 869 (plurality opinion). . . . Women, it is now acknowledged, have the talent, capacity, and right "to participate equally in the economic and social life of the Nation." *Id.,* at 856. . . . Their ability to realize their full potential, the Court recognized, is intimately connected to "their ability to control their reproductive lives." *Ibid.* Thus, legal challenges to undue restrictions on abortion procedures do not seek to vindicate some generalized notion of privacy; rather, they center on a woman's autonomy to determine her life's course, and thus to enjoy equal citizenship stature.

. . . .

We have . . . ruled that a State must avoid subjecting women to health risks not only where the pregnancy itself creates danger, but also where state regulation forces women to resort to less safe methods of abortion. See *Planned Parenthood of Central Mo. v. Danforth,* 428 U.S. 52, 79, 96 S.Ct. 2831, 49 L.Ed.2d 788 (1976) (holding unconstitutional a ban on a method of abortion that "force[d] a woman . . . to terminate her pregnancy by methods more dangerous to her health"). . . . In *Stenberg,* we expressly held that a statute banning intact D & E was unconstitutional in part because it lacked a health exception. . . . We explained [that] . . . division in medical opinion "at most means uncertainty, a factor that signals the presence of risk, not its absence." [*Stenberg,* 530 U.S. at 937.]

. . . .

C

. . . .

During the District Court trials [involving this Act], "numerous" "extraordinarily accomplished" and "very experienced" medical experts explained that, in certain circumstances and for certain women, intact D & E is safer than alternative procedures and necessary to protect women's health. . . . According to the expert testimony plaintiffs introduced, the safety advantages of intact D & E are marked for women with certain medical conditions, for example, uterine scarring, bleeding disorders, heart disease, or compromised immune systems . . . , for women with certain pregnancy-related conditions, such as placenta previa and accreta, and for women carrying fetuses with certain abnormalities, such as severe hydrocephalus.

. . . .

[E]ach of the District Courts to consider the issue rejected Congress' findings as unreasonable and not supported by the evidence. . . . The District Courts' findings merit this Court's respect. . . .

. . . .

II

A

. . . .

Delivery of an intact, albeit nonviable, fetus warrants special condemnation, the Court maintains, because a fetus that is not dismembered resembles an infant. But so, too, does a fetus delivered intact after it is terminated by injection a day or two before the surgical evacuation, . . . or a fetus delivered through medical induction or cesarean. . . . Yet, the availability of those procedures—along with D & E by dismemberment—the Court says, saves the ban on intact D & E from a declaration of unconstitutionality. Never mind that the procedures deemed acceptable might put a woman's health at greater risk.

. . . .

Notably, the concerns expressed are untethered to any ground genuinely serving the Government's interest in preserving life. . . . Revealing in this regard, the Court invokes an antiabortion shibboleth for which it concededly has no reliable evidence: Women who have abortions come to regret their choices, and consequently suffer from "[s]evere depression and loss of esteem."[1] . . . The solution the Court approves, then, is *not* to require doctors to inform women, accurately and adequately, of the different procedures and their attendant risks. . . . Instead, the Court deprives women of the right to make an autonomous choice, even at the expense of their safety.

This way of thinking reflects ancient notions about women's place in the family and under the Constitution—ideas that have long since been discredited. . . .

B

In cases on a "woman's liberty to determine whether to [continue] her pregnancy," this Court has identified viability as a critical consideration. See *Casey,* 505 U.S., at 869–870, 112 S.Ct. 2791 (plurality opinion). . . . Today, the Court blurs that line . . . Instead of drawing the line at viability, the Court refers to Congress' purpose to differentiate "abortion and infanticide" based not on whether a fetus can survive outside the womb, but on where a fetus is anatomically located when a particular medical procedure is performed.

. . . .

The Court's hostility to the right *Roe* and *Casey* secured is not concealed. Throughout, the opinion refers to obstetrician-gynecologists and surgeons who perform abortions not by the titles of their medical specialties, but by the pejorative label "abortion doctor." . . . A fetus is described as an "unborn child," and as a "baby," . . . ; second-trimester, previability abortions are referred to as "late-term," . . . ; and the reasoned medical judgments of highly trained doctors are dismissed as "preferences" motivated by "mere convenience" . . . Instead of the heightened scrutiny we have previously applied, the Court determines that a "rational" ground is enough to uphold the Act. . . . And, most troubling, *Casey's* principles, confirming the continuing vitality of "the essential holding of *Roe,*" are merely "assume[d]" for the moment, . . . rather than "retained" or "reaffirmed." *Casey,* 505 U.S., at 846, 112 S.Ct. 2791.

III

. . . .

B

[T]he Court offers no clue on what a "proper" [as-applied] lawsuit might look like. . . . Surely the Court cannot mean that no suit may be brought until a woman's health is immediately jeopardized by the ban on intact D & E. A woman "suffer[ing] from medical complications," needs access to the medical procedure at once and cannot wait for the judicial process to unfold.

. . . .

IV

. . . .

In sum, the notion that the Partial-Birth Abortion Ban Act furthers any legitimate governmental interest is, quite simply, irrational. The Court's defense of the statute provides no saving explanation. In candor, the Act, and the Court's defense of it, cannot be understood as anything other than an effort to chip away at a right declared again and again by this Court—and with increasing comprehension of its centrality to women's lives. . . . When "a statute burdens constitutional rights and all that can be said on its behalf is that it is the vehicle that legislators have chosen for expressing their hostility to those rights, the burden is undue." *Stenberg,* 530 U.S., at 952, 120 S.Ct. 2597 (GINSBURG, J., concurring) (quoting *Hope Clinic v. Ryan,* 195 F.3d 857, 881 (C.A.7 1999) (Posner, C. J., dissenting)).

NOTES

1. The Court is surely correct that, for most women, abortion is a painfully difficult decision. But "neither the weight of the scientific evidence to date nor the observable reality of 33 year of legal abortion in the United States comports with the idea that having an abortion is any more dangerous to a woman's long-term mental health than delivering and parenting a child that she did not intend to have. . . ." Cohen, Abortion and Mental Health: Myths and Realities, 9 Guttmacher Policy Rev. 8 (2006). . . .

Questions and Comments

1. Why does the Supreme Court in *Stenberg* overturn the Nebraska late-term abortion statute as unconstitutional? What part(s) of the statute offended the Constitution, according to the Court?

2. According to Oliveri, how did the proponents of the federal late-term abortion statute misrepresent the truth about the use of such abortions? How did the opponents of the statute likewise misrepresent reality? What was the factual reality that lay between these two misrepresentations?

3. Why did opponents of the federal statute attempt to hide the facts about who uses late-term abortions? What would Angela Davis (see chapter 7) say about their approach? Why does Oliveri think the approach ultimately hurt, rather than helped, their cause? What is the broader problem with the pro-choice movement that, according to Oliveri, is illustrated by her analysis of its approach to late-term abortion?

4. In *Stenberg v. Carhart*, the U.S. Supreme Court held the Nebraska "partial birth abortion" statute unconstitutional because it lacked a health exception. What did Justice Kennedy, writing for the majority in *Gonzales*, say about the absence of a health exception in the federal statute at issue in that case? Why, according to the Court, did the lack of a health exception *not* render the federal act unconstitutional? Is the Court's analysis in *Gonzales* consistent with the holding in *Stenberg*? Does *Gonzales* fundamentally change abortion law?

5. Justice Ginsburg, dissenting in *Gonzales*, writes that the majority's opinion "reflects ancient notions about women's place in the family and under the Constitution. . . ." What specific notions is she referring to? Do you agree that Justice Kennedy's opinion reflects those notions?

6. Justice Ginsburg also states that lawsuits challenging abortion restrictions "center on a woman's autonomy to determine her life's course, and thus to enjoy equal citizenship stature." In making this argument, as well as the one mentioned above in question 5, what approach to abortion jurisprudence is Justice Ginsburg taking, the privacy approach or the equality approach?

2. Minors' Access to Abortion

Chapter 19

Politics and Pregnancy
Adolescent Mothers and Public Policy

Deborah L. Rhode

Although teenage pregnancy has recently emerged as a major social "problem," its frequency is by no means a recent social phenomenon. The appropriate age for sexual relations and parenthood has always been a matter of cultural definition, and in the United States it has varied considerably across time, region, class, race, ethnicity, and gender. Over the last two centuries, the age at which childbirth is biologically possible has declined, while the period of adolescents' economic dependence has increased. One result has been a growing cultural conflict over reproductive choices during the transition to adulthood. During the past two decades, the rising birth rate among unmarried teenagers has prompted increasing national concern, but no coherent policy. Much of the problem stems from disputes over the nature of the problem. Is the primary issue morality, fertility, or poverty? What choices should adolescents make in sexual relationships, what role should the state play in shaping the choices available, and who should decide those questions?

This essay explores public policies on adolescent pregnancy against their broader historical, legal, and socioeconomic background. Its central premise is that such policies have frequently misdescribed the problem and have misled as to the solution. Too often, decision-makers have located the problem at the individual level, and faulted teens who want "too much too soon" in sexual relations. Insufficient attention has focused on the societal level, on structures that offer female adolescents "too little too late": too little reason to stay in school, too little assistance in birth control, too little opportunity for childcare, health services, vocational training or decent jobs, and too little understanding of the responsibilities of single parenthood. Both legislative and judicial decisionmaking has proceeded without adequate information on the experience of women or the consequences of various public policies.

To understand the limitations of current frameworks, some historical background is useful. Since specific policies toward adolescent pregnancy are a recent development, their evolution must be understood in terms of broader reproductive, family, and regulatory patterns. Although extended historical analyses are available elsewhere, a brief overview is helpful here in highlighting dynamics that are especially relevant

Deborah Rhode, "Politics and Pregnancy: Adolescent Mothers and Public Policy," 1 S. CAL. REV. L. & WOMEN'S STUD. 99 (1991). The essay excerpted here is adapted from a chapter entitled "Adolescent Pregnancy and Public Policy," in ANNETTE LAWSON AND DEBORAH L. RHODE (eds.), THE POLITICS OF PREGNANCY 301–335 (1993).

to contemporary debates. In particular, it is worth underscoring the variation in cultural norms concerning teenage sexuality and the class and racial biases in public policy responses.

. . . .

III

The late 1960s and early 1970s witnessed the first perception of teenage pregnancy as a major social problem. The increase in public concern was not a function of increases in adolescent fertility. In fact, rates of childbirth among females ages fifteen to nineteen dropped almost 45% between 1957 and 1983, largely because of liberalization of contraceptive and abortion policy.[1] Although the birth rate began to rise again in the late 1980s, it still remained substantially lower than in the decade before the *Roe* decision. When teenage childbearing became a focus of attention, the reasons had less to do with its frequency than with a cluster of volatile issues involving sexuality, abortion, family values, and welfare policy.

During the last quarter-century, although fewer adolescents were having children, more were having sex and more were becoming pregnant. More of those who gave birth were raising their child outside of marriage. By the late 1980s, the United States had the highest teenage pregnancy rate in the developed world. Approximately 45% of females between fifteen and nineteen were sexually active before marriage, an increase of over 15% since 1971, and substantial numbers used contraceptives intermittently or ineffectively.[2] The result was a million teenage pregnancies each year, and about four-fifths of these were unintentional.[3] An estimated four out of every ten American women were becoming pregnant at least once before age twenty, a rate that has doubled since 1950.[4] About half of that group were carrying their pregnancy to term (20% of all adolescents), and half of those who did so were unmarried (10% of all adolescents).[5] Recent estimates indicate that less than 5% of all unmarried teens and less than 1% of blacks were placing their child for adoption, a dramatic shift from earlier eras.[6] The rate of teenage childbirth among blacks is almost two and one-half times greater than among whites; among Hispanics, the rates are almost twice as great. Over a quarter of single black women have had at least one child by the age of eighteen.[7] Although teens under age fifteen have accounted for only 2% of all teenage mothers, their rate of pregnancy has been increasing.[8]

Such patterns are widely assumed to constitute a social problem, but there is no consensus on its cause or cure. At the risk of some oversimplification, it makes sense to distinguish two dominant positions in public debate. Most liberals "begin with the premise that teenagers should not have babies [while most] conservatives begin with the premise that single teenagers should not have sex."[9] For conservatives, the problem involves primarily moral and fiscal concerns; premarital sexuality is not only objectionable in itself, it promotes other objectionable practices—either abortion and the destruction of fetal "life," or nonmarital childbearing and the destruction of traditional values as well as the erosion of financial self-sufficiency. For liberals, the problem involves primarily health and socioeconomic status; single parenthood is linked with disrupted education, reduced employment opportunities, and an increased likelihood of poverty for mothers, as well as heightened medical risks and developmental difficulties for their children.

Each of these definitions of the problem is itself problematic on both descriptive and prescriptive levels. Most conservative and liberal accounts distort the dynamic they seek to counteract. Both constituencies have overstated the adverse consequences of adolescent pregnancy and understated the barriers to addressing it. Such distortions are in some sense endemic to the American political process. The most effective way of getting an issue onto the policy agenda is usually to paint it as a crisis that can be addressed without major political conflict or financial expenditure. Yet the construction of the issue best suited to attracting public notice and building coalitions for reform is often ill-suited to generating adequate policy responses. That is clearly the case with adolescent pregnancy. Conflicting definitions of the problem have resulted in political compromises that are inadequate to serve societal needs.

From conservatives' perspective, the increase in teenage sexuality, pregnancy, and nonmarital childbirth is both a cause and consequence of deeper social difficulties. This view presents the problem primarily in moral terms and attributes blame to the rise in cultural permissiveness, the decline in parental authority, and the weakening of community sanctions against out-of-wedlock births. Public policies on birth control are also held accountable for legitimating conduct they should seek to prevent. According to New-Right legislators such as former Senator Jeremiah Denton, author of the federal Adolescent and Family Life Act, "the most effective oral contraceptive yet devised is the word 'no.'"[10] From conservatives' vantage, any outreach program designed to prevent pregnancy rather than sex appears counterproductive; it encourages the activity that creates the problem.

Most available research, however, fails to support such claims. Studies of contraceptive and abortion services generally find no evidence that their availability has increased sexual activity.[11] The vast majority of adolescents seek assistance only after they have engaged in sexual intercourse. Comparative data underscore the point. Many European countries have rates of adolescent sexual activity equivalent to those in the United States, but substantially higher rates of contraceptive use and lower rates of adolescent pregnancy and abortion.

Although liberals tend to be more permissive toward teenage sexual activity, they are typically no less judgmental than conservatives about teenage childbirth. Both groups share assumptions about the experience of adolescent pregnancy that rest on dubious factual premises. Most public debate conflates unintended and unwanted pregnancy and ignores data indicating that adolescent attitudes fall across a spectrum. As noted earlier, the frequent caricature of children having children is highly distorted: two thirds of all births are to eighteen- and nineteen-year-olds and only a tiny percentage are to mothers under sixteen.[12] The equally common assumption that early pregnancy constitutes a "direct path to poverty" is equally exaggerated. The leading longitudinal study by Furstenberg, Brooks-Gunn, and Morgan involving predominantly black adolescent mothers in Baltimore, found that the majority were eventually able to obtain a high-school education, secure full-time employment, and avoid welfare dependency.[13] About two thirds of their children have completed or are close to completing comparable levels of schooling, and only a quarter have become teenage parents themselves.[14]

So, too, many factors commonly assumed to be consequences of early pregnancy—educational difficulties, low self-esteem, poverty, and unemployment—appear also to be partial causes. For example, although adolescent mothers are more likely to drop out of school than peers of similar socioeconomic backgrounds, it is unclear how much of this difference is due to childbearing and how much to lower academic commitment and competence. Recent studies suggest that most young mothers leave school before becoming pregnant, rather than the converse, and that mothers who give birth while in school are as likely to graduate as their peers.[15] If such findings are confirmed, then labeling early parenthood as the paramount problem will misrepresent the solution.

A growing number of scholars have also suggested that early pregnancies are more "adaptive" for economically and racially subordinate groups than is commonly acknowledged. According to researchers such as Arline Geronimus, Mary Edwards, and Mark Testa, teenagers who are no longer in school may find advantages in having their most intensive parenting demands during a period when they have fewest employment opportunities and greatest access to childcare assistance from their relatives.[16] Since young black mothers are likely to live in an extended family, they often have better access to networks of kin support and childcare than older mothers. From a physiological standpoint, early motherhood is far less problematic than conventional accounts imply. Most health risks currently associated with teenage childbirth are attributable to socioeconomic status and the failure to obtain adequate prenatal care. If such care were available, some analysts believe that childbearing between ages sixteen and nineteen by poor women would pose fewer risks to mothers or newborns than later childbearing because many medical problems associated with poverty increase with age.

Such claims have themselves become matters of considerable dispute. Some commentators challenge the conclusions regarding health difficulties and claim that if risks to infants after the first few months of birth are considered, early childrearing carries significant disadvantages. Recent research also suggests that a substantial number of young mothers remain outside of support networks and find family childcare inadequate. Even if . . . most adolescent mothers are eventually able to achieve financial independence, a significant number experience enduring poverty and many face prolonged periods of severe hardships. Children of teenage mothers also have disproportionate difficulties, such as high rates of delinquency and low rates of educational attainment. Although it is unclear how much of the problem is attributable to socioeconomic variables and how much to parental age and capacity, at least some evidence suggests that young adolescents are less well equipped for certain childrearing demands. In any event, the existence of such controversies highlights the need for qualifications largely missing in current policy debates.

Similar qualifications are necessary in assessing conventional solutions for the adolescent pregnancy "problem." Recent data call into question the widespread assumption that economically and racially subordinate groups gain substantial benefits from deferring parenthood until marriage or the completion of education. Divorce is frequent among these young couples, and various factors, including relatively high rates of unemployment, violence, suicide, and substance abuse have reduced the pool of eligible male partners. Although the extent to which such factors explain current racial differences in family formation is subject to debate, marriage clearly is not an adequate "solution" for many pregnant adolescents.

Moreover, women of color, who are concentrated in occupations offering low pay and little return for completion of secondary education, often have relatively little to lose from early childbirth. Thus, some longitudinal studies have found that the labor market positions of black women who gave birth in their teens do not substantially vary from the positions of those who did not.[17] Similar findings have emerged from research comparing adolescents who became mothers with sisters who delayed childbearing; deferral of parenthood and additional schooling did not significantly increase income or reduce welfare dependency.[18] By contrast, a recent study of largely black Baltimore teenagers found that those who obtained abortions did better economically and educationally than adolescents who gave birth, even after controlling for various demographic and motivational factors.

Although such conflicting data underscore the need for further research, one general point attracts widespread consensus. Childbirth patterns are responsive to socioeconomic and cultural factors that vary considerably across class, race, and ethnicity. Expectations about future opportunities play an important role in shaping collective norms and individual choices, frequently at preconscious levels.

The point of this discussion is not, as Arline Geronimus emphasizes, that "in the best of all possible worlds, teen childbearing would be personally or socially optimal. . . ." Rather, as she suggests, "we are very far from the best of all possible worlds, and . . . there are serious flaws in the logic of current policy approaches intended to get us there."[19] As the following discussion makes clear, conflict and confusion over the nature of the adolescent pregnancy "crisis" has seriously compromised societal responses.

IV

. . . .

In a series of cases during the late 1970s and early 1980s, the Supreme Court held that states could require parental consent or notification for abortion services to unemancipated minors as long as adjudicative procedures were available to bypass such requirements under certain circumstances. To a majority of Justices, parental involvement rules were justified by the "peculiar vulnerability" of adolescence and the importance of preserving family ties. However, a minor should be able to avoid consent and notice requirements by establishing in court either that she is sufficiently mature and well-informed to make an independent decision concerning abortion or that, even if she is immature, the abortion would be in her best interest.

In 1990, a sharply divided Court sustained further restrictions on adolescent's [sic] abortion rights. A majority of Justices in *Hodgson v. Minnesota*[20] upheld a requirement that both parents be notified prior to an adolescent's abortion if a judicial procedure is available to bypass that requirement.* In *Ohio v. Akron Center for Reproductive Services*,[21] the Court sustained a legislative scheme that required physicians personally to notify one parent; that placed heightened burdens of proof on minors seeking judicial bypass of the notice requirement; that imposed delays of up to 22 days for bypass applicants; and that failed to insure confidentiality. In upholding the reasonableness of such regulations, the majority concluded:

> It is both rational and fair for the State to conclude that, in most instances, the family will strive to give a lonely or even terrified minor advice that is both compassionate and mature. . . . It would deny all dignity to the family to say that the State cannot take this reasonable step in regulating its health professions to ensure that, in most cases, a young woman will receive guidance and understanding from a parent.[22]

On a symbolic level, this resolution is understandable. . . . [M]ost parents feel that they should be involved in matters that call for mature guidance. A notice-plus-bypass procedure affirms the value of parental involvement, but also recognizes that in some instances such involvement may result in punitive or otherwise counterproductive measures. Yet on a practical level, such a compromise carries significant costs, and law has offered a poor forum for assessing them. Legislative and judicial decision-making generally has proceeded without demanding or assembling adequate data on the effects of notice or consent requirements. Do they result in greater communication on matters involving sexuality and birth control? What are the consequences for teenagers? How many experience better parental relations, how many suffer increased physical risks from self-help or delayed decisions to abort, how many decide not to abort, and what are the effects of that decision? Finally, how well are legal procedures likely to function? How many minors evade consent requirements by seeking abortions out-of-state? Do petitions to bypass parental involvement result in thoughtful exercise of judicial discretion? Or could the resources consumed by courts and counsel in bypass cases be directed to more constructive approaches such as pregnancy prevention services?

Although initial legislative and judicial decision-making proceeded without systematic evidence on these points, subsequent research has provided partial answers. Yet the data available have had disturbingly little policy impact. For example, parental knowledge does not correlate with more effective contraceptive practices on the part of adolescents.[23] About half of all adolescents seek birth control services without informing their parents, and about half that group (a quarter of all teens) will not seek such assistance if parents must consent or receive notification.[24] Only 2% of surveyed adolescents indicate that policies requiring parental involvement would cause them to restrict their sexual activity.[25] Statutory notice requirements do not significantly increase the likelihood that teenagers will consult their parents on birth control matters.[26]

---

* *Editor's note*: Most judicial bypass statutes authorize the judge to allow the abortion either if the judge finds that the petitioner is sufficiently "mature" to make the decision herself or if the judge finds that the abortion (or, sometimes, having the right to make the decision) is in the petitioner's best interests.

Nor have judicial bypass procedures usefully contributed to adolescent decision-making. . . . Of the first 1300 Massachusetts abortion cases involving petitions to bypass parental consent, courts found the adolescent to be mature in 90% of all cases and in all but five of the remaining cases, held that abortion was in her best interest. Four cases were either overturned on appeal or the consent was obtained through another judge. In the single case where the court refused to authorize termination of the pregnancy, the petitioner obtained an abortion in another state. Although the frequency of adolescent abortion has declined in Massachusetts since the implementation of consent requirements, almost all of the decline appears attributable to an increase in teenagers resorting to out-of-state abortions.

Studies of other state notification procedures similarly find that all but a tiny percentage of bypass petitions are granted but that the procedure itself imposes substantial barriers, particularly for poor, nonwhite, and very young teenagers. . . . Adolescents have often been deterred by the lack of information about legal assistance, the risk of public exposure, the costs of multiple trips to distant locations, and the fear of courtroom interrogations. This fear is understandable given the judicial questions that some minors encounter, such as: How will you feel about having a "dead child"? Are you aware that abortion can jeopardize your future fertility? Would your parents be willing and able to raise your baby? Notice and consent requirements increase the risk of physical abuse, psychological trauma, medically-threatening delays, and unwanted childbirths. In effect, such rules compound the "peculiar vulnerability" they are designed to address.

Those who administer consent regulations express little support for their requirements. Criteria for assessing teens' maturity and best interests have been arbitrary and inconsistent, while judicial cross examination has often increased the guilt and misery that accompanies unwanted pregnancies. As the dissent in *Hodgson* recognized, and the results in bypass cases reflect, it is almost impossible to identify circumstances in which a minor is too immature to make an abortion decision for herself and in which her best interest lies in having a child that she does not want.[27] . . . In case studies of Massachusetts and Minnesota regulations, participants in the legal process overwhelmingly agreed that resources now spent on obtaining judicial rubber stamps of bypass petitions should be allocated to more productive strategies.[28]

This is not to understate the value of fostering better communication between parents and their children concerning responsible sexual behavior. It is rather to suggest that involuntary notification is an ineffective means of fostering such communication. Virtually every major professional study has concluded that compulsory parental involvement ill services adolescent needs and family relationships. A preferable strategy would be voluntary parental outreach programs. Such programs seek to improve family communication and adolescent decision-making skills while avoiding the notice or consent requirements that deter teenagers from seeking assistance. Yet all too often, legislative, judicial, and administrative analysis has proceeded without consideration of such alternative strategies for parental involvement. As in the design of other teenage pregnancy initiatives, policy makers have offered compromises more responsive to the symbolic politics than to practical needs.

. . . .

NOTES

1. MARIS VINOVSKIS, AN "EPIDEMIC" OF ADOLESCENT PREGNANCY? 25 (1988); ELISE JONES, ET AL., TEENAGE PREGNANCY IN INDUSTRIALIZED COUNTRIES 37 (1986).

2. Elise Jones, et al., *Teenage Pregnancy in Developed Countries: Determinants and Policy Implications,* 17 FAM. PLANNING PERSPECTIVES 53, 57 (1985) [hereinafter *Teenage Pregnancy in Developed Countries*]; RISKING THE FUTURE: ADOLESCENT SEXUALITY, PREGNANCY, AND CHILDBEARING 15, 40 (Cheryl Hayes, ed. 1987) [hereinafter RISKING THE FUTURE].

3. RISKING THE FUTURE, supra note 2 at 1, 52.

4. Id.

5. *Teenage Pregnancy in Developed Countries,* supra note 2, at 56.

6. CLAIRE BRINDIS & RITA JEREMY, ADOLESCENT PREGNANCY AND PARENTING IN CALIFORNIA: A STRATEGIC PLAN FOR ACTION 32–41 (1988) (discussing increase in sexually active teens and divergence in estimated adoption rates of .4% for black teens and 12.2% of whites); Jane Gross, Anti-Abortion Revival: Homes for the Unwed, N.Y. Times, July 23, 1989, at 25 (quoting the President of the National Committee for Adoption).

7. RISKING THE FUTURE, supra note 2, at 53–67; CHILDREN'S DEFENSE FUND, TEENAGE PREGNANCY: AN ADVOCATE'S GUIDE TO THE NUMBERS 22 (1988) [hereinafter ADVOCATE'S GUIDE].

8. ADVOCATE'S GUIDE, supra note 7, at 11.

9. CAROL JOFFE, THE REGULATION OF SEXUALITY: EXPERIENCES OF FAMILY PLANNING WORKERS 45 (1986) (*quoting* CONNAUGHT MARSHNER, THE NEW TRADITIONAL WOMAN 9 (1982)).

10. ROSALIND PETCHESKY, ABORTION AND WOMAN'S CHOICE: THE STATE, SEXUALITY, AND REPRODUCTIVE FREEDOM 270 (1990) (quoting Orrin Hatch and Jeremiah Denton).

11. HARRELL RODGERS, JR., POOR WOMEN, POOR FAMILIES: THE ECONOMIC PLIGHT OF AMERICA'S FEMALE-HEADED HOUSEHOLDS 92–93 (1986); Eve Paul & Dara Klassa, *Minors' Right to Confidential Contraceptive Services: The Limits of State Action,* 10 WOMEN'S RTS. L. REP. 45, 46 n.11 (1987); Brigid Rentoul, *Cognitus Interruptus: The Courts and Minors' Access to Contraceptives,* 5 YALE L. & POL. REV. 212, 231–32 nn.99–100 (1986). *See also* Ann Harper, *Teenage Sexuality and Public Policy: An Agenda for Gender Education,* in FAMILIES, POLITICS, AND PUBLIC POLICY: A FEMINIST DIALOGUE ON WOMEN AND THE STATE 220 (Irene Diamond ed. 1983).

12. Diana Pearce, *Children Having Children: Teen Pregnancy and Public Policy and Women's Perspectives* in THE POLITICS OF PREGNANCY: ADOLESCENT SEXUALITY AND PUBLIC POLICY (A. Lawson & D. Rhode eds.) (1993) [hereinafter THE POLITICS OF PREGNANCY].

13. FRANK FURSTENBERG, JR., JEANNE BROOKS-GUNN, & S. PHILIP MORGAN, ADOLESCENT MOTHERS IN LATER LIFE (1987)....

14. Id.; Frank Furstenberg, Mary Elizabeth Hughes, & Jeanne Brooks-Gunn, *The Next Generation: Children of Teenage Mothers Grow Up,* in EARLY PARENTHOOD AND THE TRANSITION TO ADULTHOOD (Margaret K. Rosenheim & Mark F. Testa eds.) [1992] [hereinafter EARLY PARENTHOOD].

15. For school drop-out findings, see Randall Olsen & George Farkas, *Endogenous Covariates in Duration Models and the Effect of Adolescent Childbirth on Schooling,* 19 J. HUM. RESOURCES 39 (1989); Dawn Upchurch & James McCarthy, *The Timing of First Birth and High School Completion,* 55 AM. SOC. REV. 224 (1990).

16. See Arline Geronimus, *On Teenage Childbearing and Neonatal Mortality in the United States,* 13 POPULATION AND DEV. REV. 245 (1987); Mary G. Edwards, Teenage Childbearing: Redefining the Problem for Public Policy, August 30, 1990 (paper delivered before the American

Political Science Association); Mark Testa, *Racial Variation in the Early Life Course of Adolescent Welfare Mothers,* in EARLY PARENTHOOD, supra note 14.

17. See Elaine McCrate, *Labor Market Segmentation and Relative Black/White Teenage Birth Rates,* REV. BLACK. POL. ECON. 37 (Spring 1990); Shelly Lundberg and Robert B. Plotnick, Teenage Childbearing and Adult Wages, Discussion Paper No. 90–24 (1989) (finding that premarital birth reduces wages for white but not black women).

18. See Arline Geronimus & Sanders Korenman, The Socioeconomic Consequences of Teen Childbearing Reconsidered, Research Report 90–109 (Population Studies Center, Sept. 1990).

19. Geronimus, supra note 16, at 273 n.14.

20. 110 S. Ct. 2926 (1990).

21. 110 S. Ct. 2972 (1990).

22. 110 S. Ct. at 2984.

23. Asta Kenney, Jacqueline Forrest, & Aida Torres, *Storm over Washington: The Parental Notification Proposal,* 14 FAM. PLAN. PERSP. 185, 190 (1982). . . .

24. Id. at 189.

25. Id.

26. Robert Blum, Michael Resnick, & Trisha Stark, *The Impact of a Parental Notification Law on Adolescent Abortion Decision-Making,* 77 AM. J. PUB. HEALTH 619, 620 (1987) (comparing 65% rate of notification in Minnesota, which has a notification law, and 62% rate in Wisconsin, which does not). . . .

27. 110 S. Ct. at 2926.

28. Robert M. Mnookin, Bellotti v. Baird: *A Hard Case,* in IN THE INTEREST OF CHILDREN 258 (R. Mnookin ed. 1985).

Chapter 20

Sex Education

Politicians, Parents, Teachers, and Teens

AND

Understanding "Abstinence"

Implications for Individuals, Programs, and Policies

Cynthia Dailard

Sex Education: Politicians, Parents, Teachers, and Teens

In 1981 Congress passed, and President Reagan signed into law, the Adolescent Family Life Act (AFLA). Through AFLA, the federal government for the first time invested on a small scale in local programs designed to prevent teenage pregnancy by encouraging "chastity and self-discipline" among teenagers. AFLA helped usher in 20 years of debate at the federal, state and local level over whether sexuality education should exclusively promote abstinence or should take a more comprehensive approach.

In the late 1990s, federal investment in this area increased significantly after Congress, as part of the 1996 welfare reform law, created a federal-state program funded at $440 million over five years to support local sexuality education programs that condemn *all* sex outside of marriage—for people of any age—and prohibit any positive discussion of contraception. Four years later, conservative lawmakers secured an additional victory when Congress approved a *third* abstinence-only education program funded at $50 million over two years through a set-aside in the maternal and child health block grant.

Yet this major increase in federal funding occurred despite evidence that shows that more comprehensive sexuality education, rather than abstinence-only education, helps teenagers to delay sexual activity ("Fueled by Campaign Promises, Drive Intensifies to Boost Abstinence-Only Education Funds," *TGR* [The Guttmacher Report], April 2000, page 1). It also occurred without clear pictures of either local sexuality education policies or the content of classroom instruction. Several studies published

---

This chapter excerpts two pieces by the same author, written two years apart: Cynthia Dailard, *Sex Education: Politicians, Parents, Teachers, and Teens,* The Guttmacher Report on Public Policy, February 2001; and Cynthia Dailard, *Understanding 'Abstinence': Implications for Individuals, Programs and Policies,* The Guttmacher Report on Public Policy, December 2003.

within the past year fill in these gaps, highlighting a significant disparity between the inclinations of policymakers and the needs and desires of both students and parents. This research also suggests that there is a large gap between what teachers believe should be taught regarding sexuality education and what is actually taught in the classroom.

Local Policy

More than two out of three public school districts have a policy mandating sexuality education, according to research published in 1999 by The Alan Guttmacher Institute (AGI). Most of these policies—more than eight in 10—were adopted during the 1990s. . . .

This AGI research, based on a nationwide survey of school superintendents, found that local policies overwhelmingly encourage abstinence. Eighty-six percent of school districts with a sexuality education policy require promotion of abstinence; 51% require that abstinence be taught as the preferred option but also permit discussion of contraception as an effective means of protecting against unintended pregnancy and sexually transmitted diseases (STDs); and 35% require abstinence to be taught as the only option for unmarried people, while either prohibiting the discussion of contraception altogether or limiting discussion to contraceptive failure rates. Only 14% have a truly comprehensive policy that teaches about both abstinence and contraception as part of a broader program designed to prepare adolescents to become sexually healthy adults.

. . . .

Clearly, state and local policymakers have strongly supported abstinence promotion for some time; the AGI study was conducted even before states began implementing abstinence-only programs funded under the 1996 welfare reform law. Districts that switched their policies during the 1990s were twice as likely to adopt a more abstinence-focused policy as to move in the other direction. Half of school superintendents surveyed cited state directives as the most important factor influencing their current policy; approximately four in 10 cited school boards or special committees.

Teachers

Not surprisingly, this shift in policy has had an impact on teachers and the content of sexuality education. A second AGI study, based on a survey of public school teachers, shows that since the late 1980s, sexuality education in secondary schools has become more focused on abstinence and less likely to provide students with information about contraception. The survey results, published in 2000, show that the percentage of public school teachers in grades 7–12 who teach abstinence as the only way of preventing pregnancies and STDs rose dramatically between 1988 and 1995—from one in 50 to one in four. Additionally, nearly three in four present abstinence as the preferred way to avoid unintended pregnancy and STDs.

Teachers are also emphasizing different topics than they did in the past. Compared

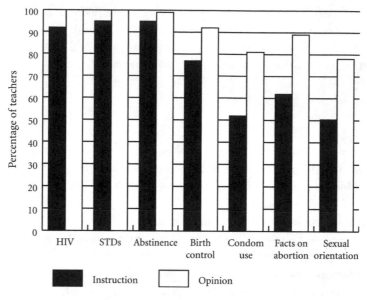

Fig. 20.1. *Thinking vs. Doing.* There is a large gap between what teachers think should be taught and what they teach when it comes to birth control, abortion and sexual orientation. *Source:* Darroch, J.E., Laundry, D.J., and Singh, S. Changing emphasis in sexuality education in U.S. public secondary schools, 1988–1999, *Family Planning Perspectives,* 2000, 32(5):204–211 & 265.

with teachers in the late 1980s, teachers today are more likely to teach about abstinence, STDs and resisting peer pressure to have sex, but are significantly less likely to discuss more "controversial" subjects such as birth control, abortion and sexual orientation. . . .

Although more than nine in 10 teachers believe that students should be taught about contraception (and half believe that contraception should be taught in grade seven or earlier), one in four are instructed not to teach the subject. And while the vast majority also believe that sexuality education courses should cover where to go for birth control, information about abortion, the correct way to use a condom, and sexual orientation, far fewer actually cover these topics. . . .

Even if teachers are allowed to cover these sensitive topics, they may avoid them because they fear adverse community reaction; more than one-third report such concerns. All in all, these pressures and limitations lead one in four teachers to believe that they are not meeting their students' needs for information. A similar percentage of fifth- and sixth-grade teachers who teach sexuality education believe that schools are not doing enough to prepare students for puberty or to deal with pressures and decisions regarding sexual activity. Finally, a study published last year by the Centers for Disease Control and Prevention found that a significant proportion of health educators in secondary schools want additional training in the areas of pregnancy, STD and HIV prevention.

Parents

Most parents (65%) believe that sex education should encourage young people to delay sexual activity but also prepare them to use birth control and practice safe sex once they do become sexually active, according to interviews conducted for the Kaiser Family Foundation in 2000. In fact, public opinion is overwhelmingly supportive of sexuality education that goes beyond abstinence (see chart). Moreover, public opinion polls over the years have routinely showed that the vast majority of Americans favor broader sex education programs over those that teach only abstinence.

Kaiser reports that among the one-third of parents who say that adolescents should be told "only to have sex when they are married," an overwhelming majority also say that schools should teach adolescents how to get tested for HIV/AIDS and other STDs (86%), how to talk to a partner about birth control and STDs (77%), how to use condoms (71%), and where to get and how to use other birth control methods (68%). This suggests that parents and policymakers differ in their understanding of what it means to present abstinence as the only option outside of marriage, and that policies that prohibit any discussion of contraception or that portray it as ineffective may not reflect the desires of most parents.

In addition to topics that are routinely covered in sexuality education classes— such as the basics of reproduction, HIV and STDs, and abstinence—parents want schools to cover topics often perceived to be controversial by school administrators and teachers. Kaiser found that at least three-quarters of parents say that sexuality education classes should cover how to use condoms and other forms of birth control, abortion, sexual orientation, pressures to have sex and the emotional consequences of having sex. Three in four parents believe that these topics should be "discussed in a

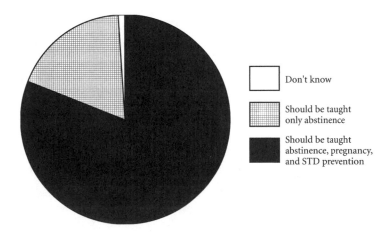

Don't know

Should be taught only abstinence

Should be taught abstinence, pregnancy, and STD prevention

Fig. 20.2. *Public Opinion.* Americans overwhelmingly favor broader sexuality education programs over those that discuss only abstinence. *Source:* The Henry J. Kaiser Family Foundation/ABC Television, *Sex in the 90s: 1998 National Survey of Americans on Sex and Sexual Health,* Sept. 1998.

way that provides a fair and balanced presentation of the facts and different views in society." Yet most of these topics tend to be the very ones that teachers shy away from or are prohibited from teaching. Finally, most parents believe that the amount of time being spent on sexuality education should be significantly expanded.

Students

According to Kaiser, students report that they want more information about sexual and reproductive health issues than they are receiving in school. Approximately half of students in grades 7–12 report needing more information about what to do in the event of rape or sexual assault, how to get tested for HIV and other STDs, factual information on HIV/AIDS and other STDs, and how to talk with a partner about birth control and STDs. Two in five also want more factual information on birth control, how to use and where to get birth control, and how to handle pressure to have sex. Yet a significant percentage report that these topics are not covered in their most recent sexuality education course, or that they are not covered in sufficient depth. Moreover, Kaiser found that students whose most recent sex education course used an abstinence-only approach were less knowledgeable about pregnancy and disease prevention than were those whose most recent sex education was more comprehensive.

Research on teenage males published by The Urban Institute in 2000 suggests that although sexuality education has become almost universal, students are not receiving even general information early enough to fully protect themselves against unintended pregnancy and STDs. According to the Institute . . . 30% of teenage males still do not receive any sexuality education prior to first intercourse, with the rate as high as 45% for black teenage males. . . .

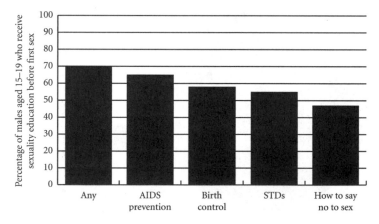

Fig. 20.3. *Knowledge Gap.* Many young men do not receive sexuality education before they have sexual intercourse for the first time. *Source:* Lindberg, L.D., Ku, L., and Sonenstein F., Adolescents' reports of reproductive health education, 1988–1995, *Family Planning Perspectives,* 2000, 32(5):220–226.

Finally, The Urban Institute found that levels of communication between parents and their teenage sons remain low. Only half of young men today report ever having spoken to either of their parents about AIDS, STDs, birth control or what would happen if their partner became pregnant. Given parents' reticence, it is no wonder that they count on teachers and schools to convey the critical information that teenagers need to protect themselves when they do become sexually active.

Conclusion

This growing body of research highlights a troubling disconnect: While politicians promote abstinence-only education, teachers, parents and students want young people to receive far more comprehensive information about how to avoid unintended pregnancy and STDs, and about how to become sexually healthy adults.
. . . .

Understanding "Abstinence": Implications for Individuals, Programs, and Policies

The word "sex" is commonly acknowledged to mean different things to different people. The same can be said for "abstinence." The varied and potentially conflicting meanings of "abstinence" have significant public health implications now that its promotion has emerged as the Bush administration's primary answer to pregnancy and sexually transmitted disease (STD) prevention for all people who are not married.

For those willing to probe beneath the surface, critical questions abound. What is abstinence in the first place, and what does it mean to use abstinence as a method of pregnancy or disease prevention? What constitutes abstinence "failure," and can abstinence failure rates be measured comparably to failure rates for other contraceptive methods? What specific behaviors are to be abstained from? And what is known about the effectiveness and potential "side effects" of programs that promote abstinence? Answering questions about what abstinence means at the individual and programmatic levels, and clarifying all of this for policymakers, remains a key challenge. Meeting that challenge should be regarded as a prerequisite for the development of sound and effective programs designed to protect Americans from unintended pregnancy and STDs, including HIV.

Abstinence and Individuals

What does it mean to use abstinence? When used conversationally, most people probably understand abstinence to mean refraining from sexual activity—or, more specifically, vaginal intercourse—for moral or religious reasons. But when it is promoted as a public health strategy to avoid unintended pregnancy or STDs, it takes on a different connotation. Indeed, President Bush has described abstinence as "the surest way, and the only completely effective way, to prevent unwanted pregnancies and sexually transmitted disease." So from a scientific perspective, what does it mean to abstain

Contraceptive Effectiveness Rates for Pregnancy Prevention

Contraceptive Method	Perfect Use[a]	Typical Use[a]
Abstinence	100	???
Female Sterilization	99.5	99.5
Oral Contraceptive	99.5–99.9[b]	92.5
Male Condom	97	86.3
Withdrawal	96	75.5

[a] Percentage of women who successfully avoid an unintended pregnancy during their first year of use.

[b] Depending on formulation.

Sources: Perfect use—Hatcher, RA, et al., *Contraceptive Technology*, 17th ed., 1998, page 216. Typical use—AGI, *Fulfilling the Promise: Public Policy and U.S. Family Planning Clinics*, 2000, page 44.

from sex, and how should the "use" of abstinence as a method of pregnancy or disease prevention be measured?

Population and public health researchers commonly classify people as contraceptive users if they or their partner are consciously using at least one method to avoid unintended pregnancy or STDs. From a scientific standpoint, a person would be an "abstinence user" if he or she *intentionally* refrained from sexual activity. Thus, the subgroup of people consciously using abstinence as a method of pregnancy or disease prevention is obviously much smaller than the group of people who are not having sex. The size of the population of abstinence users, however, has never been measured, as it has for other methods of contraception.

When does abstinence fail? The definition of an abstinence user also has implications for determining the effectiveness of abstinence as a method of contraception. The president, in his July 2002 remarks to South Carolina high school students, said "Let me just be perfectly plain. If you're worried about teenage pregnancy, or if you're worried about sexually transmitted disease, abstinence works every single time." In doing so, he suggested that abstinence is 100% effective. But scientifically, is this in fact correct?

Researchers have two different ways of measuring the effectiveness of contraceptive methods. "Perfect use" measures the effectiveness when a contraceptive is used exactly according to clinical guidelines. In contrast, "typical use" measures how effective a method is for the average person who does not always use the method correctly or consistently. For example, women who use oral contraceptives perfectly will experience almost complete protection against pregnancy. However, in the real world, many women find it difficult to take a pill every single day, and pregnancies can and do occur to women who miss one or more pills during a cycle. Thus, while oral contraceptives have a perfect-use effectiveness rate of over 99%, their typical-use effectiveness is closer to 92% (see chart). As a result, eight in 100 women who use oral contraceptives will become pregnant in the first year of use.

Thus, when the president suggests that abstinence is 100% effective, he is implicitly citing its perfect-use rate—and indeed, abstinence *is* 100% effective if "used" with perfect consistency. But common sense suggests that in the real world, abstinence as a contraceptive method can and does fail. People who intend to remain abstinent may "slip" and have sex unexpectedly. Research is beginning to suggest how difficult abstinence can be to use consistently over time. For example, a recent study presented at the 2003 annual meeting of the American Psychological Society (APS) found that over 60% of college students who had pledged virginity during their middle or high school years had broken their vow to remain abstinent until marriage. What is not known is how many of these broken vows represent people consciously choosing to abandon abstinence and initiate sexual activity, and how many are simply typical-use abstinence failures.

To promote abstinence, its proponents frequently cite the allegedly high failure rates of other contraceptive methods, particularly condoms. By contrasting the perfect use of abstinence with the typical use of other contraceptive methods, however, they are comparing apples to oranges. From a public health perspective, it is important both to subject abstinence to the same scientific standards that apply to other contraceptive methods and to make consistent comparisons across methods. However, researchers have never measured the typical-use effectiveness of abstinence.

Therefore, it is not known how frequently abstinence fails in the real world or how effective it is compared with other contraceptive methods. This represents a serious knowledge gap. People deserve to have consistent and accurate information about the effectiveness of all contraceptive methods. For example, if they are told that abstinence is 100% effective, they should also be told that, if used correctly and consistently, condoms are 97% effective in preventing pregnancy. If they are told that condoms fail as much as 14% of the time, they should be given a comparable typical-use failure rate for abstinence.

What behaviors should be abstained from? A recent nationally representative survey conducted by the Kaiser Family Foundation and *seventeen* magazine found that half of all 15–17-year-olds believed that a person who has oral sex is still a virgin. Even more striking, the APS study found that the majority (55%) of college students pledging virginity who said they had kept their vow reported having had oral sex. While the pledgers generally were somewhat less likely to have had vaginal sex than nonpledgers, they were equally likely to have had oral or anal sex. Because oral sex does not eliminate people's risk of HIV and other STDs, and because anal sex can heighten that risk, being technically abstinent may therefore still leave people vulnerable to disease. While the press is increasingly reporting that noncoital behaviors are on the rise among young people, no research data exists to confirm this.

Abstinence Education Programs

Defining and communicating what is meant by abstinence are not just academic exercises, but are crucial to public health efforts to reduce people's risk of pregnancy and STDs. For example, existing federal and state abstinence-promotion policies typically neglect to define those behaviors to be abstained from. The federal government will provide approximately $140 million in FY 2004 to fund education programs that exclusively promote "abstinence from sexual activity outside of marriage" ("Abstinence Promotion and Teen Family Planning: The Misguided Drive for Equal Funding," *TGR*, February 2002, page 1). The law, however, does not define "sexual activity." As a result, it may have the unintended effect of promoting noncoital behaviors that leave young people at risk. Currently, very little is known about the relationship between abstinence-promotion activities and the prevalence of noncoital activities. This hampers the ability of health professionals and policymakers to shape effective public health interventions designed to reduce people's risk.

There is no question, however, that increased abstinence—meaning delayed vaginal intercourse among young people—has played a role in reducing both teen pregnancy rates in the United States and HIV rates in at least one developing country. Research by The Alan Guttmacher Institute (AGI) indicates that 25% of the decrease in the U.S. teen pregnancy rate between 1988 and 1995 was due to a decline in the proportion of teenagers who had ever had sex (while 75% was due to improved contraceptive use among sexually active teens). A new AGI report also shows that declines in HIV-infection rates in Uganda were due to a combination of fewer Ugandans initiating sex at young ages, people having fewer sexual partners and increased condom use. . . .

But abstinence proponents frequently cite both U.S. teen pregnancy declines and the Uganda example as "proof" that abstinence-only education programs, which exclude accurate and complete information about contraception, are effective; they argue that these programs should be expanded at home and exported overseas. Yet neither experience, in and of itself, says anything about the effectiveness of programmatic interventions. In fact, significant declines in U.S. teen pregnancy rates occurred prior to the implementation of government-funded programs supporting this particularly restrictive brand of abstinence-only education. Similarly, informed observers of the Ugandan experience indicate that abstinence-only education was not a significant program intervention during the years when Uganda's HIV prevalence rate was dropping. Thus, any assumptions about program effectiveness, and the effectiveness of abstinence-only education programs in particular, are misleading and potentially dangerous, but they are nonetheless shaping U.S. policy both here and abroad. . . .

Accordingly, key questions arise about how to measure the success of abstinence-promotion programs. For example, the administration is defining program success for its abstinence-only education grants to community and faith-based organizations in terms of shaping young people's intentions and attitudes with regard to future sexual activity. In contrast, most public health experts stress the importance of achieving desired behavioral outcomes such as delayed sexual activity.

To date, however, no education program in this country focusing exclusively on abstinence has shown success in delaying sexual activity. Perhaps some will in the future. In the meantime, considerable scientific evidence already demonstrates that certain types of programs that include information about both abstinence and contraception help teens delay sexual activity, have fewer sexual partners and increase contraceptive use when they begin having sex. It is not clear what it is about these programs that leads teens to delay—a question that researchers need to explore. What is clear, however, is that no program of any kind has ever shown success in convincing young people to postpone sex from age 17, when they typically first have intercourse, *until marriage*, which typically occurs at age 25 for women and 27 for men. Nor is there any evidence that the "wait until marriage" message has any impact on young people's decisions regarding sexual activity. This suggests that scarce public dollars could be better spent on programs that already have been proven to achieve delays in sexual activity of any duration, rather than on programs that stress abstinence until marriage.

Finally, there is the question of whether delays in sexual activity might come at an unacceptable price. This is raised by research indicating that while some teens promising to abstain from sex until marriage delayed sexual activity by an average of 18 months, they were more likely to have unprotected sex when they broke their pledge than those who never pledged virginity in the first place. Thus, might strategies to promote abstinence inadvertently heighten the risks for people when they eventually become sexually active?

Difficult as it may be, answering these key questions regarding abstinence eventually will be necessary for the development of sound and effective programs and policies. At a minimum, the existing lack of common understanding hampers the ability of the public and policymakers to fully assess whether abstinence and abstinence education are viable and realistic public health and public policy approaches to reducing unintended pregnancies and HIV/STDs.

Questions and Comments

1. What does Rhode mean when she says the problem of teen pregnancy should be looked at from the societal level, rather than the individual level?
2. According to Rhode, liberal and conservative analysts see teen pregnancy similarly. In what way are their assumptions similar? How does Rhode differ from them?
3. What implications does Rhode's argument have for the way teen access to abortion should be regulated?
4. Many states require pregnant minors to notify or obtain consent from one or more parents before they can obtain an abortion. Constitutionally, such requirements must be accompanied by the option of a "judicial bypass"—where the minor who does not want to involve her parents can obtain permission for the abortion from a judge instead. In some states, judges must grant such permission if they find that the minor is sufficiently mature and that the abortion is in her best interests. In others, the judge must find that the minor is mature and that *the exclusion of the parents* (rather than the abortion) is in her best interests. Some states require both. Which approach is preferable? Could a minor ever be *not* sufficiently mature to consent to an abortion on her own, and yet sufficiently mature to bear the child and become a mother? That is, does it make sense for a court to find that the minor is immature, and yet that the *abortion* is *not* in her best interest? *See* Jamin B. Raskin, "The Paradox of Judicial Bypass Proceedings," 10 Am. U. J. Gender, Soc. Pol'y. & L. 281, 281 (2002).
5. What is Dailard's argument about abstinence "failure"? According to that argument, in what way do abstinence proponents overstate this approach's effectiveness by ignoring its "failure" rates?
6. Do abstinence-only programs run by public schools violate the privacy rights of students in those schools? In other words, do they violate the students' right to reproductive autonomy?
7. In *Bowen v. Kendrick,* 108 S.Ct. 2562 (1988), the U.S. Supreme Court held that the Adolescent and Family Life Act, which provides grants to both religious and secular institutions to run abstinence-only programs, did not violate the Establishment Clause of the First Amendment. The Court concluded, "The Act's approach toward dealing with adolescent sexuality and pregnancy is not inherently religious, although it may coincide with the approach taken by certain religions." 108 S.Ct., at 2564.

3. Wrongful Birth and Selective Abortion

Chapter 21

Not Your Garden Variety Tort Reform

Statutes Barring Claims for Wrongful Life and Wrongful Birth Are Unconstitutional under the Purpose Prong of Planned Parenthood v. Casey

Julie F. Kowitz

At the age of 36, Julie Sejpal gave birth to a daughter with Down syndrome. Ms. Sejpal, a teacher of differently-abled children, had expressed concern throughout her pregnancy that she was at increased risk for fetal anomalies because of her age. Still her obstetricians discouraged her from getting amniocentesis, assuring her that the test would not be necessary unless other prenatal tests suggested a problem. Two months later, a routine prenatal blood test showed that Ms. Sejpal faced a greater than normal risk of giving birth to a child with Down syndrome. The laboratory result specifically warned that the patient should be advised about the availability of amniocentesis and genetic counseling.

Ms. Sejpal's physicians never advised her about the availability of amniocentesis, nor did they refer her for genetic counseling. In fact, when a sonogram indicated that her pregnancy was not progressing normally, one of her obstetricians misinformed her that the fetus's small size suggested only that her pregnancy was less advanced than he had thought. When Ms. Sejpal asked if the blood test should be repeated, he told her it was unnecessary.

On August 30, 1989, Erica Sejpal was delivered by Cesarean section. Julie Sejpal saw Erica only briefly before a nurse whisked the baby off under the pretext that Erica needed oxygen. The medical personnel told both Julie Sejpal and her husband that Erica was fine; no one alerted them to Erica's condition. The obstetrician then proceeded to sterilize Ms. Sejpal by tubal ligation, a procedure to which Ms. Sejpal had consented the week before. Ms. Sejpal did not find out until hours after Erica's delivery and the sterilization that her baby had been born with Down syndrome.

Julie Sejpal and her husband sued her physicians and the hospital for wrongful birth. They also sued on behalf of Erica for wrongful life. The Sejpals alleged that Ms. Sejpal would have had the information necessary to decide whether to terminate her pregnancy but for the physicians' and hospital's acts. They further asserted that if Ms.

Julie F. Kowitz, "Not Your Garden Variety Tort Reform: Statutes Barring Claims for Wrongful Life and Wrongful Birth Are Unconstitutional under the Purpose Prong of *Planned Parenthood v. Casey*," 61 Brook. L. Rev. 235 (1995).

Sejpal had known of her fetus's condition, she would have sought an abortion and would not have consented to being sterilized.

The Sejpals filed suit in Pennsylvania state court. Unfortunately for the Sejpals, Pennsylvania bars wrongful life and birth claims by statute. Accordingly, the physicians and the hospital sought to dismiss these claims. In response to the motion, the Sejpals asserted that the statutes violated their Fourteenth Amendment right to privacy, which encompassed Julie Sejpal's right to choose abortion as established in *Roe v. Wade*. The Court of Common Pleas rejected this assertion, finding that the statutes did not infringe on any Fourteenth Amendment rights, and dismissed the claims for wrongful life and wrongful birth.

Whether and to what degree the Fourteenth Amendment prevents a state from restricting the right to choose abortion would soon become an issue of national debate. One month after the Court of Common Pleas' decision, in April 1992, a nation in the midst of this divisive and vitriolic debate listened anxiously to the most passionate argument before the United States Supreme Court since *Brown v. Board of Education*. Two months later, the Court released its now landmark decision in *Planned Parenthood of Southeastern Pennsylvania v. Casey* (hereinafter *Planned Parenthood v. Casey*), in which a plurality affirmed the "essential holding" of *Roe v. Wade* while upholding considerable restrictions on a woman's right to terminate her pregnancy. Most significantly, the *Casey* plurality altered abortion jurisprudence radically with its ruling that restrictions on a woman's right to choose abortion were no longer subject to strict scrutiny, but instead to a newly-minted and less stringent "undue burden" standard of review.

At the same time as the *Casey* plurality lowered the constitutional standard of review for laws that affect the right to choose abortion, *Casey* expanded the scope of legislation that would be subject to that review. The joint opinion defined an undue burden as "a state regulation (that) has the purpose or effect of placing a substantial obstacle in the path of a woman seeking an abortion of a nonviable fetus." This disjunctive language—"purpose or effect"—provides two alternative and independent bases for review of legislation affecting reproductive choice. Prior to *Casey*, purpose was not an independent inquiry. After *Casey*, legislation affecting abortion rights is unconstitutional if it is passed with either the purpose of substantially obstructing women seeking abortions or when the legislation has that effect.

Statutes that bar wrongful life and wrongful birth claims are passed with precisely the purpose that *Casey* proscribes. The express purpose of these statutes is to remove physicians' liability for these birth-related torts. On its face, this legislation appears to be standard tort reform. The legislative history of Pennsylvania's wrongful life and birth statutes, however, illustrates that the Pennsylvania legislature's actual reason for banning wrongful life and birth actions was not tort reform, but to deter women from having abortions. The legislature intended to accomplish this purpose by encouraging physicians to withhold information from women about the health of their fetuses— information that might lead women to seek abortions. This legislative purpose—to prevent a woman from making an informed choice about whether to terminate her pregnancy—is proscribed by the purpose prong of *Planned Parenthood v. Casey*.

This Note argues that under the effect prong of *Casey*, statutes that bar wrongful life and wrongful birth claims have an indirect but impermissible effect on a woman's right to choose abortion. That effect may be difficult to prove, however, under the effect prong analysis that *Casey* requires. These statutes' impermissible legislative purpose, however, is eminently clear. . . .

The Development of the Wrongful Birth and Wrongful Life Causes of Action

Wrongful life and wrongful birth actions arise when a physician's negligent care leads to the birth of a child that the parents might have chosen to abort had they been given access to all available information earlier in the pregnancy. In such suits, the physician usually fails to provide the parents with correct information about or diagnosis of a genetic aberration or developmental abnormality in the fetus. Alternatively, a claim may arise when the physician fails to diagnose a parent's genetic condition properly. In this circumstance, the physician's act or omission leads to a pregnancy that otherwise could have been prevented by contraception.

A wrongful life action is brought by or on behalf of the child born with congenital anomalies. The child alleges that but for the negligent diagnosis or the withheld information, he or she would not have been conceived or would not have been born. The child sues for damages resulting from his or her birth, including pain and suffering, and for lifetime financial support. Often, the parents bring a wrongful birth action on their own behalf in conjunction with the wrongful life action. They allege that the physician's failure to provide adequate medical information deprived them of the opportunity to make a meaningful decision whether to conceive or bear a differently abled child. The parents typically seek damages for expenses related to the child's condition, including the extraordinary costs of the child's medical care and special educational needs. The parents may also seek damages for the emotional distress which they suffer.

. . . .

Almost universally, courts have upheld the validity of wrongful birth claims. Wrongful life claims have not fared as well; only four state courts have recognized this tort.

The recognition of wrongful birth and life suits prompted pro-life organizations to lobby heavily for legislation barring the claims. Influenced, at least in part, by these efforts, twenty-one states introduced legislation to prohibit wrongful birth or wrongful life actions. Although the majority of these laws were not enacted, nine states have statutes barring wrongful birth claims, wrongful life claims, or both. Only a handful of cases have challenged the constitutionality of these statutes,[1] and no majority opinion has held them to be unconstitutional. In four of the nine states that bar wrongful life and birth claims, the statutes have never been challenged.

While few cases have considered the constitutionality of the impact that statutes barring wrongful life and wrongful birth claims have on the right to abortion, those cases that have justify upholding them on two bases—because the statute's bar does not affect the right to terminate pregnancy, or because the statute's effect does not constitute state action. . . . The Fourteenth Amendment protects individuals against action taken by the states, not against action taken by private parties. Courts that have [based their rulings on a lack of state action reason] that private physicians, and not the state, are the actors in the wrongful life scenario. Courts also have rejected the argument that by removing physician liability, the statutes encourage physicians to withhold information. . . .

Courts that have surpassed the threshold state action issue to consider the merits of challenges to statutes barring wrongful life and birth claims have held that the statutes do not affect abortion rights. These cases—almost all of which were decided prior to *Casey*—use the analysis developed in *Roe*. They interpret *Roe* to govern only legislation that directly impacts on abortion rights and therefore reject challenges to statutes barring wrongful life and birth claims because such statutes do not regulate or affect abortion directly. Analysis of these statutes under the undue burden test developed in *Casey*, however, yields a significantly different result.

An Analysis of Wrongful Life and Birth Statutes under Casey: Purpose and Effect

The Importance of the Purpose Prong

While *Planned Parenthood v. Casey* restricted the right to abortion by permitting broader state regulation of the procedure, *Casey*'s purpose prong generated a new, independent basis to challenge legislation that impinges on the right to choose abortion. Courts have continued to ignore the purpose prong, however, perhaps because the plurality in *Casey* did not perform a purpose analysis of the Abortion Control Act. This oversight notwithstanding, a purpose test for legislation that affects abortion rights is important in several respects.

First, purpose prong analysis is distinct from the extensive fact-based, effect prong analysis applied by the Supreme Court and lower courts post-*Casey*. Under the effect prong, because only a substantial obstacle constitutes an undue burden, the court must ascertain not only whether an obstacle exists, but the "size" of the obstacle. The "effect" of a restriction must be calculable. Furthermore, courts must distinguish between a particular burden and an undue burden; only an undue burden is unconstitutional.

This calculation becomes increasingly difficult if the challenged law is not an abortion regulation, but still affects the right to choose abortion indirectly. Statutes that bar wrongful life and birth claims fall in this category. The "effect" of such an indirect regulation of abortion can be either difficult to measure, or too conflated with other factors to satisfy a *Casey* effect prong analysis. Moreover, effect prong analysis relies on highly case-specific factors; the outcome of the analysis may vary from state to state. A virtually identical restriction might pose a substantial obstacle in one state and not in another. These shifting, case-specific considerations, the vagueness of the term "substantial" and the difficulty of accurately measuring the effect of abortion restrictions make the effect prong of *Casey* unpredictable, difficult to prove, and highly prone to result-oriented judicial decision-making. In contrast, purpose prong analysis avoids this quagmire because it does not rely on such immeasurable, case-specific, and manipulable factors.

. . . .

Furthermore, inasmuch as legislators do not pass laws arbitrarily but with a desired end in mind, a finding of impermissible purpose can buttress a litigant's efforts to prove the unconstitutional effect of an abortion regulation. When a competent legislature intends to place a substantial obstacle in the path of a woman seeking an abortion, one can presume that the resulting legislation will successfully effectuate that end. A finding of unconstitutional legislative purpose, while not dispositive, may be indicative of that legislation's unconstitutional effect. . . .

Finally, analysis of the legislative purpose of a statute resolves the state action problem. . . . When the state intends for a statute to have an impermissible impact on constitutionally protected rights, the statute no longer regulates individual conduct alone. While the conduit for the state's act may be a private individual—such as the physician in a wrongful life or birth suit—if the state intends for that individual to violate another's constitutional rights, it is as if the state itself has acted. Passage and enforcement of such a statute therefore constitutes state action. In the case of statutes barring wrongful birth and life suits, an analysis of those statutes' purpose is essential to overcoming the state action problem.

Analysis of Wrongful Birth and Life Statutes under *Casey*'s Effect Prong

. . . .

[Under *Casey,* an] acceptable regulation becomes an impermissible infringement on a woman's right to liberty only when it has the "effect of placing a substantial obstacle in the path of a woman seeking an abortion." Therefore, statutes that bar wrongful birth or life suits must have the effect of substantially obstructing a woman from obtaining an abortion in order to be invalid under the effect prong of *Casey.*

. . . .

The *Casey* plurality repeatedly emphasized that informed choice is central to a woman's right to abortion, and encouraged states to pass legislation "aimed at ensuring a decision that is mature and informed."[2] Moreover, *Casey* stressed the centrality of the doctor-patient relationship for creating the necessary forum for informed consent. The Court stressed that the state-mandated information provided by physicians must be "truthful and not misleading"[3] as well as "calculated to inform the woman's free choice, not hinder it."[4]

A physician's failure to disclose accurate information about fetal health to a pregnant woman is as misleading as providing false information. . . . Moreover, the particular information withheld—the health of the fetus—is so integral to informed choice that its omission substantially obstructs a woman's right to choose abortion. By posing such an obstacle, statutes barring wrongful life and birth claims unduly burden a woman's right to choose abortion and are unconstitutional. . . . [However,] *Casey* demands a highly detailed factual showing to prove substantiality. Gathering the requisite evidence in these circumstances is difficult for several reasons. First, courts are likely to demand that a litigant establish that the affected group of women absolutely would have chosen to terminate their pregnancies had they known of the fetal defect. If the affected women might have carried the fetus to term, courts are likely to view the information withheld as not substantial, or perhaps as no obstacle at all. Moreover, although it is a question of fact, the average woman probably cannot predict accurately her reaction to the knowledge that she carries a child with mental or physical anomalies. Courts are apt to view women's speculations as unreliable.

Similarly, showing that the affected group chose not to abort based solely on physician omission presents equally thorny problems. The decision to abort is uncomplicated for many women, but not for all. For some women, the choice between carrying to term and terminating a pregnancy is dependant on a combination of many factors: her health, her financial resources, her desire to have a child, her relationship status, if any, and the timing of the pregnancy. Health of the fetus is only one, albeit a highly significant, factor. A court is unlikely to be inclined toward or capable of parsing out the omitted information's effect from the effect of other factors. . . .

Analysis of Wrongful Life and Wrongful Birth Statutes under *Casey*'s Purpose Prong

Under the purpose prong of *Casey*, a challenge to wrongful life and birth statutes may be successful. As noted above, *Casey* forbids legislation that has the "purpose . . . of placing a substantial obstacle in the path of a woman seeking an abortion." Legislation with this purpose violates a woman's Fourteenth Amendment liberty interest in abortion. In the abortion context, specific legislative purposes are presumptively valid: for example, the state can attempt to discourage women from seeking abortions to further its interest in potential life. When the state's purpose surpasses mere encouragement and reaches the intent to substantially obstruct a woman's abortion decision, the legislation becomes unconstitutional under *Casey*. Close examination of the purpose of legislation affecting abortion rights is necessary to distinguish permissible from impermissible state goals.
. . . .

The legislative history of Pennsylvania's wrongful birth and life statute both exposes and exemplifies [the statute's] impermissible legislative intent. . . . In support of the House version, Representative [Stephen] Freind testified that "until *Roe* . . . is reversed, those in the pro-life movement must be as aggressive and creative as possible in drafting and passing legislation which regulates and restricts abortion as much as possible."[5] Representative Freind emphasized that the legislation was designed to protect those pro-life physicians who would refuse to perform amniocentesis if they believed it would influence a woman's decision whether to carry to term or to abort. One such pro-life physician, testifying to the same committee, urged passage of the House bill to protect physicians, who, like himself, would not "order tests and studies on a pregnant woman, the sole purpose of which is to destroy the unborn child."[6] This physician further testified that he would not participate in treatment that could possibly result in abortion. This testimony amply shows that the bill's sponsors did not have tort reform in mind, but fully intended for the bill to obstruct women's right to abortion.

In House debate, Representative Freind argued that wrongful life and birth suits force physicians to recommend eugenic abortions. He consistently reiterated that even if a physician intentionally and knowingly lied to a woman about the health of her fetus, under the proposed legislation, the woman would not have a cause of action for infringement of her right to abortion. Furthermore, he argued that "no law . . . requires a doctor on any treatment for any condition to fully disclose the information to the patient."[7] Regardless of the veracity of such statements pre-*Casey*, *Casey* clearly dictates that the information physicians provide to pregnant women about their options be "truthful and not misleading." Supporters of the bill bluntly advocate violations of that principle.

Supporters of the Senate bill made similar arguments to those of its House proponents. Senator Joseph Rocks, the bill's sponsor in the Senate, for example, defined the legislature's objective in barring wrongful life and birth claims as preventing physicians from being "coerced into accepting eugenic abortion as a condition for avoiding [a lawsuit]."[8] Another proponent saw the function of a statute barring wrongful life and birth suits as "a simple question of whether [the legislature] should or should not save the life of an unborn child."[9]

Opponents of both the House and Senate bills expressed grave concern about the detrimental effect of such legislation on a woman's informed consent. . . . Senator Greenwood criticized the bill, stating:

> (I)t is ironic that the proponents of this legislation, who have argued so relentlessly about the need for informed consent for those who would have an abortion, who have argued that any woman who is about to have an abortion must be told every last detail about the risks of the abortion, about the details of the abortion, about the possible complications of an abortion, that same woman should be kept in the dark . . . and not given informed consent about some of the medical tools available to her in her pregnancy. The way this bill does that is by providing immunity from wrongful birth suits for physicians who withhold that information.[10]

. . . .

This legislative history demonstrates that the legislative purpose of section 8305 is to substantially obstruct women from seeking abortions. This purpose is prohibited under the purpose prong of *Casey*. The proponents of section 8305 aim to reduce the number of abortions by allowing physicians to withhold information that might lead women to abort their fetuses. Because *Casey* insists that women be given accurate, nonmisleading information about their pregnancies, and because these statutes have the purpose of encouraging physicians to mislead women, they violate a woman's Fourteenth Amendment right to liberty.

. . . .

NOTES

1. See, e.g., Hickman v. Group Health, Inc., 396 N.W.2d 10 (Minn. 1986); Edmonds v. Western Pa. Hosp. Radiology Assocs., appeal denied, 607 A.2d 1083 (Pa. Super. Ct. 1992), 621 A.2d 580 (Pa. 1993), cert. denied, 114 S. Ct. 63 (1993). At least one court has interpreted a conscience clause

statute, which allows physicians and nurses to refuse to perform abortions, as indicating legislative leaning toward disfavor of wrongful life and wrongful birth claims. See Azzolino v. Dingfelder, 337 S.E.2d 528 (N.C. 1985), cert. denied, 479 U.S. 835 (1986) (barring wrongful life and wrongful birth claims based on conscience clause provision).

2. 112 S. Ct. 2791, 2824 (1992).

3. See Casey, 112 S. Ct. at 2823.

4. Id. at 2820.

5. Hearing on H.B. 1361, Idaho Code S 5–334 (1986) (testimony of Representative Freind).

6. Id. (statement of Dr. Samuel H. Henck, family practitioner).

7. See, e.g., Pa. House Leg. J. 310, 313 (Feb. 24, 1988).

8. Pa. Senate Leg. J. 1961 (March 22, 1988).

9. Id. at 1963 (statement of Senator Clarence Bell).

10. Id. at 1960 (statement of Senator James C. Greenwood).

Chapter 22

Disability Rights and Selective Abortion

Marsha Saxton

Disability rights activists are now articulating a critical view of the widespread practice of prenatal diagnosis with the intent to abort if the pregnancy might result in a child with a disability. . . . [Activists have begun] to challenge a basic tenet of disability oppression: that disability *causes* the low socioeconomic status of disabled persons. Collective consciousness-raising has made it clear that stigma is the cause. . . .

Effective community organizing by blind, deaf, and mobility-impaired citizen groups and disabled student groups flourished in the late 1960s and resulted in new legislation. In 1973 the Rehabilitation Act Amendments (Section 504) prohibited discrimination in federally funded programs. The Americans with Disabilities Act of 1990 (ADA) provides substantial civil rights protection and has helped bring about a profound change in the collective self-image of an estimated 4.5 million Americans. Today, many disabled people view themselves as a part of a distinct minority and reject the pervasive stereotypes of disabled people as defective, burdensome, and unattractive.

It is ironic that just when disabled citizens have achieved so much, the new reproductive and genetic technologies are promising to eliminate births of disabled children—children with Down syndrome, spina bifida, muscular dystrophy, sickle cell anemia, and hundreds of other conditions. . . .

Reproductive Rights in a Disability Context

There is a key difference between the goals of the reproductive rights movement and the disability rights movement regarding reproductive freedom: the reproductive rights movement emphasizes the right to have an abortion; the disability rights movement, the right *not to have* an abortion. Disability rights advocates believe that disabled women have the right to bear children and be mothers, and that all women have the right to resist pressure to abort when the fetus is identified as potentially having a disability.

Women with disabilities raised these issues at a conference on new reproductive technologies (NRTs) in Vancouver in 1994. For many of the conference participants,

Marsha Saxton, "Disability Rights and Selective Abortion," in RICKIE SOLINGER (ed.), ABORTION WARS: A HALF CENTURY OF STRUGGLE, 1950–2000, 374, 374–393 (1998).

we were an unsettling group: women in wheelchairs; blind women with guide dogs; deaf women who required a sign-language interpreter; women with scarring from burns or facial anomalies; women with missing limbs, crutches, or canes. I noticed there what we often experience from people who first encounter us: averted eyes or stolen glances, pinched smiles, awkward or overeager helpfulness—in other words, discomfort accompanied by the struggle to pretend there was none.

It was clear to me that this situation was constraining communication, and I decided to do something about it. I approached several of the non-disabled women, asking them how they felt about meeting such a diverse group of disabled women. Many of the women were honest when invited to be: "I'm nervous. Am I going to say something offensive?" "I feel pretty awkward. Some of these women's bodies are so different!" One woman, herself disabled, said that she'd had a nightmare image of a disabled woman's very different body. One woman confessed: "I feel terrible for some of these unfortunate disabled women, but I know I'm not supposed to feel pity. That's awful of me, right?"

This awkwardness reveals how isolated the broader society and even progressive feminists are from people with disabilities. . . . In the United States this information void has yielded a number of unexamined assumptions, including the belief that the quality and enjoyment of life for disabled people is necessarily inferior, that raising a child with a disability is a wholly undesirable experience, that selective abortion will save mothers from the burdens of raising disabled children, and that ultimately we as a society have the means and the right to decide who is better off not being born.

What the women with disabilities were trying to do at the Vancouver conference, and what I wish to do in this essay, is explain how selective abortion or *eugenic abortion,* as some disability activists have called it, not only oppresses people with disabilities, but also hurts all women.

Eugenics and the Birth Control Movement

The eugenic interest that stimulates reliance on prenatal screening and selective abortion today has had a central place in reproductive politics for more than half a century. In the nineteenth century, eugenicists believed that most traits, including such human "failings" as pauperism, alcoholism, and thievery, as well as such desired traits as intelligence, musical ability, and "good character," were hereditary. . . .

Leaders in the early birth control movement in the United States, including Margaret Sanger, generally embraced a eugenic view, encouraging white Anglo-Saxon women to reproduce while discouraging reproduction among nonwhite, immigrant, and disabled people. Proponents of eugenics portrayed disabled women in particular as unfit for procreation and as incompetent mothers. In the 1920s Margaret Sanger's group, the American Birth Control League, allied itself with the director of the American Eugenics Society, Guy Irving Burch. The resulting coalition supported the forced sterilization of people with epilepsy, as well as those diagnosed as mentally retarded and mentally ill. . . .

Disability-Positive Identity Versus Selective Abortion

It is clear that some medical professionals and public health officials are promoting prenatal diagnosis and abortion with the intention of eliminating categories of disabled people, people with Down syndrome and my own disability, spina bifida, for example. . . .

The resistance to [such] selective abortion in the disability activist community is ultimately related to how we define ourselves. . . . [W]e've come to realize that the stereotyped notions of the "tragedy" and "suffering" of "the disabled" result from the *isolation* of disabled people in society. Disabled people with no connections to others with disabilities in their communities are, indeed, afflicted with the social role assignment of a tragic, burdensome existence. It is true, most disabled people I know have told me with certainty, that the disability, the pain, the need for compensatory devices and assistance can produce considerable inconvenience. But the inconvenience becomes minimal once the disabled person makes the transition to a typical everyday life. It is discriminatory attitudes and thoughtless behaviors, and the ensuing ostracism and lack of accommodation, that make life difficult. That oppression is what's most disabling about disability.

. . . .

[T]he "Baby Doe" cases of the 1980s caught the attention of the growing disability rights movement. These cases revealed that "selective nontreatment" of disabled infants (leaving disabled infants to starve because the parents or doctors chose not to intervene with even routine treatments such as antibiotics) was not a thing of the past. In this same period, we also took note of the growing number of "wrongful birth" suits—medical malpractice suits brought against physicians, purportedly on behalf of disabled children, by parents who feel that the child's condition should have been identified prenatally. These lawsuits claim that disabled babies, once born, are too great a burden, and that the doctors who failed to eliminate the "damaged" fetuses should be financially punished. . . .

Many who resist selective abortion insist that there is something deeply valuable and profoundly human (though difficult to articulate in the sound bites of contemporary thought) in meeting and loving a child or adult with a severe disability. Thus, contributions of human beings cannot be judged by how we fit into the mold of normalcy, productivity, or cost-benefit. People who are different from us (whether in color, ability, age, or ethnic origin) have much to share about what it means to be human. We must not deny ourselves the opportunity for connection to basic humanness by dismissing the existence of people labeled "severely disabled."

Mixed Feelings: Disabled People Respond to Selective Abortion

The disability *activist* community has begun to challenge selective abortion. But among disabled people as a whole, there is no agreement about these issues. After all, the "disability community" is as diverse as any other broad constituency, like "the working class" or "women." . . .

People with different kinds of disabilities may have complex feelings about prenatal screening tests. While some disabled people regard the tests as a kind of genocide, others choose to use screening tests during their own pregnancies to avoid the birth of a disabled child. But disabled people may also use the tests differently from women who share the larger culture's anti-disability bias.

Many people with dwarfism, for example, are incensed by the idea that a woman or couple would choose to abort simply because the fetus would become a dwarf. When someone who carries the dwarfism trait mates with another with the same trait, there is a likelihood of each partner contributing one dominant dwarfism gene to the fetus. This results in a condition called "double dominance" for the offspring, which, in this "extra dose of the gene" form, is invariably accompanied by severe medical complications and early death. So prospective parents who are carriers of the dwarfism gene, or are themselves dwarfs, who would readily welcome a dwarf child, might still elect to use the screening test to avoid the birth of a fetus identified with "double dominance."

Deafness provides an entirely different example. There is as yet no prenatal test for deafness, but if, goes the ethical conundrum, a hearing couple could eliminate the fetus that would become a deaf child, why shouldn't deaf people, proud of their own distinct sign-language culture, elect for a deaf child and abort a fetus (that would become a hearing person) on a similar basis?

Those who challenge selective or eugenic abortion claim that people with disabilities are the ones who have the information about what having a disability is like. The medical system, unable to cure or fix us, exaggerates the suffering and burden of disability. The media, especially the movies, distort our lives by using a disability as a metaphor for evil, impotence, eternal dependence, or tragedy—or conversely as a metaphor for courage, inspiration, or sainthood. Disabled people alone can speak for the women facing these tests. Only we can speak about our real lives, our ordinary lives, and the lives of disabled children.

"Did you get your Amnio yet?": The Pressure to Test and Abort

. . . .

The reproductive technology market has, since the mid-1970s, gradually changed the experience of pregnancy. Some prenatal care facilities now present patients with their ultrasound photo in a pink or blue frame. Women are increasingly pressured to use prenatal testing under a cultural imperative claiming that this is the "responsible thing to do." . . . As feminist biologist Ruth Hubbard put it, "Women are expected to implement the society's eugenic prejudices by 'choosing' to have the appropriate tests and 'electing' not to initiate or to terminate pregnancies if it looks as though the outcome will offend."[1] . . .

[S]ome doctors and counselors do make a good-faith effort to explore with prospective parents the point at which selective abortion may seem clearly "justifiable," with respect to the severity of the condition or the emotional or financial costs involved. These efforts are fraught with enormous social and ethical difficulty. Often, however, unacknowledged stereotypes prevail, as does a commitment to a libertarian view ("Let people do whatever they want!"). Together, these strains frequently push prospective parents to succumb to the medical control of birth while passively colluding with pervasive disability discrimination.

Among the most common justifications of selective abortion is that it "ends suffering." . . . What is too often missed in medical training and treatment are the *social factors* that contribute to suffering. Physicians, by the very nature of their work, often have a distorted picture of the lives of disabled people. They encounter disabled persons having health problems, complicated by the stresses of a marginalized life, perhaps exacerbated by poverty and race or gender discrimination, but because of their training, the doctors tend to project the individual's overall struggle onto the disability as the "cause" of distress. Most doctors have few opportunities to see ordinary disabled individuals living in their communities among friends and family.

Conditions receiving priority attention for prenatal screening include Down syndrome, spina bifida, cystic fibrosis, and fragile X, all of which are associated with mildly to moderately disabling clinical outcomes. Individuals with these conditions can live good lives. There are severe cases, but the medical system tends to underestimate the functional abilities and overestimate the "burden" and suffering of people with these conditions. Moreover, among the priority conditions for pre-natal screening are diseases that occur very infrequently. Tay-Sachs disease, for example, a debilitating, fatal disease that affects primarily Jews of eastern European descent, is often cited as a condition that justifies prenatal screening. But as a rare disease, it's a poor basis for a treatment mandate.

. . . .

It may be difficult for some to resist the argument that it is their duty to "save scarce health care dollars," by eliminating the expense of disabled children. But those who resist these arguments believe the value of a child's life cannot be measured in dollars. It is notable that families with disabled children who are familiar with the actual impact of the disabilities tend not to seek the tests for subsequent children. The bottom line is that the cost-benefit argument disintegrates when the outlay of funds required to provide services for disabled persons is measured against the enormous resources expended to test for a few rare genetic disorders. In addition, it is important to recognize that promotion and funding of prenatal tests distract attention and resources from addressing possible environmental causes of disability and disease.

Disabled People and the Fetus

I mentioned to a friend, an experienced disability activist, that I planned to call a conference for disabled people and genetics professionals to discuss these controversial issues. She said, "I think the conference is important, but I have to tell you, I have trouble being in the same room with professionals who are trying to eliminate my people." I was struck by her identification with fetuses as "our people." . . . The connection disabled people feel with the "disabled fetus" may seem to be in conflict with the pro-choice stance that the fetus is only a part of the woman's body, with no independent human status.

Many of us with disabilities might have been prenatally screened and aborted if tests had been available to our mothers. I've actually heard people say, "Too bad that baby with [x disease] didn't 'get caught' in prenatal screening." (This is the sentiment of "wrongful birth" suits.) It is important to make the distinction between a pregnant woman who chooses to terminate the pregnancy because she *doesn't want to be pregnant* as opposed to a pregnant woman who *wanted to be pregnant* but rejects a particular fetus, a particular potential child. Fetuses that are wanted are called "babies." Prenatal screening results can turn a "wanted baby" into an "unwanted fetus."

. . . .

Our resistance to the systematic abortion of "our young" is a challenge to the "non-humanness," the non-status of the fetus. This issue of the humanness of the fetus is a tricky one for those of us who identify both as pro-choice feminists and as disability rights activists. Our dual perspective offers important insights for those who are debating the ethics of the new reproductive technologies.

Disentangling Patriarchal Control and Eugenics from Reproductive Freedom

The issue of selective abortion is not just about the rights or considerations of disabled people. Women's rights and the rights of all human beings are implicated here.

When disability rights activists challenge the practice of selective abortion, as we did in Vancouver, many feminists react with alarm. They feel "uncomfortable" with language that accords human status to the fetus. . . . In the disability community[, however,] we make a clear distinction between our views and those of anti-abortion groups. There may have been efforts to court disabled people to support anti-abortion ideology, but anti-abortion groups have never taken up the issues of expanding resources for disabled people or parents of disabled children, never lobbied for disability legislation. They have shown no interest in disabled people after they are born.

But a crucial issue compels some of us to risk making people uncomfortable by discussing the fetus: we must clarify the connection between control of "defective fetuses" and the control of women as vessels or producers of quality-controllable products. . . . A consideration of selective abortion as a control mechanism must include a view of the procedure as a wedge into the "quality control" of all humans. If a condition (like Down syndrome) is unacceptable, how long will it be before experts use selective abortion to manipulate—eliminate or enhance—other (presumed genetic) socially charged characteristics: sexual orientation, race, attractiveness, height, intelligence? Pre-implantation diagnosis, now used with in vitro fertilization, offers the prospect of "admission standards" for all fetuses. . . . [A]s anthropologist Rayna Rapp notes, "Private choices always have public consequences."[2] When a woman's individual decision is the result of social pressure, it can have repercussions for all others in the society. . . . For those with "disability-positive" attitudes, the analogy with sex selection is obvious. Oppressive assumptions, not inherent characteristics, have devalued who this fetus will grow into.

. . . .

To blame a woman's oppression on the characteristics of the fetus is to obscure . . . the different access to "choice" of different groups of women. At conferences I've been asked, "Would I want to force a poor black woman to bear a disabled child?" That question reinforces what feminists of color have been saying, that the framework of "choice" trivializes the issues for nonprivileged women. It reveals distortions in the public's perception of users of prenatal screening; in fact, it is the middle and upper class who most often can purchase these "reproductive choices." It's not poor women, or families with problematic gene traits, who are creating the market for tests. Women with aspirations for the "perfect baby" are establishing new "standards of care." Responding to the lure of consumerism, they are helping create a lucrative market that exploits the culture's fear of disability and makes huge profits for the biotech industry.

Some proponents argue that prenatal tests are feminist tools because they save women from the excessive burdens associated with raising disabled children. This is like calling the washer-dryer a feminist tool; technological innovation may "save time," even allow women to work outside the home, but it has not changed who does the housework. Women still do the vast majority of child care, and child care is not valued as real work. . . . Selective abortion will not challenge the sexism of the family structure. . . .

I believe that at this point in history the decision to abort a fetus with a disability even because it "just seems too difficult" must be respected. A woman who makes this decision is best suited to assess her own resources. But it is important for her to realize this "choice" is actually made under duress. Our society profoundly limits the "choice" to love and care for a baby with a disability. This failure of society should not be projected onto the disabled fetus or child. No child is "defective." A child's disability doesn't ruin a woman's dream of motherhood. Our society's inability to appreciate and support people is what threatens our dreams. . . .

Women sometimes conclude, "I'm not saintly or brave enough to raise a disabled child." This objectifies and distorts the experience of mothers of disabled children. . . . It doesn't take a "special woman" to mother a disabled child. It takes a caring parent to raise any child. . . .

A Proposal for the Reproductive Rights Movement

. . . .

Our tasks are to gain clarity about prenatal diagnosis, challenge eugenic uses of reproductive technologies, and support the rights of all women to maintain control over reproduction. Here are some suggestions for action:

. . . .

- We must recognize disability as a feminist issue. All females (including teenagers and girls) will benefit from information and discussion about disability *before* they consider pregnancy, so they can avoid poorly informed decisions.
- Inclusion of people with disabilities must be part of the planning and outreach of reproductive rights organizations . . . [including] *involvement of disabled people* as resources. . . .

- We must support family initiatives—such as parental leave for mothers and fathers, flex-and part-time work, child care resources, programs for low-income families, and comprehensive health care programs—that help *all* parents and thus make parenting children with disabilities more feasible.
- We must convince legislatures, the courts, and our communities that fetal anomaly must never be used again as a justification or a defense for safe and legal abortion. This is a disservice to the disability community and an insupportable argument for abortion rights.
- We must make the case that "wrongful life" suits should be eliminated. "Wrongful birth" suits (that seek damages for the cost of caring for a disabled child) should be carefully controlled only to protect against medical malpractice, not to punish medical practitioners for not complying with eugenic policy.
- We must break the *taboo* in the feminist movement against discussing the fetus. Getting "uncomfortable" will move us toward clarity, deepening the discussion about women's control of our bodies and reproduction.

  . . . .

- We can help ourselves and each other gain clarity regarding the decision to abort a fetus with a disability. To begin with, we can encourage women to examine their motivations for having children, ideally before becoming pregnant. We can ask ourselves and each other: What needs are we trying to satisfy in becoming a mother? How will the characteristics of the potential child figure into these motivations? What opportunities might there be for welcoming a child who does not meet our ideals of motherhood? . . . Do we have sufficient knowledge about disability, and sufficient awareness of our own feelings about disabled people, for our choices to be based on real information, not stereotypes?

Taking these steps and responding to these questions will be a start toward increasing our clarity about selective abortion.

Caring about Ourselves and Each Other

. . . .

The message at the heart of widespread selective abortion on the basis of prenatal diagnosis is the greatest insult: some of us are "too flawed" in our very DNA to exist; we are unworthy of being born. This message is painful to confront. It seems easier to take on easier battles, or even just to give in. But fighting for this issue, our right and worthiness to be born, is the fundamental challenge to disability oppression; it underpins our most basic claim to justice and equality—we are indeed worthy of being born, worth the help and expense, and we know it! The great opportunity with this issue is to think and act and take leadership in the place where feminism, disability rights, and human liberation meet.

NOTES

1. Ruth Hubbard, The Politics of Women's Biology (New Brunswick, N.J.: Rutgers University Press, 1990), 197.

2. Rayna Rapp, "Accounting for Amniocentesis," in Knowledge, Power, and Practice: The Anthropology of Medicine in Everyday Life, ed. Shirley Lindenbaum and Margaret Lock (Berkeley: University of California Press, 1993).

4. Reproductive Rights of Women in Prison

Chapter 23

Searching for the State
Who Governs Prisoners' Reproductive Rights?

Rachel Roth

. . . .

[T]he contemporary penal state is rife with problems of accountability and transparency that undermine women's reproductive health and rights. . . . [T]he proliferation of confinement institutions—and the web of relationships among them and between them and private organizations and for-profit businesses—has changed the landscape and introduced new challenges to holding state actors accountable. I argue that the multifaceted nature of the state, characterized by decentralization, delegation, and discretion, makes justice elusive for imprisoned women who experience threats to their reproductive rights.

. . . .

[I]mprisoned women have to contend with a qualitatively different kind of state control than women in the "free world." [U]nderstand[ing] the constitution of state authority is a challenge, in part because prisons are closed institutions, operating largely, as an editorial recently put it, "in the shadows, outside public scrutiny" (New York Times 2004). Yet doing so is important, because understanding who, what, and where "the state" lies is necessary to foster any kind of accountability for women deprived of their liberty.[1] Although the scale of imprisonment makes this problem particularly acute in the United States, the shift to privatization under way in many countries, including the privatization of prisons operated by multinational corporations, may complicate questions of the state's identity and accountability in many places.

. . . .

Most women in prison are poor and will return to poor communities after serving their time. They tend to be relatively young, mothers of at least one child, and disproportionately African American, Latina, and Native American. . . . The permanent disadvantages that come with having a prison record in the United States, especially a felony drug record, should be of interest to welfare scholars as well as scholars of punishment. . . . Because jails and prisons are part of the fabric of life for many families and communities, ignoring prisoners distorts analysis of the needs, experiences, and rights of women of color and lower-income women in general.

Rachel Roth, "Searching for the State: Who Governs Prisoners' Reproductive Rights?" 11 SOCIAL POLITICS 411 (2004).

Searching for the State in the Field

. . . .

Penal policy . . . is characterized by local discretion. "Local" has two meanings. First, about 40 percent of women are confined in local jails—some 3,300 of them, run largely without state oversight by sheriffs or other municipal officials. Second, legislative bodies typically delegate broad powers to those who run prison systems, whether public or private. Although the federal prison sector has expanded greatly since the 1980s, crime is still primarily a state matter in the United States. State governments may neither require nor allow for public involvement in policy making about prisons. In Colorado, for instance, Department of Corrections (DOC) policies are statutorily exempt from the standard rule-making procedures that guide the regulatory process. . . .

These high levels of decentralization, delegation, and discretion often obscure the locus of official decision-making authority over reproduction. Are relevant policies formalized and written down? Are they publicly available? . . . In many cases, the answer to these questions is no.

The lack of transparency and accountability is deeply troubling because reproductive rights are critically important for prisoners. Demographically, the typical prisoner is in her late twenties or early thirties—in other words, someone for whom reproductive health and control is very salient. An estimated 5–10 percent of women enter prison and jail pregnant, and others become pregnant while they are imprisoned. Because few states permit conjugal visits—and prisoners must be legally married to qualify—most women are getting pregnant with someone who works on the inside.[2]

. . . .

[I]t has become increasingly common for prisoners to find themselves farmed out under contractual arrangements to institutions in other states or localities. When the Alabama DOC sent 200 women to a private prison in Louisiana, for instance, the women missed out on visits from their families and found themselves without access to education programs or even Alabama legal materials (Crowder 2003). Whether and to what extent prisoners can assert rights under the policies of their home state is an evolving question legally and an open question practically.

Finally, privatization further undermines accountability. Although relatively few women are confined in private prisons, many have to rely on private companies for medical care. . . . Privatization introduces a profit motive into the provision of treatment, and prisoners are an especially vulnerable group because of their serious health needs as well as their structural position. Privatized services are rarely monitored adequately and rarely save money; indeed, proper monitoring makes any contract more expensive. Whether private contractors can be held liable for medical neglect or abuse under state law varies by state; private contractors are not immune from challenges under the federal civil rights law governing actions against state and local governments (42 U.S.C. Section 1983). The Supreme Court has held, however, that private corporations that run prisons under federal contract are shielded from lawsuits for constitutional violations—a decision that blurs the distinction between the "state" and "nonstate" actors to prisoners' disadvantage (Alexander 2003).

. . . .

Bearing in mind these complex institutional arrangements, what do we find when trying to make sense of state power in the lived experiences of women negotiating reproductive health needs in prison? Because written policies are a critical element of transparency, the next two sections are organized according to whether women's conflicts with the state arise from the absence of official written policy or despite official policies.

. . . .

Governing by Unwritten Rules

Two recent conflicts over abortion access illustrate the kinds of obstacles imprisoned women confront when state authority rests in unwritten rules. In early 2003, a county sheriff in Texas transferred a woman to state prison to avoid dealing with her abortion request, an action that may suggest at least tacit cooperation among state agents (Lamoreaux 2003; Ruiz 2003a, 2003b). Confined in a Houston jail for violating her probation and facing two years in state prison, this woman sought to terminate her first-trimester pregnancy. During her three weeks at the jail, she was told that she would not be taken to a clinic for an abortion without a court order. Neither the woman nor the ACLU, which intervened on her behalf, ever succeeded in obtaining a written copy of the jail's policy. Lo and behold, the county sheriff transferred the woman to state prison the day after she filed a lawsuit in federal court, a move that rendered the case moot, because she was no longer in the sheriff's custody.

. . . .

Although this particular woman may be better off in the state prison system, which has written guidelines to handle abortion requests, her transfer by the sheriff leaves other women coming to the jail vulnerable to the same arbitrary treatment she experienced there.[3] . . .

The second case, spanning fall 2002, concerns a young Missouri woman sent to the St. Louis County jail because she missed a meeting with her probation officer (Lieberman 2003a, 2003b). When her pregnancy test came back "positive," she immediately asked for an abortion—and kept asking. Told "we don't do that," she filled out medical requests and grievances. As October gave way to November, she grew increasingly worried. Somehow, in early December, she found her way to the National Abortion Federation (NAF) hotline, and used all of her allotted telephone time to call the staff there. NAF contacted the ACLU Reproductive Freedom Project in New York, which contacted the legal director of the local ACLU, Denise Lieberman; NAF also relayed Lieberman's contact information to the jailed woman.

Initially, Lieberman did not fare much better with the powers that be than Lamoreaux had in Houston. Both the medical director at the jail (before she stopped talking to Lieberman) and the county attorney maintained that they were not required to provide the woman with an abortion, calling it a purely elective procedure, "like plastic surgery," and not medically necessary. Then finally, on the day before Christmas, the county attorney agreed to transport the woman to a local clinic for an abortion— just as Lieberman was digging her car out of the snow to go to the federal courthouse and file a lawsuit. But even this did not end the negotiations—more ensued over whether the woman would be shackled during the procedure (the clinic refused), and whether the guard would stand inside the room or outside the door. Because the county would not pay, Lieberman scrambled to raise the money from emergency abortion funds and a network of local women attorneys.

The county never produced any kind of written policy statement, leaving all other women confined in the jail in the same insecure position. In 2002, the jail admitted more than 1,500 women, a majority of whom were African American.[4] A less determined person than the subject of this story might have given up. The irony, if such a term is even appropriate, is that she was due to be released in three weeks anyway— but those extra three weeks would have pushed her to need a more expensive, more complicated, and less accessible abortion. Although we can never know precisely how many other women have encountered such problems, news reports and court documents identify similar conflicts between women and local penal authorities in at least twelve additional states: Arizona, California, Florida, Georgia, Idaho, Louisiana, New Jersey, New York, Ohio, Oregon, Pennsylvania, and Virginia. Some of these women never managed to obtain abortions.

As a matter of constitutional law, federal courts have consistently held that prisoners retain the right to abortion, yet corrections informants in several states indicated that they would review women's abortion requests on a case-by-case basis or that their practice is to allow minimum-security prisoners out on furlough, suggesting that higher-security prisoners would not be able to get an abortion (Roth 2004b). At the state level, some fourteen state DOCs lack official written abortion policies, and others will not release their policies to the public ("for security reasons"); at the federal level, the BICE [Bureau of Immigration and Customs Enforcement] has no publicly available policy about detained immigrants' access to abortion services. Because abortion is a time-sensitive need, the status quo in these states represents serious potential problems for women. To run through the obvious candidates, would the medical staff, the warden of the prison, the medical director for the central DOC, or some other DOC official get to decide? What if the medical provider is a private company and nothing about abortion was written into the contract?

In an opinion that belies the reality of negotiating for medical care behind bars, the U.S. Fifth Circuit Court of Appeals recently held that a jail can require a woman to obtain a court order authorizing her to be released or transported for an abortion. This decision also rests on the notion that abortions are elective medical procedures that jails are not required to provide. In contrast, the Third Circuit Court of Appeals has held that it is unreasonable to require a court order for an abortion.[5] The Third Circuit is also the one federal appellate court to consider the question of public funding; it ruled that if prisoners cannot pay for an abortion, then the state must do so (in this specific case, the Monmouth County Jail in New Jersey), because prisoners cannot fend for themselves and the state is obligated to provide for prisoners' serious medical needs (Monmouth County Correctional Institute Inmates v. Lanzaro, 34 F.2d 326 [3rd Cir. 1987], cert. denied 486 U.S. 1006). As a matter of official or default policy, though, many states impose on women all of the costs of transportation, security, and abortion—a significant burden, compounded by the concentration of abortion services in urban areas, and the concentration of prisons in rural areas.

The impact of privatization on abortion and pregnancy care is an area about which we know especially little but have reason to be concerned. Although financial incentives would lead to policies freely permitting abortion, because an abortion costs less than pregnancy care and giving birth in a hospital, this is not necessarily the case. One state corrections informant told me that CMS [Correctional Medical Services, the nation's largest private vendor of medical care to prisons] is antichoice, for instance. Privatization thus raises questions about whether abortion policy in a contracted medical setting emanates from the state, and even more so whether state or private actors make decisions in individual women's cases.

. . . .

Governing by Written Rules

Of course it would be naive to assume that written policies in and of themselves always suffice to guarantee reproductive rights. Policies may be unclear, contravene women's rights, or bear little resemblance to practice. Official written abortion policies, for instance, are models of neither transparency nor accountability. First, almost all formal state-level abortion policies are devised and approved without going through the regular administrative rule-making process, and the results may be inaccessible or incomplete. The Idaho DOC, for instance, posts the full text of its pregnancy testing and prenatal care policies on its Web site, but not the full text of its abortion policy. Alaska has a provision banning abortion funding in its overall "scope of [medical] services" policy, but no specific guidelines on abortion, including how a woman can get one with her own money. States may not define the category of therapeutic abortions for which, according to policy statements, they pay. Second, written policies may clearly limit women's abortion rights or burden them to the point where they cannot be exercised. Only two state policies, in Minnesota and Wisconsin, explicitly mention that they pay for abortions if a woman has been raped, making prison policies stingier than even federal Medicaid policy. Others make women pay for all of the costs associated with an abortion—transportation, security, and the procedure itself—which may put an abortion out of reach, especially if there is no local provider and if state law mandates in-person counseling by the clinic or other requirements necessitating more than one trip to the clinic.

. . . .

Although women's abortion claims may evoke more political controversy, women who need pregnancy care, preventive health care to preserve their fertility, and treatment for reproductive health problems also find their reproductive rights jeopardized by imprisonment. Because few jail or prison officials would say they do not provide prenatal and gynecological care, the problems here are more likely to be about standards of care, monitoring, and accountability than official policy. As one example, according to a lawsuit brought in 2002 by women in Alabama, the DOC and its private vendor NaphCare discourage women from seeking medical treatment, and the contract is designed to discourage the company from providing treatment. To discourage women, for instance, the prison holds sick call in the middle of the night (Laube v. Haley, second amended complaint, December 18, 2002). To discourage spending money on treatment, the contract defers to "physician judgment" on whether to treat preexisting conditions; a woman sentenced to prison after surgery for breast cancer received no chemotherapy for eighteen months (Cason 2002).

. . . .

[Another serious problem is] the gap between [official] written policy and practice, [as illustrated by] . . . women's inability to get into community-based prisons. The California DOC currently runs three Community Prisoner Mother Programs (CPMP) designed for pregnant women and women with children under the age of six. Although pregnant women are eligible for transfer to these facilities under the terms of a settlement agreement and other official state policy, they have reported for several years that they cannot get into the programs until after they give birth because the prison doctor will not sign off on their transfer. The doctor apparently tells women that they are too "high-risk" to travel for several hours to reach the program sites. As one woman writes: "I have a full duty paper from the doctor which states that I can work any job that is give[n] to me. Examp. Kitchen where there is water all over and very dangerous. And to me that's more of a high risk than traveling on a bus or van."[6]

Getting into one of these programs before having the baby is important to minimize the chance that something will go wrong. That is, women who have already transferred to CPMP can bring their baby back with them after they give birth. If they are still in the regular prison, and no one in the family is available to pick up the baby from the hospital on short notice, then the state would assume custody, creating the potential for problems later on when someone tries to claim the baby. Most pregnant women are sentenced to Valley State Prison for Women in California's San Joaquin Valley. Relatives may have to travel long distances to reach the hospital in Madera, where the women give birth. Madera is more than 215 miles from Los Angeles and about 180 miles from San Francisco; add up to 365 miles for those living north of the Bay Area, making the journey especially difficult for anyone who does not have a car. Even though women are aware of their rights, they are virtually powerless, by themselves, to hold the state accountable.

Women's problems with the state do not stop when they are released from prison. . . . [A] complicated and ever-widening net of official federal and state policies jeopardizes women's access to public goods and services that they, as low-income mothers, may need to regain custody of their children—benefits such as public housing, public assistance, food stamps, and student loans, not to mention employment. This is assuming they have been able to maintain their parental rights in the first place, escaping the impact of the 1997 Adoption and Safe Families Act (ASFA), which speeds up the process of terminating a parent's rights if her children are in foster care. No systematic research about the impact of ASFA has yet been done (and will be very difficult, as family court proceedings are closed to the public, unless they go up on appeal), but the anecdotal evidence from California to New York is that the law has hurt prisoners. Given the disproportionate number of African American children brought into the foster care systetm, some advocates consider fast-track adoption a modern form of genocide or political subordination (McCray 2003; Roberts 2002). In addition to ASFA, many states have their own statutes and court decisions that allow incarceration to be taken into account in proceedings concerning child placement or even target prisoners for termination of parental rights. Together, these policies continue to exact punishment even after someone has served her time. Paying one's debt to society becomes a permanent condition of life that undermines women's rights to be mothers.

Governing by Other Means: Pregnant Women in the Belly of the Beast

Pregnant women's encounters with staff members, in both security and custody roles and in medical roles, illustrate the ways that individuals wield the discretionary power of the state, cutting across the written/unwritten divide. Consider two examples that women brought to the attention of Legal Services for Prisoners with Children (LSPC), an organization that works with women and their families in California. As home to the two largest women's prisons in the world, California's policies and practices affect the lives of a significant number of prisoners in the country. Although California may be unusual in the size of its prison apparatus and the level of organized advocacy on behalf of women, the problems plaguing its medical system are by no means unique to the state.

One woman described going into labor during count—a surveillance ritual, performed several times each day, where each prisoner is locked in her cell and counted. Because the guards would not let her go to the infirmary until count was complete, she wound up giving birth alone twenty minutes after she got to the infirmary instead of at the hospital. Her story highlights how tensions between security and medicine are "resolved" in favor of security: here, the prison staff subordinated the woman's need for immediate medical attention to concerns with following standard security practices.

Another woman writes of her experience several months into her pregnancy:

> I went for my monthly checkup. They couldn't find my baby's heartbeat. . . . [Five days later] I was in a lot of pain and was spotting a lot. I told my housing staff and he called the MTA. She told him I didn't have proof, that she wouldn't see me. At that time the bleeding slow down so I put a pad on. It was blood on it but not good enough for her. She told me that All Pregnant Women Bleed. I told her that I was a high risk and when I seen the doctor last week he couldn't find a heartbeat. So she called the doctor and he told her to send me back to my unit. [Three days later at 3:00 A.M.] I lost my baby in my bathroom.[7]

MTA stands for medical technical assistant, a corrections officer who has trained to be a licensed vocational nurse. As this story shows, the MTAs work as gatekeepers to medical services, and critics argue that they render judgments far outside their licensed scope of practice. Contrary to medical and corrections ethics, they maintain dual roles as medical and security staff (American Nurses Association 1995). As LSPC medical advocacy coordinator Heidi Strupp says, "It's a fundamental conflict to have the person who can spray pepper spray in your eyes be the person to clean it out" (Strupp 2003). The MTA position is unique to California, a gift to the state's powerful corrections union, but other jurisdictions are creating positions that blur the lines.

In Chicago, the county jail has begun training corrections officers to serve as doulas, birth attendants whose purpose is to support and advocate for pregnant women (Christy Hall, personal communication 2004). Again, institutional loyalties would seem to undermine this role.

These two women's stories serve as stark reminders that jails and prisons limit women's movement, dramatizing the powerful and literal ways that prisons control women. Recall the story of the woman who fought so persistently for her abortion rights in the St. Louis County Jail. The jail is a "direct supervision" facility featuring pod construction, where guards bring meals and daily medications to the pod, instead of having prisoners move about the facility. A guard also picks up prisoners' requests for medical care and brings them to the medical unit. The woman who sought an abortion suspects that the guard did not deliver all of her requests and reports that he tore one up right in front of her. Because she was not free to move about the jail and deliver her requests herself, this woman was severely constrained in her efforts to be her own advocate.

. . . .

Conclusion

. . . .

Putting the state at the center of analysis points us in a promising direction to determine just how it is that prisons constrain women's lives and rights. From an advocacy perspective, it is important to know who is responsible for what, to determine the best avenues to press for accountability and change. Depending on the problem and the prison, advocates may fare best by working through the courts, legislature, or bureaucracy or by appealing directly to the public to build community support and public pressure. From a scholarly perspective, attending to prisons yields a more complete understanding of the state and of women's relationships with the state. . . . So, too, are prisons a critical arena for feminist scholars who reject "choice" as a framework for reproductive politics. Nowhere is it truer that simple invocations of choice are insufficient to guarantee women's reproductive rights than in prisons, where women are literally held captive by the state. The stories that emanate from women's prisons, including reports of unnecessary and unauthorized hysterectomies, evoke an earlier era and speak powerfully to the vulnerabilities wrought by racism, poverty, and state control. In a contemporary parallel, a perverse and ultimately false pronatalism characterizes the treatment of women in prison and the treatment of poor women outside—one that interferes with abortion so that women will have babies but then fails to support the children and families that result.

To borrow a phrase from anthropologist Jane Guyer, prisons are arenas where we feel "the presence of the state even in its absence" (personal communication 2002). By this I do not mean that the state is truly absent but that its seeming absence is itself one manifestation of contemporary state power. As this article has shown, at the most basic level the state is always present: After all, prisons have the power to hold women and limit their contact with the outside world, and individuals as well as institutions embody that power. Yet the state's contours and workings may be opaque, disjointed, and ambiguous, especially as states contract out the power to treat, confine, and punish. Some manifestations challenge our very ideas of what a prison is—for instance, "secure" community-based "facilities" for mothers and children that are run by private nonprofit organizations but also staffed by members of the state's corrections union. By interrogating both the absence and presence of official state power, feminist scholarship on prisons may generate new insights into the ways that states govern women's lives and secure a greater measure of justice for imprisoned women.

NOTES

1. Although beyond the scope of this article, men also have interests in reproduction, which prison officials may arbitrarily deny. A few men have tried unsuccessfully to claim the right to procreate with their wives outside of prison (Roth 2004a). Although imprisonment forecloses the hopes and dreams of both women and men of having children in the future, women experience distinctive dilemmas by virtue of already being pregnant when they come under state control and because they can become pregnant in prison.

2. I am inclined to argue that there is no such thing as consensual sex between prisoners and prison staff or volunteers. See Human Rights Watch (1996) and Amnesty International (1999, 2001).

3. There is no public record of what happened to this woman after her transfer to the state prison.

4. St. Louis County Department of Justice Services e-mail correspondence 2004. The department reports that 930 women were African American; 641 were white; and two were unknown or "other."

5. Compare Monmouth County Correctional Institute Inmates v. Lanzaro (1987), covering Delaware, New Jersey, and Pennsylvania, with Victoria W. v. Larpenter (2004 WL 928682, 5th Cir. [La.]), covering Louisiana, Mississippi, and Texas. . . .

6. Letter to LSPC [Legal Services for Prisoners with Children], quoted by permission.

7. Letter to LSPC, summarized and quoted by permission; emphasis in original.

SOURCES CITED

Alexander, Elizabeth. 2003. "Private Prisons and Health Care: The HMO from Hell." In Capitalist Punishment: Prison Privatization and Human Rights, ed. Andrew Coyle, Allison Campbell, and Rodney Neufeld, chap. 6. Atlanta: Clarity Press.

American Nurses Association. 1995. Scope and Standards of Nursing Practice in Correctional Facilities. Washington, D.C.: American Nurses Association.

Amnesty International. 1999. "Not Part of My Sentence": Violations of the Human Rights of Women in Custody. New York: Amnesty International.

———. 2001. Abuse of Women in Custody: Sexual Misconduct and Shackling of Pregnant Women. New York: Amnesty International.

Cason, Mike. 2002. "Inmates Claim Medical Care Lax." Montgomery Advertiser, December.

Coyle, Andrew, Allison Campbell, Rodney Neufeld, eds. 2003. Capitalist Punishment: Prison Privatization and Human Rights. Atlanta: Clarity Press.

Crowder, Carla. 2003. "Alabama Women Dislike Newer, Safer Prison: Inmates Miss Family Visits, Jobs at Crowded Tutwiler." Birmingham News, May 11.

Human Rights Watch. 1996. All Too Familiar: Sexual Abuse of Women in U.S. State Prisons. New York: Human Rights Watch.

Lamoreaux, Annette. 2003. Interview with regional director, ACLU of Texas, in Washington, D.C., June 9.

Lieberman, Denise. 2003a. "Legal Director's Report: Fighting for Equality, Free Speech, and Bodily Integrity." Liberties (newsletter of the ACLU of Eastern Missouri) 33 (1): 3.

———. 2003b. Interview with legal director of the ACLU of eastern Missouri, in St. Louis, July 17.

McCray, Ida. 2003. Interview with director of Families with a Future, in San Francisco, April 29.

New York Times. 2004. "The Dark Side of America" (editorial). May 17.

Roberts, Dorothy. 2002. Shattered Bonds: The Color of Child Welfare. New York: Basic Civitas Books.

Roth, Rachel. 2004a. "'No New Babies'? Gender Inequality and Reproductive Control in the Criminal Justice and Prison Systems." American University Journal of Gender, Social Policy, and the Law 12(3), forthcoming.

———. 2004b. "Do Prisoners Have Abortion Rights?" Feminist Studies 30(2), forthcoming.

Ruiz, Rosanna. 2003a. "County Inmate Suing for Right to Get Abortion." Houston Chronicle, February 6.

———. 2003b. "Inmate Who Sued to Get Abortion Is Transferred." Houston Chronicle, February 7.

Strupp, Heidi. 2003. Interview with medical advocacy coordinator, Legal Services for Prisoners with Children, in San Francisco, April 21.

Questions and Comments

1. Kowitz argues that statutes prohibiting wrongful birth claims violate women's reproductive rights under *Casey*. Which prong of the *Casey* test—the "purpose" or the "effect" prong—does she think provides the stronger argument against such statutes? Why? Do you agree with her?

2. If one accepts Kowitz's argument against prohibition of wrongful birth claims, does that mean one must accept sex-based selective abortions? That is, would a law prohibiting a woman from seeking an abortion because she doesn't want a child of the sex of her fetus necessarily be inconsistent with Kowitz's position? Would it violate the reproductive rights of women to prohibit such abortions? For a discussion of sex-selective abortions, *see* April Cherry, "A Feminist Understanding of Sex-Selective Abortion: Solely a Matter of Choice?" 10 Wis. Women's L.J. 161 (1995).

3. In *Acuna v. Turkish,* 894 A. 2d 1208 (N.J. Super, A.D. 2006), the plaintiff sued her physician, Sheldon Turkish, for medical malpractice (among other claims), arguing that he failed to obtain adequate informed consent before performing an abortion on her. In her complaint, she alleged that the defendant failed "to advise her that her pregnancy, although in the embryonic stage, i.e., within the first eight weeks, 'was a complete, separate, unique and irreplaceable human being' and that the 'abortion did not prevent a human being from coming into existence but [was] actually killing an existing human being.'" Abbott S. Brown, "How Much Information Is Enough? Decision Explores the Meaning of 'Informed Consent' in the Context of Abortion," 185 N.J.L.J. 1061 (2006). The Superior Court, Appellate Division, of New Jersey denied the defendant's motion for summary judgment, allowing the case to continue to trial. The court stated, "Here, Acuna alleges that her consent to an abortion was 'uninformed' because Turkish failed to accurately answer her question, '[I]s the baby already there?'" Id. Because this question of what information the doctor should provide was an issue of fact, the court concluded, it had to be decided by a jury. What impact are rulings like *Acuna* likely to have on abortion providers?

4. Is there a policy that would both avoid the dehumanization of the disabled that Saxton describes and yet protect the rights of patients to be protected from negligent—sometimes *grossly* negligent—treatment by physicians? Would it make a difference to your assessment of these issues if health insurance were widely available, and if it provided adequate support for disabled children throughout those children's lives?

5. In her article about the reproductive rights of women in prison, Roth observes that the prison is "a critical arena for feminist scholars who reject 'choice' as a framework for reproductive politics." What does she mean by this? Is Roth's approach to her topic more consistent with liberal individualism or critical constructivism?

Motherhood Denied
Legal Regulation of Conception

Introduction to Part III

Part III, "Motherhood Denied: Legal Regulation of Conception," examines the flip side of the issue of abortion: limitations and constraints imposed upon women who affirmatively want to have a child. Section A addresses the wide variety of punitive restrictions on the reproductive behavior of low-income women and women of color, highlighting the extent to which reproductive rights are not only a "gender" issue but also an issue of race and class. An excerpt from Rickie Solinger's *The Politics of Pregnancy* puts the discussion in historical context, showing how reproduction-related legal rules from the earliest era of this country (rules governing slavery and the treatment of indigenous North Americans) enforced regimes of gender, race, and class subordination. Next, in her article, "The Social Meaning of the Norplant Condition: Constitutional Considerations of Race, Class, and Gender," Catherine Albiston argues against the late-twentieth-century practice of mandating Norplant (a type of temporary sterilization) as a condition of probation in crimes of child abuse and neglect. Albiston contends that the individual responsibility focus of such mandatory sterilization practices reflects historical biases against poor women of color as bad mothers, and diverts attention from the systemic causes of child abuse. She also canvasses Equal Protection and fundamental rights arguments suggesting that requiring Norplant as a condition of probation is unconstitutional. Although Norplant has not been commercially available in this country since 2002, Albiston's piece is still important, both because of what it reveals about the race and class biases that motivated this modern form of forced sterilization and because its constitutional analysis could be relevant to other, new forms of coercive sterilization that might arise in the future.

Finally, section A concludes with Lucy A. Williams's article, "The Ideology of Division: Behavior Modification Welfare Reform Proposals," continuing these themes in an analysis of the child exclusion policies ("family caps") that are used in various welfare programs around the country. These provisions prohibit certain women who have children while on welfare from receiving the additional increment of support that they would normally be due because of the increase in their family size. Williams's contemporaneous critique of the rhetoric behind the family cap proposals, written when they first surfaced, rings equally true today. She demonstrates that, like the Norplant condition, family caps divert attention from the structural causes of poverty, incorrectly attributing poverty to "deviant" actions by the poor, such as "irresponsible" child bearing.

Section B of part III turns to another, very different, set of issues about whether the government can and should regulate women's efforts to have children: alternative reproduction. This section first covers "surrogate" motherhood and other alternative reproductive technologies. The first chapter is an excerpt from Martha Ertman's "What's Wrong with a Parenthood Market?," which explores the benefits of "commodification"—allowing market transactions (contracts) to create parent relationships. Exploring medical practices surrounding both artificial insemination (AI) and in vitro fertilization (IVF), Ertman argues that taking such alternative reproduction methods —especially AI—out of the market harms single women, gay couples, and others who benefit from intent-based definitions of parenthood. Following Ertman, an excerpt from Dorothy Roberts's influential book, *Killing the Black Body,* suggests a critique of the market-based approach, as it analyzes the racial dynamics at work in the legal rules and social practices surrounding alternative reproduction issues. Finally, section B turns to another type of reproductive technology, excerpting Lori Andrews's article, "Is There a Right to Clone? Constitutional Challenges to Bans on Human Cloning." In that piece, the author focuses on reproductive cloning (cloning to create a human being, rather than to create tissue for therapeutic medical use), highlighting the policy concerns and constitutional issues raised by this still-nascent form of alternative reproduction.

A. Punitive Policies

Regulation of Conception by Low-Income
Women and Women of Color

Chapter 24

Racializing the Nation

From the Declaration of Independence to the Emancipation Proclamation, 1776–1865

Rickie Solinger

. . . .

During the eighteenth century in the American colonies and then in the United States, . . . [l]egislators crafted laws to regulate sexual intimacy for a society in which some people were the property of other people, and in which race and property and population growth all interacted with each other, as reproductive matters.

The early laws show us what all laws show: lawmakers' worries about what ordinary people will do if their behavior is not regulated. The laws show what, in fact, people were actually doing in an unregulated state. The first colonial laws forbidding marriage between white women and African men, for example, suggest that at the time these laws were enacted in the first half of the seventeenth century, white women were forming intimate relations, including marriage, with Africans, even with enslaved African men. If these everyday relations had been rare or non-existent, no laws like these would have been necessary.

. . . .

[T]he founders did not debate which race was destined to populate and to rule the continent. This goal was a certainty beyond debate. If the United States were to be a "white country," laws and practices would have to make it—and keep it—that way. Laws would ensure that whites alone were citizens and property-owners. Laws would ensure that enslaved Africans were—both as labor and as property—the producers but not the owners of wealth. Laws and military victories would ensure that native populations were "removed" from properties that whites could use to consolidate their holdings and their territorial supremacy. All of these laws would depend on defining and policing race by regulating reproductive practices, what I call "racializing the nation."

Degrading African and Native Reproduction

At the end of the 18th century, racial theorists defined race as a quality inhering in the body, a biologically-conditioned characteristic, not an environmentally-conditioned

Rickie Solinger, *Pregnancy and Power: A Short History of Reproductive Politics in America* 27–62 (2005).

attribute. They described the color—or the race—of enslaved Africans in the late 18th century as a biological marker of permanent inferiority. Theorists also imposed a biologically-based interpretation of inferiority on Indians at this time, an interpretation that precluded assimilation.

. . . .

Whites used somatic or body-based ideas about racial inferiority to justify the physical domination and exploitation of Africans and Indians whose labor and land they were determined to command. Domination relied at its heart on controlling the reproduction of enslaved and native women.

. . . .

[T]he reproductive capacity of enslaved and native women was the resource whites relied on to produce an enslaved labor force, to produce and transmit property and wealth across generations, to consolidate white control over land in North America, and to produce a class of human beings who, in their ineligibility for citizenship, underwrote the exclusivity and value of white citizenship.

. . . .

[A]rguably the serial decisions—the formal and informal regulations—to treat Black women as breeders with no formal rights or control over their own bodies, their sexual experiences, and their children, constituted the ultimate degradation of enslaved persons and provided the foundation of the slavery system. The first of these laws was enacted in the Virginia colony in 1662, "An Act Defining the Status of Mulatto Bastards." The law read: "Whereas some doubts have arrisen whether children got by an Englishman upon a negro woman should be slave or Free, Be it therefore enacted and declared by this present grand assembly, that all children borne in this country shall be held bond or free only according to the condition of the Mother. And that if any christian shall committ Fornication with a negro man or woman, hee or shee soe offending shall pay double the Fines imposed by the former act."[1]

. . . .

[T]he Virginia colony's law was a radical innovation, adapting an old practice to meet the labor and other needs of an under-populated land. Under the new system, if the father was enslaved and the mother was enslaved, the child was born enslaved. If the father was a free man and the mother was enslaved, the child would be born enslaved. The older law would have classified the offspring of this union as a free child. Clearly, after 1662 the fertility of the enslaved woman became the basis for the increase of human property. Just as clearly, the new law encouraged white men to seek power, pleasure, and profit by impregnating enslaved women.

. . . .

The new law also went some distance toward clarifying and hardening racial boundaries. Consider, for example, an enslaved child who could show that while his mother was enslaved, his father was white and free. After 1662 this fact . . . became entirely irrelevant. As legal scholar Adrienne Dale Davis has put it: "Showing that one's father was white was [now] no defense to enslavement."[2]

But what of the children of free white mothers and Black enslaved fathers? These were children born from mothers the courts believed were beneath contempt. According to the law, following their mother's racially elevated though sexually degraded status, these children were free. But they were not "white." Consequently, in colonial communities throughout the North American colonies, these children enlarged the population of free Blacks.

. . . .

A . . . practical, labor-oriented, and profitable solution to the growing number of free Blacks was widely adopted: to hold mixed race children—typically the offspring of servants—in extended, though impermanent bondage. Traditionally, children of indentured servants could be held in servitude till the age of twenty-one if a white boy, and the age of eighteen if a white girl. A mixed-race child of a white mother was bound out by law until the age of thirty-one. Historian Kristin Fischer notes, "mixed-race children, though they might be nominally free, effectively spent most of their productive and reproductive years as servants."[3] In addition, mixed-race children were marked indelibly as illegitimate, unable to inherit property or names from their fathers.

These early Virginia laws set the pattern for colonial and then state legislatures for nearly two hundred years: using sexual regulations—who had the right to have sex and reproduce with whom—to reinforce and police racial boundaries. These laws also played a major role in allowing whites to construct and dominate the labor system. These laws sexualized race and racialized sex. . . . One state's law allowed the formally acknowledged illegitimate child of a deceased owner and his "concubine" to be freed at the owner's death only if the value of the child did not exceed the portion of the estate's value that such a child was entitled to. If the child were worth a substantial sum on the slave market, or if the master's estate were paltry, the master's illegitimate slave child would have to remain enslaved. The law was written to protect the property interests of the dead slave owner's white family in this way.

The experience of giving birth to a child who was the property of one's owner was a devastatingly complex event for enslaved parents. In many cases, the birth was the outcome of coerced sex, forced on an enslaved woman by her owner, a man who might or might not acknowledge a child born of that rape.

. . . .

The child embodied the enslaved mother's sexual degradation and also her degradation as human property. The child defined her as chattel who reproduced a commodity, not a person, at the will of the owner. The owners' freedom to rape enslaved women depended on the traditional definition of sexual violation as a crime against a man's legal rights over an economic dependent: his property. When a slave owner raped his own possession, no man's property interests were hurt. As historian Kathleen Brown writes, "The only man with legal claims to a female slave's labor and reproductive capacity was her master. Rape did not jeopardize his investment,"—and may well, in fact, have increased it.[4] . . . And yet, in addition to symbols of degradation, that same enslaved child could represent for his or her mother "the continuity of a people," the extension, the enrichment, and the potential of the community of Black people, and its renewal: a new life. From the owner's perspective, the new interracial child enlarged his slave holdings, but at the same time, represented a threat to racial status—a "monstrous amalgam." No matter that the slave owner was more often than not the father of this "monster." Elite whites were horrified that by sometimes appearing "white," though not legally "white," the interracial child represented racial corruption. Such children, breaching the borders of "white," symbolized abominable "infractions against the color line" and became the occasion for new laws—ever more finely calibrated definitions of whiteness—ensuring the continuing degradation of interracial children. The sexual behavior of owners created new opportunities for elite whites to tighten the noose of slavery.

. . . .

[S]ex and reproduction were central to social practices of racial degradation and racial privilege . . . during the slavery regime. . . . To begin with, as we've seen, often the enslaved woman did not have the right to choose her sexual partner. With no reliable contraception, many enslaved women, therefore, did not have the right to choose their procreating partner. In American slave society then, making such deeply intimate partnering decisions was a racial privilege.

Because I use the term "racial privilege" repeatedly in this chapter, I want to be clear about what I mean by this expression. I am using "racial privilege" in this discussion as a way of describing a status or an opportunity that the law and other instruments of power reserved for whites and generally denied women of color, on the basis of race. I am not suggesting that all white women were able freely, for example, to choose their sexual partners in a male-dominant society. But I do mean to indicate that white women were very much more likely than women of color to be able to exercise preference or claim personal dignity in this and other related matters discussed in this chapter. I also mean to indicate that denying African Americans these opportunities or privileges was key to racial degradation and enslavement.

. . . .

If the slave child was a commodity, then the womb of the enslaved woman was a manufactory, a site of value only if it churned out product. . . . Owners of small numbers of enslaved persons often made their slave property "marry abroad," to an available enslaved person on a different plantation so that valuable reproduction could proceed.

. . . .

Even given their value as "golden geese," the reproductive experiences of many enslaved women, particularly those on small plantations, show how reproductive health was a racial privilege under slavery. Of course not all white women lived out their pregnancies in health or with access to decent food, shelter, and medical attention in this era. Still, most enslaved women were forced by their slave status into reproductive danger. Dunaway shows how these women were endangered: "On average, a pregnant slave was removed from field work only about twenty days throughout her entire pregnancy." She worked until a week before delivery, in some places working to fill cotton baskets weighing 75 to 100 pounds. "In contrast, Southern doctors recommended that affluent pregnant women limit their physical exertion to activities no more strenuous than those conducted 'in carriage' and elite women took regular afternoon naps."[5]

. . . .

Historian Richard Follett has found that on Louisiana sugar plantations terrible work conditions and other factors created reproductive havoc. He wrote, "Overwork induced miscarriage and stillbirths shortened birth intervals, high levels of infant mortality ensured that women would resume early menses, inadequate postnatal care further limited the delay between births, while relatively poor nutritional content and quantity of the slave mother's milk probably triggered early weaning and shorter birth intervals."[6]

One formerly enslaved woman, Josephine Bacchus, looked back, remembering: "I ain't never been safe in de family way." She recalled experiencing constant hunger and rape, and being pressed back into the fields soon after childbirth. Not surprisingly, all of her babies except one died at birth. Under this regime, mothers died too. Edward De Bieuw, an enslaved man in Lafourche Parish, Louisiana recalled, "My ma died 'bout three hours after I was born. . . . Pa always said they made my ma work too hard. . . . He said ma was hoein.' She told the driver she was sick; he told her to just hoe-right-on. Soon, I was born, and my ma die[d] a few minutes after dey brung her to the house."

Women were also forced to perform the reproductive labor of wet-nursing, that is, nursing a baby born to another woman. Ellen Betts, an enslaved woman, reported, "I don't do nothing all my days, but nuss, nuss, nuss, nuss. I nuss so many chillen it done went and stunted my growth and dat's why I ain't nothin' but bones to dis day." The system also stunted enslaved babies, many of whom, especially on the sugar plantations, were born tiny.

. . . .

Slavery established the right to choose a sexual and procreating partner as the privilege of whites. It also established the right to marry and raise one's children with one's marital partner as a similar privilege. The slave code forbade enslaved persons from contracting marriage and disregarded the meanings of partnering practices among enslaved persons. Codes referred to slave matrimony as "the association which takes place among slaves, and is called marriage, [but is] . . . properly designated by the word contubernium, a relation which has no sanctity, and to which no civil rights are attached."[7] A by-product of disallowing slave marriage was the denial of "legitimacy" status to all enslaved children, rendering "legitimacy" the privilege of whites. In addition, by denying enslaved people the right to marry, owners protected themselves and the church against the need to reconsider the meaning of marriage and of sin. This was especially relevant if an owner sold a man but wanted that man's "wife" to continue increasing his slave holding by having more children. If the owner had allowed marriage, how could he—and the church—define the woman's relationship to the man he paired her with after selling her husband? Also, by denying enslaved people the right to both "religious ceremony and public recording," owners justified their claim that "blacks didn't construct families that were moral and cultural equivalents of whites.'"[8]

. . . .

Whether an enslaved person lived in a sustained, loving relationship or an imposed arrangement, the slave owner's economic and labor calculations could end a family arrangement as easily as they could construct them, so making family itself a white privilege. Especially in the slave-exporting states, where enslaved persons were the most valuable commodity small farmers "produced," the right to family was particularly violated. These owners sold children much more often than owners in the Lower South and regularly structured labor arrangements for men that sent them away from

home. . . . Under the slavery system, the right to be the mother of one's child was, on top of everything else, a racial privilege—that is, a privilege reserved for white women.
. . . .

Most tragically, unlike a white mother, an enslaved mother did not have the privilege to protect her children from sale, or in many cases, to maintain a relationship with her children. On plantations large and small, family breakup was a distinct possibility. One former slave described an auction at which his enslaved mother's children were sold off, one by one, while the mother looked on "in an agony of grief." Next, the mother herself was on the block:

> My mother was then separated from me, and put up in her turn. She was bought by a man named Isaac R. . . . and then I was offered to the assembled purchasers. My mother half distracted with the parting forever from all her children, pushed through the crowd while the bidding for me was going on, to the spot where R. was standing. She fell at his feet, and clung to his knees, entreating him in tones that a mother only could command to buy her Baby as well as herself, and spare to her one of her little ones at least. Will it, can it be believed that this man, thus appealed to, was capable not merely of turning a deaf ear to her supplication, but of disengaging himself from her with such violent blows and kicks as to reduce her to the necessity of creeping out of his reach and mingling the groan of bodily suffering with the sob of a broken heart.[9]

. . . .

Recent research has shown that between 1820 and 1860, as the cotton kingdom boomed, one-tenth of all Upper South slaves were relocated to the Lower South each decade. Nearly one out of three children living in the Upper South in 1820 was gone by 1860. Thus a very high percentage of slave families were broken in this era by owners' strategies for maximizing profits.
. . . .

When possible, enslaved women nevertheless did what they could, within their circumstances, to assert ownership over their own bodies and their reproductive capacities. This meant trying to protect themselves "totally beyond the control of the master," sometimes by resisting rape, by choosing one's own sexual or life partner, by attempting self-abortion or seeking the services of knowledgeable enslaved people on the plantation, or by other means. In studies of slavery and resistance, a Georgia physician is much-quoted because what he had to say in 1849 was so revealing about both white fears of Black reproductive autonomy and about the constant need of enslaved women to manage their fertility. He said that "slave women had far more abortions and miscarriages than did his white patients, either because of the excessive work slaves were compelled to perform or, 'as the planters believe,' because slaves were possessed of a secret by which they destroy the fetus at an early stage of gestation."[10]

Historian Stephanie Shaw has defined efforts of enslaved women to exert reproductive control as expressions of maternal responsibility:

> [E]ven when slave women had abortions, refused to conceive or committed infanticide in order to protect children from a life time of slavery, they often did so in the interests

of mothering. And even when they made such decisions without considering the child's future, they made mothering decisions—decisions not to mother.

This is a bold interpretation, in part because anti-abortion rights forces in the United States today have effectively pressed many people in this country to imagine the act of terminating a pregnancy as an irresponsible and selfish act. Here we need to consider the relationship between reproductive autonomy and maternal judgment.[11]

. . . .

At the same time that the laws, policies, and practices of the slavery system racialized the nation, the United States was also racialized by cultural and military violence waged against Native Americans. The age of the cotton boom and slavery expansion and rampant marketing in the bodies of enslaved persons overlapped the age of Indian "removal." As early as 1802 President Thomas Jefferson had supported the idea of transporting Indians from their tribal lands east of the Mississippi River to western destinations. In 1830, President Andrew Jackson signed The Indian Removal Act that empowered the military to carry out massive movement of Native Americans westward, "beyond the chartered boundaries of states."[12] Tribal disputes, court cases, an important treaty, and political opposition delayed government action. But in the winter of 1838–1839, the U.S. military rounded up approximately 14,000 Cherokees and forced them to walk one thousand miles to the Oklahoma Territory. For between one-quarter and one-third of these people, this was a death march.

. . . .

[Historian Theda] Perdue shows how the prestige or status of women declined sharply as whites penetrated Cherokee land and culture and worked hard to "civilize" and Christianize these people. In the late eighteenth and early nineteenth centuries, women's power as reproducers and their power as members of the Cherokee polity were reciprocally diminished. To a significant degree, government officials and Christian missionaries defined their task as interrupting old meanings associated with communal property, clan-based power, and female reproduction. In the 1820s, for example, as part of the program of bringing "civilization" to Indians, missionaries and their Cherokee allies restricted then outlawed polygamy, a practice Perdue and others associate with strong female bonds. In 1825, matrilineality, a foundational source of female power, was seriously compromised when the Cherokee council allowed "the children of Cherokee men and white women, living in the Cherokee nation as man and wife" to become citizens of the Cherokee nation.

Fundamentally, whites who concerned themselves with Indian culture and nation measured the value of Indian women against a standard that governed early Victorian-American, white women's lives: enforced dependency and gentility. Ironically, "policy makers, agents, and missionaries" found Indian women "degraded" because they were not politically powerless and economically dependent like proper white women. Therefore, a first task in civilizing Indians was to raise the status of their women "to its proper rank and influence" by restricting female authority. A minister in 1822 expressed his belief that Indian women who "nurse and nourish every one that cometh into the world" were in a special position to do God's work, exercising "authority over the mind in its most pliant state." This was the most important task Cherokee women could perform. Their social roles should be constructed accordingly.[13]

. . . .

Historical evidence shows that Cherokee women resisted land agreements with the U.S. government, that is, treaties providing for the trade of ancestral land in the East for tracts a thousand miles away. Women argued from a position of power derived from reproductive and maternal capacity. They spoke forcefully about how their "duties as mothers" gave them the right to speak to "Chiefs and warriors in council."

. . . .

Historians have preserved records of the terrible wrenching of a people from their land and of the "Trail of Tears," the ghastly forced-march of Cherokee to the Oklahoma Territory. Here is one account of what happened when the United States military arrived to "remove" the Cherokee: "Men working in the fields were arrested and driven to stockades. Women were dragged from their homes by soldiers whose language they could not understand. Children were often separated from their parents and driven into the stockades with the sky for a blanket and the earth for a pillow." Violations of Cherokee life- and death-related rituals began at once: "One family was forced to leave the body of a child who had just died," and the distraught mother "collapsed of heart failure." Another mother "could only carry her dying child in her arms a few miles." Eventually she had to "consign her much loved babe to the cold ground." Accounts of life along the trail have been described as "a litany of the burial of children, some born in an 'untimely' way."

One can imagine that along the trail, all rituals and rules governing birth—what women ate, who saw them, who attended birth, and the many other traditional prescriptions—were distressfully suspended. But birth went on. A variety of sources report that nearly seventy newborn babies were among the Cherokees who arrived in Oklahoma Territory. Perhaps it is surprising that so many infants were born and survived. After all, a missionary reported that "troops frequently forced women in labor to continue [marching] until they collapsed and delivered 'in the midst of the company of soldiers.'"[14]

. . . .

Far from regretting [the harsh reproductive effects of these policies], many prominent white Americans approved. Charles Francis Adams, Jr., a descendant of presidents, and himself an important industrialist in the late nineteenth century, judged U.S. Indian policy as harsh but efficacious because it "saved the Anglo-Saxon stock from being a nation of half-breeds." Prominent missionaries such as Rufus Anderson, secretary of the American board of foreign missions from 1832 until 1866, and author of *The Hawaiian Islands, Their Progress and Condition under Missionary Labors* (1864), approved of the reduction of the native population of that island by ninety per cent. He found the obliteration of natives only "natural," similar to "the amputation of diseased members of the body."[15]

. . . .

The United States became a racialized country in the late 18th century and beyond not simply under the mechanisms directly enforcing and perpetuating racial slavery, Indian removal, and white supremacy. The nation was fully racialized when laws and practices explicitly linked the degradation of Blacks and Indians to the elevation of whites. White privilege depended on this process. The special status of whites was built out of the rules, laws, and norms governing white sex-and-pregnancy every bit as much as the slave system and Indian degradation depended on reproductive control of non-white people. The social privileges and protections of white people depended on laws, policies, and attitudes continually affirming and policing racial boundaries. Often the most direct way to police these boundaries was by prescribing and monitoring the sexual and reproductive behavior of white women.

Cementing White Supremacy

For the rest of this chapter, I will look at how definitions and enforcement of white women's sex-and-pregnancy-related behavior contributed to the process of racializing the nation. To reiterate, I am using this term, racializing, to refer to the process carried out by elites whereby the nation's inhabitants were divided into racial groups. Each group was subject to special laws and rules depending on race, with the overall goal of maintaining white supremacy.

We can start the consideration of white women's reproductive experiences in the early decades of the United States by exploring changes in the meanings of white motherhood in the late 18th century. We can ask what those changes had to do with definitions of race and the nation. Second, we can look at the idea of chastity and its role in underwriting new ideas about white motherhood, as well as its dynamic role in defining the racial identity of females. Finally, we can take a look at the simultaneous rise in the United States in the first half of the 19th century of a vibrant abolitionist movement and a vibrant claim for fertility control.

In 1787, a Cherokee woman, Katteuha, wrote to Benjamin Franklin proposing a wise course for their respective nations: peace. She built her letter on a metaphor, the life-giving, revered, nation-shaping Mother of All, a woman so wise that even powerful white men such as Franklin "ought to mind" what she says. Katteuha assumed that Benjamin Franklin and his people would "have a beloved woman amongst [them] who will help put her Children right if they do wrong." Katteuha assumed that the white man would credit her trope: motherhood as a source of wisdom and state power.[16]

In truth, the Cherokee woman's metaphor described a mother who was grander and more potent than even the most endowed white mothers in the United States at the end of the 18th century. Even many of the most privileged lived in a society where married mothers could not own property, work for pay, divorce and claim custody of their children, or look for legal protection if they'd been sexually violated. Even for privileged women, motherhood could be "the last straw in enforcing women's subordination to men."[17] But throughout white culture, as the slave system hardened and spread, white motherhood increasingly appeared as Katteuha described it: an ennobled status. White mothers increasingly appeared in prescriptive literature as dependent but dignified, innocent and pious but knowing, domestic but able to shape the affairs of the nation through their child-rearing responsibilities, deeply emotional but judicious. Above all, white mothers were paragons of white purity.

....

A number of historians have written about the "rise of the moral mother" or "republican motherhood" at the end of the 18th century and into the 19th century. Popular literature at that time prescribed the "moral mother" as provider of nurturing guidance to future citizens of the republic. Writers defined motherhood as the noblest status of women. But this literature never referred to race. Clearly, though, the prescription described an exclusionary, racialized ideal. Both the moral mother's children —future citizens—and the republic they would serve were imagined white.

This venerated white mother, the wife in a patriarchal household, emerged in the late 18th century as a cultural icon for a number of reasons. First of all, by this time, infant mortality had declined, so fewer births were needed to produce a desired number of living children. Also parents understood that they had to stop subdividing their landholdings into ever-tinier plots, if their offspring were to inherit farms big enough to survive on. For these reasons, women began to try to limit their fertility. And as women had fewer children, each one seemed more precious. White motherhood became an upgraded status as infant care was now defined as complicated and demanding expertise.

....

The process of racializing the nation was complicated. We can get some sense of how complicated by looking at the situation facing poor white women who engaged in sex and reproductive activities when they were unprotected by male relatives. Like Black women, these women were excluded from the category of white nation-building mother, despite their racial identity. Unprotected impoverished white women continued to earn punishment for sex-and-pregnancy-related behaviors even though white women who were married to, or the daughters of, property-owning men no longer faced punishments by the end of the 18th century.

....

[Illustrating the lines drawn between different women, and between women and men,] the official treatment of fornication—the crime of sex outside of marriage— was complicated and ever-changing. Early in the history of the American colonies, both men and women were publicly shamed and punished for fornication. But by the middle of the 18th century, fornication had become a "female crime." As historian Cornelia Dayton described it,

> By 1740, the Puritan system of prosecuting and punishing men alongside women for fornication had collapsed. Lawyers, judges, and sexually active young white men had brought off a coup: [white] men would be exempted from confessing to philandering while women, still presented for the crime and convicted by both their confessions and their pregnancies, would continue to appear in public as repentant sinners until the end of the century.[18]

But now only some women were likely to face prosecution: only "marginal women —poor domestics, women in interracial relationships, women who repeatedly bore children without marrying" were prosecuted for committing fornication. These were white women whose behavior blurred the distinctions between slaves and free women.[19] The vulnerable fornicating female was the woman who refused or failed to be properly "white," who was not sexually restrained and enfolded within the patriarchal family. When authorities stopped bringing charges against fornicating wives and daughters of "middling sorts," that is, females attached to men owning at least some property, then only family members or the church could punish these women. Sexual misbehavior could be treated as a private matter. One could say that sexual privacy, even when unconventional sexual activities were involved, became a privilege of race and class.

Without prosecution or a trial, the male fornicator was less likely to be named in public—a highly desirable situation for the male. In fact, a woman, if she herself were respectable and protected by family, could simply threaten to name her sexual partner if the court leaned toward prosecuting her. That might well convince the magistrate to desist. On the other hand, if the girl had been raped or if she'd been abandoned, if her parents were dead or destitute, her experience in court and in the community could be "difficult or bitter." If she were a Black fornicator, she might still be whipped. Having one's sexually misbehaving body mortified in public became a mark and a definition of race and racial degradation.

The prescriptive and cautionary literature of the 18th century brought the stories of sexually errant young white women into public view. The stories demonstrated that when an unprotected white girl threw off sexual restraint and revealed her carnal nature, she was regarded like a slave. Her story was tragic because she had so much to lose in an era in which chaste white girls who became chaste white wives and mothers had a role in shaping the destiny of the nation.

. . . .

[T]he cult of white young womanhood and white motherhood utterly depended on family protection and chastity. Chastity, above all, distinguished white females from slave women who were, in the white mind, completely alienated from sexual purity. According to many abolitionists, this distinction was key to maintaining the system. The great abolitionist Sarah Grimke explained to white women that the racialized privilege of chastity was grounds for anti-slavery work. She wrote in 1838,

> The virtue of female slaves is wholly at the mercy of irresponsible tyrants, and women are bought and sold in our slave markets to gratify the brutal lust of those who bear the name of Christians. In our slave States, if . . . a woman desires to preserve her virtue unsullied, she is either bribed or whipped into compliance, or if she dares resist her seducer, her life by the laws of some of the slave States may be . . . sacrificed to the fury of disappointed passion. . . . In Christian America, the slave has no refuge from unbridled cruelty and lust.

Grimke begged every white woman to see that her own claim to moral purity and chastity was "contaminated" if she looked "at these scenes of shocking licentiousness and cruelty, and fold[ed] her hands in apathy and [said], 'I have nothing to do with slavery.'"[20]

Indeed, looking back, religious and cultural prescriptions that defined the proper sex-and-pregnancy behavior of white women seemed to guarantee one thing above all: the rules promised white females that if they behaved as instructed, they would not be *slaves*. Evangelical Protestants in the post-Revolutionary era taught that women who could suppress their innate sexual impulses would be like "angels," raised from slavery, "elevated . . . above the weakness of animal nature."[21] Chaste white women, close to God, were relieved of the dangerous lustiness of the body. And being relieved, they were free to become moral mothers, intellectual persons, the human equals of men.

In a society where white men were all-powerful, prescriptive chastity became a way of curtailing unlimited male power over white women, including the power of sexual domination. At the same time, the chastity of white women enforced white men's property interests in their wives. Only a chaste wife could ensure that her husband really was the father of his heir. Also, as one historian has put it, "a cuckolded husband unable to control his wife's sexual behavior forfeited respect as head of the household."[22] According to prescriptive literature, white chastity was key to the orderly transmission of property, to the orderly functioning of the family, generally—and thus to the order and dignity of the nation shaped by white patriarchal families, reproducing white citizens.

In 1799, Hannah More, an Englishwoman concerned about improving the education of women, wrote about the role of culture and society in categorically creating and distinguishing between free women and enslaved women. She noted that in countries where interest in the "mere person," the "mere external charms," *the sexual bodies of women,* was "carried to the highest excess," women were "slaves."[23] In white America in this era, white female chastity could stand for the self-ownership of free white women as a republican claim and an emblem of national virtue.

. . . .

By definition, slave women were not chaste. Nor were Indian women, long described by European men as sexually free and possessing secret contraceptive knowledge that allowed sex with no consequences. (Englishmen imagined native women as capable of going through childbirth without pain, another emblem of unwomanly unchasteness.) As we've seen, poor white women could be chaste or unchaste. As servants they were likely to be "unchaste," their class status opening them to sexual exploitation and marking them as sexually degraded, like slaves.

. . . .

Ultimately, in practical terms, however, prescriptive literature and racial ideologies were not enough to maintain the chastity of white womanhood in America. Ultimately powerful religious, medical, and legal authorities came to believe that white chastity depended on enforcing the strictest relationship between sex and reproduction. Authorities determined that such a relationship had to be vitalized and enforced by law: through the criminalization of abortion and the criminalization of contraception.

. . . .

The existence of these laws also represented a state policy mandating the continuation of an indivisible relationship between sex and pregnancy: the basis of white chastity. In sum, in the emancipation era, white male authorities organized strenuously to force their vision of *the race* onto the bodies of white women. In effect, doctors and legislators ensured that no matter the outcome of the Civil War, the future of slavery, or the demographic viability of the Indian, laws over women's bodies would make sure that white women would remain chaste and thus remain white.

NOTES

1. Quoted in Carol Berkin and Leslie Horowitz, *Women's Voices, Women's Lives: Documents in Early American History* (Boston: Northeastern University Press, 1998), 13.

2. Adrienne Dale Davis, "Don't Let Nobody Bother Yo' Principle: The Sexual Economy of American Slavery," in Sharon Harley and the Black Women and Work Collective, eds., *Sister Circle: Black Women and Work* (New Brunswick, NJ: Rutgers University Press, 2002), 111.

3. Kristen Fischer, *Suspect Relations: Sex, Race, and Resistance in Colonial North Carolina* (Ithaca, NY: Cornell University Press, 2002), 124.

4. Kathleen M. Brown, *Good Wives, Nasty Wenches, and Anxious Patriarchs* (Chapel Hill: University of North Carolina Press, 1996), 210.

5. Wilma A. Dunaway, *The African-American Family in Slavery and Emancipation* (New York: Cambridge University Press, 2003), 129–30.

6. Richard Follett, "Heat, Sex, and Sugar: Pregnancy and Childbearing in the Slave Quarters," *Journal of Family History* 28 (2003): 510–39.

7. E. Franklin Frazier, "The Negro Slave Family," *Journal of Negro History* 15 (1930): 246.

8. Dunaway, *African-American Family,* 118–19.

9. E. Franklin Frazier, "The Negro Slave Family," *Journal of Negro History* 15 (1930): 222–23.

10. From Herbert G. Gutman, *The Black Family in Slavery and Freedom,* quoted in Janet Farrell Brodie, *Contraception and Abortion in Nineteenth-Century America* (Ithaca, NY: Cornell University Press, 1994), 52–53.

11. Stephanie Shaw, "Mothering under Slavery in the Antebellum South," in Janet Golden and Rima Apple, eds., *Mothers and Motherhood: Readings in American History* (Columbus: Ohio State University Press, 1997), 309.

12. Theda Perdue, *Cherokee Women: Gender and Cultural Change, 1700–1835* (Lincoln: University of Nebraska Press, 1998), 190.

13. Ibid., 161.

14. Theda Perdue, *Slavery and the Evolution of Cherokee Society, 1540–1866* (Knoxville: University of Tennessee Press, 1979), 99–100.

15. David E. Stannard, *American Holocaust: The Conquest of the New World* (New York: Oxford University Press, 1992), 243–44.

16. Nancy Shoemaker, "Introduction," in Nancy Shoemaker, ed., *Negotiators of Change: Historical Perspectives on Native American Women* (New York: Routledge, 1995), 9.

17. Ellen Carol DuBois and Linda Gordon, "Seeking Ecstasy on the Battlefield: Danger and Pleasure in Nineteenth-Century Feminist Sexual Thought," *Feminist Studies* 9(1983):7–25.

18. Cornelia Hughes Dayton, *Women before the Bar: Gender, Law, and Society in Connecticut, 1639–1789* (Chapel Hill: University of North Carolina Press, 1995), 60.

19. Ibid., 161.

20. Sarah Grimke, "On the Condition of Women in the United States," in Nancy Cott, Jeanne Boydston, Anne Braude, Lori D. Ginzberg, and Molly Ladd-Taylor, eds., *Root of Bitterness: Documents on the Social History of American Women,* 2nd ed. (Boston: Northeastern University Press, 1996), 126–27.

21. Nancy Cott, "Passionlessness: An Interpretation of Victorian Sexual Ideology, 1790–1850," *Signs* 4 (1978): 219–36.

22. Fischer, *Suspect Relations*, 17.

23. Hannah More, *Strictures on the modern system of female education: with a view of the principles and conduct prevalent among women of rank and fortune* (London: T. Cadell Jun. and W. Davies, 1799).

Chapter 25

The Social Meaning of the Norplant Condition
Constitutional Considerations of Race, Class, and Gender

Catherine Albiston

> And they had the operation voluntarily, for the good of Society.
>
> —Aldous Huxley, *Brave New World*

> We protect [privacy] rights not because they contribute, in some direct and material way, to the general public welfare, but because they form so central a part of the individual's life.
>
> —Blackmun, J., dissenting, in *Bowers v. Hardwick,*
> 478 U.S. 186 (1986)

I. Introduction

. . . .

Although many child abusers are men,[1] prosecutorial attention and judicial intervention increasingly have focused on women who abuse their children. . . . [S]ome courts recently have required Norplant as a condition of probation for child abusers and for women who used drugs while pregnant.

Norplant consists of six matchstick-size silicone capsules implanted under the skin of a woman's upper arm. These capsules suppress ovulation and inhibit fertilization through the release of hormones. Implanting the contraceptive requires a local anesthetic and takes approximately fifteen minutes. Norplant is extremely effective, with a failure rate lower than that of oral contraceptives. It remains effective for five years after implantation or until the capsules are removed.

Norplant has both financial and medical drawbacks. The initial implantation cost for Norplant is relatively high—$365 for the capsules themselves and from $150 to $500 for the implantation procedure.[2] Removal costs are also high—$150 to $300,[3] or more depending on complications. The medical side effects of Norplant include headaches, depression, nervousness, enlargement of the ovaries and/or fallopian tubes, inflammation of the skin, weight gain, inflammation of the cervix, nausea, dizziness,

Catherine Albiston, "The Social Meaning of the Norplant Condition: Constitutional Considerations of Race, Class, and Gender," 9 BERKELEY WOMEN'S LAW JOURNAL 9 (1995).

acne, abnormal hair growth, tenderness of the breasts, and prolonged or irregular bleeding. Norplant is contraindicated for women who suffer from heart disease, kidney disease, liver disease, diabetes, or high blood pressure. Furthermore, Norplant capsules that are not removed after their five-year contraceptive life put the woman at risk of ectopic pregnancy and continue to interfere with the woman's fertility.

The unique characteristic of Norplant is that it removes virtually all control over contraception from the woman. In fact, it is this lack of control that makes Norplant an attractive coercive device. Once it is implanted, it does not require daily pill-taking or actions at the time of sexual activity, nor can it be discontinued without the advice and assistance of a physician. Norplant is a contraceptive that is susceptible to coercive use because it does not depend on the cooperation of the woman.

Norplant has been used to further social policy goals in part because it may be controlled by the provider. States have taken advantage of this aspect of Norplant by promoting its use among certain targeted groups. The choice of which groups to target for state mandated or sponsored uses of Norplant suggests which women's reproductive rights the state wishes to control. Some states have considered incentives or requirements for women receiving public aid to use Norplant, although none of these bills has been signed into law. In addition, Medicaid now covers Norplant in all fifty states, despite the initial concern over the racist implications of limiting the birth rate of Medicaid recipients. Some inner-city high schools with high rates of student pregnancy offer Norplant to students as a contraceptive choice. The common thread among these various programs is that they target poor women of color.

While these social programs concern voluntary use of Norplant, increasingly Norplant has been used in more coercive ways. Judges have imposed Norplant as a condition to probation for women convicted of drug use or child abuse. These women face a choice between prison or a five-year curtailment of their reproductive freedom. Norplant as a condition of probation may seem less objectionable than other Norplant policies. Probation conditions are imposed only on individual women convicted of child abuse or drug use while pregnant, whereas other social policies attempt to control the reproductive rights of poor women of color without the justification of individual culpability. Many proponents of the use of Norplant as a condition of probation argue that women who have been convicted of abusing a child or using drugs while pregnant have failed at parenting and, as a result, do not deserve to have additional children. Norplant is considered less objectionable than sterilization because it is reversible and less physically intrusive than tubal ligation. It also may save the government the costs of caring for children damaged by abuse and drug exposure in vitro.

The particular factual circumstances of cases where Norplant has been imposed, however, are disturbing. One defendant agreed to Norplant as a condition of her probation with little information about its health consequences, no consultation with a doctor, and without the presence of her lawyer. When she later appealed on the grounds that the probation condition violated her constitutional rights and that Norplant would complicate her preexisting health conditions, the judge denied her motion, finding that she had given informed consent. Another defendant was unable to tolerate the side effects of Norplant, and had her implants removed. She then obtained a tubal ligation because she believed permanent sterilization was the only way to avoid violating her probation and risking imprisonment. Both these women had no prior record of child abuse.

The systemic implications of the Norplant policy are even more disturbing than these individual cases. Although the application of Norplant as a condition of probation seems impartial, poor women of color are most likely to receive the condition because institutional biases make them most likely to be prosecuted for child abuse and drug use during pregnancy. . . .

II. Social and Historical Context of the Norplant Policy

. . . .

Society readily accepts prevention of pregnancy as a solution to child abuse because controlling the reproductive capacity of women of color is an historically accepted practice. Furthermore, the Norplant policy's focus on individual responsibility diverts attention from the systemic causes of child abuse, such as poverty, drug use, and the lack of institutional supports for families. . . .

A. Discriminatory Prosecution of Poor Women of Color

Evaluation of the Norplant policy requires considering how race and class affect who is prosecuted for child abuse and drug abuse. A number of factors make poor women of color more likely than other women to be prosecuted for drug use and child abuse. First, because poor women of color are more likely to be under government supervision through public hospitals and welfare agencies, their drug use or child abuse is more likely to be discovered. Second, the racist attitudes of some health care professionals and social workers cause them to disproportionately report women of color to the authorities. Third, prosecutorial efforts focus on the drugs used primarily by poor women of color, even though drugs used by white women, such as alcohol and marijuana, also harm fetuses when used during pregnancy. . . .

B. Stereotypes of Poor Women of Color

. . . .

Given [the] history of devaluing women of color as mothers,* it is not surprising that the judicial remedy to these problems is the prevention of motherhood. When sentencing a poor woman of color convicted of child abuse, a judge has broad discretion with the potential to make inferences based on these stereotypical images. Stereotypes of women of color as lascivious, sexually insatiable, and loose may drive the inference that a probationer is likely to become pregnant again. Stereotypes of women of color as lazy, childlike, and stupid drive the inferences that they cannot or will not use other means of birth control, and that a contraceptive such as Norplant that removes control from the woman herself is the only effective and appropriate solution.

* *Editor's note*: For that history, see Davis, chapter 7, Solinger, chapter 24, and Roberts, chapter 28, in this volume.

The historical devaluation of women of color as mothers enables the conclusion that they do not "deserve" to be parents. Furthermore, as the Norplant policy professes to "protect" children of color by preventing their conception, it resurrects the historical sterilization abuse of women of color and its eugenic goals.

C. Norplant Cannot Replace Institutional Supports for Poor Families

. . . .

Poor women of color face the formidable challenge of raising children without the basic supports on which most middle-class families depend. Women of color are more likely than white women to be single parents, raising their children in poverty, and without adequate health or child care. Furthermore, some of the social institutions ostensibly designed to assist poor women perpetuate this status. Welfare agencies require that no man, particularly one with a job, live in the household with the mother of the child receiving AFDC benefits. Medicaid benefits do not provide for abortions, and . . . [f]ederal and state assistance for child care generally consists of tax credits, which primarily benefit the middle class. . . .

Child abuse and drug use during pregnancy are in part products of this social context of poverty and minimal institutional support. The burdens of poverty, added to the normal pressures of parenthood, contribute to child abuse and neglect. The lack of affordable childcare sometimes presents a working poor woman with the choice of losing a job necessary for survival or risking charges of child neglect for leaving a young child home alone while she is at work. . . . [W]omen cannot seek help for child abuse and drug addiction, because health care professionals are likely to report them. Furthermore, most drug treatment facilities refuse to take pregnant addicts, and prenatal care for drug addicts is virtually unattainable. . . .

D. Health Implications of Imposing Norplant on Poor Women

. . . .

The poor health and inadequate access to health care of poor women create particularly serious risks for the unsupervised use of Norplant as a condition of probation. . . .

Norplant implanted as a condition of probation also raises concerns about adequate follow-up and removal of the capsules. Norplant capsules that are not removed after their five-year contraceptive life put the woman at risk of ectopic pregnancy, and continue to interfere with her fertility. In one study of the use of Norplant abroad, nearly thirty percent of the participants could not be located for follow-up after only one year. Although women on probation are intended to remain in close contact with their probation officer, in reality the contact tends to be minimal. In fact, those women who have violated their probation have a significant incentive to evade their probation officer, regardless of the risk to their health or welfare. Several poor women who have sought to have Norplant removed because of medical complications have been unable to do so because of the $150 cost. Without government assistance, poverty presents a significant barrier to removal. . . .

III. Equal Protection and the Trifurcated Identity

. . . .

A. The Equal Protection Clause of the Fourteenth Amendment

. . . .

[E]qual protection doctrine provide[s] inadequate protection for poor women of color who are the targets of the Norplant policy. The present structure of the doctrine forces a poor woman of color challenging the policy to choose among the legally recognized, and thus protected, elements of her identity. As classifications based on race historically have been subjected to closer judicial scrutiny than those based on gender, a woman's first preference may be to challenge the Norplant policy as racially discriminatory. However, this type of challenge does not address the gender-specific reason that the Norplant policy affects her—that she is capable of carrying a child. It also does not address the contribution her economic class has made to her status as a convicted drug addict or child abuser. Any poor woman of color challenging the Norplant policy will be unable to find an equal protection theory that allows her to press all her race-, class-, and gender-based claims without denying the reality of her identity. . . .

. . . .

B. Wealth- and Race-Based Classifications Are Inadequate

[In this part, the author rejects a wealth-based argument because the Supreme Court has refused to apply anything but the easily-satisfied rational basis standard of review to such classifications. She also rejects a race-based argument because, although Norplant policies disparately affect people of color, an Equal Protection claim would require proof of discriminatory intent.]

C. Gender

Because gender more precisely defines the class affected by the Norplant policy than race or wealth, a gender-based challenge is more feasible. Courts subject gender classifications to intermediate scrutiny, requiring the classification to be substantially related to an important government interest. The courts posit that real differences between men and women do exist to justify some gender classifications. Courts recognize, however, that legislators sometimes create gender classifications based on sexist stereotypes, and as a result, courts have refused to uphold such classifications. Thus, when applying intermediate scrutiny, courts inquire whether the gender classification stigmatizes women by promoting traditional stereotypes of their roles in society. These stereotypes include nonparticipation in the workforce, a primary role as mother and nurturer, and an identity derived from biological reproductive abilities. When probing for traditional gender stereotypes, a court addresses not only the harm to the particular plaintiff in the case, but also the social meaning of the perpetuated stereotype as it affects all women, including those not before the court. Gender classifications which reference traditional stereotypes harm women outside the plaintiff class because they support sexist assumptions used to deny women equal access to the benefits of society. Moreover, stereotypical assumptions regarding women's roles affect men as well, because they limit the life choices available to both men and women. . . .

Because Norplant is imposed only on women, it creates a gender classification in the application of a probation condition. This classification must be substantially related to important government interests in order to be sustained. The primary government interests served by the Norplant policy are rehabilitating the probationer and protecting the welfare of children. Assuming for purposes of this discussion that these interests are legitimate and important, the inquiry focuses on the fit between the means, namely the gender classification, and the ends of rehabilitation and child welfare. If the rationale for how the gender classification serves these ends relies on traditional stereotypes of women, it is constitutionally prohibited.

Norplant invokes traditional stereotypes of women because it focuses on their reproductive biology and social role as caretakers of children. In cases involving drug use while pregnant, the Norplant policy focuses on the reproductive ability of women, rather than men, even though the genetic material contributed by a drug-addicted man also could be harmful to the child. Some may argue that the Norplant policy relies on a real distinction between men and women rather than on a stereotype because only a woman carries a fetus and can harm the fetus while it is in the womb. Those who argue that this danger to the fetus supports greater intervention fail to acknowledge two problems with their fetal protection theory. First, fetal protection is not a recognized objective of child protection statutes and is not supported by most existing statutes. Second, even if fetal protection were a valid objective, the Norplant policy only protects potential fetuses. The woman is not yet pregnant, and Norplant is actually designed to prevent the fetus' creation. Before there is a viable fetus, the state has no interest in the welfare of the unborn child that can support regulation of the woman's behavior. With the Norplant policy there is no fetus at all, let alone a viable fetus. Thus, relying on harm that might occur to potential fetuses while in the womb would be a significant extension of child-protection laws and an unprecedented invasion of fetal-protection policies into the realm of criminal sanctions.

In cases involving child abuse, the court imposes Norplant on women not because they have the potential to become pregnant, but because they have the potential to become parents. The imposition of Norplant on women without equivalent restrictions on men implies that women, and not men, will always be the caretakers of the children they bear. This inference relies on the traditional stereotype of women as mothers and nurturers, making the classification constitutionally suspect.

By searching for traditional stereotypes of white women, current equal protection doctrine disregards the intersection of race, gender, and class in the Norplant policy. Gender discrimination claims must unidimensionally focus on the gender element to the exclusion of other applicable classifications. The particular gender stereotypes with which the Supreme Court is concerned, namely nonparticipation in the workforce, a primary role as mother and nurturer, and an identity derived from biological reproductive abilities, are stereotypes of a white, economically privileged woman. The historical experiences of poor women of color, however, do not match these stereotypes. Only an economically privileged woman would have sufficient family income to allow her to remain home with the children and be delimited as a mother and nurturer. Women of color were forced by their economic circumstances to work to support themselves and their families long before white women began entering the workforce in large numbers. Moreover, women of color have been historically devalued as mothers and nurturers, except as caretakers for white children. Finally, rather than excessive concern over and protection of their biological reproductive capacities, women of color have been subjected to systematic sterilization abuse and attempts to cut off their reproductive rights.

. . . .

Equal protection doctrine's bifurcation of identity forces women of color to bring a challenge based solely on gender, and then imposes a white standard upon them. One might argue that the Norplant policy does not perpetuate traditional gender stereotypes of white women because it does not emphasize protection of reproductive capacity, force women to take on the role of mother and nurturer, or burden a woman's ability to enter the workforce. In fact, superficially it does just the opposite: it prevents women of color from becoming mothers, allowing them to work without the "burden" of children, and protecting them from the more drastic and intrusive step of irreversible sterilization.

A more adequate equal protection doctrine would probe for the specific gender stereotypes that derive from and reinforce the historical devaluation of women of color. Once the gender standard is racialized, the relevant inquiry becomes the social meaning of the Norplant policy in reference to stereotypes of women of color. Rather than searching for glorification of motherhood and homelife, a court should look for continued devaluation of the motherhood of women of color. Rather than probing for excessive concern over biological reproductive abilities, a court should look for attempts to cut off reproductive rights and perpetuate sterilization abuse of women of color. Rather than disapproving of inferences that women are weak, sensitive, naive and unfit for the working world, a court should be vigilant against inferences that women of color are sexually promiscuous and evil. Changing the inquiry to match the relevant stereotypes requires recognition of the implicit white, economically privileged stereotypes already embodied in equal protection doctrine.

It is important to note that it does not matter if a particular woman fits the stereotype of women of color, just as it does not matter that most women actually were primary caretakers of children at the time earlier gender decisions were made. The objective of equal protection is to prevent laws from perpetuating harmful gender roles. The Norplant policy maintains the detrimental stereotypes of poor women of color as welfare queens, inadequate parents, and untreatable drug addicts.

. . . .

The Norplant policy makes pregnancy the locus of abuse in both child abuse and drug use cases, and consequently preventing pregnancy becomes the solution. Preventing women of color from becoming mothers, however, perpetuates the eugenic goals of historical sterilization abuse of women of color. The social meaning of preventing the pregnancy of poor women of color is that they and their children are inferior and expendable, and that poor women of color are inadequate to be mothers.

. . . .

Perpetuation of these stereotypes affects policy decisions in reproductive rights legislation which disadvantage women of color and affects the actions of private physicians and social workers. Defining certain women as somehow "different" and inferior makes infringement of their reproductive freedoms more palatable. . . . [It also] allows continued belief in the theory that child abuse is the result of the actions of "bad" women, and not the responsibility of society as a whole. . . .

IV. Fundamental Rights Analysis

The use of Norplant also raises concerns under the Fourteenth Amendment because it infringes on fundamental rights. Fundamental rights rooted in the Fourteenth Amendment traditionally have been divided into two strands: one stemming from the Due Process Clause, the other originating in the Equal Protection Clause. Rights considered "due process" fundamental rights include:

> the right of the individual to contract, to engage in any of the common occupations of life, to acquire useful knowledge, to marry, establish a home and bring up children, to worship God according to the dictates of his own conscience, and generally to enjoy those privileges long recognized at common law as essential to the orderly pursuit of happiness by free men.[4]

Griswold v. Connecticut and its progeny established the right to privacy, which encompasses the right to marry, to procreate, and to terminate pregnancy. The right to privacy extends to some but not all unmarried persons and relationships outside of marriage. Rights considered "equal protection" fundamental rights include the right to vote, [the] right to interstate travel, the right of access to the courts, and the right to education.

The Norplant policy impinges on the fundamental rights of the probationer by restricting her procreative freedom. . . .

A. Probation Conditions Generally

Rules governing probationary conditions generally come from state statutes. Conditions of probation must be reasonable and must be directed toward the goals of rehabilitation and public safety. A condition of probation is unreasonable if it is not related to the offender's crime, relates to conduct which is not in itself criminal, or requires or forbids conduct which is not reasonably related to future criminality.

Probation conditions requiring defendants to refrain from becoming pregnant where the offense is unrelated to pregnancy or children consistently have been found invalid. . . . [C]ourts have held that prohibiting conception is not reasonably related to forgery or grand theft and battery. Even in cases of child abuse, courts have found conditions requiring the offender to refrain from having more children invalid. For

example, in *Howland v. State*,[5] the court held that a condition prohibiting the probationer from fathering a child was only related to his crime of child abuse if he had custody of or access to the child. . . .

In summary, the Norplant policy does not enjoy a more permissive standard for infringement of fundamental liberty rights by virtue of its status as a condition of probation. Rather, probation conditions face the added statutory hurdle that they be reasonably related to rehabilitation and public safety, the permissible goals of probation.
Although standards of review for probation conditions impinging on fundamental
rights differ from jurisdiction to jurisdiction, most require that the condition further
the rehabilitation and public safety goals of probation, a requirement consistent with
substantive due process standards. Review of due process decisions addressing infringement on procreative liberty indicates that appellate courts must determine that
no less restrictive alternatives exist for avoiding future child abuse before affirming the
imposition of Norplant as a condition of probation.

B. Due Process

. . . .

Norplant implicates due process rights because it infringes on rights rooted in tradition and essential to human autonomy and dignity. The Due Process Clause of the
Fourteenth Amendment ensures procreative liberty, which includes "the right of the
individual . . . to marry, establish a home and bring up children." The right to procreative liberty is one of several rights under the umbrella of the right to privacy. . . .

. . . .

Where a privacy right protected by substantive due process is at stake, . . . the state
may only infringe on that right if it demonstrates that its intrusion is narrowly drawn
to further a compelling interest.

The state interests proffered to support the use of Norplant as a condition of probation are relatively straightforward and appear unobjectionable on their face. Recall
that statutory probation requirements combined with constitutional considerations
narrow the range of reasonable state interests to those relating to the objectives of probation. In *People v. Johnson*,[6] a typical example, the state advanced two interests in opposition to the defendant's fundamental right of procreative liberty. First, the state argued that implanting Norplant in probationers facilitates achievement of the state's
probationary goal of rehabilitation by greatly reducing the risk of an untimely childbirth. Untimely childbirth is relevant because it has been identified as a risk factor for
child abuse and neglect. Second, the state argued that Norplant "furthers the state's
compelling interest in protecting the welfare of its children."[7] This interest derives
from increasing numbers of child abuse and neglect cases.

First, consider the state's professed concern for the rehabilitation of the child abuser
or drug addict. Rehabilitation of a child abuser logically would involve some effort
to improve his or her parenting skills, while rehabilitating a drug-addicted woman
would require some kind of drug treatment. Counseling, rather than punishment,
seems a more appropriate remedy for child-abusing parents who were likely abused

themselves as children. States have shown little interest, however, in promoting programs such as in-home care, economic assistance, prenatal care, drug treatment for pregnant addicts, or counseling that are more directly rehabilitative than contraception. Norplant as a remedy focuses on one risk factor, pregnancy, to the exclusion of many others that also put stress on the family. Because Norplant is so loosely related to rehabilitation, it appears that the state's real interest is the prevention of children being born to "unacceptable" mothers—that is, to drug addicts and child abusers. Second, consider the state's interest in protecting the welfare of children. In cases of drug use during pregnancy, "protecting the welfare of children" extends into the arena of fetal protection. Although protection of unborn children finds some support in existing law, "protecting unborn children" is not a recognized objective of child abuse statutes or a valid state interest. Even if fetal protection were a valid objective of probation conditions, the Norplant policy only protects potential fetuses. Before there is a viable fetus, the state has no interest in the welfare of the unborn that can support regulation of a woman's behavior. Furthermore, it is far from clear that drug use during pregnancy always harms the fetus. Studies of cocaine-exposed babies have failed to determine the percentage of children harmed and to control for other risk factors such as socioeconomic status. More importantly, fetal protection theories often hide government interests in curtailing the activities of women—even those activities that are legal. This sudden government concern over the welfare of these fetuses is suspicious, given the historical neglect of prenatal care for poor women of color and the sterilization abuses of the past. Given that Norplant prevents conception and birth of children, rather than protecting existing children, the state's real concern may be lowering the birth rate in certain communities.

Once the state establishes a compelling interest, it must demonstrate that infringement on the fundamental right is narrowly drawn to further this interest. Part of this analysis usually includes consideration of whether less restrictive alternatives to the infringement are available. In cases of child abuse, the imposition of Norplant only marginally advances the state's interest in the welfare of children. Norplant may prevent the birth of additional children who potentially could be abused, but it does nothing to protect the children the defendant already has or to prevent the child abuser from abusing children who are not her own. Thus, Norplant will protect, by preventing their existence, only a small subset of the children at risk of abuse. . . .

Courts must recognize that less restrictive alternatives to Norplant are available. Provision of prenatal care, drug treatment facilities, and general health care—all now lacking for many women prosecuted for child endangerment through drug use— would serve the state's interests in protecting the child and rehabilitating the woman without infringing on procreative liberty. In addition, in-home family support services and parental counseling are more desirable alternatives in both child abuse and drug use cases because they may enable children to remain with their parents. These programs would reduce the cost of foster care and the damage foster care does to children. Moreover, the funding and development of these programs could benefit women who have not yet abused their children in a manner that the technological fix of Norplant cannot. . . .

C. Fundamental Rights under Equal Protection:
Equality in the Protection of Liberty

Due to an accident of history, the fundamental right to procreative liberty has roots in both equal protection and substantive due process doctrine. The right to procreative liberty developed during the Supreme Court's doctrinal transition from relying on equal protection theories to relying on substantive due process theories to expand the protection of fundamental rights. Because the protection of the fundamental right to procreative liberty bridges these two historical trends, the textual source of the right is unclear. Not surprisingly, given this history, opinions addressing the right to procreative liberty have relied on both equal protection and due process reasoning. For example, in *Skinner v. Oklahoma*,[8] the Supreme Court considered a challenge to Oklahoma's sterilization of male inmates. Recognizing the right to bear children as "one of the basic civil rights of man," the Court held that legislation requiring sterilization of an arbitrary class of criminals was invalid because it "ran afoul of the equal protection clause."[9] In *Griswold v. Connecticut*,[10] however, the Court relied on substantive due process arguments to recognize the right to privacy as one of the fundamental rights protected by the Constitution. The distinction between due process and equal protection did not remain clear. In *Eisenstadt v. Baird*,[11] although the Court discussed the right to privacy, it invalidated prohibitions on the distribution of contraception to unmarried individuals because they "violated the rights of single persons under the Equal Protection Clause of the Fourteenth Amendment."[12] Thus, a clear historical dividing line between equal protection and substantive due process does not emerge with respect to the right to privacy. . . .

There is, however, an important distinction between due process and equal protection analyses as they apply to fundamental rights. The distinction is due, in part, to the different constitutional roles these doctrines play. Substantive due process has been used to protect traditional and historical practices against infringements by the states and federal government. In contrast, equal protection doctrine attempts to protect disadvantaged groups from discriminatory practices, however historically ingrained those practices might be. Although both doctrines generate heightened scrutiny of an infringement of fundamental rights, due process focuses on balancing the state and individual interests involved, whereas equal protection focuses on the evenhandedness of the state's intrusion.

An example using the Norplant policy may illustrate this subtle but important distinction. . . . The due process analysis requires the court to evaluate the state's power to infringe on the rights of all probationers convicted of harming children. In contrast, equal protection requires the court to focus on the class distinctions drawn by the state, in this case along the lines of gender. Focusing on the uneven application of the probation condition makes the underlying criminal conduct irrelevant. As Cass Sunstein notes, "the fact that the underlying conduct can be criminalized is irrelevant to the problem; it is always immaterial to an equal protection challenge that members of the victimized group are engaging in conduct that could be prohibited on a general basis."[13] Thus, the relevant question under equal protection is not whether the state has a sufficiently compelling interest in fighting child abuse to overcome the liberty interests of probationers, but whether the state has an interest in drawing the line so as to infringe on the procreative rights of female offenders, but not those of male offenders.

Fundamental rights analysis using equal protection differs from standard equal protection analysis. Because imposing Norplant, a female contraceptive, creates a gender classification, standard equal protection doctrine requires the state to prove it has an important interest that is substantially related to the gender classification it has created. Where that classification impinges on a fundamental right, however, the scrutiny applied to the use of the classification should be increased. Thus,

> [n]o restriction, which unequally burdens some while leaving similarly situated people unaffected, can be imposed to restrain a fundamental right without a showing of compelling justification. Such a justification is independent of the compelling interest the government has to prove in order to restrict a fundamental right under due process. Here we are talking about the justification of the government to restrict a fundamental right of a particular group or class of people.[14]

The state can demonstrate a compelling interest in unequal infringement of a fundamental right only if there are no less restrictive alternatives for achieving the government's objectives. Note how this increased scrutiny ties together equal protection and due process doctrine. The importance of equality is recognized by focusing on the classification, whereas the importance of the fundamental right infringed is recognized by increasing the standard of review under equal protection to require a compelling state interest and the search for less restrictive alternatives.

. . . .

I certainly do not wish to argue that if the state curtailed the reproductive rights of men and women equally, a solution like Norplant would be acceptable. Requiring evenhanded restriction of rights, however, protects against violations of procreative liberty by affecting everyone, rather than only a powerless minority. Thus, as Cass Sunstein has recognized, "the requirement of generality operates as a political safeguard, ensuring that if the . . . majority is to burden the minority it must burden itself as well. In imposing this requirement of generality, the Equal Protection Clause . . . serves its most familiar and established function."[15] Where everyone is forced to bear the burden, the interests implicated are more carefully evaluated. . . .

Fundamental rights analysis under equal protection thus reunites the trifurcated identity of poor women of color. Poor women of color, as a class, may challenge the Norplant policy as a discriminatory infringement on their procreative liberty. Regardless of whether the relevant identity is economic class, gender, or race, the state still must demonstrate a compelling interest, rather than only an important or legitimate one, in drawing the classification. The focus of the analysis remains on Norplant's unequal infringement, however, because the equal protection analysis addresses the classifications involved, rather than balancing the fundamental rights against the state's interests.

Armed with this new constitutional theory, women challenging Norplant as a condition of probation have a greater chance of success. The Norplant policy clearly infringes on their fundamental right of procreative liberty by restricting their ability to have children. Although the state may be able to present compelling interests to outweigh a probationer's interests, this will not be enough to justify imposing this burden unevenly upon women but not men. Equal protection doctrine requires the state to demonstrate a compelling interest in imposing the Norplant condition disproportionately on women. This gender line is dubious under even intermediate scrutiny. . . .

NOTES

1. In one study conducted by the Women's Safety Project, 96% of the perpetrators of child abuse on girls under 16 were men. "Violence against Women," TORONTO STAR, July 30, 1993, at A23.

2. Reshma Menon Yaqub, "The Double-Edged Sword of Norplant," CHI. TRIB., Jan. 24, 1993, at 11.

3. Removal can cost as much as $300 and may also be very painful. Norplant's Side Effects Lead Women to Remove Device (CNN television broadcast, Apr. 25, 1992).

4. Meyer v. Nebraska, 262 U.S. 390, 399 (1923).

5. Howland v. State, 420 So. 2d 918 (Fla. App. 1982).

6. People v. Johnson, No. 29390 (Tulare County, CA, Super. Ct. Jan. 2, 1991).

7. Jim Persels, "The Norplant Condition: Protecting the Unborn or Violating Fundamental Rights?," 13 J. LEGAL MED. 237, 239 (1992) (citing Respondent's Supplemental Brief at 13, People v. Johnson, no. F015316 (Cal. App. 5th Dist.), filed Nov. 5, 1991).

8. 316 U.S. 535, 536–37 (1942).

9. Id. at 541.

10. 381 U.S. 479 (1965).

11. 405 U.S. 438 (1972).

12. Id. at 443.

13. Cass Sunstein, "Sexual Orientation and the Constitution: A Note on the Relationship between Due Process and Equal Protection," 55 U. CHI. L. REV. 1161, 1167 (1988).

14. Viktor Mayer-Schonberger, "Substantive Due Process and Equal Protection in the Fundamental Rights Realm," 33 HOW. L.J. 287, 289 (1990).

15. Sunstein, supra note 13, at 1178.

Chapter 26

The Ideology of Division
Behavior Modification
Welfare Reform Proposals

Lucy A. Williams

. . . .

The rhetoric of the current "welfare reform" debate goes something like this: Aid to Families with Dependent Children (AFDC) recipients are themselves responsible for their poverty because they have not "pulled themselves up by their bootstraps"; they are dysfunctional mothers incapable of fitting into mainstream society, and they are economically and emotionally atrophied because of their "dependence" on welfare. Proponents of "welfare reform" further argue that by withholding AFDC benefits, the government can transform present recipients into productive members of society, thereby solving the intractable problems of poverty. Consistent with this rhetoric, the current "welfare reform" proposals condition AFDC eligibility on conformity with putative moral norms of society. Underlying the proposals is the belief that the receipt of assistance is debilitating.

These concepts, always an undercurrent in American history, surfaced with new vigor in the work of conservative scholars in the early 1980's. The conservatives' ideas engendered several state demonstration projects, including Learnfare (loss of benefits if a child misses a certain number of days of school or fails to average a certain grade), Family Cap (loss of benefits for additional children), Bridefare or Wedfare (small monetary incentives given to a mother to marry the father of her child combined with the loss of benefits for additional children), incentives for recipients to use Norplant contraception, and benefit reductions if the mother pays her rent irregularly or fails to obtain medical treatment for her children. The idea behind all of these projects is the same: only those women and children who conform to majoritarian middle-class values deserve government subsistence benefits.

Because projects that condition eligibility on behavior contravene the mandated eligibility requirements set forth in the Social Security Act,[1] they require the United States Department of Health and Human Services (HHS) to waive the entitlement provisions under 42 U.S.C. § 1315. Through this administrative mechanism, President Bush embraced the use of welfare laws to attempt to modify behavior.

Lucy A. Williams, "The Ideology of Division: Behavior Modification Welfare Reform Programs," 102 YALE L.J. 719 (1992).

Being True to Our Roots: The Historical Context for Behavior Modification Proposals

The United States has always been ambivalent about assisting the poor, unsure whether the poor are good people facing difficult times and circumstances or bad people who cannot fit into society. . . . Public welfare programs in the United States originated as discretionary programs for the "worthy" poor . . . such as the blind, deaf, insane, and eventually the orphaned.

. . . .

The Great Depression provided the impetus for a national framework to provide assistance to the poor. . . . [T]he massive unemployment of previously employed, white male voters made it politically impossible to dismiss the poor as responsible for their own situation. . . . But legislators considered cash relief a temporary measure to last only until the Depression ended. . . . From its inception, the language and administration of the Social Security Act ("the Act") allowed the exclusion of African Americans from the programs. For example, Southern Congressmen defeated statutory language that would have protected African Americans from discrimination in eligibility for old-age pensions. Impelled by their fear that elderly African Americans would help support younger African Americans, who would thus become less pliant field laborers, these same Congressmen eliminated specific language requiring that old-age benefits be "a reasonable subsistence compatible with decency and health,"[2] thereby retaining state discretion over the amount of benefits. African-American leaders had argued that local standards would allow "less assistance to aged Negroes than to aged whites."[3]

The small program that covered children living with their mother, Aid to Dependent Children (ADC), assisted the children of women who were white, widowed, and had been connected to men for a substantial portion of their lives. Given that population, policymakers considered ADC a temporary program, effective until dependents could be covered under the portion of the Act dealing with male workers' old-age insurance. Although society had ambivalent feelings about supporting this population, it was willing to do so because the job of these white women was to provide good homes for their children.

The legislative history of the Social Security Act allowed the states, which administered the ADC program, to condition eligibility upon the sexual morality of ADC mothers through suitable-home or "man-in-the-house" rules.* In some states, African-American single mothers were intentionally excluded from the welfare rolls. One Southern field supervisor reported:

> The number of Negro cases is few due to the unanimous feeling on the part of the staff and board that there are more work opportunities for Negro women and to their intense desire not to interfere with local labor conditions. The attitude that "they have always gotten along," and that "all they'll do is have more children" is definite. . . . There

---

* *Editor's note*: "Suitable home" or "man in the house" rules punished women for extramarital sex by terminating welfare benefits of those living with men to whom they weren't married.

is hesitancy on the part of lay boards to advance too rapidly over the thinking of their own communities, which see no reason why the employable Negro mother should not continue her usually sketchy seasonal labor or indefinite domestic service rather than receive a public assistance grant.[4]

Contrary to the belief of the Social Security Act's drafters, the ADC program did not decline and disappear. Rather, the civil rights and welfare rights movements of the 1960's and 1970's resulted in the inclusion of many who had been excluded from the original ADC program. The early 1980's, however, saw a return to the exclusion of the "undeserving poor," now defined as those whose behavior did not adhere to middle-class values.

. . . .

Family Cap Policies

Building on the historic biases reflected in the suitable home and "man-in- the-house" rules, the Family Cap demonstration proposals attempt to influence poor women's decisions about procreation. . . . The proposals, embraced by President Bush, elimi-nate or reduce additional AFDC benefits for the support of additional children con-ceived after a mother begins receiving AFDC. New Jersey became the first state to pur-sue this course of action when it enacted Family Cap legislation on January 21, 1992.[5] It received a federal waiver on July 20, 1992.

. . . .

Wisconsin offered two reasons for testing a Family Cap Program: (1) to reduce long-term welfare dependency among families headed by male and female teen par-ents; and (2) to delay subsequent births to first-time teen parents who receive AFDC until they are emotionally and financially prepared to support additional children. The New Jersey proposal applies to all AFDC mothers regardless of age; its goal is a more extensive effort at "mutual responsibility." The proposal contends that "wel-fare recipients will be asked to make the same type of decisions based on their income that working families have to make about supporting their family based on the money they earn." The underlying goal of Family Cap programs is for people to plan for their children; the assumption is that middle-class people are intelligent enough to refrain from having children when they cannot support them and that poor women should do likewise.

. . . .

[T]he underlying assumptions of Family Cap proposals—that AFDC mothers have many children, that they have free access to medical options for family planning, and that they get pregnant in order to receive additional benefits—are unsound. In fact, as of 1990, the average AFDC family, including adults, had 2.9 members; 72.5% of all families on AFDC had only one or two children, and almost 90% had three or fewer children. These figures are no larger than those found among two-parent families in the general population.

. . . .

Furthermore, for those women who wish to terminate their pregnancies, neither abortion facilities nor government funding are necessarily available. . . . In addition, even when a woman does obtain birth control, the failure rates for the most reliable forms of contraceptives (i.e., the pill, diaphragms, condoms) range from 6% to 16% per year.

There are many reasons why AFDC mothers become pregnant or choose to remain pregnant. These reasons include occurrences of unplanned pregnancies (whether due to a lack of information, money, or forethought), the belief that a child solidifies a relationship with the father, the assumption that children represent an economic value (e.g., to serve as agricultural workers, to support parents in their old age), the belief that the significant health problems and infant mortality rates associated with poverty increase the risk that a single woman with only one child will become childless, a sense that one's life is so hopeless that having a child gives it value and meaning, and the desire to give a grandchild to one's own mother. Many of these reasons are equally applicable to non-AFDC, middle-class women.

"Normal" women allegedly have children only when they are economically able to support them. This is not true. Most people do not view having a baby as the prize for having made it economically, nor do they have a child to gain an additional tax deduction for a dependent. Just like AFDC recipients, they want to be parents and to share their lives with a child.

. . . .

Empirical studies have consistently documented the lack of a correlation between the receipt of AFDC benefits and the child-bearing decisions of unmarried women— even for young, unmarried women.[6] In a recent study of AFDC recipients by the Center for Urban Affairs and Policy Research, 100% of the mothers said their ability to receive AFDC had no effect on the decision to have a child.[7] In addition, AFDC families are not larger in those states with larger AFDC grants, and teen birth rates are not higher in the states with higher AFDC grants.[8] The number of female-headed families has continued to grow since the early 1970's, even though AFDC benefits, adjusted for inflation, have decreased by 30%. Women receiving AFDC are less likely than non-AFDC recipients to want an additional child, less likely to have multiple pregnancies, and more likely to practice contraception.[9]

Furthermore, the incremental increase that an AFDC family receives when a new child enters the family is so small that it does not even cover such basic essentials as diapers, clothing, bottles and formula. In Wisconsin, for example, an additional third child adds $100 to the grant; in New Jersey, $64; in Mississippi, $24.[10] Thus if economics were really the driving factor in an AFDC mother's decision to have a child, she would make the "rational" decision not to do so.

If Mississippi's economic disincentive of giving only an additional $24 for another child has not reduced AFDC family size or curbed teenage birth rate, Wisconsin's reducing the grant increment from $77 to $39 is also likely to be ineffective. If poor people do not change their behavior based on the strongest economic motivator—living well below the poverty level—the additional economic incentive of a $70 AFDC reduction is certainly non-determinative.

The Method behind the Madness

. . . .

Why does American society cling to the myth that unlike the majority, welfare recipients have deviant values that can be manipulated solely by the economics of a meager AFDC grant? . . . The answer . . . lies in a New Right agenda, which I call an ideology of division, playing to America's deepest racial fears and to resentment of the poor, single, unemployed mother.

. . . .

The articulation of the "otherness" of the poor—their amorality and depravity—is longstanding. But the unique contribution of the American New Right has been to manipulate public attitudes through the subtle use of racism, scapegoating and stereotypes. It is no accident that the bulk of conservative scholarship about public assistance has focused on AFDC, the social welfare program that highlights most graphically race and gender distinctions. Thus the New Right has achieved popular acceptance for the misuse of AFDC laws, shifting our attention from national structural problems to the purported social deviance of individual women of color.[11]

In the current variation of "otherness," the average citizen considers all AFDC recipients as part of the "underclass," i.e., African-American, long-term welfare recipients who live in inner-city ghettos and regularly have babies. The stereotype also holds that unlike whites, these undeserving poor have warped values,[12] which do not include the desire for such things as good schools, jobs, or safe streets.

The New Right's success in drawing support from working and middle class whites indicates the depth and pervasiveness of the myth of deviance regarding the AFDC African-American underclass. By exploiting a stereotype based on race and demerit, the New Right encourages the average white citizen to distance herself or himself from the African-American welfare mother and her children. While a white may support income transfer programs for the elderly because she or he anticipates growing old someday, whites know that they will never be African American, fourteen years old and pregnant. They can freely discount poverty as the moral failing of urban African-American culture, rather than recognizing it as a social condition cutting across racial and geographic lines and entrapping even the morally virtuous. The myth enables whites to nourish their deeply held belief that they will never be poor because they work hard, keep their kids in school, and make rational family planning decisions.

Contrary to the myth, empirical data does [sic] not support the stereotype of welfare recipients as African Americans living in urban ghettos. Only 39.7% of all AFDC recipients in 1990 were African American.[13] Non-Hispanic whites comprised 38.1% of AFDC recipients in 1990. The percentage of African-American recipients has in fact decreased from 45.8% since 1973.[14] Moreover, only 8.9% of the total poor live in "ghettos."[15] The median stay on AFDC in 1990 was twenty-three months.[16] . . . [T]he urban "underclass" is but a small percentage of the AFDC population.

Nevertheless, by focusing on images of the underclass welfare mother, the New Right has reduced the entire poverty debate to the AFDC program.

. . . .

The New Right has played not only to racial fears and prejudice, but also to the dream of intact families and the fantasy of women as moral guardians. In the New

Right mythology, single mothers, particularly those not economically "independent," are necessarily sexually overactive and morally deviant. This gender bias, like racial stereotyping, is not new to the welfare debate. Our social welfare policy has always preferred white women who were related to a man in the labor market or were in the workforce themselves.

The demographics of the labor market, however, have changed. Since the early 1970's, as real wages fell and as buying power declined, women have entered the workplace in unprecedented numbers. They went to work outside the home not only because the women's movement opened some previously closed doors, but also because of the belief that two incomes were necessary to maintain a desired lifestyle.

A growing number of women now would prefer not to work, but feel trapped by perceived economic circumstances. Social expectations about women as domestic caretakers have not adjusted to the realities of working women. Women are still expected to do the bulk of the child care, home care, and nurturing, and they are often overwhelmed by the substantial and conflicting demands on their time.

The New Right's ideology of division channels that dissatisfaction toward welfare mothers: why should a woman who wants to be a homemaker have to work outside of the home and support through her tax dollars the AFDC recipient who has the "luxury" of staying at home to raise her children?[17] This sentiment has prompted behavioral modification proposals like Learnfare and Family Cap, which seek to punish and devalue the "nonproductive" mother for the ostensible reason that she at least should exercise some control over her children and stop getting pregnant.

This attempt to use economic motivation to create changed behavior in AFDC mothers and children leads to "solutions" that are contrary to empirical evidence and thus cannot solve the problems for which they are ostensibly designed. "Welfare reform" programs such as Learnfare and Family Cap do not solve burgeoning social problems; they reflect only political expedience and culturally biased mythology.
. . . .

NOTES

1. 42 U.S.C. § 602(a)(10)(A) (1989). . . .

2. STAFF OF SENATE COMM. ON FINANCE, 74TH CONG. 1ST SESS., SOCIAL SECURITY BILL: SUMMARY OF PROVISIONS, COMPARISON OF TEXT OF ORIGINAL BILL, AND WAYS AND MEANS REDRAFT, COMPILATIONS OF TEXT OF PROPOSED AMENDMENTS, ETC. 3 (Comm. Print 1935) (reviewing statutory language deleted by House Ways and Means Committee).

3. Economic Security Act: Hearings on S. 1130 Before the Senate Comm. on Finance, 74th Cong., 1st Sess. 489 (1935) (statement of George E. Haynes, Executive Secretary, Department of Race Relations, Federal Council of Churches).

4. Winifred Bell, Aid to Dependent Children 34–35 (1965).

5. Act of Jan. 21, 1992, ch. 526, 1991 N.J. Sess. Law. Serv. 526 (West). In New Jersey, mothers receive $64 per month for the support of each additional child. 1992 GREEN BOOK, STAFF OF HOUSE COMM. ON WAYS AND MEANS, 102D CONG., 2D SESS., OVERVIEW OF THE ENTITLEMENT PROGRAMS: BACKGROUND MATERIAL AND DATA ON PROGRAMS WITHIN THE JURISDICTION OF THE COMM. ON WAYS AND MEANS 639 (1992) [hereinafter 1992 GREEN BOOK]. Under its Family Cap statute, any AFDC recipient who has a child while eligible for AFDC would receive no additional benefits.

6. Kristin A. Moore, The Urban Institute, Policy Determinants of Teenage Childbearing 62 (1980); The Effect of Government Policies on Out-of-Wedlock Sex and Pregnancy, 9 FAM. PLAN. PERSP. 164 (1977). See also WILLIAM JULIUS WILSON, THE TRULY DISADVANTAGED 78–81 (1987). But see Robert D. Plotnick, Welfare and Out-of-Wedlock Childbearing: Evidence from the 1980s, 52 J. MARRIAGE & FAM. 735 (1990). This is an excellent example of how the scope of the inquiry defines the debate; by focusing on whether AFDC fosters pregnancy, discussion is diverted from true solutions for teenage pregnancy.

7. Fay Lomax Cook et al., Center for Urban Affairs and Policy Research, Northwestern University, Convergent Perspectives on Social Welfare Policy: The Views from the General Public, Members of Congress, and AFDC Recipients 5–40 (1989).

> I didn't decide [to have a baby]. I didn't know anything about babies at the time. I wanted to be with [my boyfriend]. . . . My mom said no. I snuck out and saw him anyway and BINGO! I got pregnant. I had my cake and had to eat it too.

Id. at 5–40 (quoting unnamed AFDC recipient).

8. The five states with the highest teen birth rates for 18–19 year olds (Arizona, Arkansas, Mississippi, Nevada, and New Mexico) all have AFDC benefits below the national median; the five states with the lowest 18–19 year old teen birth rates (Massachusetts, Minnesota, New Hampshire, North Dakota, and Vermont) all have AFDC benefits above the national median. CHILD TRENDS, INC., FACTS AT A GLANCE 1, 5 (TABLE 2) (JAN. 1992); U.S. DEPARTMENT OF HEALTH AND HUMAN SERVICES, SOCIAL SECURITY ADMINISTRATION, SOCIAL SECURITY BULLETIN, ANNUAL STATISTICAL SUPPLEMENT 108, 306 (1992).

9. Paul J. Placek & Gerry E. Hendershot, Public Welfare and Family Planning: An Empirical Study of the "Brood Sow" Myth, 21 SOC. PROB. 658, 666, 668 (1974).

10. 1992 GREEN BOOK, supra note 5, at 669.

11. The AFDC cuts that are publicly supported are those that address behavioral modification and values. . . . The same poll that showed support for Learnfare and Family Cap indicated opposition to direct cuts in AFDC grants. Vlae Kershner, California Split over Governor's Welfare Plan, S.F. CHRON., Feb 4, 1992, at A.1. . . . Polls consistently show support for helping the "needy" and "assistance to the poor." FRANK BLOCK ET AL., THE MEAN SEASON: THE ATTACK ON THE WELFARE STATE 46–47 (1987); 1991 National Opinion Research Center Poll, Sept. 1991, available in DIALOG, File No. 468. . . .

12. A 1990 study showed that 62% of whites thought African Americans tended to be lazy, while 54% thought Hispanics likely to be lazy. Seventy-eight percent thought African Americans and 72% thought Hispanics preferred to live off welfare. TOM W. SMITH, NATIONAL OPINION RESEARCH CENTER, UNIVERSITY OF CHICAGO, ETHNIC IMAGES 9 (1990).

13. 1992 GREEN BOOK, supra note 5, at 670.

14. Id., at 670.

15. THE URBAN UNDERCLASS (Christopher Jencks & Paul E. Peterson eds.) 251 (1991) (defining "ghetto" as metropolitan census tract having poverty rate above 40%).

16. 1992 GREEN BOOK, supra note 5, at 670.

17. See 133 CONG. REC. H11, 515–16 (daily ed. Dec. 16, 1987) (remarks of Rep. Roukema) (opposing Family Support Act). In 1972, 49% of adults surveyed believed that mothers receiving welfare should be required to take any job offered them. Gallup Poll, May 1972, available in DIALOG, File No. 468. In 1991, 79% favored requiring all mothers on welfare to do work for their welfare checks. Gallup Poll, November, 1991, available in DIALOG, File No. 468. By 1992, 80% favored such a requirement. Gallup Poll, April 1992, available in DIALOG, File No. 468. The stereotype of the perennially unemployed mother again uses only a subset of the AFDC population as a symbol of the unworthy poor. Thirty-nine percent of single AFDC mothers in a recent

study either combined work with welfare, or alternated between them during a two-year period. The race of the mother was not a predictor of whether the mother would go into the labor market. INSTITUTE FOR WOMEN'S POLICY RESEARCH, COMBINING WORK AND WELFARE: AN ALTERNATIVE ANTI-POVERTY STRATEGY 9–19 (1992).

It is not surprising that at the same time that policymakers are trying to use the minuscule AFDC budget to address major systemic problems of poverty, states are not spending even the money already appropriated under the Family Support Act to implement job programs designed to move AFDC mothers into the labor force. JAN L. HAGEN & IRENE LURIE, THE NELSON A. ROCKEFELLER INSTITUTE OF GOVERNMENT, STATE UNIVERSITY OF NEW YORK, IMPLEMENTING JOBS: INITIAL STATE CHOICES, SUMMARY REPORT 6 (1992).

Questions and Comments

1. According to Solinger, how have laws regulating human reproduction "racialized" the United States? What are some examples of the racial impacts such laws have had? How have they served to reinforce both the material interests and the putative superiority of whites?
2. Since New Jersey's family cap was adopted in 1993, twenty-two additional states have established similar policies. "New Jersey Family Cap Upheld by State Supreme Court," National Conference of State Legislatures, available at http://www.ncsl.org/statefed/welfare/NJfamilycap.htm.
3. Are there similarities between the images of poor women that were invoked to justify requiring Norplant as a condition of probation and those that have been invoked to justify family caps? How do those images relate to the stereotypes of such women described in other readings in this volume?
4. If the authors in this section have convinced you that Norplant and family cap policies rely on, and reinforce, disparaging and inaccurate stereotypes of women of color, do you think such policies should be considered a prohibited form of race discrimination? Traditionally, constitutional law has required proof of intent in order to establish that an actor has unconstitutionally discriminated on the basis of race. If that interpretation of the Constitution precludes a finding that governmental policies based on harmful racial stereotypes constitute race discrimination, is it too narrow?
5. How do Albiston and Williams explain the behavior of women subjected to Norplant conditions and family cap provisions, respectively? Are their explanations more consistent with the liberal individualist approach to reproductive justice or the critical constructivist view?

B. Assisted Reproduction
Regulation of "Surrogacy" and Cloning

Chapter 27

What's Wrong with a Parenthood Market?
A New and Improved Theory of Commodification

Martha M. Ertman

Most people believe parenthood should not be bought and sold. A quarter century ago, Richard Posner and Elisabeth Landes defended, against a strong consensus, the economic efficiency of paying for babies in adoption.[1] Outraged readers decried their analysis, suggesting it epitomized the bloodless approach to human affairs that, they argued, fatally flawed legal economics. But using a baby as a club to beat commodification over the head is misguided. Contrary to Margaret Jane Radin's claim that "conceiving of any child in market rhetoric wrongs personhood,"[2] a parenthood market, in some circumstances, can be a good thing.[3] Specifically, the sale of parental rights through the alternative insemination market facilitates the formation of families based on intention and function rather than biology and heterosexuality. Consequently, people who believe that same-sex couples and single parents can and do form families should reconsider their assumption that a parenthood market is always contrary to human flourishing.[4]

. . . .

I begin by describing ways in which parental rights are already commodified through alternative insemination ("AI"). . . . Adoption and reproductive technologies reveal a gap between the rhetoric condemning the sale of parenthood and people's actual practices. The blanket condemnation of the parenthood market as a species of slavery simply does not comport with the way we live and regulate these transactions.

The next part elaborates on this point, describing in some detail the transactions involved in buying and selling sperm for alternative insemination. It illustrates how the market for male gametes operates as a relatively free market, "an economic activity in which buyers and sellers come together and the forces of supply and demand affect prices."[5]

One could respond to this analysis by determining to decommodify adoption and reproductive technology transactions to bring rhetoric condemning baby selling in line with legal and social practices. Because of the considerable benefits of marketizing parental rights and obligations, at least in the alternative insemination context, I reject the anti-commodification approach.

. . . .

Martha M. Ertman, "What's Wrong with a Parenthood Market? A New and Improved Theory of Commodification," 82 N.C. L. Rev 1 (2003).

I. Describing Parenthood Markets

Academic hand wringing about whether selling parenthood would be a good thing implies that we do not already buy and sell it. But the practice is alive and well in various guises, direct and indirect. People routinely exchange funds to obtain parental rights and obligations through adoption and reproductive technologies. Thus, there is a functioning market. In the case of reproductive technologies, especially in vitro fertilization and alternative insemination, this market is a relatively free market, operating as it does largely unhampered by legal regulation. At least in the case of alternative insemination the very fact that this market operates as a free market furthers human flourishing by allowing gay and single people to become parents.
. . . .

B. Reproductive Technologies

. . . .

Alternative insemination, like adoption and other reproductive technologies, involves the exchange of money for parenthood. Sperm banks pay donors about $60 for each donation, and the donors agree to provide regular donations over a period of time. . . . All told, alternative insemination can cost between $500 and $1000 for the first insemination and between $300 and $700 for each subsequent insemination.[6]

Seventy to seventy-five percent of women get pregnant using alternative insemination within six tries, a rate that is considerably higher than for IVF.[7] Thus, assuming pregnancy on the sixth insemination and the possibility of conception at home rather than in a doctor's office, a woman may acquire parental rights through alternative insemination for between $1,000 and $4,500 (plus shipping costs of between $72 and $600).[8]
. . . .

II. The Alternative Insemination Market

The alternative insemination market differs from surrogacy and adoption in that AI is a literal market and a relatively free, open market. The free market aspects of alternative insemination transactions play a crucial role in making this branch of the parenthood market particularly beneficial to marginalized groups.
. . . .

[A] relatively low price for the gametes and lack of regulation means that it is both an open market in which a large number of people can participate, and a free market that flourishes because of its comparative freedom from regulation. Taken together, these factors illustrate how the alternative insemination market makes positive contributions to both law and society. Of course, this relative lack of regulation also has potential drawbacks, including the lack of government oversight that could provide quality control and the lack of subsidies that could broaden the range of people who have access to parenthood through reproductive technologies.

A. Buyers and Sellers Exchange Money for Male Gametes

Alternative insemination generally involves at least two separate transactions. The sperm bank first purchases sperm from a donor and subsequently sells the sperm to a woman who uses it to become a mother. Both transactions (which I will refer to as the bank/donor and bank/recipient transactions) involve the exchange of money for goods and services. While the transactions differ in important respects, both transactions commodify gametes, and in doing so commodify parental rights and responsibilities. . . .

The bank's provision of goods and services begins with the careful screening of potential donors. . . . Also, sperm banks provide information about many other donor characteristics, including ethnicity, hair color, hair texture, eye color, height, weight, blood type, skin tone, years of education, occupation or major in college, and, in many cases, baby pictures and audio tapes of the donor's voice.

. . . .

In addition to selling this medical and character trait information, the banks sell anonymity, the freedom to become a parent with little risk that the biological father will interfere with the intended family. Anonymity is crucial because family law often links biology to parental rights and responsibilities. Anonymity allows a donor to donate without risk that the donation will result in the financial or social responsibilities of fatherhood and allows a recipient to conceive without the risk of unwanted intervention in the family by a stranger.

. . . .

Both legal doctrine and the structure of the alternative insemination market contribute to anonymity in sperm sales. On a doctrinal level, statutes often terminate the donor's rights and responsibilities regarding the child. . . . Contract law provides an additional basis for anonymity. Sperm bank contracts routinely provide for this anonymity.

. . . .

B. Alternative Insemination as a Free, Open Market

. . . .

Compared to other markets, the alternative insemination market is a relatively free market as it is subject to very limited legal regulation through statute or administrative rule. While some commentators think that public law should interfere with the operation of this market, I think that the private law nature of alternative inseminations, on balance, furthers human flourishing because statutory regulations would likely reflect majoritarian bias against single parents and gay people. . . . On the other hand, regulation could increase access by subsidizing assisted reproduction, and improve the quality of services by dictating minimum standards for obtaining, storing, and shipping samples, as well as the actual insemination.

. . . .

A number of aspects of alternative insemination make it a particularly striking example of how privatization opens up possibilities for marginalized people to skirt the majoritarian moral bias of public law. First, both technologies and deregulation open the market to a wide range of people. The technologies mean that recipients in isolated areas can obtain sperm. . . . The number of banks, coupled with technological innovations, reflects a high supply of sperm, which translates to a relatively low price for this method of becoming a parent. The low price, in turn, makes alternative insemination a technology that most middle class women can afford (unlike, for example, IVF or adoption). Moreover, access is facilitated by the possibility of insemination at the recipient's home.

. . . .

III. Mixed Valences of the Alternative Insemination Market

. . . .

A. Negative Implications of the Alternative Insemination Market

At least four aspects of the AI market could be described as negative. First, the donor selection process appears to be highly racialized, raising eugenic concerns. Second, poor women lack access to the market. Third, anonymity may deprive some children of the opportunity to know their biological fathers and also deprive them of potential financial support. Fourth and finally, a parenthood market might harm children by treating them like chattel. I address these concerns in turn below, concluding that while they are serious, especially with respect to objectification, they do not justify a blanket condemnation of the AI market, either because they are not unique to the AI market, or because addressing the concern would itself trigger other negative effects.

1. EUGENIC CONCERNS

The marketization of particular characteristics, such as race (especially whiteness as evidenced by archetypally white features such as blue eyes and blonde hair), a university education, and height, suggests that people who have these characteristics are more valuable than other people. The property value of whiteness is part and parcel of the legacy of white supremacy. While sperm is not priced on the basis of race, the alternative insemination market does seem to be racialized in other ways.

The California Cryobank's May 2001 Donor Catalog lists donors in sections based on the donor's race. . . . The [catalogue] . . . states that specimens donated by Caucasian donors are stored in vials with "WHITE caps and are shipped in WHITE canes." Similarly, . . . Black/African-American [specimens] and Asian . . . specimens, respectively, are stored in vials with "BLACK caps and are shipped in BLACK canes" and with "YELLOW caps and are shipped in YELLOW canes."[9] . . . Most striking in this large sperm bank's inventory is the over-representation of Asian donors and under-representation of African-American donors.

While the seeming paucity of donors of color (especially Black/African-American) would give many people pause, further investigation indicates that the California Cryobank's inventory does not appear to be tailored to maximize replication of an Aryan ideal. A review of the Catalog's other racialized designations of donors, such as hair color and eye color, suggests that recipients do not select donors who conform to a blonde, blue-eyed ideal. Of the 115 Caucasian donors listed, only 10% are blonde, and 23% are listed as having blue eyes.[10] . . . [H]owever, this brief discussion does give a sense of some eugenic aspects of the alternative insemination market. The next question is whether law or culture might have a response to the apparent racial disparity in available sperm.

. . . .

It could be that sperm banks screen donors for racial characteristics based on perceived or actual higher demand for Caucasian, blonde, and/or blue-eyed donors. . . . Although a social norm against discrimination might challenge banks' racial screening, it seems unlikely that racial screening would run afoul of legal rules.

. . . .

This analysis changes little when we consider the possibility that recipients, rather than banks, are discriminating on racial grounds in selecting Caucasian donors over donors of color. At least as a legal matter, women should be able to select the race of their child without state intervention.[11] Still, as a normative, cultural matter, some people might object when white women choose to have white babies through alternative insemination, in a market that monetizes whiteness and other characteristics as superior.

But if we condemn would-be mothers for selecting donors who, they believe, will transmit what they deem to be socially optimal genes to their children, then we could ask the same question of both men and women who select their partners on similar grounds. If we scrutinize white single mothers' selection of white sperm donors, we should also critique white men who choose to marry white women or Harvard graduates who prefer to marry others who attended elite colleges. If this level of meddling seems ridiculous, it is hard to see how it is appropriate when the insemination occurs technologically rather than coitally.

Moreover, while the concerns about sperm banks discriminating against donors of color are serious, the pricing of parental rights based on the child's race or other characteristics, if it does exist, is not unique to alternative insemination, nor even reproductive technologies generally. The adoption market for example, already differentiates fees based on children's characteristics.

2. ACCESS CONCERNS

A second negative element of the alternative insemination market is that many people do not have access to the market. . . . While most middle class women can afford the $1,000 to $4,500 or so that alternative insemination may cost, working class and poor women are left out.

Like eugenic concerns, problems of access are not unique to the alternative insemination market. Working class and poor people have more limited access to all kinds of goods and services, from basic needs like housing to luxuries like beach vacations. Moreover the alternative insemination market is less exclusive than other markets for parental rights. . . . [A]doption can cost between $4,000 and $30,000, surrogacy fees alone can cost between $10,000 and $20,000, and in vitro fertilization can cost between $44,000 and $211,000, while alternative insemination can cost as little as $1,000 to $4,500.

To say the AI market should be terminated because poor and working class people cannot access it would be to punish middle class users of alternative insemination simply for being middle class and either single or gay. Specifically, a concrete good (extending parenthood to people otherwise excluded from that life experience) would be snuffed out to serve an end that is so grand (wealth redistribution) as to be aspirational rather than practical.

3. ANONYMITY CONCERNS

. . . .

The prevalence of adopted children tracking down their birth parents illustrates the importance that some people place on knowing their genetic parents. However, not all adoptees seek this connection, and those who succeed in reconnecting with their birth families sometimes find that the fantasy of the perfect family was just that, a fantasy. Moreover, many children of divorced or single mothers have little or no contact with their genetic fathers. Given these considerations, it seems unfairly burdensome to impose a standard of two-biological-parent families for children conceived through AI that is not imposed on parents who conceive coitally.

. . . .

4. OBJECTIFICATION CONCERNS

Importantly, purchasing gametes to conceive a child could cause the child to feel that he or she has been purchased like a new car. Radin claims that "conceiving of any child in market rhetoric harms personhood."[12] This statement asks us to consider whether the parenthood market, as manifested through adoption and reproductive technologies, treats children like chattel, thus harming their personhood.

. . . .

However, this analysis suggests a monolithic market in which all transactions are interchangeable. . . . Becoming a parent invokes a raft of obligations quite different from those entailed in car ownership. Legally speaking, parents are obliged to, among other things, feed, clothe, shelter and educate their child, keep the child out of wage labor, and refrain from discipline that rises to the level of abuse. From an ethical standpoint, parents have the duty to help the child develop a healthy sense of self, become an independent adult, and learn how to be a good citizen. While a car owner is obliged to maintain insurance and refrain from using the car to sell illegal drugs, that owner is also free to destroy the car if she chooses, or run it into the ground through lack of maintenance. Parents are obviously not free to do the same.

In sum, while one might want to guard against language and transactions that treat children as chattel, the mere existence of a market in parenthood does not pose that particular danger. If it did, wage labor would be akin to chattel slavery.[13] Indeed, wage labor is the opposite of slavery, an insight that shows how slavery is problematic as an instance of both *over*-commodification (treating people as things for exchange) and *under*-commodification (refusing to pay people for their labor). In both labor and parenthood markets, the market's character depends on the obligations and rights built into it.

. . . .

B. Positive Implications of the Alternative Insemination Market

While the market for parenthood has negative effects, it also has positive ones.

. . . .

The practical effect of new family structures is profound. While it is difficult, if not impossible, to estimate the number of new families that exist by virtue of AI, one can look to increases in single motherhood recorded by the Census and social science data to note the increasing numbers of children born to gay couples and single gay people. These families take various forms, including two same-sex parents, a gay male couple and a lesbian couple coparenting, a lesbian and a gay man coparenting, a single lesbian (or heterosexual woman) coparenting with a gay male couple, a heterosexual woman coparenting with a gay man, and a lesbian or bisexual woman coparenting with a heterosexual man.

The increasing prevalence of these new families is positive in several ways. First, as parenthood is an important social and personal experience, opening that option to previously excluded individuals facilitates human flourishing for those people and thus for society as a whole. . . . . Finally, these new families undermine the traditional family, a form that is central to both gender and sexual orientation subordination.
. . . .

One important effect of new family forms is that they increase agency for women and gay people generally by undermining patriarchal understandings of family. As these new families live their lives, interacting with schools, neighbors, employers, employees, and other families, the social definition of what counts as a family inevitably evolves. To the chagrin of some social conservatives, family begins to mean the group that people choose rather than one ordained by nature or a divine authority.

The market is a key player in this transformation. If public law was the sole determinant of who could become a parent through alternative insemination or other reproductive technologies, then many gay people would likely be excluded from that opportunity. While American law leaves AI to the market, other countries regulate it, generally excluding gay people from becoming parents through AI. Importantly, many of these bans allow opposite-sex unmarried couples to use reproductive technologies, revealing majoritarian bias against gay people as parents even in countries that recognize them as partners. While some jurisdictions, such as Holland, allow lesbian couples to alternatively inseminate, this rule excludes single lesbians from becoming parents through AI. The majoritarian moral bias of this regulation turns on its genesis in a public decision-making process. Since European health care is socialized, public bodies decide who has access to services such as AI. In the United States, in contrast, privatized health care leaves access issues to the market. As long as lesbians can purchase AI in the U.S. system, they may become parents by this method.
. . . .

In addition to these practical, positive effects, the alternative insemination market has positive theoretical implications. Most important is that these new family forms, made possible by webs of contracts and a relatively free market, supplement our notions of family as natural with notions of family as intentional or functional. In short, alternative insemination, and reproductive technologies generally, contribute to the replacement of status-based understandings of family with contractual models.
. . . .

Second . . . most scholarship on commodification assumes that women and other marginalized people will be the sellers of contested commodities, while men or other socially powerful people will be the buyers. But the alternative insemination market defies this generalization, inverting feminist concerns with the commodification of sex and reproduction. Feminists have articulated concerns that surrogacy harms women by tempting poor women to sell something precious they would not otherwise sell. Similarly, anti-prostitution and anti-pornography feminists contend that both the actual sellers and women generally are harmed when women sell their bodies for male sexual gratification. In each instance, the feminist concern is that poor women will be objectified by selling intimate parts of themselves out of economic necessity. In the alternative insemination context, in contrast, men are the sellers and women are the buyers. Men sell an intimate part of themselves, generated in an act that remains sexual even in the sterile environs of a doctor's office, to women. While the gametes are objectified, rendered commodities that are exchanged for value, so are the men, or at least the proceeds of their desire. Women, for a change, are the subjects in the transaction, rather than the objects.

. . . .

NOTES

1. Elisabeth M. Landes and Richard A. Posner, "The Economics of the Baby Shortage," 7 J. Leg. Stud. 323 (1978).

2. Margaret Jane Radin, Contested Commodities: The Trouble with Trade in Sex, Children, Body Parts, and Other Things 139 (1996).

3. Terminology is important in this discussion. I use "parenthood market" to mean a transfer of parental rights and responsibilities for a price. Posner and Landes used the phrases "market in adoption" and "free market in babies." See Landes and Posner, supra note 1, at 324. But Posner later altered his terminology, suggesting that the transaction is better described as the sale of parental rights. See Richard A. Posner, Economic Analysis of Law 167–70 (5th ed. 1998). He also has clarified that he "did not advocate a free market in babies." See Richard A. Posner, "Mischaracterized Views," 69 Judicature 321, 321 (1986). . . .

4. The phrase "human flourishing" echoes Margaret Jane Radin's language in her canonical critique of commodification. See Radin, supra note 2, at 64.

5. Merriam-Webster's Collegiate Dictionary 712 (10th ed. 1993).

6. Rachel Pepper, The Ultimate Guide to Pregnancy for Lesbians 45, 51 (1999).

7. New York State Task Force on Life and the Law, Assisted Reproductive Technologies: Analysis and Recommendations for Public Policy 76, 78 (1998). . . .

8. Pepper, supra note 6, at 51. . . . [H]ealth insurance covers alternative insemination by women with male partners more frequently than the same procedures for lesbians. See Laurie A. Rompala, Note, "Abandoned Equity and the Best Interests of the Child: Why Illinois Courts Must Recognize Same-Sex Parents Seeking Visitation," 76 Chi.-Kent L. Rev. 1933, 1938 n.25 (2001).

9. California Cryobank, Inc., When You Succeed, We Succeed (promotional brochure) available at http://www.cryobank.com/pdf/fds.pdf, at 1–7. The Catalog similarly notifies buyers that donors of mixed race or "unique ancestries" are stored in vials with "RED caps and are shipped in RED canes." Id.

10. California Cryobank, Inc., Donor Catalog Index, at http://www.cryobank.com/catalog/index.cfm (last visited Nov. 3, 2003) (on file with the North Carolina Law Review). Eleven donors are listed as having blonde hair, and twenty-seven are listed as blue-eyed. While it is diffi-

cult to get reliable information on the prevalence of hair color, a hair color company, Clairol, estimates that 19% of American females are naturally blonde. Kristi Turnquist, "Oh, Lighten Up! More and More People are Dyeing to Be Blondes," Oregonian, July 13, 2000, at E01.

11. See Palmore v. Sidoti, 466 U.S. 429, 433 (1984); Loving v. Virginia, 388 U.S. 1, 2 (1967).

12. RADIN, supra note 2, at 139.

13. Transferring something for a price does not allow the transferee to do whatever she wants with it. A worker transfers her promise to work in return for wages, and legal doctrine prevents the employer from endangering the employee through, for example, unsafe conditions. See 29 U.S.C.A. §§ 651–78 (2003). If the employer were not so constrained, wage labor would look more like slavery.

Chapter 28

Race and the New Reproduction

Dorothy Roberts

At bottom, the argument against surrogacy rests on the peculiar nature of childbearing that makes its sale immoral. Legal theorist Margaret Jane Radin and other scholars argue that surrogacy impermissibly alienates a fundamental aspect of one's personhood and treats it as a marketable commodity. In Radin's words, "Market-inalienability* might be grounded in a judgment that commodification of women's reproductive capacity is harmful for the identity aspect of their personhood and in a judgment that the closeness of paid surrogacy to baby-selling harms our self-conception too deeply."[1] . . . Surrogacy treats women as objects rather than as valuable human beings by selling their capacity to bear children for a price. The practice places a specific dollar value on the surrogate's personal traits. Directories display photographs of and vital information (height, hair color, racial origins) about women willing to be hired to gestate a baby. Barbara Katz Rothman notes how the term "product of conception," often used to describe the fertilized egg to be implanted in a surrogate mother, reflects this commodification: "It is an ideology that enables us to see not motherhood, not parenthood, but the creation of a commodity, a baby."[2]

Moreover, pregnancy impresses a surrogate's body into paid service to a degree distinct from other work. Unlike most paid laborers, the surrogate mother cannot separate herself from the service she performs. As Kelly Oliver puts it, "Surrogacy is a twenty-four-hour-a-day job which involves every aspect of the surrogate's life. . . . Her body becomes the machinery of production over which the contractor has ultimate control."[3] Commercial surrogacy can be seen as liberating when liberation is measured by the individual's freedom and ability to buy and sell products and labor on the market. But women's wombs and pregnancy are not ordinary products or labor. Like children, organs, or sexual intimacy, women's reproductive capacities should not be bartered in the market

The relationship between race and reproduction further illuminates this market inalienability. It demonstrates how surrogacy both misvalues and devalues human beings. First, . . . Radin [and others] argue that surrogacy values women and children in the wrong way. Why do they conclude that paying women for their gestational services will produce this harmful conception of women and their reproductive capacity? It is also possible, as John Robertson suggests, that we could view gestators as "worthy col-

Dorothy Roberts, *Killing the Black Body: Reproduction, and the Meaning of Liberty* 277–93 (1997).

* *Editor's note*: Radin uses "market inalienability" to refer to a legal prohibition against selling something for money.

laborators in a joint reproductive enterprise from which all parties gain, with money being one way that the infertile couple pays its debt or obligation to the surrogate."[4] ... Radin's sense of the immorality of commercial surrogacy may arise from the features it shares with the American institution of slavery. The experience of surrogate mothers is not equivalent to slavery's horrors, dehumanization, and absolute denial of self-determination. Yet our understanding of the evils inherent in marketing human beings stems in part from the reduction of enslaved Blacks to their physical service to whites.

The quintessential commodification of human beings was the sale of slaves on the auction block to the highest bidder. Slaves were totally and permanently commodified. Slaves bore all of the legal attributes of property: just like a horse, a necklace, or a piece of furniture, they could be "transferred, assigned, inherited, or posted as collateral."[5] ...

Slave women were treated as surrogate mothers in the sense that they lacked any claim to the children whom they bore and whom they delivered to the masters who owned both mother and child. As the contemporary surrogate mother takes the place of an infertile wife, the economic appropriation of slave women's childbearing was the only way for the slave economy to produce and reproduce its laborers. It is the enslavement of Blacks that enables us to imagine the commodification of human beings, and that makes the vision of fungible breeder women so real.

The issue of race illuminates the harm of surrogacy in a second way. The feminist arguments against surrogacy focus on the commodification of women's wombs. Just as critical, however, is the commodification of the genetic tie, based on a valuation of its worth. In his discussion of egg donation, John Robertson defends recipients' desire to "receive good genes" from women who "appear to be of good stock."[6] He advocates perfecting the technology of egg donation because it will "enhance the ability to influence the genetic makeup of offspring." "Eugenic considerations are unavoidable," Robertson concludes, "and not inappropriate when one is seeking gametes from an unknown third party." Although this process devalues all women, it devalues Black women in a particular way.

Feminist opponents of surrogacy miss an important aspect of the practice when they criticize it for treating women as *fungible* commodities. A Black surrogate is not exchangeable for a white one. ... Surrogacy ... is so troubling precisely because its commercial essence lays bare how our society actually *does* value people. We must assess both the liberating and the oppressive potential of surrogacy, not in the abstract realm of reproductive choice, but in the real world that devalues certain human lives with the law's approval.

The Black Gestational Surrogate

Gestational surrogacy separates the biological connection between mother and child into two parts—the gestational tie and the genetic tie. In gestational surrogacy, the hired gestator is implanted with an embryo produced by fertilizing the contracting mother's egg with the contracting father's sperm using [in vitro fertilization]. The child therefore inherits the genes of both contracting parents and is genetically unrelated to her birth mother. This type of surrogate is treated even more like an "incubator" or "womb for rent" than paid gestators who contribute an egg to the deal. Gestational surrogacy disconnects the parents' valuable genes from the gestator's exploited reproductive capacity.

Gestational surrogacy allows a radical possibility that is at once very convenient and very dangerous: a Black woman can give birth to a white child. White men need no longer rely on white surrogates to produce their valuable white genetic inheritance. This possibility reverses the traditional presumptions about a mother's biological connection to her children. The law has always understood legal parentage to arise definitively from female, but not male, biology. The European-American tradition identifies a child's mother by the biological act of giving birth: at common law, a woman was the legal mother of the child she bore. But Black gestational surrogacy makes it imperative to legitimate the genetic tie between the (white) father and the child, rather than the biological, nongenetic tie between the (Black) birth mother and the child.

In *Johnson v. Calvert,* a gestational surrogacy dispute, the court legitimated the genetic relationship and denied the gestational one in order to reject a Black woman's bond with the child.[7] The birth mother, Anna Johnson, was a former welfare recipient and a single mother of a three-year-old daughter. The genetic mother, Crispina Calvert, was Filipina, and the father, Mark Calvert, was white. The press, however, paid far more attention to Anna Johnson's race than to that of Crispina Calvert. It also portrayed the baby as white. During her pregnancy, Anna changed her mind about relinquishing the baby and both Anna and the Calverts filed lawsuits to gain parental rights to the child.

Judge Richard N. Parslow, Jr., framed the critical issue as determining the baby's "natural mother." Johnson's attorney relied on the historical presumption that the woman who gives birth to a child is the child's natural, and legal, mother. All states except Arkansas and Nevada apply an irrebuttable presumption of legal parenthood in favor of the birth mother. Yet Judge Parslow held that Johnson had no standing to sue for custody or visitation rights, and granted the Calverts sole custody of the baby. His reasoning centered on genetics. Judge Parslow described the Calverts as "desperate and longing for their own genetic product."[8] He noted the need for genetically related children and compared gestation to a foster parent's temporary care for a child who is not genetically hers. (Robertson has similarly argued that the gestational surrogate is a "trustee" for the embryo and should be kept to "her promise to honor the genetic bond."[9])

Judge Parslow also equated a child's identity with her genetic composition: "We know more and more about traits now, how you walk, talk, and everything else, all sorts of things that develop out of your genes."[10] On appeal, the California court of appeals also saw genetics as "a powerful factor in human relationships," writing, "The fact that another person is, literally, developed from a part of oneself can furnish the basis for a profound psychological bond. Heredity can provide a basis of connection between two individuals for the duration of their lives."[11] The California Supreme Court affirmed this view, reducing the legal significance of gestation to mere evidence of the determinative *genetic* connection between mother and child.

The California courts reduced legal motherhood to the contribution of an egg to the procreative process. But the law need not place such primacy on genetic relatedness. There is little doubt, for example, that a court would not consider a woman who donated her eggs to an infertile couple to be the legal mother, despite her genetic connection to the child. By relying on the genetic tie to determine legal parenthood, the courts in the *Johnson* case ensured that a Black woman would not be the "natural mother" of a white child.

In Europe, different circumstances have also produced controversy concerning a Black woman bearing a white child. Black women in England and Italy have been implanted with a white woman's eggs in order to bear a child of their own. It was reported that the British woman used a white woman's eggs because of the shortage of Black women who donate their eggs to infertile couples. She resorted to eggs of a different race only after waiting four years for a Black donor. In her mind, the *egg* donor's race was not determinative: because the father was of mixed racial heritage, the child would be of mixed race as well—regardless of the egg donor's race. As the clinic director noted, "all you are going to do by having a white woman's egg is have a slightly paler shade of coffee colour rather than a darker shade of coffee colour."[12]

In Italy, an African woman's choice of a white woman's egg was far more momentous. Because her husband, whose sperm fertilized the egg, was white, her baby was also white. The second woman deliberately selected the donor's race because she believed that "the child would have a better future if it were white."[13] Unlike gestational surrogacy, egg donation and marriage to the father gave this woman a solid legal claim to the white child she bore. Yet the shock of a Black woman giving birth to her own white child was great enough to make international news and to send experts pondering about the ethics of such "designer babies." A wide spectrum of commentators condemned even the British woman's selection of a white egg donor. Conservative British politician Jill Knight maintained that choosing a child's ethnic identity was "plain and unvarnished genetic engineering."[14] The chairman of the British Medical Association's ethics committee called for Parliament to debate the issue. And a spokesman for the Catholic media center stated that "the Catholic Church would be opposed to such interference with the natural processes."[15]

It is regrettable that the woman in Italy refused to give birth to a Black child. Seduced by the misleading allure of the new reproduction, she unfortunately sought a technological solution to the problem of racism. On the other hand, the furor over her racial selection of eggs overlooked the fact that most white couples also choose to have a white child when they select the race of a sperm or egg donor or surrogate mother. Race is the sperm donor characteristic most likely to be matched to recipient specifications, and virtually all sperm banks are willing to meet this request. It was most hypocritical for white ethicists and politicians to lash out at this Black woman for picking the most popular type of donor eggs.

Gestational surrogacy invokes the possibility that white middle-class couples will use Black women to gestate their babies. Since contracting couples need not be concerned about the gestator's genetic qualities (most important, her race), they may favor hiring the most economically vulnerable women in order to secure the lowest price for their services. Black gestators would be doubly disadvantaged in any custody dispute: besides being less able to afford a court battle, they are unlikely to win custody of the white child they bear, as the *Johnson* case demonstrates. Writer Katha Pollitt speculates that this legal advantage might have been the Calverts' motive for choosing a Black gestational surrogate in the first place. "Black women have, after all, always raised white children without acquiring any rights to them," Pollitt notes. "Now they can breed them, too."[16]

Some writers had already predicted a caste of breeders, composed of women of color whose primary function would be to gestate the embryos of more valuable white women. . . . Slave women were similarly compelled to breed children who would be owned by their masters and to breast-feed their masters' white infants, while neglecting their own children. In fact, Anna Johnson's lawyer likened the arrangement Johnson made with the Calverts to "a slave contract."[17]

. . . .

Magnifying Racial Inequities

So far I have argued that use of new reproductive technologies reflects an already existing racial caste system. High-tech means of procreation may also magnify racial inequities by enhancing the power of privileged whites and contributing to the devaluation of Blacks. With only 40,000 babies in the United States conceived through IVF since 1981,[18] the racial disparity in its use will hardly alter the demographic composition of the country. Rather, the harm occurs at the ideological level—the message it sends about the relative value of Blacks and whites in America. But this is not an imaginary harm: ideology has a real effect on social policy and consequently on the material conditions of people's lives. By strengthening the ideology that white people deserve to procreate while Black people do not, the new reproduction may worsen racial inequality.

We should not dismiss the possibility of more tangible harms, however. The ability to select or improve the genetic features of one's offspring carries material as well as symbolic advantages. Modern genetic technologies allow parents who can afford them to secure the health and physical abilities of their children. Without government subsidies, this could produce a society where only the poor bear children with genetic disorders. Concentrating the power of genetic enhancement in the hands of an already privileged class would exacerbate differences in the status and welfare of social groups.

While birth control has been the tool for imposing negative eugenics, the new reproduction is the instrument for achieving positive eugenics—increasing the number of births from superior parents. According to Noel Keane, the doctor who assisted in the first public surrogacy arrangement explained his participation in terms of eugenics: "I performed the insemination because there are enough unwanted children and children of poor genetic background in the world."[19]

The March 1934 issue of *Scientific American* reported that each year between 1,000 and 3,000 American women requested sperm for artificial insemination, a procedure used by women with sterile husbands since the mid-nineteenth century. Noting that the women usually wanted the most biologically fit donors, the article extolled the eugenic potential of this reproductive technology: "Some 10,000 to 20,000 babies [could] be born every year from selected sources, while less than 500 babies per year are now being born to the men of real talent in our country. What will be the eugenic effect on the race, if this same tendency grows?"[20]

The eugenic possibilities of artificial insemination were explored most notably by Hermann J. Muller, a zoologist who won the Nobel Prize in 1946 for his discovery that radiation causes gene mutations. . . . Muller estimated that artificial insemination could enable 50,000 children to inherit the genes of a single "transcendently estimable man" and the majority of the population to possess the innate qualities of such men as Lenin, Newton, Pasteur, Beethoven, and Marx.[21] Unlike most eugenicists, Muller rejected the notion that socially lower classes or less advanced races had genetically inferior intelligence, attributing differences among groups to their environment.

. . . .

[F]our years after Muller's death, a right-wing millionaire named Robert K. Graham realized Muller's fantasy by establishing the Hermann J. Muller Repository for Germinal Choice. (Muller had disavowed the repository prior to his death because of his concern about biased solicitations.) Graham originally stocked the bank with sperm donated exclusively by Nobel laureates, including William Shockley, but later began accepting donations from other scientists.

Singapore provides a contemporary example of a positive eugenics program. The Singapore government responded to the country's falling birthrate by investing in the rapid development of new reproductive technologies, including the world's first egg bank. . . . Fueled by concern over Singapore's growing Malay and Indian populations, the program aims at increasing the fertility of the educated elite, particularly those of Chinese ancestry.

. . . .

What Should We Do?

. . . .

What exactly does race mean for our understanding of the new reproduction? Let us consider three possible responses for social policy. First, we might acknowledge that race influences the use of reproductive technologies, but decide this does not justify interfering with individuals' liberty to use them. Second, we could work to ensure greater access to these technologies by providing public assistance or including them in insurance plans. Finally, we might determine that these technologies are harmful and that their use should therefore be discouraged.

The Liberal Response: Setting Aside Social Justice

One response to this racial disparity is to note that it stems from the economic and social structure, not from individuals' use of reproductive technologies. Protection of individuals' procreative liberty should prohibit government intervention in the choice to use IVF and other high-tech services, as long as that choice itself does not harm anyone. Because protecting individual liberty from state intrusion is so central to liberal philosophy, I call this the liberal response. Currently, there is little government supervision of reproduction-assisting technologies, and many proponents fear legal regulation of these new means of reproduction. In their view, financial and social barriers to IVF are unfortunate but inappropriate reasons to interfere with those fortunate enough to have access to this technology. Nor, according to the liberal response, does the right to use these technologies entail any government obligation to provide access to them. Just as current constitutional jurisprudence recognizes no right to public funding of abortions or other reproductive health services, there is no constitutional right to government subsidies for high-tech fertility treatment. . . . Furthermore, if for cultural reasons Blacks choose not to use these technologies, this is no reason to deny them to people who have different cultural values.

Perhaps we should not question infertile couples' motives for wanting genetically related children. After all, people who have children the old-fashioned way may also practice this type of genetic selection when they choose a mate. It would be hypocritical to condemn people who resort to new reproductive technologies for having the same desires for their children as more conventional parents, whose decisions are not so scrutinized. The desire to share genetic traits with our children may not reflect the eugenic notion that these particular traits are *superior* to others; rather, as Barbara Berg notes, "these characteristics may simply symbolize to the parents the child's connection to past generations and the ability to extend that lineage forward into the future."[22] Several people have responded to my concerns about race by explaining to me, "White couples want white children not because of any belief in racial superiority, but because they want children who are like them."

Moreover, the danger of government scrutiny of people's motives for their reproductive decisions may override concerns about racism. This danger leads some commentators who oppose the practice of using abortion as a sex-selection technique to nevertheless oppose its legal prohibition. As Tabitha Powledge put it, "To forbid women to use prenatal diagnostic techniques as a way of picking the sexes of their babies is to begin to delineate acceptable and unacceptable reasons to have an abortion. . . . I hate these technologies, but I do not want to see them legally regulated because, quite simply, I do not want to provide an opening wedge for legal regulation of reproduction in general."[23] It would similarly be unwise to permit the government to question individuals' reasons for deciding to use reproduction-assisting technologies.

The Distributive Solution

. . . .

Another approach to procreative liberty places more importance on reproduction's social context than does the liberal focus on the fulfillment of individual desires. Procreative liberty cannot be separated from concerns about equality. . . . Policies governing reproduction not only affect an individual's personal identity; they also shape the way we value each other and interpret social problems. The social harm that stems from confining the new reproduction largely in the hands of wealthy white couples might be a reason to demand equalized access to these technologies.

This view also recognizes the social constraints on individuals' ability to make reproductive decisions. The concept of the already autonomous individual who acts freely without government intrusion is a fallacy that privileges decisionmaking by the most wealthy and powerful members of society. It ignores the communities and social systems that both help and hinder an individual in determining her reproductive life.

Obviously, the unequal distribution of wealth in our society prevents the less well off from buying countless goods and services that wealthy people can afford. But there may be a reason why we should be especially concerned about this result when it applies to reproduction. . . . Reproduction is special. Government policy concerning reproduction has tremendous power to affect the status of entire groups of people. This is why the Supreme Court in *Skinner v. Oklahoma* declared the right to bear children to be "one of the basic civil rights of man."[24] This is why in their *Planned Parenthood v. Casey* opinion Supreme Court Justices O'Connor, Kennedy, and Souter stressed the importance that the right to an abortion had for women's equal social status. It is precisely the connection between reproduction and human dignity that makes a system of procreative liberty that privileges the wealthy and powerful particularly disturbing.

Because procreative liberty is such an important right, so central to "personal identity, to dignity, and to the meaning of one's life,"[25] its infringement by forces other than the state should also be addressed. Why must we adopt the baseline of existing inequalities? Why should the deepening of these inequalities not weigh heavily in balancing the benefits and harms of assisted reproduction? Procreative liberty's importance to human dignity is a compelling reason to guarantee the equal distribution of procreative resources in society. Moreover, addressing the power of unequal access to these resources to entrench unjust social hierarchies is no less important than allowing wealthy individuals alone to fulfill expensive procreative choices. We might therefore address the racial disparity in the use of reproductive technologies by ensuring through public spending that their use is not concentrated among affluent white people. Government subsidies, such as Medicaid, and legislation mandating health insurance coverage of fertility services would allow more diverse and widespread enjoyment of the new reproduction.

Should We Discourage the New Reproduction?

If these technologies are in some ways positively harmful, will expanding the distribution of fertility services solve the problem? Will distributing more of the technologies be enough to redress the racist social arrangements that make these technologies dangerous? . . . Although the more equalized distribution of resources would alleviate many social problems, it alone cannot eliminate oppressive social structures. My racial critique of the new reproduction is more unsettling than its exposure of the maldistribution of technologies. It also challenges the importance that we place on genetics and genetic ties. Eradicating the harmful aspects of new reproductive technologies, then, may require deterring people from using them.

But can we limit individuals' access to these technologies without critically trampling on individual freedom from unwarranted government intrusion? After all, government has perpetrated much injustice on the theory that individual interests must be sacrificed for the public good. This was the rationale justifying the eugenic sterilization laws enacted earlier in this century. According to eugenicists, the law could restrict the reproductive liberty of the unfit in the interest of improving the genetic quality of the nation.

Even for liberals, individuals' freedom to use reproductive technologies is not absolute. Most liberals would place some limit on their use, perhaps by identifying the legitimate reasons for procreation. John Robertson, for example, concedes that the state may prevent parents from cloning offspring or using genetic screening to intentionally diminish the health of their children (intentionally bearing a deaf child, for example).[26] He justifies this restriction by arguing that these uses of reproduction-assisting technologies do not further the core value of procreation of producing "normal, healthy children" for rearing.[27] If such a core view of reproduction can limit individuals' personal procreative decisions, then why not consider a view that takes into account the new reproduction's role in social arrangements of wealth and power? If the harm to an individual child or even to a core notion of procreation can justify barring parents from using the technique of their choice, then why not the new reproduction's potential for worsening group inequality? The magnitude of harm that can result from the unequal use of these technologies, an inequality rooted partly in racism, justifies government regulation.

Some have concluded that the harms caused by certain reproduction-assisting practices even justify their prohibition. In 1985, for example, the United Kingdom passed the Surrogacy Arrangements Act banning commercial contract pregnancy arrangements and imposing fines and/or imprisonment on the brokers who negotiate these agreements. The authors of the act reasoned that "[e]ven in compelling medical circumstances the dangers of exploitation of one human being by another appears [sic] to the majority of us far to outweigh the potential benefits, in almost every case."[28] Some Marxist and radical feminists agree that paid pregnancy contracts should be criminalized to prevent their exploitation and commodification of women and children. Surrogacy contracts are void and unenforceable in five states in this country; three others prohibit commercial surrogacy.

On the other hand, the government need not depart at all from the liberal noninterference model of rights in order to discourage or refuse to support practices that contribute to social injustice. Even the negative view of liberty that protects procreative choice from government intrusion leaves the state free to decide *not* to lend assistance to the fertility business or its clients. Indeed, liberals who argue that the state *must* facilitate the use of these technologies, by enforcing paid pregnancy contracts for instance, contradict their own precepts.

We should therefore question a system that channels millions of dollars into the fertility business, rather than spending similar amounts on programs that would provide more extensive benefits to infertile people. . . . The fact that new reproductive technologies facilitate procreative decisions is not reason enough to exempt them from government supervision; obstetrics and abortion services are subject to regulation. Taking these social justice concerns more seriously would justify government efforts to reallocate resources away from expensive reproductive technologies toward activities that would benefit a wider range of people.

Indeed, we can no longer avoid these concerns about the social costs and benefits of IVF. Such calculations are now part of the debate surrounding the advisability of state laws requiring insurance companies to include the cost of fertility treatment in their coverage. . . . Covering the costs of expensive high-tech procedures means raising the price of insurance for everyone. The Massachusetts Association of Health Maintenance Organizations says its members pay $40 million more in premiums to cover infertility treatment for 2,000 couples.[29] . . . Moreover, providing insurance for expensive fertility treatments but not adoption (which can also cost thousands of dollars) ironically makes these technologies the only alternative some people can afford.

A study recently reported in the *New England Journal of Medicine* calculated the real cost of IVF at approximately $67,000 to $114,000 per successful delivery.[30] For older couples with more complicated conditions, the cost rose to $800,000. . . . (The high incidence of risky multiple births with IVF dramatically boosts hospital charges.) The authors concluded that the debate about insurance coverage must take into account these economic implications of IVF, as well as ethical and social judgments about resource allocation. Yes, insurance coverage increases access to these technologies to some degree. But can we justify devoting such exorbitant sums to a risky, nontherapeutic procedure with an 80 percent failure rate when so many basic health needs go unmet?

Research designed to reduce infertility, programs that facilitate adoption, and the general provision of basic human needs are examples of expenditures that would help a far broader range of people than IVF. The federal government has done little to combat the epidemic spread of chlamydia, an STD that affects millions of people and contributes to especially high infertility rates among young Black women. . . . The medical establishment has much more to gain from developing expensive technological interventions that foster a dependent clientele than from research directed at the causes and prevention of infertility. The IVF clinic at New York Hospital–Cornell Medical Center, for example, generates a $2 million annual surplus for the Cornell Medical College that enables its physicians to earn up to $1 million a year.[31] This kind of profit creates a strong incentive to push infertile couples toward repeated attempts at a high-tech solution, despite abysmal success rates that only drop with each try.

Black women in particular would be better served by a focus on the improvement of basic conditions that lead to infertility, such as occupational and environmental hazards, diseases, and complications following childbirth or abortion. . . .

The concentration of effort on the new reproduction diverts attention from the interests of poorer Black women in another, more subtle way. Although the "biological clock" metaphor is grossly exaggerated, one reason for infertility among white, educated, high-income women is their postponement of childbearing in order to pursue a career. The cause of these women's infertility is not biological; rather, it is a workplace that makes it virtually impossible for women to combine employment and childrearing. These women can . . . afford to bypass the structural unfairness to mothers through technological intervention. Similarly, many affluent white women gained entry to the male-dominated workplace by assigning female domestic tasks to low-paid dark-skinned nannies. These luxuries, which most Black women cannot afford, take the place of widespread reforms that would increase *all* women's employment options. Relying on expensive interventions to resolve the tension between child-raising and work destroys the possibility of unity in women's struggle for fundamental change in the sexual division of labor.

. . . .

There is no question that the way we view the freedom to create children technologically, as well as "naturally," is shaped by race. . . . While too much fertility is seen as a Black woman's problem that must be curbed through welfare policy, too little fertility is seen as a white woman's problem to be cured through high-tech interventions. The new reproduction is designed for the creation of white babies.

We must address the contribution that this disparity makes to racial injustice in America. Staunch civil libertarians object that intervening might unfairly limit the choices of wealthy white people. I, too, am wary of state interference in reproductive decision making; after all, Black women are the most vulnerable to such government abuse. But our vision of procreative liberty must include the eradication of group oppression, and not just a concern for protecting the reproductive choices of the most privileged. . . .

NOTES

1. Margaret Jane Radin, "Market-Inalienability," *Harvard Law Review* 100 (1987), p. 1932.

2. Barbara Katz Rothman, "Reproductive Technology and the Commodification of Life," in Baruch et al., *Embryos, Ethics, and Women's Rights* (New York: Harrington Park Press, 1988), pp. 95, 96.

3. Kelly Oliver, "Marxism and Surrogacy," in Holmes and Purdy, *Feminist Perspectives in Medical Ethics* (Bloomington: Indiana University Press, 1992), pp. 274–75.

4. John A. Robertson, "Procreative Liberty and the State's Burden of Proof in Regulating Noncoital Reproduction," *Law, Medicine, and Health Care* 16 (1988), p.22.

5. Cheryl I. Harris, "Whiteness as Property," *Harvard Law Review* 106 (1993), p. 1720.

6. John A. Robertson, "Technology and Motherhood: Legal and Ethical Issues in Human Egg Donation," *Case Western Reserve Law Review* 39 (1988–89), pp. 1, 31.

7. 5 Cal. 4th 84, Cal. Rptr 2d 494 (1993), *cert. denied,* 114 S. Ct. 206 (1993).

8. *Johnson v. Calvert,* No. X-633190, slip opinion, p. 21 (Cal. App. Dept. Super Ct. Oct 22, 1990), aff'd, *Anna J. v. Mark C.,* 12 Cal. App. 4th 977, 286 Cal. Rptr 369 (1991), aff'd, *Johnson v. Calvert,* 5 Cal. 4th 84, 19 Cal. Rptr 494 (1993), *cert. denied,* 114 S. Ct. 206 (1993).

9. John A. Robertson, "Embryos, Families, and Procreative Liberty: The Legal Structure of the New Reproduction," *Southern California Law Review* 59 (1986), pp. 942, 1015.

10. *Johnson v. Calvert,* slip opinion, p. 8.

11. Anna J. v. Mark C., supra note 8.

12. Jill Serjeant, "Clinic Blames Shortage of Black Eggs for Baby Row," *Reuters World Service,* Dec. 31, 1994.

13. Abbie Jones, "Fertility Doctors Try to Egg On Donors," *Chicago Tribune,* March 6, 1994, p. F1.

14. David Fletcher et al., "Black Woman Awaits Implant to Have Mixed-Race Baby," *Daily Telegraph,* Dec. 31, 1993, p. 1.

15. Ibid.

16. Katha Pollit, "Checkbook Maternity: When Is a Mother Not a Mother?" *The Nation,* Dec. 31, 1990, pp. 825, 842.

17. David Behrens, "It's a Boy! But Whose? Surrogate and Genetic Parents in Tug-of-War," *New York Newsday,* Sept. 21, 1990, pp. 1, 15.

18. Trip Gabriel, "High-Tech Pregnancies Test Hope's Limit," *New York Times,* Jan. 7, 1996, p. 18.

19. Noel P. Keane and Dennis L. Breo, *The Surrogate Mother* (New York: Everest House, 1981), p. 36.

20. John Harvey Caldwell, "Babies by Scientific Solution," *Scientific American* 150 (March 1934), pp. 124–25.

21. Hermann J. Muller, *Out of the Night: A Biologist's View of the Future* (New York: Vanguard, 1935).

22. Barbara J. Berg, "Listening to the Voices of the Infertile," in Callahan, ed., *Reproduction, Ethics, and the Law* (Bloomington: Indiana University Press, 1995), pp. 80, 82.

23. Tabitha M. Powledge, "Unnatural Selection: On Choosing Children's Sex," in Helen B. Holmes et al., eds., *The Custom-Made Child? Women-Centered Perspectives* (Totowa, N.J.: Humana, 1981), pp. 193, 197.

24. Skinner v. Oklahoma, 316 U.S. 535, 541 (1942).

25. John A. Robertson, *Children of Choice: Freedom and the New Reproductive Technologies* (Princeton: Princeton University Press, 1995), p. 24.

26. Ibid., pp. 167–69.

27. Ibid., p. 167.

28. Ibid., p. 64.

29. ABC World News Tonight, Transcript #6038, Feb. 22, 1996.

30. Peter J. Neuman et al., "The Cost of a Successful Delivery with In Vitro Fertilization," *New England Journal of Medicine* 331 (1994), p. 239.

31. Gabriel, "High-Tech Pregnancies Test Hope's Limit," p. 1.

Chapter 29

Is There a Right to Clone?

Constitutional Challenges to Bans on Human Cloning

Lori B. Andrews

> Perhaps in recognition of the surrealistic circumstances
> they should have spelled it D-A-L-I, instead of D-O-L-L-Y.
> —Ray Suarez, *Talk of the Nation*

On December 5, 1997, Richard Seed shocked the scientific community by announcing that he intended to begin cloning human beings. Seed planned to use the techniques that Ian Wilmut and Keith Campbell had used to create Dolly the sheep, the first cloned mammal. Dolly resulted from a transfer of the nucleic DNA of an adult mammary tissue cell to the enucleated egg cell of an unrelated sheep, and gestation in a third, surrogate mother sheep.

Governments worldwide reacted strongly to the idea of human cloning. Nineteen European countries signed an accord banning cloning. President Clinton denounced Seed's plan in a national radio address and renewed his efforts to get Congress to adopt a moratorium on human cloning. When Dolly's birth was first announced in February 1997, President Clinton issued an executive order banning the use of federal funding for human cloning[1] and asked his newly formed National Bioethics Advisory Commission ("NBAC") to prepare a comprehensive report on the scientific, ethical, and legal issues raised by human cloning.[2] When the NBAC report was released in July 1997, Harold T. Shapiro, NBAC Chair, indicated that further public discussion of this matter is important. . . .[3]

The NBAC report recommended that Congress enact federal legislation banning the creation of a child through cloning—no matter what the source of funds—for three to five years, at which time the issue should be reconsidered. President Clinton forwarded a bill to Congress based on that recommendation. . . . By April 1, 1998, seven other bills had been introduced in Congress and eighteen states were considering cloning laws.*

Lori B. Andrews, "Is There a Right to Clone? Constitutional Challenges to Bans on Human Cloning," 11 HARV. J. LAW & TECH. 643 (1998).

* *Editor's note*: At the time of this book's publication, no federal law had been enacted by Congress, but President Clinton's moratorium on federal funding was still in place.

. . . .

Many medical organizations surveyed by the NBAC, including the American Medical Association, the World Medical Association, and the World Health Organization, find cloning human beings to be unacceptable. In fact, the majority of the thirty-two scientific societies surveyed opposed the procedure, although, notably, the infertility professional societies did not join in advocating a ban. Certain religious groups oppose the procedure as well. In reaction to the cloning of Dolly the sheep, the Vatican stated that a "person has the right to be born in a human way. . . .[4]

. . . .

I. The Goals and Potential Impacts of Cloning Research

A. What Is Cloning and Why Might It Be Desirable?

Mammalian "cloning" is the manipulation of a cell from an animal or human in such a way that it grows into a virtual copy of that animal or human with identical nucleic DNA. One way to think about it is that cloning is a way to create later-born twins of an individual who is living or has already lived. Unlike naturally occurring twins, however, the clone will not be one hundred percent genetically identical because it will have mitochondrial DNA from the donor of the enucleated egg. In the case of Dolly the sheep, an adult mammary cell containing a copy of every gene needed to make the lamb was extracted, then starved of its nutrients, forcing the cell into a quiescent state. This cell was then fused with an enucleated egg cell—one in which the nucleus has been extracted—and an electric current was run through the fused cell, activating it and causing it to begin to divide. These active cells were then implanted into a surrogate mother and carried to term.

Cloning may be an attractive means of creating a child to people in a variety of situations. If one or both members of a couple are infertile, cloning presents one viable reproductive option. If one member of the couple has a genetic disorder that the couple does not wish to pass on to a child, they could clone the unaffected member of the couple. If both husband and wife are carriers of a recessive genetic disease and are unwilling to run the twenty-five percent risk of bearing a child with the disorder, they may seek to clone one or the other of them. This may be the only way in which the couple will be willing to have a child that will carry on their genetic line.

Even people who could reproduce coitally may desire to clone for a variety of reasons. People may want to clone themselves, deceased or living loved ones, or individuals with favored traits. A wealthy childless individual may wish to clone himself or herself to have a genetic heir or to pass on control of a family business. Parents who are unable to have another child may want to clone their dying child.

People might wish to clone individuals with desired traits, such as Mother Teresa, Michael Jordan, or Michelle Pfeiffer. Less well-known individuals could also be cloned for specific traits, such as a high pain threshold or resistance to radiation. Those who can perform a particular job well, like soldiers or athletes, might also make good candidates. One biologist even suggested cloning legless men for the low gravitational field and cramped quarters of a space ship.

Clones could be created to donate non-essential organs like kidneys or bone marrow. John Fletcher, former bioethicist at the National Institutes of Health, argues, "[t]he reasons for opposing this are not easy to argue."[5] Going further with this idea, John Robertson advocates cloning a "back up supply of embryos from which tissue or organs could be obtained if a tragedy befell a first child."[6]

Cloning also broadens the options available to non-traditional family units. Clone Rights United Front, a group of gay activists based in New York, demonstrated against the proposed New York legislation that would ban nuclear transplantation research and human cloning because they see human cloning as a significant breakthrough for same-sex reproduction.[7] ...

Ursula Goodenough, a cell biologist from Washington University, raised an additional application of cloning—reproduction without men. If females cloned themselves, men would be superfluous in reproduction, leading to a world where men may eventually be phased out entirely—the ultimate feminist utopia. Ann Northrop, a columnist for the New York gay newspaper, LGNY, says that cloning is enticing to lesbians because it offers them a means of reproduction and "has the potential of giving women complete control over reproduction."[8] "This is sort of the final nail in men's coffins. . . . Men are going to have a very hard time justifying their existence on this planet, I think. Maybe women may not let men reproduce."[9]

B. The Potential Physical Risks in Cloning Humans

Many scientists, including Dolly's creators, are concerned that it would be premature to begin human cloning without first addressing the many safety concerns through animal research. . . . [T]here are technical questions which can only be answered by continued animal research. Of 277 attempts in the sheep cloning experiment, only one—Dolly—survived.

Reactivating the genes of a cell is risky. An adult cell which has already been differentiated contains a complete complement of genes, but only a small proportion are activated in order to do the specialized task of that cell. Activating the slumbering genes may reveal hidden mutations. Mutations are "a problem with every cell, and you don't even know where to check for them," according to Ralph Brinster of the University of Pennsylvania.[10] . . . Also, if all the genes in the adult DNA are not properly reactivated, there could be a problem for the clone at a later developmental stage. The high rate of laboratory deaths suggests that cloning may in fact damage the DNA of a cell, and scientists urge that Dolly should be closely monitored for abnormal genetic anomalies that did not kill her as a fetus but may have long-term harmful effects.

Furthermore, because scientists do not fully understand the cellular aging process, they do not know what "age" or "genetic clock" Dolly inherited. On a cellular level, when the report of her existence was published in *Nature,* was she a normal seven month old lamb, or was she six years old (the age of the mammary donor cell)? There is speculation that Dolly's cells most likely are set to the genetic clock of the nucleus donor, and therefore are comparable to those of her six year old progenitor. One commentator stated that if the hypotheses of a cellular, self-regulating genetic clock were correct, clones would be cellularly programmed to have much shorter life spans than the "original." This could . . . lead people to view cloned animals and humans as short-lived, disposable copies. This concern for premature aging has lead Dr. Sherman Elias, geneticist and obstetrician at the Baylor College of Medicine, to call for further animal testing of nuclear transplantation as a safeguard to avoid subjecting human clones to premature aging and the potential harms associated with aged cells.[11]

The history of animal cloning from embryonic and fetal cells also suggests caution before cloning humans. . . . [W]hen the Grenada Corporation in Texas began the cloning of cows from differentiated embryonic cells, some of the cloned calves were abnormally large. Some weighed up to one hundred and eighty pounds at birth, more than twice the normal seventy five pound birth weight of this breed. Also, some of these calves were born with diseases such as diabetes and enlarged hearts, and eighteen to twenty percent of these calves simply died after birth.

. . . .

The gross deformities and early deaths among cloned animals raise concerns that initial trials in human nuclear transplantation will also meet with disastrous results. Dr. Wilmut is specifically concerned with the ethical issues raised by any such defective births. He responded to the announcement that Dr. Richard Seed intended to clone human beings within the next two years by stating: "Let me remind you that ¼ of the lambs born in our experiment died within days of birth. Seed is suggesting that a number of humans would be born but others would die because they didn't properly develop. That is totally irresponsible."[12] . . . [M]any scientific groups are voluntarily observing a moratorium on human cloning because "the chance of abhorrent offspring is high."

C. The Potential Psychological Impacts of Cloning

Concerns about the psychological impact of cloning focus on the parent/child relationship, the undermining of the clone's autonomy and free will, and the later-born twin's loss of ability to control private information.

The unique origins of a clone might create unreasonable expectations about her. When a clone is created from a dead child, the parents might expect the second child to be a replacement for the first. . . . But the clone will invariably be different. The parents will be older—even if just by a few years—than they were when rearing the first child. They will also have suffered an indelible grief, the death of their child, and thus may have a tendency to overprotect the clone. They may also narrow the experiences of the clone, exposing it only to the type of food, toys, or classes that the first child liked.

These two problems—the specter of difference, leading to disappointment, and the narrowing of experiences—are likely to haunt all cloning arrangements. Consider, for example, what might happen if a couple cloned a famous basketball player. If the clone breaks his knee at age ten, would his parents consider him a disappointment? Would he view himself as a failure?

. . . .

Family relationships could also be altered by the fact that a cloned child may seem more like an object than a person, since he or she is "designed and manufactured as a product, rather than welcomed as a gift."[13] As the NBAC observed, "[s]omatic cell nuclear transfer cloning, some fear, offers the possibility of virtually complete control over one important aspect of a child's development, his or her genome, and it is the completeness of this control . . . [that] invokes images of manufacturing children according to specification."[14] It might diminish the personhood of a clone if he were created to satisfy the vanity of the nucleic DNA donor or to meet the needs of a pre-existing individual, such as a child needing bone marrow. In attempting to cull out from the resulting child the favored traits of the loved one or celebrity who has been cloned, the social parents might limit the environmental stimuli to which the child is exposed. "Arguably a person cloned from a departed loved one . . . has less chance of being loved solely for his own intrinsic worth."[15]

Some scientists argue that these concerns are unfounded, because a clone will be invariably different from the original. The NBAC report observes that "the idea that one could make through somatic cell nuclear transfer a team of Michael Jordans, a physics department of Albert Einsteins, or an opera chorus of Pavarottis, is simply false."[16]

However, we are in an era of genetic determinism. James Watson, co-discoverer of deoxyribonucleic acid ("DNA") and the first director of the Human Genome Project, has stated, "[w]e used to think our fate was in our stars. Now we know, in large measure, our fate is in our genes."[17] Harvard zoologist Edward O. Wilson asserts that the human brain is not tabula rasa later filled in by experience, but rather "an exposed negative waiting to be slipped into developer fluid."[18]

. . .

Whether or not genetics actually play such a large role in human development, parents may raise a clone as if they do. After all, regardless of their belief in genetic determinism, the only reason people want to clone (as opposed to adopting or using an egg or sperm donor in the case of infertility) is to assure that a child has a certain genetic make-up. It seems absurd to think that they would forget about that genetic make-up once the clone was born. We already limit parents' genetic foreknowledge of their children because we believe it will improperly influence their rearing practices. Medical genetics groups often caution parents against having their children tested for late-onset genetic disorders, because a child who tested positive could "grow up in a world of limited horizons and may be psychologically harmed even if treatment is subsequently found for the disorder."[19]

Cloning could undermine human dignity by threatening the replicant's sense of self and autonomy. A vast body of developmental psychology research has demonstrated children's need to have a sense of an independent self. This might be difficult for the clone of a parent or of a previous child who died. . . .

Clones are very different from naturally-occurring twins. With twins:

> [E]ach life begins ignorant of what [the genome's determinative effects] will be, and so remains as free to choose a future as are individuals who do not have a twin. In this line of reasoning, ignorance of the effect of one's genome on one's future is necessary for the spontaneous, free, and authentic construction of a life and self.[20] . . .

Another problem is that a clone cannot control disclosure of intimate personal information. . . . [A]n individual might be stigmatized or discriminated against based on foreknowledge of her genotype. If an individual were cloned and later died young of an inheritable disease, the clone might suffer from insurance or employment discrimination.

D. The Potential Societal Impacts of Cloning Humans

The prospect of cloning humans raises several serious concerns about its overall effect on society. Cloning may interfere with evolution, because it promotes genetic uniformity, thus increasing the danger that a disease might arise in the future to which clones would have no resistance. . . . Genetic adaptation has allowed the human species to survive; producing genetically identical humans may therefore be threatening to the species. Further, although Dolly the sheep has gotten pregnant, the possibility that human clones would be sterile is another concern. Despite these overall risks, some commentators argue that if human cloning is restricted to very rare cases, then the evolution of the human species should not be stunted nor the human gene pool disturbed any more than the gene pool is currently affected by naturally occurring identical twins.

Cloning might also bring detrimental changes to the institution of the family. Boston College theologian Lisa Sowhill Cahill is concerned that cloning may lead to the commodification of human beings and their genes and to the manipulation of human genetics to achieve more socially desirable children.[21] . . . Other opponents envision a world where clones are "cannibalized for spare parts"—made solely for medical purposes and asked to donate their organs.

Cloning may also have negative impacts on broader legal concepts. [Francis] Pizzulli points out that ". . . cloning might have macroeffects upon society by eroding the concept of individuality which is at the core of our notions of privacy and autonomy."[22]

. . . .

IV. Would a Ban on Cloning Infringe upon the Right to Make Reproductive Decisions?

A variety of personal desires may motivate people to utilize cloning. The NBAC report suggests it would be "understandable, or even, as some have argued desirable,"[23] to create a child from one adult if both members of the couple have a lethal recessive gene; from a dying infant if his father is dead and the mother wants an offspring from her late husband; or from a terminally ill child to create a bone marrow donor.[24] Some of the experts testifying before the NBAC also suggested that cloning should be appropriate in exceptional circumstances. Rabbi Dorff opined that it would be "legitimate from a moral and a Jewish point of view" to clone a second child to act as a bone marrow donor so long as the "parents" raise that second child as they would any other. Rabbi Tendler raised the scenario of a person who was the last in his genetic line and whose family was wiped out in the Holocaust. "I would certainly clone him," said Tendler.[25] In contrast, the Catholic viewpoint is that cloning "is entirely unsuitable for human procreation even for exceptional circumstances."

The right to make decisions about whether or not to bear children is constitutionally protected under the constitutional right to privacy and the constitutional right to liberty. The Supreme Court in 1992 reaffirmed the "recognized protection accorded to liberty relating to intimate relationships, the family, and decisions about whether or not to beget or bear a child."[26] Early decisions protected a married couple's right to privacy to make procreative decisions, but later decisions focused on individuals' rights as well: "If the right of privacy means anything, it is the right of the individual, married or single, to be free from unwarranted governmental intrusion into matters so fundamentally affecting a person as the decision whether to bear or beget a child."[27]

A federal district court has indicated that the right to make procreative decisions encompasses the right of an infertile couple to undergo medically-assisted reproduction, including in vitro fertilization and the use of a donated embryo. Lifchez v. Hartigan held that a ban on research on fetuses was unconstitutional not only because it was impermissably [sic] vague, but also because it impermissibly infringed upon a woman's fundamental right to privacy.[28] Although the Illinois statute banning embryo and fetal research at issue in the case permitted in vitro fertilization, it did not allow embryo donation, embryo freezing, or experimental prenatal diagnostic procedures. The court stated: "It takes no great leap of logic to see that within the cluster of constitutionally protected choices that includes the right to have access to contraceptives, there must be included within that cluster the right to submit to a medical procedure that may bring about, rather than prevent, pregnancy."[29]

Using similar logic, some commentators argue that the Constitution also protects the right to create a child through cloning. As Pizzulli points out, "[i]n comparison with the parent who contributes half of the sexually reproduced child's genetic formula, the clonist is conferred with more than the requisite degree of biological parenthood, since he is the sole genetic parent."[30]

John Robertson argues that cloning is not qualitatively different from the practice of medically assisted reproduction and genetic selection that is currently occurring.[31] Consequently, he argues that "cloning . . . would appear to fall within the fundamental freedom of married couples, including infertile married couples to have biologically related offspring."[32] Similarly, June Coleman argues that the right to make reproductive decisions includes the right to decide in what manner to reproduce. . . . [33]

However, cloning is too qualitatively different from normal reproduction and from the types of assisted reproduction protected by the Lifchez case to simply assume the same Constitutional protections apply. . . . Cloning is not a process of genetic mix, but of genetic duplication. In even the most high-tech reproductive technologies available, a mix of genes occurs to create an individual with a genotype that has never before existed on earth. Even in the case of twins, their futures are unknown and the distinction between the offspring and their parents is acknowledged. In the case of cloning, however, the genotype in question has already existed. Even though it is clear that a clone will develop into a person with different traits because of different social, environmental, and generational influences, there is strong speculation that the fact that he or she has a genotype that already existed will affect how the resulting clone is treated by himself, his family, and social institutions.

. . . .

[E]ven if a fundamental constitutional right to clone were recognized, any legislation that would infringe unduly upon this right would be permissible if it were narrowly tailored to further a compelling state interest.[34] As demonstrated by the discussion in Part I, the potential physical and psychological risks of cloning an entire individual are sufficiently compelling to justify banning the procedure. Further, the notion of replicating existing humans seems to fundamentally conflict with our legal system, which emphatically protects individuality and uniqueness.

Some commentators argue that the potential harm to the cloned child should not matter because the child would not have been born otherwise and thus cloning is beneficial to that child. But there are obviously some harms that are worse than non-existence, as courts recognize in wrongful life cases. If this were not the case, any amount of pain and suffering could be inflicted on a child, so long as the parents claimed they would not have given birth to him otherwise.

Similarly, it has been argued that, because the risk of physical harm of cloning is no different from risks with normal reproduction from certain genetic disorders, cloning should not be restricted any more than other forms of reproduction. This analogy is not apt, though. Parents might conceive a child who was unable to walk due to the genetic anomaly of spina bifida. But if they intervened with a child, by beating her, and caused the same result, the moral analysis would be much different. To the extent that cloning is a purposeful intervention that causes harm, it should be viewed differently from traditional reproduction.

The government could also assert a compelling interest in protecting against broader social harms. For example, the government could assert an interest in preserving evolution and thus forbid cloning because it could lessen diversity in society. The government may also assert an interest in diversity as a cultural good independent of its value for evolution.

. . . .

Additionally, the creation of persons to be used as "spare parts" for transplantation would not only be socially repugnant, but might be violative of the clone's Thirteenth Amendment rights against involuntary servitude. The clone's right to bodily integrity and personal property are also violated by the notion of spare organ part banking.

Francis Pizzulli points out that a ban on cloning individuals might be constitutional if it were not based on a religious rationale but on "the valid secular purpose of safeguarding a normative view of human identity," resting upon the personal privacy and individual autonomy values of the Thirteenth and Fourteenth Amendments.[35] "Implicit in the prohibition of clonal humans is the rationale that certain types of humans ought not to exist, either because they have inalienable rights to nonexistence or because their presence would erode important social values."[36]

Some commentators argue that potential psychological and social harms from cloning are too speculative to provide the foundation for a governmental ban. Elsewhere, I have argued that speculative harms do not provide a sufficient reason to ban reproductive arrangements such as in vitro fertilization or surrogate motherhood.[37]

But the risks of cloning go far beyond the potential psychological risks to the original whose expectations are not met by the clone, or the risks to the child of having an unusual family arrangement if the original was not one of his or her rearing parents.

The essential difference with cloning is the risk of hubris, of abuse of power. Cloning represents the potential for "[a]buses of the power to control another person's destiny—both psychological and physical—of an unprecedented order."[38] As Pizzulli suggests, legal discussions of whether the replicant is the property of the cloned individual, the same person as the cloned individual, or a resource for organs all show how easily the replicant's own autonomy can be swept aside.[39]

In that sense, maybe the best analogy is [sic] cloning is incest. Arguably, reproductive privacy and liberty are threatened as much by a ban on incest as by a ban on cloning. Arguably the harms are equally speculative. Yes, incest creates certain potential physical risks to the offspring, due to the potential for lethal recessive disorders. But no one seriously thinks that this physical risk is the reason we ban incest. A father and daughter could avoide [sic] that risk by contracepting or agreeing to have prenatal diagnosis and abort the affected fetuses. There might even be instances in which, because of their personalities, there is no psychological harm to either party. Yet we ban incest—despite the speculative nature of the harm—because it allows an exercise of excessive power of parents over children.

. . . .

VI. Conclusion

In May of 1971, Dr. James Watson, the Nobel Prize winner for co-discovering the structure of DNA, authored the seminal article for *The Atlantic* called *Moving Toward the Clonal Man*. He explained how cloning could be done and he tried to alert ethicists and scientists that [sic] the realization that human cloning was "a matter far too important to be left solely in the hands of the scientific and medical communities."[40] When President Clinton assigned the task of making recommendations about cloning to the National Bioethics Advisory Commission, he noted that "any discovery that touches upon human creation is not simply a matter of scientific inquiry, it is a matter of morality and spirituality as well."[41]

. . . .

This article has addressed the potential barriers that may block federal and state attempts to prohibit human cloning such as constitutional challenges based on the Commerce Clause, scientists' right of inquiry, or individuals' or couples' privacy or liberty rights to make reproductive decisions. In each case, it has been shown that human cloning could permissibly be restricted based on compelling potential harms to the clone or to the society as a whole.

NOTES

1. See Transcript of Clinton Remarks on Cloning, U.S. NEWSWIRE, Mar. 4, 1997, available in 1997 WL 571115.

2. See Letter from President William J. Clinton to Dr. Harold Shapiro, Chairman, National Bioethics Advisory Commission (Feb. 24, 1997) (on file with author), reprinted in NATIONAL BIOETHICS ADVISORY COMMISSION, CLONING HUMAN BEINGS: REPORT AND RECOMMENDATIONS OF THE NATIONAL BIOETHICS ADVISORY COMMISSION, at preface (1997) [hereinafter CLONING HUMAN BEINGS].

3. CLONING HUMAN BEINGS, supra note 2.

4. Id. at 56.

5. See Jeffrey Kluger, "Will We Follow the Sheep?," TIME, Mar. 10, 1997, at 66, 70 (quoting John Fletcher).

6. John Robertson, Address to the National Bioethics Advisory Commission (Mar. 14, 1997), available at http://www.all.org.nbac/70313b.htm [hereinafter Robertson Statement].

7. See Anita Manning, "Pressing a 'Right' to Clone Humans, Some Gays Foresee Reproduction Option," USA TODAY, Mar. 6, 1997, at 1D.

8. Id. (quoting Northrup).

9. Liesl Schilinger, "Postcard from New York," INDEPENDENT (London), Mar. 16, 1977, at 2 (quoting Northrop).

10. Sharon Begley, "*Little Lamb, Who Made Thee?*" Newsweek, Mar. 10, 1997, at 53, 59.

11. See Terence Monmaney, "Prospect of Human Cloning Gives Birth to Volatile Issues," L.A. TIMES, Mar. 2, 1997, at A1.

12. "Seed's Human Cloning Bid Draws Edgy World Reactions," MEDICAL INDUSTRY TODAY, Jan. 8, 1998, available in LEXIS, News Library, Curnws File (quoting Dr. Wilmut).

13. CLONING HUMAN BEINGS, supra note 2, at 52 (citing Gilbert Meilaender, Testimony Before the National Bioethics Advisory Commission, Mar. 13, 1997).

14. Id. at 69.

15. Francis C. Pizzulli, Note, "Asexual Reproduction and Genetic Engineering: A Constitutional Assessment of the Technology of Cloning," 47 S. CAL. L. REV. 476, 503 n.140 (1974).

16. CLONING HUMAN BEINGS, supra note 2, at 33.

17. Leon Jaroff, "The Gene Hunt," TIME, Mar. 20, 1989, at 217.

18. Tom Wolfe, "Sorry, but Your Soul Just Died," FORBES ASAP, Dec. 2, 1996, at 210.

19. Dorothy Wertz et al., "Genetic Testing for Children and Adolescents: Who Decides?," 272 JAMA 875, 878 (1994).

20. See CLONING HUMAN BEINGS, supra note 2, at 68 (citing HANS JONAS, PHILOSOPHICAL ESSAYS: FROM ANCIENT CREED TO TECHNOLOGICAL MAN (1974)).

21. See Kenneth L. Woodward, "Today the Sheep . . . ," NEWSWEEK, Mar. 10, 1997, at 60.

22. Pizzulli, supra note 15, at 498.

23. CLONING HUMAN BEINGS, supra note 2, at 79.

24. See id. at 80.

25. Id. at 55. . . .

26. Planned Parenthood v. Casey, 505 U.S. 833, 857 (1992).

27. Eisenstadt v. Baird, 405 U.S. 438, 453 (1972).

28. See Lifchez v. Hartigan, 735 F. Supp. 1361, 1376–77 (N.D. Ill. 1990), aff'd mem., 914 F.2d 260 (7th Cir. 1990).

29. Id. at 1377 (citations omitted). The court also held that the statute was impermissibly vague because of its failure to define "experiment" or "therapeutic." See id. at 1376.

30. Pizulli, supra note 15, at 550 n. 357.

31. See Robertson Statement, supra note 6. This seems to be a reversal of Robertson's earlier position that cloning "may deviate too far from prevailing conception[s] of what is valuable about reproduction to count as a protected reproductive experience. At some point attempts to

control the entire genome of a new person pass beyond the central experiences of identity and meaning that make reproduction a valued experience." John A. Robertson, CHILDREN OF CHOICE: FREEDOM AND THE NEW REPRODUCTIVE TECHNOLOGIES 169 (1994).

32. Robertson Statement, supra note 6.

33. See June Coleman, Comment, "Playing God or Playing Scientist: A Constitutional Analysis of Laws Banning Embryological Procedures," 27 PAC. L.J. 133, 1364 (1996).

34. See Roe v. Wade, 410 U.S. 113, 155 (1973).

35. Pizzulli, supra note 15, at 583.

36. Id. at 493.

37. See Lori B. Andrews, "Surrogate Motherhood: The Challenge for Feminists," 16 L., MED. & HEALTH CARE 72 (1988).

38. Pizzulli, supra note 15, at 492.

39. See id.

40. James D. Watson, "Moving toward the Clonal Man," ATLANTIC, May 1971, at 50, 53.

41. Transcript of Clinton Remarks on Cloning, supra note 1.

Questions and Comments

1. According to Ertman, how does an "intent-based" definition of parenthood benefit nontraditional parents such as single individuals and gay men? How might her argument apply to surrogacy?

2. An intent-based definition of parenthood essentially enforces the choices that individuals make about becoming parents. As was discussed in the introduction to this volume, critical constructivists criticize choice-based approaches to reproductive justice. Drawing on such critiques, what disadvantages to the intent-based definition of parenthood can you identify? What do you think Roberts would say about an intent-based definition?

3. According to Roberts, how does surrogacy devalue human beings? Why does she see gestational surrogacy (as contrasted with traditional surrogacy) as especially dangerous to Black women? For example, what does she mean by "positive" eugenics, and why does she believe surrogacy raises the specter of such eugenics?

4. In *Skinner v. Oklahoma,* discussed by Albiston in the previous subpart, the U.S. Supreme Court held that the right to procreate is a fundamental right under the Constitution. Should that right to procreate include the right of infertile individuals to try to have children using assisted reproductive technologies (ARTs), such as in vitro fertilization, surrogacy, and cloning? In this context, it's interesting to note that the Supreme Court has held that the ability to reproduce is a "major life activity" under the Americans with Disabilities Act (ADA). *Bragdon v. Abbott,* 524 U.S. 624 (1998). Thus, someone whose ability to reproduce is "substantially limited" is considered "disabled" under the act and is thereby entitled to accommodation of his or her disability. Infertile couples have used this precedent to argue that an employer's failure to provide health insurance that covers infertility treatments violates the ADA. The courts are currently split on the answer to this question. See, The International Council on Infertility Information Dissemination, Inc., "Insurance and Advocacy," available at http://www.inciid.org/article.php?cat=benefits&id =414.

5. As Andrews describes it, does human cloning offer the prospect of new and varied family formations along the lines that Ertman envisions? Or, does it instead raise concerns about "positive" eugenics and the devaluing of certain groups of people similar to those Roberts discusses?

The Disciplining of Mothers-to-Be
Legal Regulation of Behavior during Pregnancy

Introduction to Part IV

Part IV, the final part of this book, is entitled "The Disciplining of Mothers-to-Be: Legal Regulation of Behavior during Pregnancy." This part exposes how legal regulation of behavior during pregnancy—including regulation of the actual process of carrying and delivering a child—perpetuates and facilitates the control of women's behavior in the service of coercive gender, race, and class norms. Section A focuses on workplace discrimination against pregnant women, beginning with the infamous case of *Troupe v. May Dept. Stores,* in which a company's firing of a woman who had been absent due to morning sickness and was about to take maternity leave was not considered to raise an issue of sex discrimination. That case is followed by Ruth Colker's "Pregnancy, Parenting, and Capitalism," which criticizes *Troupe* and argues that a choice-based approach to such issues fails to protect the interests of future children (and their mothers), as well as unfairly imposing only on women the burdens of reproducing the citizenry of the society. Then Regina Austin's article, "Sapphire Bound!," examines a case in which a pregnant Black woman was fired on the grounds that she constituted a "bad role model" for Black teens. Austin argues that such actions by employers actually reproduce the harm from which they're trying to protect teen mothers in the first place, for they assure that unwed teen parenthood will have an economically disastrous impact. Like Rhode's analysis of teen pregnancy, Austin's piece emphasizes that the *effects* of teen parenthood are not natural and inevitable, but rather flow from specific social conditions and practices.

Next, section B of part IV turns to tort and criminal liability for prenatal behavior. It starts off with *Stallman v. Youngquist,* in which the Supreme Court of Illinois refused to allow a pregnant woman to be subjected to suit for negligent driving that caused harm to her fetus. This case is followed by another excerpt from Dorothy Roberts's *Killing the Black Body,* in which she analyzes the criminal prosecution of women for using illegal substances during pregnancy. Roberts argues that such prosecutions violate the right to reproductive autonomy of poor, Black women, and punish them for having babies.

Finally, the book concludes with section C's treatment of the topic of court-ordered Cesarean sections. In the excerpt from her piece entitled "The Colonization of the Womb," Nancy Ehrenreich argues that medical practices involving Cesarean sections not only enforce a flawed medical model of childbirth but also reinforce the subordination of both privileged, white women (who consent to far too many Cesarean surgeries) and low-income women of color (who are disproportionately subjected to mandatory, court-ordered C-sections). This discussion reminds us of both the variations and the *connections* between the reproductive lives of different groups of women, and of the importance of working together to find policies and practices that will serve the interests of all.

A. Pregnancy and Fertility Discrimination in the Workplace

Chapter 30

Troupe v. May Department Stores Co.

POSNER, Chief Judge.

In 1978, Congress amended Title VII of the Civil Rights Act of 1964 to prohibit discrimination on account of pregnancy: "women affected by pregnancy, childbirth, or related medical conditions shall be treated the same for all employment-related purposes, including receipt of benefits under fringe benefit programs, as other persons not so affected but similar in their ability or inability to work." . . .

The plaintiff, Kimberly Hern Troupe, was employed by the Lord & Taylor department store in Chicago as a saleswoman in the women's accessories department. She had begun working there in 1987, initially working part time but from July 1990 full time. Until the end of 1990 her work was entirely satisfactory. In December of that year, in the first trimester of a pregnancy, she began experiencing morning sickness of unusual severity. The following month she requested and was granted a return to part-time status, working from noon to 5:00 p.m. Partly it seems because she slept later under the new schedule, so that noon was "morning" for her, she continued to experience severe morning sickness at work, causing what her lawyer describes with understatement as "slight" or "occasional" tardiness. In the month that ended with a warning from her immediate supervisor, Jennifer Rauch, on February 18, she reported late to work, or left early, on nine out of the 21 working days. The day after the warning she was late again and this time received a written warning. After she was tardy three days in a row late in March, the company on March 29 placed her on probation for 60 days. During the probationary period Troupe was late eleven more days; and she was fired on June 7, shortly after the end of the probationary period. She testified at her deposition that on the way to the meeting with the defendant's human resources manager at which she was fired, Rauch told her that "I [Troupe] was going to be terminated because she [Rauch] didn't think I was coming back to work after I had my baby." Troupe was due to begin her maternity leave the next day. We do not know whether it was to be a paid maternity leave but at argument Lord & Taylor's counsel said that employees of Lord & Taylor are entitled to maternity leave with half pay. We must assume that after Troupe was fired she received no medical benefits from Lord & Taylor in connection with her pregnancy and the birth of her child; for she testified without contradiction that she received no monetary benefits of any kind, other than unemployment benefits, after June 7, 1991. We do not know whether Lord & Taylor was less tolerant of Troupe's tardiness than it would have been had the cause not been

Troupe v. May Department Stores Co. 20 F.3d 734 (7th Cir. 1994).

a medical condition related to pregnancy. There is no evidence on this question, vital as it is.

. . . .

Different kinds and combinations of evidence can create a triable issue of intentional discrimination ("disparate treatment," in the jargon of discrimination law), the only kind of discrimination alleged in this case. One kind is evidence that can be interpreted as an acknowledgment of discriminatory intent by the defendant or its agents. . . . Such evidence is indeed direct evidence as distinct from circumstantial; and since intent to discriminate is a mental state and mind reading not an accepted tool of judicial inquiry, it may be the only truly direct evidence of intent that will ever be available. But circumstantial evidence is admissible too, to provide a basis for drawing an inference of intentional discrimination.

. . . .

[In order to survive] summary judgment a plaintiff must produce . . . evidence from which a rational trier of fact could reasonably infer that the defendant had fired the plaintiff because the latter was a member of a protected class, in this case the class of pregnant women.

We must examine the record in the light of these principles. The great, the undeniable fact is the plaintiff's tardiness. Her lawyer argues with great vigor that she should not be blamed—that she was genuinely ill, had a doctor's excuse, etc. That would be pertinent if Troupe were arguing that the Pregnancy Discrimination Act requires an employer to treat an employee afflicted by morning sickness better than the employer would treat an employee who was equally tardy for some other health reason; this is rightly not argued. If an employee who (like Troupe) does not have an employment contract cannot work because of illness, nothing in Title VII requires the employer to keep the employee on the payroll.

Against the inference that Troupe was fired because she was chronically late to arrive at work and chronically early to leave, she has only two facts to offer. The first is the timing of her discharge: she was fired the day before her maternity leave was to begin. Her morning sickness could not interfere with her work when she was not working because she was on maternity leave, and it could not interfere with her work when she returned to work after her maternity leave because her morning sickness would end at the latest with the birth of her child. Thus her employer fired her one day before the problem that the employer says caused her to be fired was certain to end. If the discharge of an unsatisfactory worker were a purely remedial measure rather than also, or instead, a deterrent one, the inference that Troupe wasn't really fired because of her tardiness would therefore be a powerful one. But that is a big "if." We must remember that after two warnings Troupe had been placed on probation for sixty days and that she had violated the implicit terms of probation by being as tardy during the probationary period as she had been before. If the company did not fire her, its warnings and threats would seem empty. Employees would be encouraged to flout work rules knowing that the only sanction would be a toothless warning or a meaningless period of probation.

Yet this is only an interpretation; and it might appear to be an issue for trial whether it is superior to Troupe's interpretation. But what is Troupe's interpretation? Not (as we understand it) that Lord & Taylor wanted to get back at her for becoming pregnant or having morning sickness. The only significance she asks us to attach to the timing of her discharge is as reinforcement for the inference that she asks us to draw from Rauch's statement about the reason for her termination: that she was terminated because her employer did not expect her to return to work after her maternity leave was up. We must decide whether a termination so motivated is discrimination within the meaning of the pregnancy amendment to Title VII.

Standing alone, it is not. (It could be a breach of contract, but that is not alleged.) Suppose that Lord & Taylor had an employee named Jones, a black employee scheduled to take a three-month paid sick leave for a kidney transplant; and whether thinking that he would not return to work when his leave was up or not wanting to incur the expense of paying him while he was on sick leave, the company fired him. In doing so it might be breaking its employment contract with Jones, if it had one, or violating a state statute requiring the payment of earned wages. But the company could not be found guilty of racial discrimination unless (in the absence of any of the other types of evidence of discrimination that we have discussed) there was evidence that it failed to exhibit comparable rapacity toward similarly situated employees of the white race. We must imagine a hypothetical Mr. Troupe, who is as tardy as Ms. Troupe was, also because of health problems, and who is about to take a protracted sick leave growing out of those problems at an expense to Lord & Taylor equal to that of Ms. Troupe's maternity leave. If Lord & Taylor would have fired our hypothetical Mr. Troupe, this implies that it fired Ms. Troupe not because she was pregnant but because she cost the company more than she was worth to it.

The Pregnancy Discrimination Act does not, despite the urgings of feminist scholars, e.g., Herma Hill Kay, "Equality and Difference: The Case of Pregnancy," 1 *Berkeley Women's L.J.* 1, 30–31 (1985), require employers to offer maternity leave or take other steps to make it easier for pregnant women to work—to make it as easy, say, as it is for their spouses to continue working during pregnancy. Employers can treat pregnant women as badly as they treat similarly affected but nonpregnant employees, even to the point of "conditioning the availability of an employment benefit on an employee's decision to return to work after the end of the medical disability that pregnancy causes." *Maganuco v. Leyden Community High School Dist.* 212, 939 F.2d 440, 445 (7th Cir.1991). *Maganuco* and other cases hold that disparate impact is a permissible theory of liability under the Pregnancy Discrimination Act, as it is under other provisions of Title VII. Id. at 443. But, properly understood, disparate impact as a theory of liability is a means of dealing with the residues of past discrimination, rather than a warrant for favoritism.

The plaintiff has made no effort to show that if all the pertinent facts were as they are except for the fact of her pregnancy, she would not have been fired. So in the end she has no evidence from which a rational trier of fact could infer that she was a victim of pregnancy discrimination. The Supreme Court noted recently that the age discrimination *"law requires the employer to ignore an employee's age . . . ; it does not specify further characteristics that an employer must also ignore,"* such as pension expense. *Hazen Paper Co. v. Biggins,* 507 U.S. 604, 612, 113 S.Ct. 1701, 1707, 123 L.Ed.2d 338 (1993) (emphasis in original). The Pregnancy Discrimination Act requires the employer to ignore an employee's pregnancy, but . . . not her absence from work, unless the employer overlooks the comparable absences of nonpregnant employees . . . in which event it would not be ignoring pregnancy after all. Of course there may be no comparable absences, but we do not understand Troupe to be arguing that the reason she did not present evidence that nonpregnant employees were treated more favorably than she is that . . . there is no comparison group of Lord & Taylor employees. What to do in such a case is an issue for a case in which the issue is raised. (We do not even know how long Troupe's maternity leave was supposed to be.) We doubt that finding a comparison group would be that difficult. Troupe would be halfway home if she could find one nonpregnant employee of Lord & Taylor who had not been fired when about to begin a leave similar in length to hers. She either did not look, or did not find. Given the absence of other evidence, her failure to present any comparison evidence doomed her case.

. . . .

Chapter 31

Pregnancy, Parenting,
and Capitalism

Ruth Colker

Judicial decisions in the United States have been hostile to discrimination claims by pregnant women. Rejecting the notion that pregnancy-based discrimination is sex-based, United States courts have refused to consider such discrimination as part of the law of sex discrimination. . . . Since the Pregnancy Discrimination Act ("PDA")[1] was passed to specify that pregnancy-based discrimination in employment should be considered to be sex-based discrimination, some United States courts have imposed impossible burdens of proof on female plaintiffs. Other courts have used the PDA as an opportunity to rule for male plaintiffs, overturning special treatment rules for pregnant women. . . . United States law also does little to protect fetuses from hazards at the workplace while women are pregnant. Federal antidiscrimination law requires no accommodations for pregnant women.

. . . .

Finally, the United States stands alone in the western world in its failure to require employers to provide paid leave to parents following the birth of a child. Until quite recently, women could be fired who took unpaid, medical leave following the birth of a child. After almost a decade of political struggle to pass the Family and Medical Leave Act ("FMLA"),[2] parents who work for large employers are now entitled to twelve weeks of unpaid leave following the birth or adoption of a child. This statute provides few genuine options for the overwhelming number of poor, or even middle-class women, who cannot afford to take unpaid leave and still pay the bills. Their only solace is that, if they work for a large employer, they, at least, will have a job to which they can return after taking the most minimal possible medical leave.

. . . .

I. The Economic Debate

Economic discourse has dominated the arguments both for and against paid parenting leave and health insurance coverage for pregnant women.

. . . .

Ruth Colker, "Pregnancy, Parenting, and Capitalism," 58 Ohio L.J. 61 (1997).

Judge Richard Posner . . . argues:

The requirement that the employer not differentiate among its employees on the basis
of pregnancy is analytically the same as a requirement that the employer pay the same
retirement benefits to male and female employees despite women's superior longevity,
or a requirement that the employer grant maternity leave (in other words, agree to re-
instate female employees who take time off to have or take care of their babies). In all
three cases, the law compels the employer to ignore a real difference in the average cost
of male and female employees. The result is inefficient, but a more interesting point is
that it may not benefit women as a whole.[3]

Posner acknowledges at the end of his article that the cost of laws such as the PDA
may be offset "by gains not measured in an economic analysis—gains in self-esteem."[4]
Never does he consider, however, whether the benefits of such laws might be measured
in the well-being of our next generation. And, not surprisingly, as we will soon see,
Posner's hostility to the PDA is reflected in his decisions as a jurist.

Arguments in support of increased benefits for pregnant women also often speak
in purely economic terms.

. . . .

[But] parents do not make child care (or pregnancy) decisions on a purely economic basis. If they did consider economics seriously, most adults, of course, would
forego parenting altogether. But even after having decided to partake in the psychic
and emotional rewards of parenting, they do not always even seek to minimize the
costs of parenting. They sometimes choose highly uneconomical options in the early
years of a child's life out of their concern for the child's well-being.

. . . .

Poor women's decisions can also be understood as reflecting decisions about child
care rather than economics. Some working class women, who earn minimum wage
salaries, find that it makes more sense to quit their jobs and go on welfare after the
birth of a child than to stay at paid employment. With the inadequate system of child
care and health insurance that is available to poor women, staying at home to raise
their child is the only way to safeguard their child's well-being. . . . The language of the
welfare debate, however, condemns them as bad mothers without understanding the
rationality of their decisions from the perspective of the child's well-being.

. . . .

In Canada, the federal Unemployment Insurance Act provides fifteen weeks of maternity benefits for the biological mother and a ten-week parenting benefit which can
be taken by either parent. Canadian parents thus receive compensation for nearly six
months of leave following the birth of a child. . . . [A] portion of this leave is available
to either parent; the justification is not simply the biological needs of the pregnant
woman. The effect of the Canadian legislation is to help make it possible for parents to
care for their children themselves for the first six months, and possibly first year, of
their child's life. It is the interests of the young child, not the pregnant woman, that
justifies such a lengthy leave period for either parent.

. . . .

Nearly every European country provides women with at least eight weeks of paid leave following the birth of a child which is then followed by a period of paid parental leave. It is clear from the language of these statutes that even the maternity leave is justified, in part, by the needs of the child. . . . And, unlike the United States, none of the European countries exempt small businesses from statutory coverage.

. . . .

II. Special Treatment/Equal Treatment Discourse

. . . .

A. Pregnancy Leave

The PDA has generally been interpreted to incorporate an equal treatment rather than a special treatment model. In doing so, the PDA sometimes helps prevent overt discrimination against pregnant women, but never helps accommodate the needs of the child following birth. A case that reflects this pattern is *Maganuco v. Leyden Community High School District 212.*[5] Plaintiff Maganuco was a pregnant school teacher who wanted to use her accumulated paid sick leave before taking an unpaid maternity leave. School policy forbade an individual who took maternity leave from combining it with paid sick leave. She argued that this rule violated the PDA by creating a disparate impact against women in the workplace. Drawing a distinction between plaintiff's medical needs and her child care needs, the court ruled against the plaintiff:

> Teachers who choose not to take maternity leave, and decide instead to return to teaching as soon as their period of pregnancy-related disability ends, are unaffected by the policy that Maganuco challenges. The impact of the leave policy that Maganuco contests, then, is dependent not on the biological fact that pregnancy and childbirth cause some period of disability, but on a Leyden schoolteacher's choice to forego returning to work in favor of spending time at home with her newborn child. However, this choice is not the inevitable consequence of a medical condition related to pregnancy, and leave policies that may influence the decision to remain at home after the period of pregnancy-related disability has ended fall outside the scope of the PDA.[6]

The Seventh Circuit's description of Maganuco's choice to stay home with the newborn makes it sound like she is staying home to engage in optional play activity. (Maybe the court should also have mentioned her choice not to relinquish the child for adoption so that she would not incur child care needs at all.) Earlier in the opinion, the court described her as needing only ten days of post-delivery recuperation to recover from her pregnancy. Purportedly, she should then have returned to work full-time, although no daycare center will even consider taking a child until he or she is at least six weeks old. Once ten days have passed, and her medical needs have purportedly ended, the PDA's concern for her treatment at the workplace expires. This uncaring and callous consideration of the needs of the newborn is entirely possible in the equal treatment regime of the United States, in which we can disregard that most pregnant women give birth to a child who will have significant parental child care needs.

Even when the PDA was flexibly interpreted to arguably accommodate special treatment, it did so under the guise of considering only the needs of the pregnant woman. The facts were distorted to hide the actual benefits to the child. In *California Federal Savings & Loan Ass'n v. Guerra*,[7] the United States Supreme Court was faced with the question of whether California's Fair Employment and Housing Act was inconsistent with the PDA by requiring that California employers provide women with four months of unpaid disability leave following the birth of a child even if they did not offer disability leave for any other condition. The case was dubbed a special treatment case because California was requiring that a benefit be provided to (formerly) pregnant women that was not provided to other employees.

The United States Supreme Court interpreted the PDA to permit such special treatment while also defining the special treatment narrowly to include only the interests of the pregnant woman. "We emphasize the limited nature of the benefits § 12945(b)(2) provides. The statute is narrowly drawn to cover only the period of actual physical disability on account of pregnancy, childbirth, or related medical conditions."[8] The language of the statute and facts of the case, however, are inconsistent with this interpretation of the statute. The statute required up to four months of leave following the birth of a child, which it termed disability leave. Yet, there was no requirement that the woman provide medical certification for this leave. The Ninth Circuit's opinion reflects that Lillian Garland took a four-month pregnancy disability leave, but contains no evidence that she had a medical reason for four months of leave. Of course, it is possible that she had substantial medical complications following the birth of her child; however, it is far more likely that she could not find any suitable alternative child care arrangement for that time period and decided that it was in the best interest of the child for her to stay home and engage in that care herself. Interestingly, the Seventh Circuit presumed that women need only ten days to recover from childbirth while the Supreme Court engaged in the fantasy that it takes women's bodies four months to recover from childbirth. By indulging in that fantasy, the Supreme Court ignored a likely rationale of the California statute—to facilitate child care in the first four months of a child's life. Thus, the Supreme Court's special treatment holding ignored those who are the real beneficiaries of special treatment—children.

Canadian courts have not been mired down in the special treatment/equal treatment debate when confronted with fact patterns analogous to *Maganuco*. For example, in *Alberta Hospital Ass'n v. Parcels*, the Alberta Court of Queen's Bench . . . [stated,] "Those who bear children and benefit society as a whole should not be economically or socially disadvantaged by this activity. . . . It is unfair to impose all of the costs of procreation on one-half of the population. The function of anti-discrimination legislation is to remove this unfair burden from women."[9] Rather than view the case as one of special treatment for women, the Alberta court viewed the case as achieving the appropriate apportionment of the burdens of bearing children. Women will still be the ones who undergo the physical and emotional burdens of pregnancy, but the *Parcels* decision helps spread those burdens throughout society.

. . . .

C. Pregnancy Accommodations

The only federal statute that applies a special accommodation principle—the Americans with Disabilities Act ("ADA")[10]—does not cover . . . requests by pregnant women because pregnancy is a normal, rather than disabling, condition. Federal law thereby imposes no standards on the workplace to facilitate women giving birth to healthy newborns who will then, in turn, have an opportunity to obtain good care in the first year of life. Because there are no nonpregnant employees with comparable responsibilities for another's life, employers are permitted to ignore entirely the needs and interests of fetuses and newborns when setting workplace policies.

One fundamental problem with the equal treatment approach, which dominates United States caselaw on the rights of pregnant workers, is that it forces plaintiffs to engage in an impossible comparison with nonpregnant persons who face similar problems. A case that illustrates this problem is *Troupe v. May Department Stores*,[11] authored by Judge Richard Posner. The plaintiff, Kimberly Hern Troupe, was employed as a saleswoman in the women's accessories department at Lord & Taylor. Her employment record was "entirely satisfactory" until she became pregnant and began to experience what the court calls "morning sickness of unusual severity."[12] Her nausea, however, does not appear to have been limited to the morning. Even when she received an adjustment in her schedule so that she did not need to report to work until noon, she frequently reported late to work or had to leave early. She was fired the day before she was to begin her maternity leave. Citing a statement by her supervisor, Troupe argued that she was fired because her employer did not want to leave her position open during her maternity leave. The lower court granted the defendant's motion for summary judgment and Troupe appealed. The court of appeals affirmed, concluding that she had failed to sustain a prima facie case of discrimination because she could not "find one nonpregnant employee of Lord & Taylor who had not been fired when about to begin a leave similar in length to hers."[13]

The tone of the *Troupe* opinion is to place all the blame on the plaintiff for her problems at work and in litigation. For example, the court explains her morning sickness by suggesting that she caused it to last until noon because "she slept later under the new schedule, so that noon was 'morning' for her."[14] Of course, the court does not explain why she also had to frequently leave work early due to her nausea. Was she napping at the cosmetic counter? As for her inability to provide comparative evidence of discrimination, the court "doubts that finding a comparison group would be that difficult. . . . She either did not look, or did not find."[15] But what was she supposed to find—a nonpregnant employee with a sudden record of tardiness after a nearly spotless work record who also had scheduled a lengthy leave? Other than a pregnant woman, it is hard to imagine a proper comparison. Yet, she is blamed for not looking, just as she was blamed for having nausea beyond the morning hours.

. . . .

In fact, comparative evidence is not required in all PDA cases; direct evidence of pregnancy-related animus can also prove unlawful discrimination. Had Posner not insisted on an unreasonably narrow interpretation of the PDA, direct evidence of pregnancy animus should have gotten the case to the jury (or judge) for ultimate decision under what is termed a "mixed motives theory"—that an impermissible factor, along with an arguably permissible factor, motivated her discharge. Instead, the Seventh Circuit never even considered the possibility of a mixed motives theory, pretending that the PDA only permits a finding of liability through the introduction of comparative evidence.

Although the *Troupe* case is technically a termination case, it can also be seen as a pregnancy leave case. Troupe was doing her utmost to maintain paid employment until the date of her pregnancy leave (when she would most likely not be earning compensation). Her tardiness and early departures from work suggest that paid employment had become extremely difficult for her. Yet, she continued to try to work. Why? She probably needed the money, especially anticipating her increased costs and forthcoming leave of absence due to childbirth. The consequence of the discharge was to leave her without a job upon the completion of her pregnancy leave. In other words, her employer made it impossible for her to combine job security and child care. The price of her decision to take maternity leave after the birth of her child was her employment. If her termination was lawful, even the FMLA would not protect her right to return to work after an unpaid pregnancy leave.
. . . .

III. Conclusion

In the United States, it is virtually unthinkable that we would mandate paid leave for pregnant women and their partners, require accommodations during pregnancy, and insist on the availability of pregnancy-related insurance benefits for all women. Yet, these kinds of benefits (plus more) are routine in Canada and Western Europe. The basic style of discourse in discussing these pregnancy-related issues in the United States is unique. United States law on pregnancy and childbirth is imbued in the tenets of laissez-faire economics—that we should solely consider the autonomy rights of corporations or adults in our society in deciding whether to mandate benefits.

In Canada and Western Europe, by contrast, the starting premise to this discussion is quite different. The needs of children both before and after birth are at the center of the discussion, although the equality rights of women and men in society are also emphasized. This focus on children, without the expectation that we will pass on all the costs of childbearing and childrearing to women and their partners, results in an entirely different set of social policies than we see in the United States. Workplace accommodations during and after pregnancy become possible not as special treatment for women but as special treatment for fetuses and newborns. Adhering to a strict laissez-faire philosophy, the United States is not simply passing on the costs of pregnancy and childbirth to parents, especially female parents, but is endangering the welfare of our children.

My point is not that we should ignore the equality interests of adult women and men, but that we should also work harder to incorporate the needs of children into those equality rights. Parenting leave is not simply about giving women a chance to recover from the physical demands of pregnancy and childbirth, but is also about facilitating the care of children following birth. Accommodating pregnant women at the workplace is not simply about protecting their right to work while pregnant, but is also about creating a workplace that is safe for fetuses. Canada and Western Europe have managed to find solutions which protect the interests of children as well as female employees. That conversation has not even begun in the United States.

NOTES

1. Pregnancy Discrimination Act, Pub. L. No. 95–555, 95 Stat. 2076 (1978) (codified as amended at 42 U.S.C. § 2000e(k) (1994)).

2. Family and Medical Leave Act of 1993, Pub. L. No. 103–3, 107 Stat. 6 (1993) (codified as amended at 29 U.S.C. §§ 2601–2654 (1994)).

3. Richard A. Posner, "An Economic Analysis of Sex Discrimination Laws," 56 U. Chi. L. Rev. 1311, 1332 (1989).

4. Id. at 1335.

5. 939 F.2d 440 (7th Cir. 1991).

6. Id. at 444–45.

7. 479 U.S. 272 (1987).

8. Id. at 290 (emphasis in original).

9. [1992] 90 D.L.R. 4th 703, 709 (Alta. Ct. of Queen's Bench).

10. 42 U.S.C. §§ 12101–12213 (1994).

11. 20 F.3d 734 (7th Cir. 1994).

12. Id. at 735.

13. Id. at 739.

14. Id. at 735.

15. Id. at 739.

Chapter 32

Sapphire Bound!

Regina Austin

. . . .

II. A Sapphire Named Crystal

. . . .

[In] *Chambers v. Omaha Girls Club*[1] . . . [t]he plaintiff, Crystal Chambers, was employed by the defendant Girls Club of Omaha (the Club) as an arts and crafts instructor at a facility where approximately ninety percent of the program participants were black. Two years later, Chambers, an unmarried black woman in her early twenties, was discharged from her job when she became pregnant. Her dismissal was justified by the Club's so-called "negative role model rule" which provided for the immediate discharge of staff guilty of "negative role modeling for Girls Club Members," including "such things as single parent pregnancies."[2]

. . . .

The district court ruled against Crystal Chambers because it concluded that the Club's role model rule was the product of its dedication to the goal of "helping young girls reach their fullest potential."[3] Programmatic concerns provided adequate support for the rule.

. . . .

The Club's goal was to expose its members "to the greatest number of available positive options in life."[4] "Teenage pregnancy was contrary to this purpose and philosophy"[5] because it "severely limits the available opportunities for teenage girls."[6]

. . . .

The Club pointed to the reaction of two members to the earlier pregnancies of other single staffers in accounting for the genesis of the rule. In one case, a member who stated "that she wanted to have a baby as cute" as that of a staff member became pregnant shortly thereafter. In the second, a member became upset upon hearing of the pregnancy of an unmarried staff member.

As painted by the court, there were numerous indications that the operative animus behind the role model rule was paternalistic, not racist or sexist. The North Omaha facility was "purposefully located to better serve a primarily black population."[7] Although the Club's principal administrators were white, the girls served were black, the staff was black, and Crystal Chambers' replacement were [sic] black. "Great sensitivity" was shown to the problems of the staff members, including those who were

Regina Austin, "Sapphire Bound!" 1989 WIS. L. REV. 539 (1989)

black, pregnant, and unmarried. Plaintiff was even offered help in finding other employment after she was fired.

. . . .

A.

For those who have no understanding of the historical oppression of black women and no appreciation of the diversity of their contemporary cultural practices, the outcome of the *Chambers* case might have a certain policy appeal, one born of sympathy for poor black youngsters and desperation about stemming "the epidemic" of teenage pregnancy that plagues them. According to such an assessment, the Club's hope that its members could be influenced by committed counselors who, by example, would prove that life offers more attractive alternatives than early pregnancy and single parenthood was at worst benign, if it was not benevolent.

But for better informed, more critical evaluators, the opinions are profoundly disturbing. Firing a young unmarried, pregnant black worker in the name of protecting other young black females from the limited options associated with early and unwed motherhood is ironic, to say the least. The Club managed to replicate the very economic hardships and social biases that, according to the district court, made the role model rule necessary in the first place. Crystal Chambers was not much older than some of the Club members and her financial and social status after being fired was probably not that much different from what the members would face if they became pregnant at an early age, without the benefit of a job or the assistance of a fully employed helpmate. On the other hand, she was in many respects better off than many teen mothers. She was in her early twenties and had a decent job. Chambers' condition became problematic because of the enforcement of the role model rule.

The material consequences that befell Crystal Chambers, and that plague other black women who have children despite their supposed role modeling responsibilities, are not inherent by-products of single pregnancy and motherhood. The condemnation and the economic hardships that follow in its wake are politically and socially contingent. Furthermore, they are not the product of a consensus that holds across race, sex, and class boundaries.

Judged by the values and behavior that are said to be indigenous to low-income, black communities of the sort from which the Club members came, sacking pregnant unmarried Crystal Chambers was not a "womanly" move. It was cold. The Club's actions stand in stark contrast to the tolerance pregnant teens and young single mothers report receiving from their female relatives and peers. Although disapproving of teenage pregnancy, black culture in general does not support abandoning the mothers or stigmatizing their offspring. Allowing for cultural heterogeneity, it is entirely possible that the black people of Omaha approved of the Club's actions. By and large, however, excluding young mothers and their children from good standing in the community would not strike most black women as being fair, feasible, or feminine.

This perspective is informed by a broader understanding of the exaggerated hostility that is generated by the pregnancies of poor, young, unmarried black females whose customs and conventions concerning childbearing and motherhood diverge from those of the mainstream. . . . If young unmarried black pregnant workers are to be adequately protected, the pregnancy discrimination law, in conjunction with provisions directed at racial and sexual oppression, must assure them working conditions that acknowledge the reproductive norms not only of females as opposed to males, but also of blacks as opposed to whites, of the young as opposed to the old, and of poor and working folks as opposed to the middle class.

Implicit in the *Chambers* decision, however, is an assumption that the actual cultural practices and articulated moral positions of the black females who know the struggles of early and single motherhood firsthand are both misguided and destructive. The older women are apparently so outrageous that they represent a grave threat to their own daughters. Yet, for some of us, their portrayal in the *Chambers* opinions is more flattering than the authors intended. . . . A black feminist jurisprudential analysis of *Chambers* must seriously consider the possibility that young, single, sexually active, fertile, and nurturing black women are being viewed ominously because they have the temerity to attempt to break out of the rigid economic, social, and political categories that a racist, sexist, and the class-stratified society would impose upon them.

Although the outcome hinged upon it, the opinions are awfully vague about the adverse effect continued employment of an unmarried pregnant arts and crafts instructor would have had in promoting teenage pregnancy among the young black Club members. I want to suggest a few possible relationships whose plausibility is attributable to a deep suspicion of black women's sexuality and an intense desire to control their "excessive" promiscuity and fecundity.

. . . .

There is a widespread belief that poor black women who raise children alone in socially and economically isolated enclaves encourage teenage pregnancy by example, subsidize it through informal friendship and extended family networks, and justify it by prizing motherhood, devaluing marriage, and condoning welfare dependency.

. . . .

Furthermore, the Club's conduct is indicative of the way in which the battle to curb black teenage pregnancy via the use of role models has become a pretext for continuing and expanding the economic and ideological war on unwed black mothers. The stress on the impact on teenage pregnancy of single middle-class role models who opt to have children is furnishing the opportunity to add a new twist to the historical efforts to ridicule and control black women's sexuality and reproduction.

. . . .

In sum, then, faulty conceptions of "role modeling" lie at the heart of the policy basis of the *Chambers* decision. In the sections that follow, I elaborate on the themes outlined above. Poor black teenagers who become pregnant are doing more than merely mimicking their mothers. In Part B, I illustrate this by considering the sociological data that identifies the material conditions and cultural practices which are correlated with black adolescent pregnancy. In Part C, I explore the contemporary effort to control the sexual and reproductive freedom of single black mothers who are said to be role models by blaming them for increased black teenage pregnancy. I explore parallels between the parts that model black women are supposed to play and historical stereotypes of black females as workers and sexual beings. In Part D, I question the propriety of blacks' accepting the guise of model assimilationists.

B.

. . . .

Blame for black teenage pregnancy must be shared by an educational system that fails to provide black youngsters with either the desire or the chance to attend college, a labor market that denies them employment which will supply the economic indicia of adulthood, and a health care system that does not deliver adequate birth control, abortion, or family planning services.

The impact of these structural factors does not make the problems constricting the lives of black adolescents entirely beyond their locus of control, however. The cultures of poor young blacks play a role in the reproduction of their material hardship. Their cultures also have strengths and virtues.

. . . .

By and large, investigators who have considered teens in various urban communities across the country suggest that they are responding to their unique material and social circumstances with conventions that seem to be of their own devising. The object is to make their lives better through means within their power. This passage from Daniel Frank's *Deep Blue Funk & Other Stories* (which is based on Frank's work in Evanston, Illinois) summarizes the typical explanations:

Being pregnant means being the center of attention, wanting to keep a boyfriend, or wanting to create something special. Getting a girl pregnant is often an attempt to prove to peers and parents that one is a man. . . . A teenager wants to have a baby in order to feel important and dignified, to feel good about herself because she has not felt good enough before. Becoming a parent is an attempt to secure intimacy, love, and safety, to claim identity and a new status. Or, it may be an attempt to save one's family from violence, separation, or divorce by creating a crisis around which the whole family must unite.[8]

Teenage pregnancy is a product of the teens' contradictory pursuit of romance, security, status, freedom, and responsibility within the confines of their immediate surroundings. The black urban adolescent culture described by sociologist Elijah Anderson, whose research was conducted in Philadelphia, is one in which young men and women manipulate each other because they have little influence over external circumstances.

[G]irls and boys alike scramble to take what they can from each other trusting, not in each other but often in their own ability to trick the other into giving them something that will establish or perpetuate their version of the good life, the best life they feel they can put together for themselves in the innercity social environment.[9]

For the females, sex is a means of capturing the affection, exclusive attention, and potential lasting economic assistance of a male partner. Enmeshed in dreamy notions of settling down with a good man, raising a family, and having a fine home, the females endeavor to make a soap opera of real life. For the males, sexual conquests substitute for successful economic engagement outside of the confines of the community.

"Casual sex with as many women as possible, impregnating one or more, and getting them to 'have your baby' brings a boy the ultimate in esteem from his peers and makes him a man."[10] Status is accorded to those who make a fool out of the ladies and creatively avoid efforts to make them "play house."

Parenthood does not always produce the results the teenagers hoped for prior to the birth of the child. Writes Frank of his informants:

> Too late they learn that being a parent is different from being pregnant. Feelings change; the reality only becomes clear upon giving birth. . . . Becoming a parent . . . means sharing or even losing that centerstage spotlight to the baby; it means being a mother when one still needs to be mothered; it means discovering one's lack of the financial and emotional resources to live up to the vision of what a "real" man, a "real" father does.[11]

Statistically speaking, teenage pregnancy is associated with a litany of economic and social disadvantages and adverse physical and psychological consequences for both mothers and children. Pregnancy and motherhood are problematic for black teenagers and young adults in part because "younger mothers tend to have less education, less work experience, and thus fewer financial resources."[12] Their economic status is weakened by the difficulty they encounter in securing child care and child support. Black babies are dying at an alarming rate and those born to adolescent mothers may be slightly more vulnerable.

But then again, things could be worse. Being a mother is certainly better than committing suicide or getting hooked on drugs. The young women often rise to the demands of the role of mother. The responsibilities of motherhood, of having someone to care for and someone who cares for them, have a positive effect on them in terms of their schooling and commitment to the workforce. Young men are sometimes favorably affected as well. They provide whatever economic assistance they can. Those who are gainfully employed take on the role of father and supporter.

In too many cases, the odds are against poor black adolescents, and the outcome of their sexual behavior is not in doubt. The females will be poor and overly burdened with responsibility. The males will be poor and overly burdened with feelings of inadequacy. The hardships will be more than they can overcome. To a certain extent, the adversity that they encounter is preordained because they and their parents do not control the material, social, and political resources that make for meaningful choice. Yet, these consequences are also the product of shared understandings and practices knowingly and voluntarily engaged in. The teenagers' cultures function in a way that make their ultimate oppression and subordination seem consensual.

Nonetheless, black teenagers are not simply pawns of the system. They create a culture of their own that is weighted with contradictions and ambivalence, promise and peril. They both accept and reject aspects of the culture of the dominant society which finds their behavior highly deviant, if not tragic. Moreover, the culture of the black adult community, which may be less disapproving, but seems no more helpful in aiding the teenagers to lead full and meaningful lives, is also selectively followed.

For example, the teens' interest in romance and materialism reflects the influence of mass culture. At the same time, having a child is a "symptom of alienation," "a rejection of the larger society's value system regarding what is *rational* and *irrational* behavior."[13] The adolescents' concern with familial responsibility is the product of their ties to past and future generations of poor black people. They have also absorbed quasi-religious notions and folk wisdom that tell them that contraception poses medical risks or is unacceptable because it reflects an immoral conscious, premeditated decision to be sexually active. At the same time, the powerlessness that afflicts their parents is something they criticize and would like to avoid. What seems to be missing is a politicized assessment of the sources of that economic and social vulnerability.

While some of their goals might be resistant and potentially liberating, the practices by which poor black teenagers pursue them are limited. Restricted to exploiting the factors at hand—the welfare system, the underground economy, their parents, their children, and each other—poor black teenagers become unintentional and effective accomplices of the forces that would confine them to marginal existences.

On a personal or micro-level, poor black female adolescents need help in separating what it is that they want in the way of material and emotional security and familial and communal obligation from the means they presently employ to achieve them. They need to confront the disparity between what they hope to achieve and the consequences that their cultural practices, in conjunction with their material conditions and the dominant ideology, produce. Fine and Zane note that "when female students are encouraged to analyze the contradictions that organize their lives—the vast space between desire and reality—their voices carry important critical insights into what is, and creative thoughts about what could be."[14] Their aspirations can provide the basis for the critique not only of the larger society but of their own cultural practices as well.

On a societal or macro-level, those interested in the welfare of poor black female adolescents should develop mechanisms that expand their opportunities for achieving what they want, which will no doubt change as their material circumstances improve. Helping them to devote their energies to attacking the institutions and organizations that control the resources they need to survive and thrive should enlarge their sense of hope and power. In the *Chambers* case in particular, the courts should have been more concerned about chastising employers like the Club for restricting the employment opportunities of young unmarried black mothers than with reinforcing the Club's message that single pregnancies and parenthood are not appropriate modes of conduct for young black women. The Club's motives, and the means by which it undertook to further them, seem less lofty in light of the rationality of the choices that produce teenage pregnancy. The courts ignored the disparity between the Club's hopes for its members and the structural impediments to their achievement. Furthermore, the courts compounded the obstacles for the plaintiff and others by failing to relate the Club's position to those impediments, and by passing up an opportunity to condemn systemic racial, sexual, and economic injustice on behalf of young unmarried black mothers.

C.

The Club is not alone in leveling the charge of "negative role modeling" against unmarried black adult pregnant women and mothers who are said to be adversely affecting adolescent black females. . . . Liz Walker, an unmarried black news anchorwoman in Boston, was extensively criticized for becoming pregnant and giving news interviews announcing her pregnancy in order to preempt speculation about her changing physical appearance. The *New York Times* reported that "[m]any of the critics . . . said, that as a black woman, Ms. Walker had a special responsibility as a role model for black teen-agers, who are responsible for a disproportionately large share of out-of-wedlock births."[15] Carl Rowan, in a nationally syndicated column, mentioned the controversy, labeled teen parenthood "a national social tragedy," and concluded that he could not "see how a TV anchorwoman in Boston or anyplace else would feel comfortable adding to it."[16]

. . . .

In any event, the condemnation of black unwed motherhood is so deeply embedded in mainstream thought that its invocation in connection with teenage pregnancy may be considered uncontroversial. Single black mothers get blamed for so much that there is little reason not to blame them for teenage pregnancy as well. The accusation of negative role modeling on the part of black single mothers represents an extension of long-standing indictments that are the product of the unique variants of patriarchy that apply to black women alone. Poor and low-income black females who have children, maintain families of their own, and for whatever reason (whether because of choice or necessity) head households of their own have been labeled "matriarchs." In the mid-1960s, Daniel Patrick Moynihan argued that "the matriarchal structure" of the black family was an aspect of the "tangle of pathology" gripping the "Negro community" because it "seriously retards the progress of the group as a whole, and imposes a crushing burden on the Negro male and, in consequence, on a great many Negro women as well."[17] After "the Moynihan Report," the term "matriarch" became a slur even among blacks, an accusation that a woman was both anti-male and anti-black. Matriarchs are disloyal to the black men with whom they share the common experience of racial oppression because they deny the men the opportunity to assert a semblance of masculine supremacy in a context that white people theoretically do not control. In addition, matriarchs are traitors to the cause of black liberation, the success of which depends on black males, first before others, securing parity of status with white men.

. . . .

Other analyses of black single motherhood set up a conflict along both gender and class lines. The current hysteria over negative role modeling extends the stigma of unwed pregnancy and motherhood that has long plagued black women of the lower classes to those who are older (arbitrarily over 24), "highly educated," and middle-class.

. . . .

At bottom, unmarried black woman workers who have babies are being accused of carrying on like modern-day Jezebels when they should be acting like good revisionist

Mammies. Though not totally divorced from reality, Jezebel and Mammy were largely ideological constructs that supported slavery. Each pertained to black female slaves' intertwined roles as sexual beings and workers. Each justified the economic and sexual exploitation of black female slaves by reference to their character traits, rather than to the purposes of the masters. Jezebel was the wanton, libidinous black woman whose easy ways excused white men's abuse of their slaves as sexual "partners" and bearers of mulatto offspring. Jezebel was both "free of the social constraints that surrounded the sexuality of white women," as to whom she represented a threat, and "isolated from the men of her own community."[18]

In contrast, Mammy was "asexual," "maternal," and "deeply religious."[19] Her principal tasks were caring for the master's children and running the household. Mammy was said to be so enamored of her white charges that she placed their welfare above that of her own children. Mammy was "the perfect slave—a loyal, faithful, contented, efficient, conscientious member of the family who always knew her place; and she gave the slaves a white-approved standard of black behavior."[20] She was "the personification of the ideal slave, and the ideal woman, . . . an ideal symbol of the patriarchal tradition. She was not just a product of the 'cultural uplift' thoery [sic] [which touted slavery as a means of civilizing blacks], but she was also a product of the forces that in the South raised motherhood to sainthood."[21]

Commentators have emphasized the negative implications of the Mammy stereotype. Writes Elizabeth Fox-Genovese:

> If implicitly the idea of the Mammy referred to motherhood and reproduction, it also claimed those privileges for the masters rather than for the slaves themselves. Just as Buck signaled the threat [to] master-slave relations, Mammy signaled the wish for organic harmony and projected a woman who suckled and reared white masters. The image displaced sexuality into nurture and transformed potential hostility into sustenance and love. It claimed for the white family the ultimate devotion of black women, who reared the children of others as if they were their own. Although the image of the Mammy echoed the importance that black slaves attached to women's roles as mothers, it derived more from the concerns of the master than from those of the slave.[22]

bell hooks sounds a similar theme:

> The mammy image was portrayed with affection by whites because it epitomized the ultimate sexist-racist vision of ideal black womanhood—complete submission to the will of whites. In a sense whites created in the mammy figure a black woman who embodied solely those characteristics they as colonizers wished to exploit. They saw her as the embodiment of woman as passive nurturer, a mother figure who gave all without expectation of return, who not only acknowledged her inferiority to whites but who loved them.[23]

. . . .

As if to resemble the role model Genovese says Mammy could have been, Crystal Chambers was supposed to expose the young Club members, the beneficiaries of white benevolence, to images congruent with traditional notions of patriarchy that were not entirely consistent with the norms of the black community. She was supposed to be an accomplice in regulating the sexuality of other young black females, in much the same way that she was expected to tolerate the regulation of her own. The courts would have us believe that the Club acted for the good of the girls who would miss out on a host of opportunities if they became teen mothers. Yet the distinction between paternalism and oppression is hardly crisper now than it was during slavery. It may be that the young women of the Club set are not fully informed that there is an increasing demand for their labor and are misreading the material landscape. On the other hand, they could be well informed and reaching more negative assessments of their actual economic prospects. If their options are indeed no greater than they imagine, the effort to repress their fertility may stem from its being dysfunctional for the larger society. Declining to live out the myth of the modern Mammy, Crystal Chambers refused to accept the yoke of either paternalism or oppression for herself and thereby freed the Club girls, to a small extent, from manipulation of their productive and reproductive capacities. Crystal Chambers then became valueless to her employers and was in essence expelled from the big house and returned to the field.

. . . .

NOTES

1. 629 F. Supp. 925 (D. Neb. 1986), aff'd, 834 F.2d 697 (8th Cir. 1987), reh'g denied, 840 F.2d 583 (1988).

2. 834 F.2d at 699 n.1.

3. 629 F. Supp. at 943.

4. Id. at 950.

5. Id.

6. Id.

7. Id. at 934.

8. D. FRANK, DEEP BLUE FUNK & OTHER STORIES: PORTRAITS OF TEENAGE PARENTS 11 (1983).

9. Anderson, "Sex Codes and Family Life among Poor Inner-City Youths," ANNALS, Jan. 1989, at 59, 76.

10. Id. at 77.

11. FRANK, supra note 8, at 11–12.

12. W. WILSON, THE TRULY DISADVANTAGED: THE INNER CITY, THE UNDERCLASS, AND PUBLIC POLICY 70 (1987).

13. L. DASH, WHEN CHILDREN WANT CHILDREN: THE URBAN CRISIS OF TEENAGE CHILDBEARING 31 (1989).

14. Fine & Zane, "Bein' Wrapped Too Tight: When Low Income Women Drop Out of High School," in DROPOUTS FROM SCHOOLS: ISSUES, DILEMMAS & SOLUTIONS (L. Weis ed.) (1989).

15. "Pregnant, Unmarried and Much in the Public Eye," N.Y. Times, July 12, 1987, §§ 1, at 27, col. 4.

16. Rowan, "Bostonians Are in Swivet over Role Model Behavior," Atlanta Constitution, June 18, 1987, at 19A, col. 1.

17. Office of Planning and Policy Research, U.S. Dep't of Labor, The Negro Family: The Case for National Action 29 (1965).

18. E. FOX-GENOVESE, WITHIN THE PLANTATION HOUSEHOLD: BLACK AND WHITE WOMEN OF THE OLD SOUTH 292 (1988).

19. D. White, Ar'n't I a Woman? Female Slaves in the Plantation South, 46, 46 (1985).

20. E. Genovese, Roll, Jordan, Roll: the World the Slaves Made 356 (1972).

21. D. White, supra note 19, at 58 (alteration in original).

22. E. Fox-Genovese, Within the Plantation Household: Black and White Women of the Old South, supra note 18, at 291–92.

23. B. Hooks, Ain't I a Woman: Black Women and Feminism 84–85 (1981).

Questions and Comments

1. Why was Kimberly Hern Troupe fired by her employer? Was it for tardiness? Or was it because she was about to take maternity leave? Given that summary judgments are not supposed to be granted if there is a dispute about a material fact, should the court have granted a summary judgment in the *Troupe* case?

2. As Colker points out, although federal statutes (title VII and the Pregnancy Discrimination Act) bar workplace discrimination based on sex (including discrimination based on pregnancy), they do not create an affirmative right to the *accommodation* of pregnancy. Pregnant workers are only entitled to be treated no worse than nonpregnant employees who are similarly able or unable to work.

3. Pregnancy-based discrimination in the workplace continues to place barriers in the way of women seeking to successfully combine career and motherhood. In a recent case alleging this sort of discrimination, Laura Walker filed a complaint with the Equal Employment Opportunity Commission, claiming that her former employer, a Red Lobster restaurant in Evansville, Ind., discriminated against her by cutting her work hours and ridiculing her because she sought to pump breast milk at work. Jodi Kantor, "On the Job, Nursing Mothers Are Finding a 2-Class System," NEW YORK TIMES, Sept. 1, 2006, pp.A1, A14. Judge Posner said Troupe was fired not because she was pregnant but because she was late. If Laura Walker were fired for pumping breast milk, would that constitute sex-(and pregnancy-)based discrimination, according to Posner's logic?

4. Pregnancy is often considered to be inherently harmful for young, unmarried women. How does Austin criticize this view? What, in her opinion, is the central cause of the challenges faced by young single mothers, especially Black mothers?

B. Tort and Criminal Liability for Prenatal Behavior

Chapter 33

Stallman v. Youngquist

Justice CUNNINGHAM delivered the opinion of the court:

Plaintiff, Lindsay Stallman, brought suit by her father and next friend, Mark Stallman, against defendant Bari Stallman and codefendant Clarence Youngquist (not a party to this appeal) for prenatal injuries allegedly sustained by plaintiff during an automobile collision between Bari Stallman's automobile and the automobile driven by Clarence Youngquist. Defendant Bari Stallman is the mother of plaintiff. Defendant was approximately five months pregnant with plaintiff and was on her way to a restaurant when the collision occurred.

. . . .

For the reasons developed below, this court does not recognize a cause of action brought by or on behalf of a fetus, subsequently born alive, against its mother for the unintentional infliction of prenatal injuries. This decision requires us to hold that the circuit court was correct when it granted defendant's motion for summary judgment. . . .

Case Background

. . . .

Count II of plaintiff's . . . complaint, the subject matter of this appeal, charged defendant with negligence, the direct and proximate result of which caused the fetus (the unborn plaintiff) to be thrown about in the womb of her mother (defendant) resulting in serious and permanent injury to plaintiff.

. . . .

The [appellate court] noted that in Illinois an infant who is born alive and survives may bring a tort action to recover damages for prenatal injuries resulting from another's negligence. The court then simply stated that its holding "simply allows plaintiff to litigate count II of her complaint, naming her mother as a defendant." 152 Ill.App.3d at 694, 105 Ill.Dec. 635, 504 N.E.2d 920. The . . . court cited a Michigan court of appeals case which held, "a child's mother bears the same liability for negligent conduct, resulting in prenatal injuries, as would a third person. *Grodin v. Grodin* (1981), 102 Mich.App. 396, 301 N.W.2d 869." 152 Ill.App.3d at 694.

. . . .

Prenatal Negligence

The issue whether a cause of action exists by or on behalf of a fetus, subsequently born alive, against its mother for the unintentional infliction of prenatal injuries is an

Stallman v. Youngquist, 531N.E.2d 335 (Ill. 1988).

issue of first impression in this court. We begin with a review of the area of tort liability for prenatal negligence as it has developed in regards to third persons.

It was not until 1884, in *Dietrich v. Northampton* (1884), 138 Mass. 14, that such a case came before a court in the United States alleging a cause of action for prenatal injuries. In *Dietrich,* Judge Oliver Wendell Holmes held that the common law did not recognize a cause of action in tort for prenatal injuries to a fetus. Judge Holmes denied that such an action may lie primarily because the fetus "was a part of the mother at the time of the injury, [and] any damage to it which was not too remote to be recovered for at all was recoverable by her." 138 Mass. at 17. After *Dietrich* and until 1946, all courts in the United States which considered the question agreed: no action would lie for injuries sustained by a fetus which became apparent on its birth.

This court was one of the first to consider the question of the liability of third persons for prenatal negligence after the *Dietrich* case. In *Allaire v. St. Luke's Hospital* (1900), 184 Ill. 359, 56 N.E. 638, it was held that no action would lie for injuries to a fetus, only days away from birth, due to the negligence of the defendant hospital where the mother of the plaintiff was a patient awaiting the delivery of the plaintiff. In *Allaire,* this court affirmed the opinion of the appellate court, which had stated, " 'That a child before birth is, in fact, a part of the mother and is only severed from her at birth, cannot, we think, be successfully disputed.' " 184 Ill. at 368, 56 N.E. 638. This court adopted the reasoning of the appellate court that the plaintiff, at the time of the injury, did not have a distinct and independent existence from his mother; the injury was to the mother and not to the plaintiff.

Allaire is primarily remembered today for the dissent of Mr. Justice Boggs, who asked the question: "Should compensation for his injuries be denied on a mere theory, known to be false, that the injury was not to his [or her] person but to the person of the mother?" 184 Ill. at 374, 56 N.E. 638 (Boggs, J., dissenting).

The rule recognizing the right to bring an action for injuries inflicted on a fetus by a person not its mother is as pervasive and established now as was the contrary rule before 1946. This court overruled *Allaire* in *Amann v. Faidy* (1953), 415 Ill. 422, 114 N.E.2d 412, and recognized a cause of action under the wrongful death statute for the death of an infant who, while in a viable condition, sustained a prenatal injury due to the negligence of a third person. Later, in *Rodriguez v. Patti* (1953), 415 Ill. 496, 114 N.E.2d 721, this court recognized a common law right of action for personal injuries to an infant, a viable fetus, when wrongfully injured due to the negligence of third persons. Much later, in *Chrisafogeorgis v. Brandenberg* (1973), 55 I11.2d 368, 304 N.E.2d 88, this court held that a wrongful death action could be maintained on behalf of a stillborn child who sustained injuries due to the negligence of third persons while a viable fetus.

The early reliance by courts on viability as a point at which with certainty it could be said that the fetus and the woman who is the mother of the fetus are two separate entities proved to be troublesome. Most courts have since abandoned viability as a requirement for a child to bring an action for prenatal injuries inflicted by third persons.
. . . .

The above case law has grown out of circumstances in which the defendant was a third person and not the mother of the plaintiff. Plaintiff in the instant case asserts that she should be able to bring a cause of action for prenatal injuries against her mother just as she would be able to bring a cause of action for prenatal injuries against a third person. The [appellate] court noted that the Michigan court of appeals, in *Grodin v. Grodin,* held that a child's mother bears the same liability for negligent conduct which results in prenatal injury as would a third person. In *Grodin,* a child brought suit against his mother for prenatal negligence. The plaintiff in *Grodin* had developed brown and discolored teeth because the defendant mother had taken tetracycline during the time when she was pregnant with the plaintiff. The suit alleged failure on the part of the mother to request from a doctor a pregnancy test, failure to seek proper prenatal care, and failure to report to a doctor that the mother was taking tetracycline. . . . .

The *Grodin* court would have the law treat a pregnant woman as a stranger to her developing fetus for purposes of tort liability. The *Grodin* court failed to address any of the profound implications which would result from such a legal fiction and is, for that reason, unpersuasive. . . .

This court has never been asked to decide if, by becoming pregnant, a woman exposes herself to a future lawsuit by or on behalf of the fetus which will become her child. . . . In the path which some courts have taken on the road which has recognized recovery for a child for injuries inflicted on it as a fetus, there has been an articulation of a "legal right to begin life with a sound mind and body." The articulation of this right to recover against third-person tortfeasors has served to emphasize that it is not just the pregnant woman alone who may be harmed by the tortious act of another but also the fetus, whose injuries become apparent at its birth.

It is clear that the recognition of a legal right to begin life with a sound mind and body on the part of a fetus which is assertable after birth against its mother would have serious ramifications for all women and their families, and for the way in which society views women and women's reproductive abilities. The recognition of such a right by a fetus would necessitate the recognition of a legal duty on the part of the woman who is the mother; a legal duty, as opposed to a moral duty, to effectuate the best prenatal environment possible. The recognition of such a legal duty would create a new tort: a cause of action assertable by a fetus, subsequently born alive, against its mother for the unintentional infliction of prenatal injuries.

It is the firmly held belief of some that a woman should subordinate her right to control her life when she decides to become pregnant or does become pregnant: anything which might possibly harm the developing fetus should be prohibited and all things which might positively affect the developing fetus should be mandated under penalty of law, be it criminal or civil. Since anything which a pregnant woman does or does not do may have an impact, either positive or negative, on her developing fetus, any act or omission on her part could render her liable to her subsequently born child. While such a view is consistent with the recognition of a fetus' having rights which are superior to those of its mother, such is not and cannot be the law of this State.

A legal right of a fetus to begin life with a sound mind and body assertable against a mother would make a pregnant woman the guarantor of the mind and body of her child at birth. A legal duty to guarantee the mental and physical health of another has never before been recognized in law. Any action which negatively impacted on fetal development would be a breach of the pregnant woman's duty to her developing fetus.

Mother and child would be legal adversaries from the moment of conception until birth.

The error that a fetus cannot be harmed in a legally cognizable way when the woman who is its mother is injured has been corrected; the law will no longer treat the fetus as only a part of its mother. The law will not now make an error of a different sort, one with enormous implications for all women who have been, are, may be, or might become pregnant: the law will not treat a fetus as an entity which is entirely separate from its mother.

. . . .

If a legally cognizable duty on the part of mothers were recognized, then a judicially defined standard of conduct would have to be met. It must be asked, By what judicially defined standard would a mother have her every act or omission while pregnant subjected to State scrutiny? By what objective standard could a jury be guided in determining whether a pregnant woman did all that was necessary in order not to breach a legal duty to not interfere with her fetus' separate and independent right to be born whole? In what way would prejudicial and stereotypical beliefs about the reproductive abilities of women be kept from interfering with a jury's determination of whether a particular woman was negligent at any point during her pregnancy?

Holding a third person liable for prenatal injuries furthers the interests of both the mother and the subsequently born child and does not interfere with the defendant's right to control his or her own life. Holding a mother liable for the unintentional infliction of prenatal injuries subjects to State scrutiny all the decisions a woman must make in attempting to carry a pregnancy to term, and infringes on her right to privacy and bodily autonomy. . . . Logic does not demand that a pregnant woman be treated in a court of law as a stranger to her developing fetus.

It would be a legal fiction to treat the fetus as a separate legal person with rights hostile to and assertable against its mother. The relationship between a pregnant woman and her fetus is unlike the relationship between any other plaintiff and defendant. No other plaintiff depends exclusively on any other defendant for everything necessary for life itself. No other defendant must go through biological changes of the most profound type, possibly at the risk of her own life, in order to bring forth an adversary into the world. It is, after all, the whole life of the pregnant woman which impacts on the development of the fetus. As opposed to the third-party defendant, it is the mother's every waking and sleeping moment which, for better or worse, shapes the prenatal environment which forms the world for the developing fetus. That this is so is not a pregnant woman's fault: it is a fact of life.

In practice, the reproduction of our species is necessarily carried out by individual women who become pregnant. No one lives but that he or she was at one time a fetus in the womb of its mother. Pregnancy does not come only to those women who have within their means all that is necessary to effectuate the best possible prenatal environment: any female of child-bearing age may become pregnant. Within this pool of potential defendants are representatives of all socio-economic backgrounds: the well-educated and the ignorant; the rich and the poor; those women who have access to good health care and good prenatal care and those who, for an infinite number of reasons, have not had access to any health care services.

The circumstances in which each individual woman brings forth life are as varied as the circumstances of each woman's life. Whether a standard of care to which a woman would be held while pregnant should vary according to whether a pregnancy was planned or unplanned, to whether a woman knew she was pregnant soon after conception or only knew after several months, to whether she had the financial resources with which to access the best possible medical care available or was unable to get any prenatal care are all questions which deserve much thought and reflection.

There are far-reaching issues of public policy inherent in the question whether to recognize a cause of action in tort for maternal prenatal negligence. Judicial scrutiny into the day-to-day lives of pregnant women would involve an unprecedented intrusion into the privacy and autonomy of the citizens of this State. This court holds that if a legally cognizable duty on the part of pregnant women to their developing fetuses is to be recognized, the decision must come from the legislature only after thorough investigation, study and debate.

. . . .

In holding that no cause of action will lie for maternal prenatal negligence, this court emphasizes that we in no way minimize the public policy favoring healthy newborns. Pregnant women need access to information about the risks inherent in everyday living on a developing fetus and need access to health care for themselves and their developing fetuses. It is, after all, to a pregnant woman's advantage to do all she can within her knowledge and power to bring a healthy child into this world. The way to effectuate the birth of healthy babies is not, however, through after-the-fact civil liability in tort for individual mothers, but rather through before-the-fact education of all women and families about prenatal development.

A cause of action by a fetus against its mother for the unintentional infliction of prenatal injuries is denied. . . .

Chapter 34

Making Reproduction a Crime

Dorothy Roberts

On February 2, 1992, twenty-eight-year-old Cornelia Whitner gave birth to a healthy baby boy named Kevin at Easely Baptist Medical Center in Pickens County, South Carolina. When the hospital staff discovered traces of cocaine in the baby's urine, they notified child welfare authorities. Two months later, Whitner was arrested for "endangering the life of her unborn child" by smoking crack while pregnant.

On the day of her hearing, Whitner met briefly in the hallway with her court-appointed attorney, Cheryl Aaron, for the first time. Aaron advised Whitner to plead guilty to the child neglect charges, promising to get her into a drug treatment program so that she could be reunited with her children. Aaron, who had previously prosecuted pregnant addicts herself as a Pickens County prosecutor, did not think to challenge the application of the child neglect statute to a fetus or the constitutionality of the charges brought against her client. In fact, scores of women across the country arrested for smoking crack while pregnant had similarly pled guilty to charges of child abuse, distribution of drugs to a minor, or lesser offenses. They were typically placed on probation and required to get drug treatment.

In this case, the lawyer's advice turned out to be terribly mistaken. . . . Judge Frank Eppes . . . sentenced Whitner to a startling eight-year prison term.

On the other side of the country, Darlene Johnson, a twenty-seven-year-old mother of four, stood before California Superior Court judge Howard Broadman for sentencing. She was eight months pregnant at the time. Johnson had already pled guilty to three counts of felony child abuse for whipping her six- and four-year-old daughters with a belt for smoking cigarettes and poking a hanger in an electrical socket. A child welfare report mentioned scars and bruises on the girls' bodies. Because Johnson had a prior criminal record for petty theft and credit card forgery, she faced serving time in state prison. At first Judge Broadman indicated he would grant Johnson's request for probation, which was also the recommendation of the probation officer assigned to the case. Then, noting that Johnson might become pregnant again while receiving welfare, he made an unexpected proposition: he gave Johnson a choice between a seven-year prison sentence or only one year in prison and three years on probation, with the condition that she be implanted with Norplant.

Johnson, whose appointed attorney was not present at the time, questioned the implant's safety. Judge Broadman assured her that Norplant was not experimental. . . .

Dorothy Roberts, *Killing the Black Body: Race, Reproduction, and the Meaning of Liberty* 150–201 (1997).

Caught off guard and fearing the prospect of spending the next seven years in prison, Johnson agreed.

Johnson returned to Judge Broadman eight days later when she learned from the public defender that her diabetes, high blood pressure, and other health problems made it dangerous for her to use Norplant and that the order might violate her constitutional rights. Broadman refused to rescind the order . . . [despite] an expert's declaration that Norplant was contraindicated for someone with Johnson's health condition . . . [and] that it would be "medically irresponsible" for any doctor to insert Norplant in a woman's arm under such coercive circumstances.

The ACLU joined Johnson's appeal of Broadman's order, arguing that state-coerced birth control violated the fundamental right to procreate. . . . Ultimately, an appellate court dismissed Johnson's appeal as moot after Johnson violated the terms of her probation by testing positive for drugs and was remanded to prison. . . .

States have recently turned their attention to reproduction as a focus for criminal punishment. The cases of Cornelia Whitner and Darlene Johnson represent two controversial ways in which the criminal justice system is penalizing pregnancy—the prosecution of women for exposing their babies to drugs in the womb and the imposition of birth control as a condition of probation. These criminal cases, which have multiplied over the past decade, have two things in common: both punish women, in effect, for having babies and both unduly involve poor Black women.

In what way do the cases punish pregnancy? When a pregnant woman is arrested for harming the fetus by smoking crack, her crime hinges on her decision to have a baby. She can avoid prosecution if she has an abortion. If she chooses instead to give birth, she risks going to prison. Similarly, when a judge gives a defendant the choice between Norplant or jail, incarceration becomes the penalty for the defendant's decision to remain fertile. If she violates probation by becoming pregnant, she will be sent to prison. Prosecutors and judges see poor Black women as suitable subjects for these reproductive penalties because society does not view these women as suitable mothers in the first place.

[Historically,] birth control policy has attempted to curtail the numbers of Black children based on the premise that Black fertility is the cause of social problems. In criminal cases, the government more directly punishes Black mothers for their children's difficulties. In this chapter, I explain why this combination of crime, race, and reproduction gravely threatens Black people's welfare as well as our concept of procreative liberty.

Punishing Crack Addicts for Having Babies

A growing number of women across the country have been indicted for criminal offenses after giving birth to babies who test positive for drugs. The majority of these women, like Cornelia Whitner, are poor and Black. Most are addicted to crack cocaine. Charges of "prenatal crime" used to occur twice a decade. Then, in the mid-1980s, prosecutors decided to tackle the panic over an alleged explosion of "crack babies" by prosecuting their mothers. Between 1985 and 1995, at least two hundred

women in thirty states were charged with maternal drug use. Creative statutory interpretations that once seemed little more than the outlandish concoctions of conservative pundits were used to punish women. The charges have included distributing
drugs to a minor, child abuse and neglect, reckless endangerment, manslaughter, and
assault with a deadly weapon.

. . . .

The prosecution of drug-addicted mothers is part of an alarming trend toward
greater state intervention into the lives of pregnant women under the rationale of protecting the fetus from harm. Increasingly, the interests of the fetus are pitted against
those of the mother. Courts have allowed children to bring tort suits against their
mothers for prenatal negligence. Pregnant women have been compelled to undergo
cesarean sections, blood transfusions, and other medical interventions for the sake of
the fetus. Employers have excluded fertile women from certain jobs to prevent fetal
exposure to workplace hazards.

. . . .

Legal scholars often approach [these] issue[s] by weighing the state's interest in
protecting the fetus against the mother's interest in her own bodily autonomy. But can
we determine whether the prosecutions are fair simply by deciding upon the duties a
pregnant woman owes to her fetus and then assessing whether the defendant has met
them? Both sides of the debate have largely overlooked a critical aspect of government
prosecution of drug-addicted mothers.

Just as important to this controversy as the politics of fetal rights is the politics of
race. Race entered the debate in the form of the crack epidemic and the frightening
image of the "crack baby" that helped to define it. Race also provided the backdrop of
hostility toward Black mothers that made prosecuting pregnant women permissible.
. . . The criminal regulation of pregnancy that occurs today is in some ways unprecedented. Yet it belongs to the continuing legacy of the degradation of Black motherhood. . . . The prosecutions are better understood as a way of punishing Black women
for having babies rather than as a way of protecting Black fetuses.

Creating the Crack Epidemic

Crack cocaine exploded on the American scene in the early 1980s, and its abuse
quickly rose to epidemic proportions. . . .

Crack's apparent confinement to inner-city neighborhoods made it the perfect
target for Reagan's ferocious War on Drugs and the media's disparagement of Black
Americans. . . . While powdered cocaine was glamorized as a thrilling amusement of
the rich and famous, crack was vilified for stripping its underclass users of every shred
of human dignity. . . .

One of crack's peculiar qualities appeared to be the drug's appeal to women. . . .

News of this surge in maternal drug use broke in 1988 when the National Association for Perinatal Addiction Research and Education (NAPARE) published the results
of a study of babies in hospitals across the country. NAPARE found that 11 percent of
newborns in thirty-six hospitals surveyed were affected by their mothers' illegal drug

use during pregnancy.[1] In several hospitals, the proportion of drug-exposed infants was as high as 15 and 25 percent. Extrapolating these statistics to the population at large, it was estimated that as many as 375,000 drug-exposed infants are born every year.[2] This figure covered all drug exposure nationwide and did not break down the numbers based on the extent of drug use or its effects on the newborn.

The media parlayed the NAPARE report into a horrific tale of damage to hundreds of thousands of babies. . . . Although NAPARE's figures referred to numbers of infants *exposed* to, not *harmed* by, maternal drug use, the *Los Angeles Times* wrote about 375,000 babies "tainted by potentially fatal narcotics in the womb each year."[3] Some articles attributed all 375,000 cases to crack, although experts estimate that 50,000 to 100,000 newborns at most are exposed specifically to cocaine (both powdered and crack) each year.[4] (In one editorial the figure ballooned to 550,000 babies having "their fragile brains bombarded with the drug.")[5]

. . . .

The pregnant crack addict was portrayed as an irresponsible and selfish woman who put her love for crack above her love for her children. In news stories she was often represented by a prostitute, who sometimes traded sex for crack, in violation of every conceivable quality of a good mother. The chemical properties of crack were said to destroy the natural impulse to mother. "The most remarkable and hideous aspect of crack cocaine seems to be the undermining of the maternal instinct," a nurse was quoted as observing about her patients.[6] The pregnant crack addict, then, was the exact opposite of a mother: she was promiscuous, uncaring, and self-indulgent.

She was also Black. In the focus on maternal crack use, which is stereotypically associated with Blacks, the media left the impression that the pregnant addict is typically a Black woman. Even more than a "metaphor for women's alienation from instinctual motherhood,"[7] the pregnant crack addict was the latest embodiment of the bad *Black* mother. . . .

The crack baby was equally hopeless. Always pictured trembling and shrieking in an overcrowded hospital ward, the crack baby suffered from multiple ailments that often killed him. But these images that induced pity for the helpless victim were eclipsed by predictions of the tremendous burdens that crack babies were destined to impose on law-abiding taxpayers. Permanently damaged and abandoned by their mothers, they would require costly hospital care, inundate the foster care system, overwhelm the public schools with special needs, and ultimately prey on the rest of society as criminals and welfare dependents. . . . [J]ust as the pregnant crack addict had no maternal instinct, the crack baby lacked an innate social consciousness.

. . . .

The data on the extent and severity of crack's impact on babies are highly controversial, to say the least. At the inception of the crisis numerous medical journals reported that babies born to crack-addicted mothers suffered a variety of medical, developmental, and behavioral problems.[8] But more recent research reveals that these early studies were seriously flawed.[9] The initial results were made unreliable by the lack of controls and the selection of poor, inner-city subjects at high risk for unhealthy pregnancies. Maternal crack use often contributes to underweight and premature births. This alone is reason for concern. But many of the problems seen in crack-exposed babies are just as likely to have been caused by other risk factors associated with their mothers' crack use, rather than the crack itself.

Women who smoke crack are often poor, homeless, malnourished, sick, and physically abused. They may smoke, drink, and use other illegal drugs besides crack. They are also likely to receive little or no prenatal care. Researchers cannot tell us which of this array of hazards actually caused the terrible outcomes they originally attributed to crack. Babies born under these wretched conditions are likely to be unhealthy whether or not their mothers smoke crack. Nor can researchers authoritatively determine the percentage of infants exposed to crack in the womb who actually experience these consequences.[10] It is impossible to predict, for example, if a child whose mother smoked crack will suffer any adverse medical effects at all. Some findings of earlier studies, such as a high incidence of sudden infant death syndrome and stroke, were not replicated in subsequent, more careful research.

Moreover, some researchers have found that the harmful effects of prenatal crack exposure may be temporary and treatable.[11] . . . Crack is not good for anyone. But these studies suggest that its potentially harmful consequences for babies can be minimized, or even prevented, by ensuring proper health care and nutrition for drug-dependent mothers.

The medical community's one-sided attention to studies showing detrimental results from cocaine exposure added to the public's distorted perception of the risks of maternal crack use. For a long time, journals tended to accept for publication only studies that supported the dominant view of fetal harm. Research that reported no adverse effects was ignored, even though it was often more reliable. . . . Now experts are denouncing the earlier rush to judgment. Reviewing the literature of the past decade, two researchers conclude: "We think it is clear now, from a multitude of studies, that the effect of prenatal cocaine exposure is minimal at birth and is probably limited to minor growth deficits."

My point is not that crack use during pregnancy is safe, but that the media exaggerated the extent and nature of the harm it causes. News reports erroneously suggested, moreover, that the problem of maternal drug use was confined to the Black community. A public health crisis that cuts across racial and economic lines was transformed into an example of *Black* mothers' depravity that warranted harsh punishment.
. . . .

The State's Punitive Response

The crisis of drug-exposed babies cried out for action. State prosecutors, legislators, and judges around the nation responded, and their response was punitive. They have punished women who use drugs while pregnant by jailing them during their pregnancy, by seizing custody of their babies at birth, and by prosecuting them for crimes.

The most common penalty for a mother's prenatal drug use is the permanent or temporary removal of her baby. Thousands of low-income Black mothers have lost custody of their babies on the basis of a solitary drug test. About a dozen states have enacted statutes that require the reporting of positive newborn toxicologies to child welfare authorities, and many hospitals interpret child abuse reporting laws, passed thirty years ago in all fifty states to require them to report positive results. In some states, a positive drug screening automatically triggers neglect proceedings to obtain custody of the baby. As a result, child abuse and neglect petitions containing allegations of the mother's drug use quadrupled in New York City between 1986 and 1989, paralleling the onset of the crack epidemic.[12] Crack exposure is now the leading grounds for newborn foster placement in that city.[13]

In cities across the country, policymakers are debating whether newborns whose mothers smoke crack should be taken to foster care right away. . . . But a positive toxicology (which may be false) reveals only that the mother ingested drugs shortly before the delivery. It tells us nothing about the extent of the mother's drug use, any harm to the baby, or the mother's parenting abilities. Equating evidence of maternal drug use with child neglect circumvents the inquiry into the mother's competence to care for her child that is customarily necessary to deprive a parent of custody. This could mean separating a mother from her newborn based on occasional—or even a single instance of—drug use. Some mothers have lost custody of their older children as well.

Of course, the state should remove babies from drug-addicted mothers when they are at risk of harm. But it is also harmful to children to be wrongfully taken from their mothers on insufficient evidence of unfitness, often to be cast into a more perilous foster care system. . . . When foster homes run out, children are "warehoused" in overcrowded and dangerous shelters and newborns are "boarded" in hospital wards. . . . The shortage of drug treatment services and other support for drug-dependent mothers makes it difficult for them to regain custody of their children. . . .

Another penalty is the "protective" incarceration of pregnant drug addicts charged with unrelated crimes. In 1988, a Washington, D.C., judge sentenced a thirty-year-old Black woman named Brenda Vaughn, who pleaded guilty to forging $700 worth of checks, to jail for the duration of her pregnancy. The prosecutor had agreed to probation, the typical penalty for such a minor offense. Instead Judge Peter H. Wolf stated at sentencing that he wanted to ensure that the baby would be born in jail to protect it from its mother's drug abuse: "I'm going to keep her locked up until the baby is born because she'd tested positive for cocaine when she came before me. . . . She's apparently an addictive personality, and I'll be darned if I'm going to have a baby born that way."

Although the Vaughn case was picked up by the press, defendants' drug use during pregnancy often affects judges' sentencing decisions in unnoticed cases. It does not matter to these judges that the conditions in America's jails are hazardous to fetal health. Women in prison often live in filthy and overcrowded spaces, eat poorly, are exposed to contagious diseases and violence, get little or no prenatal care, and have easy access to drugs—hardly a protective environment for a developing fetus.
. . . .

Taking a more innovative route, some judges have taken custody of the *fetus* through the juvenile court system to protect it from the mother's drug use. . . . Finally, district attorneys across the country grabbed the opportunity to become front-line champions in the assault on drug use during pregnancy. In the late 1980s, criminal cases brought against women for prenatal drug exposure began to hit the headlines.

The First Conviction

When Judge O. H. Eaton, Jr., issued a verdict in a Florida courtroom on July 13, 1989, it may have seemed like a run-of-the-mill drug-trafficking conviction. But it was a landmark decision. It was this country's first criminal conviction of a mother for exposing her baby to drugs while she was pregnant. Jennifer Clarise Johnson, a twenty-three-year-old Black woman, gave birth to her son, Carl, in 1987, and to her daughter, Jessica, in 1989. Both babies appeared healthy and normal at birth. Because Johnson had admitted to her doctors that she smoked crack shortly before the deliveries, the babies were tested. Both tested positive for metabolites of cocaine. The Florida state attorney's office, which had recently embarked on a policy of prosecuting women for prenatal drug use, decided to press for a conviction. Next to South Carolina, Florida has initiated the most prosecutions for drug use during pregnancy in the country.

The state charged Johnson with two crimes: two counts of delivering a controlled substance to Carl and Jessica, a crime carrying a potential thirty-year sentence, and one count of felonious child abuse against Jessica. (Judge Eaton later threw out the child abuse charge because there was insufficient evidence that Jessica was actually harmed by her mother's drug use.) Because the relevant Florida drug law did not apply to fetuses, the prosecution had to prove that Johnson had delivered cocaine to her children *after* they were born. The prosecutor overcame this roadblock by inventing a novel interpretation of the statute.

Assistant state attorney Jeff Deen built his case of drug delivery through the testimony of the obstetricians who attended the births, Drs. Randy Tompkins and Mitchell Perlstein. Dr. Tompkins, who delivered Jessica, testified that even after delivery "maternally altered" blood circulates between the placenta and the baby through the still-attached umbilical cord. He estimated that from forty-five to sixty seconds elapsed from the time the baby had completely emerged to the clamping of the umbilical cord. Tompkins added that once Jessica was delivered from the birth canal she was a person and no longer a fetus, even though the umbilical cord was still attached. . . .

Deen . . . argued that Johnson had passed the cocaine metabolite to her babies *through their umbilical cords* after they were born, in the sixty seconds before the cords were cut.

Deen's case was built on shaky ground. First, his statutory argument posed serious due-process problems. True, Deen succeeded in presenting a theory that could be stretched to fit the words of the statute. But the plain reading of the drug delivery law did not give Johnson fair warning that it prohibited her conduct during pregnancy.

There was also a gaping hole in the circumstantial evidence against Johnson. . . . Dr. Stephen Kandall, a neonatologist at Beth Israel Medical Center in New York and president of the New York Pediatric Society, testified for the defense that it was impossible to tell from a newborn's urine sample precisely when drugs entered the body. Although it was theoretically possible that a tiny amount of cocaine metabolite traveled through the baby's umbilical cord after delivery, it was also possible that none was transferred during those crucial seconds.

Judge Eaton disregarded both problems with the state's case against Johnson. After a brief three-hour recess, he found Johnson guilty of delivering cocaine to her children. She was sentenced to one year of residential drug treatment and fourteen years probation. Although he spared Johnson jail time, Judge Eaton imposed a number of conditions to monitor her personal life. She had to submit to random drug testing, remain employed, and notify officials if she became pregnant. She was barred from frequenting any bar or restaurant that served alcohol. Johnson's conviction also carried the threat of incarceration should she fail to meet any of the probation conditions.

The South Carolina Experiment

The State of South Carolina bears the dubious distinction of prosecuting the largest number of women for maternal drug use. Many of these cases arose from the collaboration of Charleston law enforcement officials and the Medical University of South Carolina (MUSC), a state hospital serving an indigent minority population.
. . . .

The MUSC clinicians may have had intentions of helping their patients, but their input was soon overshadowed by law enforcement objectives. The approach turned toward pressuring pregnant patients who used drugs to get treatment by threatening them with criminal charges. . . . [Local solicitor Charles] Condon also pressed the position that neither the physician-patient privilege nor the Fourth Amendment to the U.S. Constitution, which prohibits warrantless searches and seizures, prevented hospital staff from reporting positive drug tests to the police.
. . . .

During the first several months, women who tested positive for crack at the time they gave birth were immediately arrested. Then Condon added an "amnesty" program to the Interagency Policy [on Cocaine Abuse in Pregnancy]: Patients testing positive for drugs were offered a chance to get treatment; if they refused or failed, they would be arrested. . . . The policy offered no second chances. Women who tested positive for drugs a second time or who delivered a baby who tested positive were arrested and imprisoned. . . . Uncooperative women who declined treatment were arrested based on a single positive result. Crystal Ferguson, for example, requested an outpatient referral because she had no one to care for her two sons at home; she was arrested for failing to comply with Nurse [Shirley] Brown's order to enter a two-week residential program with no child care.

The Interagency Policy resulted in the arrests of forty-two patients, all but one of whom were Black. (Nurse Brown noted on the chart of the sole white woman arrested that her boyfriend was Black.) The arrests were scenes one might imagine in some totalitarian regime, not the sanctity of a maternity ward. Police arrested some patients within days or even hours of giving birth and hauled them off to jail in handcuffs and leg shackles. . . .

The day after giving birth, Ellen Laverne Knight was handed papers to sign instead of her baby. "Nurse Brown was a bitch," Knight recalled. "She came and said I had to go into a room to talk to someone. It was the police. They said I have a right to remain silent. I found out I was going to jail. They brought me my clothes, they handcuffed me, they put a sheet over my hands, they pushed me out in a wheelchair. I spent the night in city jail without a sanitary napkin." Needless to say, these arrests meant tearing newborn infants away from their mothers at a crucial time for bonding and nurturance.

Women who were pregnant at the time of their arrest sat in jail cells waiting to give birth. When they went into labor, they were rushed by ambulance to the hospital, where the continued to be treated like prisoners. . . . Three weeks after her arrest, [Lori Griffin] went into labor and was taken, still in handcuffs and shackles, to MUSC. Once at the hospital, she was kept handcuffed to her bed *during the entire delivery.*

This ruthless desecration of maternity signifies the depths to which poor Black mothers have sunk in society's estimation. The sight of a pregnant Black woman bound in shackles is a modern-day reincarnation of the horrors of slave masters' control of slave women's wombs. Of course, the women's circumstances are different, as are the regulators' precise interests in guarding the fetus. But there is an eerie link between these degraded Black mothers of Charleston, South Carolina, and their foremothers who were forced to breed for slaveholders less than two centuries ago. Thinking about an expectant Black mother chained to a belt around her swollen belly to protect her unborn child, I cannot help but recall how whites forced their pregnant slaves to lie face down in a hole to protect the fetus while they whipped the mother's back. Once again, Black women give birth in chains!

The Counterassault

Most women charged with prenatal crimes are pressured into accepting plea bargains to avoid jail time. These cases quietly slip away without appellate scrutiny. When women have appealed, however, they have almost always been victorious. With one exception, every appellate court to consider the issue, including the highest court in several states, has invalidated criminal charges for drug use during pregnancy.

Most decisions center on the court's interpretation of the criminal statute cited in the indictment. Courts have held that the state's child abuse, homicide, or drug distribution law was not meant to cover a fetus or to punish prenatal drug exposure. The Florida Supreme Court, for example, threw out Jennifer Johnson's conviction in 1992 on the ground that the state legislature had not intended "to use the word 'delivery' in the context of criminally prosecuting mothers for delivery of a controlled substance to a minor by way of the umbilical cord." A few courts have held that prosecuting a woman for conduct during pregnancy violates her constitutional right of privacy.

State legislatures have also rejected the punitive bills that proliferated in the late 1980s. While some states have included prenatal drug exposure in their civil child neglect laws, none has explicitly made it a crime. Some states have enacted instead laws designed to increase women's access to drug treatment. For example, in 1991 Missouri adopted legislation that mandates treatment and education for pregnant addicts while expressly prohibiting the use of information about their drug use as a basis for criminal prosecution. This legislative trend, however, has not deterred prosecutors from bringing charges under statutes that are already on the books. By operating on their own, rather than by legislative mandate, renegade prosecutors can more easily avoid the scrutiny entailed in passing a law and impose their personal notions of criminal justice in a discriminatory fashion.

After winning a number of state court victories, Lynn Paltrow, director of special litigation for the Center for Reproductive Law and Policy in New York, decided to take the offensive. In October 1993, Paltrow filed in federal district court a class action lawsuit against the City of Charleston and MUSC on behalf of Crystal Ferguson and another Black woman who had been jailed under the Interagency Policy. The plaintiffs demanded $3 million for violations of a number of constitutional guarantees, including the right to privacy in medical information, the right to refuse medical treatment, the right to procreate, and the right to equal protection of the law regardless of race. ... On January 8, 1997, the federal jury in *Ferguson* rejected the plaintiffs' claims that the hospital had violated their Fourth Amendment and equal protection rights.

The federal government became involved several months after the federal lawsuit was filed. The National Institutes of Health found that the Interagency Policy constituted research on human subjects, which MUSC had been conducting without federally mandated review and approval. The hospital had embarked on an experiment designed to test the hypothesis that threats of incarceration would stop pregnant women from taking drugs and improve fetal health....

The Civil Rights Division of the Department of Health and Human Services (HHS) also began investigating whether MUSC had violated the civil rights of its Black patients by discriminating against them in referring patients to the solicitor for arrest and prosecution. In October 1994—five years after the policy's inception—MUSC dropped the program as part of a settlement agreement with HHS.

. . . .

Condon claimed that the program's success at getting "scores" of women off drugs made it a model that other states sought to emulate. But the lack of reliable documentation makes it impossible to verify his claims. It is just as likely that any decline in positive test results was caused by drug-dependent women avoiding MUSC's clinic out of fear of arrest....

In the summer of 1996 the South Carolina Supreme Court delivered to Condon the boost he needed to revive his assault on pregnant crack users.

The Whitner Setback

Cornelia Whitner, the South Carolina woman sentenced to eight years in prison for child abuse, did not initially appeal her conviction. She had been locked up for nineteen months in Leath Correctional Institution before a lawyer from the local ACLU contacted her ... about challenging her conviction. Lynn Paltrow, the lawyer who filed the federal class action lawsuit, flew to South Carolina to help represent Whitner. Whitner's lawyers filed a petition for postconviction relief claiming that the trial court lacked jurisdiction to accept a guilty plea to a nonexistent offense. The relevant criminal statute punished the unlawful neglect of a *child*, not a fetus, they argued.

The judge who heard the petition was persuaded. On November 22, 1993, Judge Larry Patterson threw out the conviction and released Whitner from prison. Attorney General Condon filed a notice of appeal that day.... On July 15, 1996, the South Carolina Supreme Court dealt a disastrous blow to the antiprosecution effort. In a 3 to 2 decision, the court reinstated Whitner's conviction, holding that a viable fetus is covered by the child abuse statute. The court based its conclusion on prior case law that recognized a viable fetus as a person. South Carolina courts, for example, allowed civil actions for the wrongful death of a fetus. The key criminal law precedent was *State v. Horne,* decided in 1984, concerning South Carolina's homicide law. The defendant Horne had repeatedly stabbed his wife, who was nine months pregnant, in the neck, arms, and abdomen. The woman survived, but the fetus had died by the time doctors performed an emergency cesarean section. The court upheld Horne's conviction for voluntary manslaughter, extending liability for killing a fetus from the civil to the criminal context.

According to the *Whitner* court, these precedents dictated its interpretation of the child abuse statute: "[I]t would be absurd to recognize the viable fetus as a person for purposes of homicide laws and wrongful death statutes but not for purposes of statutes proscribing child abuse." Moreover, punishing fetal abuse would further the statute's aim of preventing harm to children.

. . . .

The decision meant that Cornelia Whitner was returned to jail to serve out the remaining six years of her sentence. It also meant abandoning her son, now a healthy four-year-old living with her aunt.... Condon has visions of replicating his Charleston experiment in other hospitals across South Carolina.

The ruling also opens up a Pandora's box. If harm to a viable fetus constitutes child abuse, then an endless panoply of activities could make pregnant women guilty of a crime. "There are not enough jail cells in South Carolina to hold the pregnant women who have a drug problem, drink a glass of wine with dinner, smoke cigarettes . . . or decide to go to work despite their doctor's advice that they should stay in bed," Paltrow pointed out. "Thousands of women are now child neglecters."

Of course, the state of South Carolina will not go after thousands of pregnant women on child neglect charges. It will not even prosecute all the pregnant women who abuse drugs and alcohol. Instead, it will escalate its crusade against the women it has prosecuted in the past—poor Black women who smoke crack. I now turn to the reasons behind this blatant racial discrimination.

The Prosecutions' Racial Bias

Poor Black women nationwide bear the brunt of prosecutors' punitive approach. According to a 1990 memorandum prepared by the ACLU Reproductive Freedom Project, 70 percent of the fifty-two cases documented at that time involved Black defendants.[14] The disproportionate prosecution of Black women could be seen most clearly in the states that had initiated the most cases. In Florida, ten out of eleven criminal cases had been brought against Black women. Similarly, of eighteen women in South Carolina charged with either criminal neglect of a child or distribution of drugs to a minor, seventeen were Black. The racial disparity has not diminished in subsequent years.

The reason Black women are the primary targets of prosecutors is not because they are more guilty of fetal abuse. A study of twenty-four hospitals conducted by the South Carolina State Council on Maternal, Infant, and Child Health in 1991 found that high percentages of pregnant women were abusing marijuana, barbiturates, and opiates—drugs used primarily by white women. MUSC's own record showed that drug use among pregnant patients was evenly distributed among white and Black women. Yet nearly all of the women the hospital reported to the solicitor were Black. These local surveys showing little difference in rates of substance abuse among Black and white women during pregnancy parallel national statistics.

Rather, this discriminatory enforcement is a result of a combination of racism and poverty. Poor women, who are disproportionately Black, are in closer contact with government agencies, and their drug use is therefore more likely to be detected. Black women are also more likely to be reported to government authorities, in part because of the racist attitudes of health care professionals. In the end, it is these women's failure to meet society's image of the ideal mother that makes their prosecution acceptable.

Who Gets Reported

To charge drug-dependent mothers with crimes, the state must be able to identify those who use drugs during pregnancy. . . . The government's main source of information about prenatal drug use is hospitals' reporting of positive infant toxicologies to child welfare or law enforcement authorities. This testing is performed almost exclusively by public hospitals that serve poor minority communities.
. . . .

Physicians who practice in fancy offices . . . identify and empathize with their patients. They may find it hard to suspect their patients of drug use. Even if they do, they see their patients' addiction as a disease requiring treatment, not a criminal act deserving punishment.
. . . .

One factor that commonly triggers an infant toxicology screen is the mother's failure to obtain prenatal care, a factor that correlates strongly with race and income. . . .

Worse still, many hospitals have no formal screening procedures, relying solely on the suspicions of health care professionals. . . . The Florida reporting statute does not require documentation of maternal drug use but only "reasonable cause to suspect it." This discretion allows doctors and hospital staff to perform tests based on their stereotyped assumptions about the identity of drug addicts.
. . . .

Evidence of Racial Bias

In fact, health care professionals report Black women who use drugs during pregnancy more readily than they report their white patients. This racial bias was demonstrated in a study of pregnant women in Pinellas County, Florida, published in the prestigious *New England Journal of Medicine.*[15] . . . The study found that there was little difference in the prevalence of substance abuse by pregnant women along either racial or economic lines, nor was there any significant difference found between public clinics and private offices. . . . Despite similar rates of substance abuse, however, Black women were *ten times* more likely than whites to be reported to government authorities. Both public health facilities and private doctors were more inclined to turn in Black women than white women for using drugs while pregnant.

. . . .

Why Crack?

. . . .

The singling out of pregnant women's crack addiction for punishment cannot be justified by either its prevalence or the degree of harm to the fetus. Numerous maternal activities are potentially harmful to the developing fetus, including drinking alcohol and coffee, taking prescription and nonprescription drugs, smoking cigarettes, failing to eat properly and being obese, playing certain sports, and residing at high altitudes for prolonged periods. Conduct by people other than the pregnant woman can also threaten fetal health. A pregnant woman's exposure to secondary cigarette smoke, sexually transmitted and other infectious diseases, environmental hazards such as toxic chemicals, radiation, and lead, and physical abuse can harm the fetus.

The injury to a fetus from excessive alcohol far exceeds the harm from crack exposure. Heavy drinking during pregnancy can cause fetal alcohol syndrome, characterized by serious physical malformations and mental deficiencies. In fact, prenatal alcohol exposure is the most common known cause of mental retardation in this country. Crack does not cause anything near this pattern of severe defects. . . .

In fact, the state could make a far more solid case for prosecuting pregnant women who smoke cigarettes. Cigarette smoking has been more firmly linked than crack to spontaneous abortions and sudden infant death. . . .

The *New York Times* recently ran a story about the growing popularity of methamphetamines—also known as crank, speed, or meth—among rural and suburban women in the West and Midwest. "The biggest difference between crack and crank," the *Times* reporter noted, "is the constituency: crank users are mainly white."

. . . .

[T]hese statistics show that targeting crack use during pregnancy unfairly singles out Black women for punishment. . . . With 375,000 drug-exposed babies born every year, the prosecution of a few hundred women must be more symbolic than a real attempt to solve the problem. Could it be that blaming Black mothers who smoke crack serves other societal purposes?

First, choosing these particular mothers makes the prosecution of pregnant women more palatable to the public. Prosecutors have selected women whom society views as undeserving to be mothers in the first place.

. . . .

In addition to legitimizing fetal rights enforcement, prosecuting crack-addicted mothers shifts public attention from poverty, racism, and a deficient health care system, implying instead that poor infant health results from the depraved behavior of individual mothers. Poverty—not maternal drug use—is the major threat to the health of Black children in America. When *Newsweek* charged that "[d]rug addiction among pregnant women is driving up the U.S. infant mortality rate," it blamed Black mothers for a trend that predated the crack epidemic. Poor Black mothers are thus made the scapegoats for the causes of the Black community's ill health.

. . . .

Punishment for Having a Baby

Recognizing this backdrop of biased reporting and historical devaluation of Black motherhood, we can better understand prosecutors' reasons for punishing drug-dependent mothers. I view these prosecutions as punishing these women, in essence, for having babies. Judges such as the ones who convicted Cornelia Whitner and Jennifer Johnson are pronouncing not so much "I care about your baby" as "You don't deserve to be a mother."

It is important to recognize at the outset that the prosecutions are premised on a woman's pregnancy and not on her illegal drug use alone. . . . [P]regnant women receive harsher sentences than drug-addicted men or women who are not pregnant. . . . In most states, drug use is a misdemeanor, while distribution of drugs or child abuse is a felony.

. . . .

When a drug-addicted woman becomes pregnant, she has only one realistic avenue to escape criminal charges: abortion. Seeking drug treatment is usually not a viable alternative. It is unlikely that the pregnant addict will be able to find a drug treatment program that will accept her. . . . A woman who has an abortion will probably avoid criminal liability altogether. Even an illegal third-trimester abortion carries a lower penalty than crimes of prenatal misconduct. In South Carolina, for example, a drug-using woman who aborts a viable fetus faces a jail term of two years, compared to a possible ten-year penalty for child abuse if she gives birth to the baby.

Women who are punished for drug use during pregnancy, then, are penalized for choosing to have the baby rather than having an abortion. It is *the choice of carrying a pregnancy to term* that is being penalized. Looked at this way, we can see that when the state convicts pregnant Black women for smoking crack it is punishing them for having babies.

Identifying the Constitutional Issue

Seeing the prosecutions as punishment for reproduction changes the interests at stake. In the *Johnson* case, the prosecutor framed the constitutional issue as follows: "What constitutionally protected freedom did Jennifer engage in when she smoked cocaine?" That was the wrong question. Johnson was not convicted of using drugs. Her "constitutional right" to smoke cocaine was never at issue. Johnson was prosecuted because she chose to have a baby while she was smoking crack. Had she smoked crack during her pregnancy and then had an abortion, she would not have been charged with a crime.

The correct question, then, is "What constitutionally protected freedom did Jennifer engage in when she decided to have a baby, even though she was using drugs?"

Understanding the prosecution of drug-dependent mothers as punishment for having babies clarifies the constitutional right at stake. The woman's right at issue is not the right to abuse drugs or to cause the fetus to be born with defects. It is the right to choose to be a mother that is burdened by criminalizing conduct during pregnancy. This view of the constitutional issue reveals the relevance of race to the resolution of the competing interests. Race has historically determined the value society places on a woman's right to choose motherhood. The devaluation of Black motherhood gives the right to decide to bear a child unique significance.

. . . .

Protecting Black Fetuses?

Finding that the prosecutions infringe upon women's constitutionally guaranteed freedom to bear a child shifts the burden onto the government to justify its punitive actions. There is good reason to question the government's justification for the prosecutions—the concern for the welfare of unborn children. . . . When a nation has always closed its eyes to the circumstances of pregnant Black women, its current expression of interest in the health of unborn Black children must be viewed with distrust. The most telling evidence of the state's disregard of Black children is the high rate of infant death in the Black community. In 1989, the mortality rate of infants born to Black mothers was 18.6 deaths per thousand births—more than twice that for infants born to white mothers (8.1). Although the national rate has declined in the 1990s, the racial gap is widening: in 1992, the rate was 16.8 for Black infants, compared to 6.9 for whites.[16] . . .

The main reasons for these high mortality rates are poverty and inadequate health care, including health care for pregnant women.

. . . .

Most poor women depend on overextended public hospitals for prenatal care because of the scarcity of neighborhood physicians who accept Medicaid. . . . A quarter of Black Americans fall between the cracks, earning just enough to make them ineligible for Medicaid but working at low-paying jobs that do not offer health insurance.[17] . . . Black women's access to prenatal care actually *declined* during the 1980s due to funding cuts, at the very time prosecutors initiated their crackdown on pregnant addicts.

. . . .

But [i]f a policy of putting pregnant women in jail really led to healthier children, wouldn't we see at least an equal number of white mothers behind bars? Is it really credible that conservative Southern prosecutors are *more* interested in saving Black babies than white babies? Just as we should be skeptical of the spread of Norplant to Black women and teens on the pretext of enhancing their reproductive freedom, we should be skeptical of prosecutions of Black women on the pretext of protecting un-born Black children from harm.

. . . .

Finding Drug Treatment

Many Americans support the prosecution of pregnant addicts based on the mistaken belief that it is easy for these women to find treatment for their problem. These mothers deserve to be punished for hurting their children, it is thought, because they have irresponsibly kept smoking crack when help was available to them. The Charleston solicitor, for example, justified bringing criminal charges against MUSC patients on the grounds that they had refused the hospital's offer of drug treatment. Prosecution, he contended, was the last resort after a rehabilitative approach failed.

But had Charleston officials really done everything they could to treat patients' addiction? Women caught using drugs were simply handed a piece of paper announcing their drug treatment appointment. No provision was made for transportation to the treatment center or for child care. In fact, there was not a single residential treatment center for pregnant addicts in the entire state at the time the Interagency Policy was instituted. For a long time Charleston residents, including Police Chief Greenberg, fought to keep a residential treatment center supported by a federal grant from locating in the city.

. . . .

Protecting the welfare of drug addicts' children requires adequate facilities for the mothers' drug treatment. Yet . . . [m]ost treatment centers either refuse to treat pregnant women or are effectively closed to them because the centers are ill-equipped to meet the needs of pregnant addicts. Most hospitals and programs that treat addiction exclude pregnant women on the grounds that their babies are more likely to be born with health problems requiring specialized prenatal care. Program directors feel that treating pregnant addicts is worth neither the increased cost nor the risk of tort liability should a woman sue the clinic for harm to the baby. . . .

. . . .

In addition, there are formidable barriers facing pregnant women who seek to use centers that will accept them. Most drug treatment programs are based on male-oriented models, which are not geared to the needs of women. The lack of accommodations for children is perhaps the most imposing obstacle to treatment. . . . In addition to these barriers, long waiting lists often make it impossible for a pregnant woman to get treatment before her due date. Further, because Medicaid rarely covers the entire course of a typical treatment program, poor women may not be able to afford full treatment even at centers that will accept them.

. . . .

Until treatment is available, it is unfair to punish pregnant addicts who cannot kick their habits in time. . . . Providing treatment should not be seen as a way of justifying punishment. Waiting until a pregnant woman seeks prenatal care or delivers a baby is already too late to offer her help. Rather, devoting attention to ending the problem of women's substance abuse would preclude the need for drastic measures once a woman becomes pregnant.

The Real Harm to Unborn Children

Finally, and perhaps most important, overwhelming evidence shows that prosecuting addicted mothers will not achieve the government's asserted goal of healthier pregnancies. Indeed, the prosecutions will have just the opposite effect. . . . The threat of criminal sanctions . . . has already driven some pregnant drug users away from treatment and prenatal care.

Every leading medical and public health organization in the country has come out in opposition to the prosecutions because of these concerns. . . .

Despite these official pronouncements, many public hospitals routinely divulge confidential patient information to prosecutors and child welfare agencies. Jennifer Johnson's trial offers a chilling display of what happens when doctors become law enforcement agents. Patients have historically shared a confidential relationship with their doctors. One of the cardinal rules of medical ethics is that physicians must be loyal to their patients; with rare exceptions, they must not act as agents for other conflicting interests. Yet Johnson's own obstetricians provided the most damning evidence against her.

. . . .

Even worse, Johnson's trial sent the message that an addict's very efforts to seek treatment would be used against her in a criminal case. The state's entire proof of Johnson's criminal intent was based on her attempts to get help. The prosecutor argued that Johnson's concern showed that she knew that her crack use harmed the fetus. An ambulance driver testified that, a month before Jessica's birth, Johnson had summoned an ambulance after a crack binge because she was worried about its effect on her unborn child. Dr. Tompkins also testified that Johnson disclosed her crack use because she was concerned about its impact on Jessica's health. The prosecutor made a list of everyone Johnson turned to for help and subpoenaed them to trial.

One wonders whether Johnson would have spoken honestly with her doctors if she had known she would hear her words echoed from the stand. . . . Clearly, the threat of prosecution will make pregnant women who use drugs wary of giving health care professionals information critical to their and their children's health.

The threat of criminal charges also deters pregnant women from seeking any prenatal care or drug treatment at all. The South Carolina policy is predicated on the assumption that a crack addict who reads the warning handed out at the clinic will be scared into getting treatment. But how can a pregnant addict who wants a healthy baby guarantee she will be able to make all of the appointments? How can she be sure she will be able to overcome her habit before the fetus becomes viable? In the end, she may decide not to risk being turned in by the people she would otherwise turn to for help.

. . . .

[A General Accounting Office] study found that "some women are now delivering their infants at home in order to prevent the state from discovering their drug use."[18]

. . . .

Pregnancy is a time when women are most motivated to seek treatment for drug addiction and make positive lifestyle changes. Contrary to their depiction in the media, most are desperate to kick their habits and provide the best they can for their babies. What these women dread most about criminal charges is the possibility of losing their children. The government should capitalize on this opportunity by encouraging substance-abusing women to seek help and by providing them with comprehensive treatment. Most experts agree that the "carrot" works far better than the "stick."

. . . .

The tragedy of crack babies is initially a tragedy of crack-addicted mothers. Both are part of a larger tragedy of a community that is suffering a host of indignities, including the denial of equal respect for its members' reproductive decisions. A commitment to guaranteeing the reproductive freedom of Black women, rather than punishing them, is the true solution to the problem of unhealthy babies.

. . . .

NOTES

1. See Jean Davidson, "Drug Babies Push Issue of Fetal Rights," *L.A. Times,* Apr. 25, 1989, p. A3.

2. See Douglas Besharov, "Crack Babies: The Worst Threat Is Mom Herself," *Wash. Post,* Aug. 6, 1989, p. B1; Kathleen Nolan, "Protecting Fetuses from Prenatal Hazards: Whose Crimes? What Punishment?," 9 *Crim. Justice Ethics* 13, 14 (1990).

3. Jean Davidson, "Newborn Drug Exposure Conviction a 'Drastic' First," *L.A. Times,* July 31, 1989, p. A1.

4. Department of Health and Human Services, Office of Evaluation and Inspections, *Crack Babies* (Washington, D.C., 1990); Lou Carlozo, "Moms' Arrests Rekindle Issue of Drug Babies," *Chi. Trib.,* Jan. 27, 1995, Metro Lake section, p. 1.

5. "Ignoring Wails of Babies," *Rocky Mountain News,* July 1, 1995, p. A58.

6. Cathy Trost, "Born to Lose: Babies of Crack Users Crowd Hospitals, Break Everybody's Hearts," *Wall St. Journal,* July 18, 1989, p. A1.

7. Cynthia R. Daniels, *At Women's Expense: State Power and the Politics of Fetal Rights* 116 (Cambridge: Harvard Univ. Press, 1993).

8. Ira J. Chasnoff et al., "Temporal Patterns of Cocaine Use in Pregnancy: Perinatal Outcome," 261 *Journal of the American Medical Assn.* 1741 (Mar. 23/31, 1989); Mark G. Neerhof et al., "Cocaine Abuse During Pregnancy: Peripartum Prevalence and Perinatal Outcome," 161 *American Journal of Obstetrics and Gynecology* 633 (1989); Diana B. Petitti & Charlotte Coleman, "Cocaine and the Risk of Low Birth Weight," 80 *American Journal of Public Health* 25 (1990).

9. Linda C. Mayes et al., "The Problem of Prenatal Cocaine Exposure: A Rush to Judgment," 267 *Journal of American Medical Assn.* 406 (Jan. 1992); Barry Zuckerman & Deborah A. Frank, " 'Crack Kids': Not Broken," 89 *Pediatrics* 337 (Feb. 1992); Robert Mathias, " 'Crack Babies': Not a Lost Generation, Researchers Say," *NIDA Notes* , Jan.–Feb., 1992, p. 16.

10. Marvin Dicker & Eldin A. Leighton, "Trends in the U.S. Prevalence of Drug-Using Parturient Women and Drug-Affected Newborns, 1979 through 1990," 84 *American Journal of*

Public Health 1433 (Sept. 1994). An article by a team of research physicians concluded that "available evidence from the newborn period is far too slim and fragmented to allow any clear predictions about the effects of intrauterine exposure to cocaine on the course and outcome of child growth and development." Linda C. Mayes, et al., "The Problem of Prenatal Cocaine Exposure: A Rush to Judgment," *Journal of American Medical Assn.* 267 (Jan. 1992), p. 406.

11. Bonnie Baird Wilford & Jacqueline Morgan, *Families at Risk: Analysis of State Initiatives to Aid Drug-Exposed Infants and Their Families* 11 (Washington, D.C.: George Washington University, 1993); Ira J. Chasnoff et al., "Cocaine/Polydrug Use in Pregnancy: Two-Year Follow-up," 89 *Pediatrics* 337 (1992); Robert Mathias, "Developmental Effects of Prenatal Drug Exposure May Be Overcome by Postnatal Environment," *NIDA Notes,* Jan.-Feb. 1992, p. 14.

12. J. R. Fink, "Reported Effects of Crack Cocaine on Infants," 11 *Youth Law News* 37 (1990).

13. Daniel R. Neuspiel, "Custody of Cocaine-Exposed Newborns: Determinants of Discharge Decisions," 83 *American Journal of Public Health* 1726 (Dec. 1993).

14. See Lynn Paltrow & Suzane Shende, "State by State Case Summary of Criminal Prosecutions against Pregnant Women," unpublished memorandum to ACLU affiliates and interested parties, Oct. 29, 1990. . . . See also Gina Kolata, "Bias Seen against Pregnant Addicts," *N.Y. Times,* July 20, 1990, p. A13, indicating that of 60 women charged, 80% were minorities.

15. Ira J. Chasnoff, Harvey J. Landress & Mark E. Barrett, "The Prevalence of Illicit-Drug or Alcohol Use During Pregnancy and Discrepancies in Mandatory Reporting in Pinellas County, Florida," *New England Journal of Medicine* 322 (1990).

16. Myron Wegman, "Annual Summary of Vital Statistics—1991," 90 *Pediatrics* 835 (Dec. 1992); Ann Scott Tyson, "Counseling for Moms Aids Inner-City Infants," *Christian Science Monitor,* Oct. 15, 1996, p. A3.

17. Palela Short et al., "Health Insurance for Minorities in the United States," 1 *Journal of Health Care for the Poor & Underserved* 9 (1990).

18. U.S. General Accounting Office Report to the Chairman, Senate Committee on Finance, "Drug-Exposed Infants: A Generation at Risk," GAO/HRO-90–138, at 39 (June 1990).

Questions and Comments

1. At first blush, it might seem inconsistent to hold a *third party* liable for harming a fetus in utero without also holding a pregnant mother liable for behavior that injured or killed her own fetus. Yet the *Stallman* court rejects this parallel. What arguments does it proffer to justify refusing to extend the third-party liability rules to pregnant women who act negligently towards the offspring they carry?

2. Law professor John Robertson has argued that, once a pregnant woman has decided not to terminate her pregnancy, she should have a duty to use reasonable care to protect the fetus from harm. Violation of that duty could result in tort liability, or even criminal charges (such as for homicide or child abuse). John A. Robertson, "Procreative Liberty and the Control of Conception, Pregnancy, and Childbirth," 69 VA. L. REV. 405, 410–11, 438–39 (1983). Do you agree with Robertson's view? What are the likely pros and cons of such a duty?

3. The Centers for Disease Control recently released guidelines recommending that the health care system, and women themselves, treat all fertile women as "pre-pregnant," even if they have no intention of having a child in the near future. "Among other things, this means all women between first menstrual period and menopause should take folic acid supplements, refrain from smoking, maintain a healthy weight and keep chronic conditions such as asthma and diabetes under control." The CDC report notes that behaviors such as smoking and drinking alcohol can affect a fetus very early in a pregnancy, before the woman even knows she's pregnant. January W. Payne, "Forever Pregnant," WASHINGTON POST, May 16, 2006, p.HE01. Do these guidelines indicate that the U.S. federal government has embraced Robertson's way of thinking? Or are they just common sense advice aimed at helping prevent risk to fetuses of women who unexpectedly become pregnant?

4. In 2001, the U.S. Supreme Court declared unconstitutional the Charleston program under which Crystal Ferguson was arrested, as described by Roberts. The Court held that the city, through its program, had violated the Fourth Amendment rights of the petitioners to be free from unreasonable searches and seizures, unless the patients involved had freely consented to the tests. The hospital workers could not conduct unconsented drug testing of maternity patients if their purpose was to alert the authorities to criminal behavior. The Court remanded the case to the lower courts to determine whether, as the city alleged, consent had in fact been given by the women involved. *Ferguson v. City of Charleston,* 532 U.S. 67 (2001). On appeal from the federal district court's finding in favor of the city on that question, the U.S. Court of Appeals for the Fourth Circuit held that the women had neither knowingly nor voluntarily consented to the tests. *Ferguson v. City of Charleston,*

S.C. 308 F.3d 380 (4th Cir., 2002), *cert denied, City of Charleston, S.C. v. Ferguson,* 539 U.S. 928 (2003).

5. Roberts emphasizes the importance to her analysis of the historical devaluation of Black motherhood. Why does that history give "the right to decide to bear a child unique significance"? How do punitive drug policies affect that right?

6. Roberts says criminalization of prenatal substance abuse constitutes "punishment for having babies." How does she reach this conclusion?

7. Roberts believes that criminalizing the behavior of individual substance-abusing women lets society off the hook. According to her view, what societal ills are hidden and excused by a focus on individual punishment? In terms of protecting the health and well-being of children, what policies are more important than arresting pregnant women for substance abuse?

8. The criminal prosecution of women of color for prenatal substance abuse continues today. In May of 2001, a South Carolina court convicted Regina McKnight of *murder* (not the less serious homicide offense of manslaughter) for the stillbirth of her child following her ingestion of crack cocaine while pregnant. Ms. McKnight, an African American woman with an IQ of 72, had never been offered treatment for her addiction. She was given a twelve-year sentence. An *amicus curiae* brief submitted by leading medical groups, including the South Carolina Medical Association, stated that there was no evidence that the stillbirth was caused by Ms. McKnight's drug use. National Advocates for Pregnant Women, "Media Advisory: Petition Filed Today Seeking U.S. Supreme Court Review of Unprecedented South Carolina Decision Treating a Woman Who Suffered a Stillbirth as a Murderer," available at: http://www.advocatesforpregnantwomen.org/issues/prmcknight.htm.

C. Court-Ordered Cesarean Sections

Chapter 35

The Colonization of the Womb

Nancy Ehrenreich

. . . .

Introduction

When a friend of mine, whom I will call Jessica Norton, became pregnant, I was struck by . . . her explanation for why she had attended a conference in another city late in her pregnancy. "The doctor gave me permission to fly," she said, "so I went." Years later, I came across a very different account of a woman's attitude towards the physician who delivered her child. This woman was Kimberly Hardy, who was prosecuted for delivery of drugs to a minor after she freely admitted that she had smoked crack shortly before giving birth. "If I'd known things would have turned out this way," she said, "I would have taken the easier, softer way out and not told anybody. What woman wouldn't be afraid to tell her doctor if she had the threat of prosecution hanging over her?"[1]

Jessica Norton and Kimberly Hardy had little in common when they made these statements. One was a 32-year-old, upper-middle-class academic having her first child, the other, a 23-year-old, unemployed mother of three. One is European-American, the other, African-American. One hired a private physician to supervise her pregnancy and help deliver her baby, the other had limited prenatal care and went to the local county hospital for the birth. . . .

For Jessica Norton, the physician is an expert, someone who can provide information to her about how to manage her pregnancy. She did not hesitate to defer to his judgment. . . . The possibility of conflict between them, of his authority standing as a threat to her autonomy, is completely absent from her vision—as is the mechanism by which medical judgments are enforced against patients, the law.

In contrast, Kimberly Hardy's statement is explicitly about power and how to avoid its coercive exercise. Having seen her own visit to a hospital for birthing assistance result in drug testing, notification of the authorities, and the removal of her child, she no longer has any trust in medical practitioners. Given her doctors' role in triggering her criminal prosecution, it is no doubt far from clear to her that they have either her interests or those of her child at heart. To her, physicians represent the punitive power of the state, the arm of the law clearly visible behind their white coats.

Nancy Ehrenreich, "The Colonization of the Womb," 43 Duke L.J. 492 (1993).

Both of these women are oppressed, but in very different ways. Jessica Norton's implicit trust in medical professionals . . . makes her vulnerable to the biases and value preferences of modern medicine. Passively accepting her physician's conclusions about what is best for her, she might forego alternative treatments that would more closely comport with her lifestyle, family needs, health concerns, and/or level of risk averseness.

. . . .

Kimberly Hardy's oppression is, of course, easier to see. Hers is not the oppression of "false consciousness," an inability to recognize the subtle but powerful ways in which her autonomy is constrained and her alternatives limited. For she has experienced a much more direct and violent (if you will) intervention into her decision making.

. . . .

[This article explores] the effect of race and class factors on the [coercive] treatment [some] women receive [in the Cesarean context]. . . . Recognition of these attitudinal components raises the possibility that [racial bias is implicated in the cases where courts have ordered women to undergo C-sections against their will, and that], in turn, it is due to race and class privilege that high-income white women are spared such interventions.

. . . .

[For] revealed in Jessica Norton's and Kimberly Hardy's statements (as I have suggested) is not only a different view of medicine but also a different experience of it. And such differential experiences are not particular to these two individuals but endemic to modern medicine's treatment of the groups to which they belong. Women of color are often treated differently by physicians than are white women; the poor (a disproportionate number of whom are minorities) tend to receive very different medical care than the well-off. . . .

Ideology and Coercion: How Images of Outsider Women Justify Their Subordination

History

. . . .

[I]t is virtually impossible to describe a negative image of women of color without simultaneously recounting a story of coercive control over [such women's] sexual or reproductive activity [that has been justified by that sterotype]. [Examples include the use of slaves' reproductive capacities to increase owners' human "property" and the unconsented sterilization of Native American and Puerto Rican women (among others).]

. . . .

In the 1980s and 1990s, coercive control of the reproductive and sexual behavior of women of color has taken the form of forced Cesarean sections, other forced treatment during pregnancy, and prosecution for prenatal substance abuse or related offenses. . . . Nearly every one of the women prosecuted in recent years for using drugs while pregnant has been a low-income woman; 80% of them have been women of color.[2] Similar disparities exist in the forced Cesarean section cases, in which the majority of those subjected to court-ordered surgery are non-white women, many of them immigrants and refugees.

. . . .

Good Patients and Bad Patients: The Images in the Medical Context

. . . .

Several studies have found that poor women of color receive different treatment at the hands of medical professionals than do privileged European-American women, and that that treatment is associated with negative stereotypes. . . . Physicians perceive minority women not only as noncompliant patients but also as litigious ones. . . . They also are much more likely to suspect that such women are drug abusers, [even though] . . . the actual levels of drug use in the two populations [are] comparable.

As previously mentioned, in the Cesarean section context this pattern continues. The leading study in the area, a national survey covering forty-five states and the District of Columbia, found that of the women subjected to court-ordered Cesarean sections, 80% were women of color (47% African-American, 33% African or Asian) and only 20% were white Americans. Fifty percent were unmarried, and 27% did not speak English as their primary language. All of the women either were treated in a teaching-hospital clinic or were receiving public assistance.

. . . .

[T]he language used in case reports about forced Cesarean sections suggests that the doctors tend to see the women against whom they seek such orders as bad mothers. For example, in one article on the subject, four obstetricians speculated that when a woman refuses surgical intervention in her labor, "[i]t is probable that the patient hopes to be freed in this way of [a] pregnancy . . . undesired because it is an unplanned pregnancy, the woman is divorced or widowed, the pregnancy is an extramarital one, there are inheritance problems, etc."[3]

. . . .

Good and Bad Control: The Images in the Legal Context

. . . .

[L]egal assessments of [court-ordered Cesarean section] cases are affected by and reflect imagery similar to that found in medical discourse. . . .

[Law professor John] Robertson argues that once a woman decides to carry her pregnancy to term she has no constitutional right to make her own decisions about how her pregnancy and labor will be conducted.[4] Rather, she has a legal duty not to put her fetus at risk and can be subject to homicide or child abuse charges for violating that duty.[5] This obligation would not only require a pregnant woman to accede to a Cesarean section but also would preclude her refusal of "established," "safe" fetal therapy and could be grounds for prohibiting her from smoking, drinking, or otherwise failing to maintain her own health.[6]

. . . .

[I]n discussing home birth, Robertson . . . opines that "a woman's interest in an aesthetically pleasing or emotionally satisfying birth should not be satisfied at the expense of the child's safety."[7] . . . [Calling the concerns of women who resist medical interventions in their labors] . . . "aesthetic" preoccupations, he treats such women as selfish and unreasonable—concerned more with their own personal tastes than with the health and safety of their babies. . . . [I]t is clear that he believes they do not live up to the accepted moral code for pregnant women. As a result, coercive control of their reproductive activities is justified.

. . . .

The opinion of Judge Richard A. Levie in *[In re] Madyun [Fetus]*,[8] although much less judgmental in tone, nevertheless reveals a similar skepticism about the moral worth and decision making capacity of the mother involved in that case. The case of Ayesha Madyun, a 19-year-old black college student experiencing her first pregnancy, was brought before the judge when physicians concluded that her labor was progressing so slowly that there was a significant risk of infection to the fetus. Ms. Madyun and her husband[, both Muslims,] objected to the surgery. . . . [T]he judge ordered the hospital "to take such steps as are medically indicated, including but not limited to a C-section, to preserve and protect the birth and safety of the fetus."[9]

. . . .

Judge Levie . . . seemed to view [the Maduyuns'] position as selfish, contending that he could not "indulge the desires of the parents" when those desires put the fetus at risk. . . . To him, they were either well-meaning but misguided zealots or reckless risk-takers.

It is possible, of course, that Judge Levie was absolutely correct about the Madyuns. In the face of medical testimony that there was a 50% to 75% chance of fetal infection but only a 0.25% risk to the mother from a Cesarean,[10] the couple's objections to the surgery would no doubt have seemed unreasonable to many. If one accepts Judge Levie's conclusion that the situation posed "minimal" risks to the mother and "significant" risks to the fetus,[11] it is difficult indeed to understand why any parents would refuse the operation other than for selfish or irrational reasons.

The judge's reliance on the medical testimony seems less understandable, however, if one probes the assumptions that underlie it. As the next Section attempts to demonstrate, the prevailing societal image of medicine as based on neutral, scientific truth obscures the race, class, and gender biases that permeate it. . . .

Hegemony and Habit: How the Legitimacy of Modern Medicine Obscures Exercises of Power against Both Privileged and Outsider Women

. . . .

The Medical Model of Reproduction

. . . .

[M]edicine (as practiced in the United States) conceives of female reproductive processes, from menstruation to childbirth to menopause, as pathological, disease-like conditions that need to be controlled to prevent them from harming the women in whose bodies they occur (or, in the case of childbirth, the fetuses those women are carrying). . . .

Childbirth . . . is . . . seen as a dangerous, pathological, and unpredictable medical event. . . . Physicians "manage" the labor, performing various interventions to assure that it proceeds along the lines of "normal" births, lines that are derived by averaging the wide range of patterns that labor actually follows. . . . A concern with . . . elimination [of risks, especially to the fetus,] . . . is also an integral part of the medical model of reproduction.

. . . .

[But] protecting a fetus often entails imposing certain risks on the woman carrying it; a Cesarean section, for example, is at least twice as likely as a vaginal birth to result in the death of the mother.[12] Yet this risk becomes irrelevant if the cultural norm already prescribes that she be willing to sacrifice anything and everything for her children (born or unborn). . . . [T]he result is that the mother becomes a source of risks, rather than a bearer of them.

. . . .

Challenges to the Medical Model of Reproduction

. . . .

SOCIAL CONSTRUCTION OF THE MEDICAL MODEL

> Jimmy Carter was the first president of the United States to have been born in a hospital.
> —Barbara Katz Rothman, *In Labor: Women and Power in the Birthplace*

. . . .

The association of medicine with reason, facts, and objectivity has been challenged through efforts to show that medicine is in fact a product of culture . . .—that it is socially constructed. . . .

[For example,] in the areas of childbirth and infant health, the rules of thumb have changed with startling rapidity. Just a generation ago, numerous behaviors and procedures were recommended that are now considered harmful. . . . The definition of "failure to progress," one of the most common "indicators" for a Cesarean, also has changed over the years; a woman is now allowed to labor less time before she will be so labeled. Similarly, the accepted medical practice of prohibiting a woman who has undergone one C-section from delivering vaginally has now been nearly universally condemned.

These numerous and significant changes in conventional medical wisdom are not simply part of some inevitable, progressive process of improvement in medical knowledge. Many of the changes . . . came about as the result of pressure exerted by the women's health movement and proponents of alternative birthing practices. Furthermore, analysts have tied such changes in medical "truths" to changes in societal images of women.

. . . .

By identifying the cultural content of medical verities of a hundred, fifty, or even ten years ago, critics raise questions about the "truth" of those espoused today. . . . The use of Cesarean sections is particularly vulnerable to criticism, for this surgery is performed with more frequency in the United States than in almost any other industrialized nation. In less than twenty years, the rate of Cesareans performed in this country more than quadrupled, bounding from 5.5% of births in 1970 to 23.8% in 1989.[13] Other nations manage to do the surgery much less frequently while maintaining comparable (or even lower) maternal and infant mortality and morbidity rates.[14]

[Critics have] argued that the various medical interventions thought to facilitate a safe delivery often create a snowball effect: the initial intervention interferes with the progress of the labor, making additional interventions seem necessary, until eventually the labor becomes so compromised that a Cesarean section is indicated. . . .

In addition, . . . [f]ear of malpractice liability . . . accounts for the routine use of fetal monitors, which are wrong as often as they are right,[15] and is the single largest reason for physicians' performance of Cesarean sections. . . .

THE "ALTERNATIVE" MODEL OF REPRODUCTION

. . . .

[P]roponents of alternative birthing practices . . . challenge mainstream depictions of birthing by suggesting that alternative methods are in fact more effective and humane.

There is no denying that this view of . . . childbirth is as socially constructed as the view it means to supplant. But the mere presence of a coherent alternative to modern medicine casts doubt upon the convictions that drive society and the courts into accepting and enforcing one view of reproduction. . . .

The alternative model of reproduction views childbirth as a normal physiological process that cannot be completely controlled, yet only rarely is harmful. . . . Recognizing the "snowball" effect that technological interventions can have on labor, [it sees] the medical search for such control as having the potential to actually increase, rather than minimize, risk. . . . [And its proponents] believe that the best way to ensure a good result is to facilitate the control of the process by the woman herself.

. . . .

[P]roponents of the alternative model have a strong commitment to patient participation in the decisionmaking process, . . . reject[ing] the notion of a hierarchical relationship between health care provider and patient, in which the provider possesses . . . expert knowledge and therefore is usually in a better position to know what is best for the patient.

. . . .

My point, however, in describing this alternative vision of childbirth is not to argue that it represents the true, correct understanding of human reproduction. Rather, I am asserting that this vision is at least as correct, or as incorrect, as the medical model. I take this position . . . because of substantial evidence that maternal and fetal morbidity and mortality are comparable under the two approaches. . . .

BIRTHING AS AN ARENA OF SOCIAL POWER AND RESISTANCE

. . . .

[T]he alternative approach to childbirth is revolutionary. It challenges fundamental beliefs and firmly entrenched distributions of power, raising questions about what constitutes male and female, science and superstition, order and chaos. Thus, efforts to employ this alternative approach can be seen as acts of resistance to the dominant order, acts informed by an alternative set of understandings of the world that medicine purports to know.

. . . .

Once it becomes apparent that the medical model is no more "true" or "right" than the midwifery model, the choice between them is revealed as less a matter of logic than of preference. . . . In refusing a Cesarean section, a woman is resisting a patriarchal view of herself and her role in reproduction. A high-income white woman who rejects the medical model of childbirth is resisting a vision of herself as an object to be "managed," as passive, incompetent, selfless, and emotional. Moreover, she is resisting an image of the reproductive process as a pathological, flawed undertaking fraught with danger, and of her own body as incompetent, threatening, and out of control. A low-income woman of color who refuses a C-section is rejecting not only the notion that her body is dangerous but also an image of herself as stupid, irresponsible, and selfish—and as impervious to pain, discomfort, or inconvenience. Moreover, she is also engaging in an act of self-preservation, challenging the very profession that has so often hurt women like her before. In a profound way, she is claiming her humanity and fighting for her survival.

Refusal of a Cesarean not only challenges applicable gender categories but also violates the prevailing norm of obedience to medical authority. . . . [And s]ince medical authority is itself constituted as male authority, . . . [these women] are rebelling against not only medicine but patriarchy as well. [But that fact is] . . . obscured by the "neutral" image of science. Thus, judges accept unquestioningly doctors' assessments of these situations. . . .

In re Madyun Fetus as an Example

> Cesarean sections are so much a part of the standard, legitimized form of birthing that refusing to submit to one marks a woman as rejecting legitimate medical advice. . . . She will not be seen as the victim of the structural distribution of power and authority, as someone resisting the symbolic violence of the transaction.
> —Susan Irwin and Brigitte Jordan, "Knowledge, Practice, and Power:
> Court-Ordered Cesarean Sections," 1987

. . . .

[I]f one is willing to concede that there might be two different but equally valid approaches to birthing, it is possible to recognize the viability of the Madyuns' position and hence to challenge the characterization of them as bad [parents].

. . . .

It had been sixty hours since Madyun's amniotic sac had ruptured when the physicians at D.C. General Hospital asked the court to order a C-section. . . . A medical resident, Dr. John C. Cumming, testif[ying] at the hearing, . . . explicitly characterized Madyun's labor as aberrational, stating that "normal" labor lasts ten to fifteen hours and that "normal obstetrical procedures" call for a birth to be completed within 24 hours of rupture of the amniotic sac. . . . Cumming further testified that failure to adhere to the established procedures increased the risk of infection, which could ultimately be fatal to the child. . . . [Although] Ms. Madyun's "slightly elevated" temperature was the only symptom [of infection] that had been noted, . . . the doctor testified that sepsis also could set in and proceed to a dangerous level with little or no warning.

Thus, he concluded, the risk of fetal infection was between 50% and 75%, whereas "the risk to Mrs. Madyun of undergoing a Caesarean section was said to be 0.25%."[16]

In his opinion (at two pages, an unusually lengthy and thoughtful opinion for decisions in such cases), Judge Levie made it clear that he viewed the Madyuns' position that the surgery was unnecessary as unfounded.... In contrast, the judge unquestioningly accepted the doctor's conclusions....

Now, at first blush, the judge's stance is probably not surprising. After all, courts frequently rely on scientific statements about the world in reaching their decisions, and medical science is generally accepted as providing reliable information about our bodies. On second glance, however, the degree of deference given to this individual doctor is rather startling. Given the time constraints under which the hearing was conducted and the absence of opposing expert testimony—or even the opportunity to obtain that testimony—the physician's statements arguably should not have been given even the usual credence accorded to professional witnesses.

....

PATHOLOGIZING OF LABOR

The physician's medical-model assumptions are revealed most obviously in the extent to which he presented Madyun's labor pattern as abnormal and highly dangerous. For example, his statements that ... delivery more than 24 hours after the waters break is dangerous stem from the tendency of traditional medicine to systematize labor, coming up with standardized charts that represent the average traits of all women and then expecting each individual woman to conform to that norm. To the unaware, however, such statements conceal as much as they reveal. For example, ... many midwives are perfectly comfortable allowing women to labor for two or three days, or even more, and the incidence of infections in births assisted by midwives, who do not follow such standardized models, is less than that in hospital births.[17] Perhaps for this reason, some hospitals have now abandoned the "24-hour rule" altogether. In addition, ... the "failure to progress" diagnosis (which seems to be the one applied in Madyun) is widely thought to be one of the most overused and challengeable bases for performing the surgery....

Furthermore, Cumming's testimony ignores the extent to which the physicians may themselves have contributed to the problems attendant to Madyun's labor and hence makes birthing in general (and her situation in particular) seem more pathological and dangerous than it really is.... [A]lternative birth professionals ... maintain that a relaxed atmosphere is essential to the progress of a woman's labor. Thus, the atmosphere of conflict over the duration of Madyun's labor could itself have contributed to her "failure to progress."...

RISK AVERSENESS

....

From [Dr. Cumming's] testimony, it appeared clear that Madyun's situation posed an unacceptable danger to her fetus and little danger to her. Yet this conclusion is possible only if one emphasizes the risks to the fetus and deemphasizes the risks to the mother.

It is unclear from the case exactly what the doctor was referring to when he listed the risk to the mother of having a C-section as 0.25%. One study found that the risk of maternal death during birth from Cesareans was 22 per 100,000 or 0.022%.[18] In contrast, the risk of death during a vaginal delivery is one in 10,000 or 0.01%, making maternal death twice as likely in a C-section delivery.[19] The risk of serious complications due to Cesareans, however, is certainly much higher [than 0.022%], and complications are both more likely and more severe following a Cesarean than a vaginal birth. Similarly, although Dr. Cumming stated that the risk to the fetus of infection increased, in his opinion, with each passing hour, he did not specifically state (at least as far as is revealed in the court opinion) whether the risk of fetal fatality due to infection similarly increased with time. Furthermore, he apparently did not discount the risk that vaginal birth posed to the fetus by the risk that a Cesarean posed to it.

Thus, the risk data the physician presented were incomplete, if not misleading. They seem to indicate that the comparative risks of death to fetus and mother were at least 200 to 1, but the reality of the situation might have been quite different. For example, if the 50–75% risk level had to do just with the possibility of the infant contracting an infection (as opposed to dying), then it certainly does not seem "ridiculous" for someone to decide to face that risk rather than undergo a Cesarean, which itself can cause harm to the fetus in addition to the mother. In fact, the calculus of risks required in such a situation is so complicated—on the one hand, a Cesarean presents an indeterminate risk of harm (perhaps severe) to the fetus and of death (two times greater than with vaginal birth), serious complications, or severe discomfort to the mother; on the other hand, vaginal birth presents an apparently indeterminate risk (mild, serious, or deadly) of infection to the fetus and a lower risk to the mother— that what seems ridiculous is to suggest that there could be a single right answer at all. From the perspective of critics of the medical model, who emphasize that individuals must make their own risk assessments and that some degree of risk is an acceptable (indeed inevitable) part of birthing, Ms. Madyun's willingness to continue laboring is one among many acceptable ways to strike the balance of risks.

The physician's conclusory decision that the indeterminate risk of infection in the newborn outweighs the doubling in the risk of death to the mother (as well as the additional risk of complications to both) reveals an underlying assumption (perhaps unconscious) that women both are and should be self-sacrificing. . . . In short, the Madyun case confirms the possibility that when physicians order Cesarean sections, they are actually imposing a particular, contingent view of the birthing process, and of women, on their patients. Viewing the process as pathological [and controllable], . . . and assuming that mothers are, and should be, self-sacrificing, they base their "scientific" judgments on contested factual assumptions and value choices.

Yet despite the uncertain grounds for medical conclusions, judges continue to grant requests for court orders in such situations. . . . [D]efin[ing] mothers as "good" or "bad" depending on whether or not they accept "medically necessary" procedures, . . . these decisions not only stem from but also confirm pejorative stereotypes of outsider women.

. . . .

Theoretical Implications

. . . .

Power and Knowledge

. . . .

The fundamental power being exercised in these situations is the power to construct reality, to say what is happening. . . . In this sense, outsider women subjected to court-ordered Cesareans are, [like privileged women], . . . controlled by indirect rather than direct force, for it is the credibility of [medical] statements about the "reality" of their labors that both generates and legitimates the court orders through which the actual, physical violence is enacted. It is the physician's power to describe the woman physically—to say what her body is like and what is happening to it, to create a governing perception of it—that in turn produces his power to define what the woman is socially—to label her as irresponsible or irrational and to make the moral judgment that she not only requires but deserves control. It is through the medical profession's monopoly over the production of what gets recognized as knowledge about women's bodies that women, through the complicity of law, are coerced.

. . . .

NOTES

1. Isabel Wilkerson, "Woman Cleared after Drug Use in Pregnancy," N.Y. TIMES, April 3, 1991, at A15; see also "Court Dismisses Prosecution for Drug Use During Pregnancy," 3 ACLU REPROD. RTS. UPDATE, April 5, 1991, at 3.

2. Dawn Johnsen, "Shared Interests: Promoting Healthy Births without Sacrificing Women's Liberty," 43 HASTINGS L.J. 569, 613 (1992) (citing ACLU memorandum reporting that in 1990, 80% of prosecutions had been against women of color).

3. J.R. Leiberman et al., "The Fetal Right to Live," 53 OBSTETRICS & GYNECOLOGY 515, 515 (1979).

4. John A. Robertson, "Procreative Liberty and the Control of Conception, Pregnancy, and Childbirth," 69 VA. L. REV. 405, 410–11 (1983).

5. Id. at 438–39.

6. A pregnant woman could even be required to undergo prenatal diagnosis, Robertson, id. at 449–50, and could be "excluded . . . from workplaces inimical to fetal health." Id. at 443.

7. Id. at 453.

8. 114 Daily Wash. L. Rep. 2233 (D.C. Super. Ct. 1986).

9. Id. at 2240.

10. Id. at 2239.

11. Id. at 2240.

12. Compare F. GARY CUNNINGHAM ET AL., WILILIAMS OBSTETRICS 593 (19th ed. 1993) (citing a study concluding that the maternal death rate in C-sections is .022%) with NATIONAL INST. OF HEALTH, U.S. DEPT. OF HEALTH & HUMAN SERVS., PUB. NO. 82–2067, CESAREAN CHILDBIRTH 16 (1981) (concluding that maternal death rate from vaginal birth is .01%). (Other studies have concluded that the maternal death rate from C-sections is four times that of vaginal birth.)

13. Joel J. Finer, "Toward Guidelines for Compelling Cesarean Surgery: Of Rights, Responsibility, and Decisional Authenticity," 76 MINN. L. REV. 239, 275 (1991).

14. According to one study of 19 industrialized countries, "with the exception of Canada

and Australia, the U.S. rate was 50 to 200 percent higher than that of other countries." Francis C. Notzon et al., "Comparisons of National Cesarean-Section Rates," 316 New Eng. J. Med. 386, 386 (1987).

15. Nancy K. Rhoden, "The Judge in the Delivery Room: The Emergence of Court-Ordered Cesareans," 74 Cal. L. Rev. 1951, 2013–17 (1986).

16. In re Madyun Fetus, 114 Daily Wash. L. Rep. 2233, 2233, 2239 (D.C. Super. Ct. 1986).

17. A leading study found that four times as many hospital babies as home-birth babies became infected, whereas both perinatal (during birth) and neonatal (after birth) infant mortality rates for the two groups were essentially the same. Lewis E. Mehl, "Research on Alternatives in Childbirth: What Can It Tell Us about Hospital Practice?," in 1 21st Century Obstetrics now! 171, 199 (Lee Stewart & David Stewart eds., 1977).

18. Cunningham, supra note 12, at 593.

19. Warren E. Leary, "Birth Experts Caution on Repeated Caesareans," N.Y. Times, Oct. 27, 1988, at B16.

Questions and Comments

1. According to Ehrenreich, how do stereotypes of low-income women and women of color as bad mothers contribute to the phenomenon of court-ordered Cesarean sections?

2. Why might a person who embraces the "alternative" approach to birthing that Ehrenreich describes decide to ignore a physician's recommendation that she undergo a C-section? What might cause her to think that the situation is less dire than the physician might believe it to be?

3. Ehrenreich suggests that physicians and judges handling mandatory C-section cases are defining and enforcing norms of good motherhood. What is the content of those norms? That is, what traits do they associate with good mothers? According to Ehrenreich, how and why do some women resist those norms?

4. While Ehrenreich's article focuses on judicially mandated Cesareans, *voluntary* C-sections account for the majority of the surgeries. And the number of such procedures has been rising dramatically in recent years. In 2004, the Cesarean rate in the United States reached an all-time high: 29 percent. Tina Cassidy, "The Way We Live Now," NEW YORK TIMES, March 26, 2006, 620. The rate for 2005 was reportedly even higher. "Babies Born to Singles Are at Record: Nearly 4 in 10," NEW YORK TIMES, November 22, 2006, p.A22. Moreover, the use of elective C-sections—performed not for medical reasons but for the convenience of the mother or physician—is rising rapidly. Cassidy, supra. Do these surgeries raise any concerns, or does the fact that they are freely chosen by the women involved make them unproblematic?

Permissions Acknowledgments

Albiston, Catherine. "The Social Meaning of the Norplant Condition: Constitutional Considerations of Race, Class, and Gender," 9 *Berkeley Women's Law Journal* (1995). Copyright 1994 by the Regents of the University of California. Reprinted by the permission of the author and publisher.

Andrews, Lori B. "Is There a Right to Clone? Constitutional Challenges to Bans on Human Cloning," 11 *Harv. J. Law & Tech.* 643 (1998). Reprinted by permission of the author and publisher.

Austin, Regina. "Sapphire Bound!" 1989 *Wis. L. Rev.* 539 (1989). Reprinted by the permission of the author and publisher.

Chase, Cheryl. " 'Cultural Practice' or 'Reconstructive Surgery'? U.S. Genital Cutting, the Intersex Movement, and Medical Double Standards," in Stanlie M. James and Claire C. Robertson (eds.), *Genital Cutting and Transnational Sisterhood* 126 (Univ. of Ill. Press 2002). Copyright 2002 by the Board of Trustees of the University of Illinois. Reprinted by permission of the author and the University of Illinois Press.

Colker, Ruth. "Pregnancy, Parenting, and Capitalism," 58 *Ohio St. L.J.* 61 (1997). Reprinted by permission of the author and publisher.

Dailard, Cynthia. "Sex Education: Politicians, Parents, Teachers, and Teens," The Guttmacher Report on Public Policy (February 2001). Reprinted by the permission of the Alan Guttmacher Institute.

Dailard, Cynthia. "Understanding 'Abstinence': Implications for Individuals, Programs, and Policies," The Guttmacher Report on Public Policy (December 2003). Reprinted by the permission of the Alan Guttmacher Institute.

Davis, Angela. "Racism, Birth Control, and Reproductive Rights," in Marlene Gerber Fried (ed.), *From Abortion to Reproductive Freedom: Transforming a Movement* 15–26 (South End Press 1990). Copyright 1981 Angela Davis. Reprinted by permission of the author.

Ehrenreich, Barbara and Deirdre English. *For Her Own Good: 200 Years of the Experts' Advice to Women* 115–54 (Random House rev. ed. 2005). Reprinted by permission of the authors and publisher.

Ehrenreich, Nancy. "The Colonization of the Womb," 43 *Duke L. J.* 492 (1993). Copyright 1993 by Nancy Ehrenreich. Reprinted by permission of the author.

Ehrenreich, Nancy. "Surrogacy as Resistance? The Misplaced Focus on Choice in the Surrogacy and Abortion Funding Contexts," 41 *DePaul L. Rev.* 1369 (1992) (reviewing Carmel Shalev, *Birth Power: The Case for Surrogacy* (1989)). Reprinted by permission of the author and press.

Ertman, Martha M. "What's Wrong with a Parenthood Market? A New and Improved Theory of Commodification," 82 *N.C. L. Rev.* 1 (2003). Reprinted by permission of the author and press.

Gibbs, Joan, Mary M. Gundrum, Rhonda Copelon, Wendy Brown, Cathy Bell, and Barbara Wolvovitz. Brief for National Council of Negro Women, et al. as Amici Curiae Supporting Appellees, *Webster v. Reproductive Health Services*, 492 U.S. 490 (No. 88-605).

Kowitz, Julie F. "Not Your Garden Variety Tort Reform: Statutes Barring Claims for Wrongful Life and Wrongful Birth Are Unconstitutional under the Purpose Prong of *Planned Parenthood v. Casey*," 61 *Brook. L. Rev.* 235 (1995). Copyright 1995 by Brooklyn Law Review. Reprinted by permission of the author and the press.

Luker, Kristin. *Abortion and the Politics of Motherhood* 11–39 (Univ. of California Press 1984). Copyright 1984 by the University of California Press. Reprinted by permission of the author and the press.

Martin, Emily. "Body Narratives, Body Boundaries," in Lawrence Grossberg, Cary Nelson, and Paula A. Treichler (eds.), *Cultural Studies* 409–19 (Univ. of Chicago Press 1992). Copyright 1992 from Routledge/Taylor & Francis Group, LLC. Reprinted by permission of the press.

Oliveri, Rigel C. "Crossing the Line: The Political and Moral Battle over Late-Term Abortion," 10 *Yale J.L. & Feminism* 397–448 (1998). Reprinted by permission of the Yale Journal of Law and Feminism.

Petchesky, Rosalind. "Introduction," in *Abortion and Women's Choice: The State, Sexuality, and Reproductive Freedom* 2–18 (Northeastern Univ. Press rev. ed. 1990). Copyright 1990 by Rosalind P. Petchesky. Reprinted by permission of the author and the University Press of New England, Hanover, N.H.

Reagan, Leslie J. *When Abortion Was a Crime: Women, Medicine, and Law in the United States, 1867–1973* 1–18 (Univ. of California Press 1997). Copyright 1997 by the University of California Press. Reprinted by permission of the author and the press.

Rhode, Deborah. "Politics and Pregnancy: Adolescent Mothers and Public Policy," 1 *S. Cal Rev. L. & Women's Stud.* 99 (1991). Reprinted by the permission of the author and the press.

Roberts, Dorothy. *Killing the Black Body: Race, Reproduction, and the Meaning of Liberty* 150–201 and 277–93 (1997). Copyright 1997 by Dorothy Roberts. Reprinted by permission of Pantheon Books, a division of Random House, Inc.

Roth, Rachel. "Searching for the State: Who Governs Prisoners' Reproductive Rights?" 11 *Social Politics* 411 (2004). Reprinted by permission of Oxford University Press.

Saxton, Marsha. "Disability Rights and Selective Abortion," in Rickie Solinger (ed.), *Abortion Wars: A Half-Century of Struggle, 1950–2000,* 374, 374–93 (Univ. of California Press 1998). Copyright 1998 by the University of California Press. Reprinted by permission of the author and the press.

Siegel, Reva B. "Abortion as a Sex Equality Right: Its Basis in Feminist Theory," in Martha Albertson Finemen and Isabel Karpin (eds.), *Mothers in Law: Feminist Theory and the Legal Regulation of Motherhood* (Columbia Univ. Press 1995). Reprinted by permission of the author, editors, and Columbia University Press.

Solinger, Rickie. *Pregnancy and Power: A Short History of Reproductive Politics in America* 27–62 (New York Univ. Press 2005). Reprinted by permission from the author and the press.

Sullivan, Kathleen M. and Susan R. Estrich. Amicus Brief of 274 Organizations in Support of *Roe v. Wade,* in *Turnock v. Ragsdale,* in Mary Becker, Cynthia Grant Bowman, and Morrison Torrey (eds.) *Feminist Jurisprudence: Taking Women Seriously: Cases and Materials* 404–7 (3d ed. 1994). Reprinted with permission of the authors and Thomson West.

Todd, Alexandra Dundas. *Intimate Adversaries: Cultural Conflict between Doctors and Women Patients* 77–97 (Univ. of Pennsylvania Press 1989). Copyright 1989. Reprinted by permission of the University of Pennsylvania Press.

Williams, Lucy A. "The Ideology of Division: Behavior Modification Welfare Reform Programs," 107 *Yale L. J.* 719 (1992). Reprinted by permission of the author and press.

About the Contributors

Catherine Albiston is Assistant Professor of Law at the Boalt Hall School of Law at the University of California, Berkeley.

Lori B. Andrews is Distinguished Professor of Law at the Chicago-Kent College of Law at the Illinois Institute of Technology and coauthor of *The Body Bazaar: The Market for Human Tissue in the Biotechnology Age.*

Regina Austin is William A. Schnader Professor of Law at the University of Pennsylvania Law School. She is coauthor of *Black Genius: African American Solutions to African American Problems.*

Catherine E. Bell is Professor of Law at the University of Alberta and author of *An Overview of Ownership and Management of Settlement Lands.*

Wendy Brown is Professor of Political Science at the University of California, Berkeley, and author of *Regulating Aversion: Tolerance in the Age of Identity and Empire.*

Cheryl Chase is the founder and executive director of the Intersex Society of North America.

Ruth Colker is Heck Faust Memorial Chair in Constitutional Law at the Michael E. Moritz College of Law at The Ohio State University and author of several books, including *The Disability Pendulum: The First Decade of Enforcement of the Americans with Disabilities Act.*

Rhonda Copelon is Professor of Law and cofounder of the International Women's Human Rights Law Clinic at the City University of New York School of Law.

Cynthia Dailard (1968–2006) was a senior public policy associate at the Guttmacher Institute and a National Family Planning and Reproductive Health Association board member.

Angela Davis is Professor of History of Consciousness at the University of California, Santa Cruz. She is author of *Women, Race, and Class* and *Abolition Democracy: Beyond Prisons, Torture, and Empire.*

Barbara Ehrenreich is an independent writer and the author of several books, including *Nickel and Dimed: On (Not) Getting By in America* and *Dancing in the Streets: A History of Collective Joy.* She is coauthor of *For Her Own Good: Two Centuries of the Experts' Advice to Women.*

Nancy Ehrenreich is Professor of Law at the Sturm College of Law, University of Denver.

Deirdre English is Director of the Felker Magazine Center at the Graduate School of Journalism at the University of California at Berkeley and coauthor of *For Her Own Good: Two Centuries of the Experts' Advice to Women*.

Martha M. Ertman is Professor of Law at the University of Maryland School of Law and coeditor of *Rethinking Commodification: Cases and Readings in Law and Culture*.

Susan R. Estrich is Robert Kingsley Professor of Law and Political Science at the University of Southern California and author of *The Case for Hillary Clinton, Soulless: Ann Coulter and the Right-Wing Church of Hate,* and *Sex and Power*.

Joan Gibbs is Lecturer in the School of Natural and Built Environments at the University of South Australia.

Mary M. Gundrum is Managing Attorney at the Florida Immigrant Advocacy Center.

Julie F. Kowitz is Adjunct Assistant Clinical Professor of Law at Brooklyn Law School.

Kristin Luker is Professor of Jurisprudence and Social Policy at the Boalt Hall School of Law at the University of California, Berkeley, and author *of Dubious Conceptions: The Politics of Teenage Pregnancy*.

Emily Martin is Professor of Anthropology at New York University and author of *The Woman in the Body: A Cultural Analysis of Reproduction* and *Flexible Bodies: Tracking Immunity in American Culture from the Days of Polio to the Age of AIDS*.

Rigel C. Oliveri is Associate Professor of Law at the University of Missouri–Columbia School of Law.

Rosalind Pollack Petchesky is Distinguished Professor of Political Science at Hunter College and the Graduate Center, City University of New York, and author of *Global Prescriptions: Gendering Health and Human Rights*.

Leslie J. Reagan is Associate Professor of History and Medicine, as well as Associate Professor of Law and Gender and Women's Studies, at the University of Illinois, Urbana-Champaign. She is author of *When Abortion Was a Crime: Women, Medicine, and Law in the United States, 1867–1973* and coauthor of *Medicine's Moving Pictures: Medicine, Health, and Bodies in American Film and Television*.

Deborah Rhode is Ernest W. McFarland Professor of Law and Founding Director of the Center on Ethics at the Stanford University School of Law. She is coeditor of *Women and Leadership: The State of Play and Strategies for Change*.

Dorothy Roberts is Kirkland and Ellis Professor of Law, Professor of African-American Studies and Sociology (by courtesy), and Faculty Fellow at the Institute for Policy Research at Northwestern University. She is author of *Shattered Bonds: The Color of Child Welfare* and *Killing the Black Body: Race, Reproduction, and the Meaning of Liberty*.

Rachel Roth is an independent scholar and Soros Justice Fellow, and author of *Making Women Pay: The Hidden Costs of Fetal Rights*.

Marsha Saxton is Senior Researcher at the World Institute on Disabilities and coeditor of *With Wings: An Anthology of Literature by and about Women with Disabilities.*

Reva B. Siegel is Nicholas deB. Katzenbach Professor of Law at Yale University and co-author of *Processes of Constitutional Decisionmaking.*

Rickie Solinger is an independent historian and author of several books, including *Pregnancy and Power: A Short History of Reproductive Politics in America.*

Kathleen M. Sullivan is Stanley Morrison Professor of Law at the Stanford University School of Law and coauthor of *Constitutional Law* and *First Amendment Law.*

Alexandra Dundas Todd is Professor of Sociology at Suffolk University and author *of Intimate Adversaries: Cultural Conflicts between Doctors and Women Patients.*

Lucy A. Williams is Professor of Law at the Northeastern University School of Law and editor of *International Poverty Law: An Emerging Discourse.*

Barbara Wolvowitz is editor of *Civil Rights Litigation and Attorney Fees Annual Handbook* (1988).

Index